# Doing History

Now in its sixth edition, *Doing History* offers a unique perspective on teaching and learning history in the elementary and middle grades. Through case studies of teachers and students in diverse classrooms and from diverse backgrounds, it shows children engaging in authentic historical investigations, often in the context of an integrated social studies curriculum.

The book is grounded in the view that children can engage in valid forms of historical inquiry—asking questions, collecting and analyzing evidence, examining the varied perspectives and experiences of people in the past, and creating evidence-based historical accounts and interpretations. Grounded in contemporary sociocultural theory and research, the text features vignettes in each chapter showing communities of teachers and students doing history in environments rich in literature, art, writing, and discussion. The authors explain how these classrooms reflect contemporary principles of teaching and learning, and thus, the descriptions not only provide specific examples of successful activities but also place them in a context that allows teachers to adapt and apply them in a wide range of settings.

*Doing History* emphasizes diversity in two ways: Readers encounter students from a variety of backgrounds and see how their diverse experiences can form the foundation for learning, and they also see examples of how teachers can engage students with diverse experiences and perspectives in the past, including those that led to conflict and oppression. The book also discusses principles for working with English learners and newcomers, and it provides guidance in using multiple forms of assessment to evaluate the specifically historical aspects of children's learning.

Updates to this edition include updated historical and instructional examples to ensure currency, new suggestions for children's literature to support good teaching, expanded attention to teaching about oppressed groups in history, and greater attention to when historical perspective taking is and is not appropriate.

**Linda S. Levstik** is Professor Emerita in the Department of Curriculum and Instruction at the University of Kentucky, USA.

**Keith C. Barton** is Professor in the Department of Curriculum and Instruction and Adjunct Professor of History at Indiana University, USA.

# ENDORSEMENTS

As a path-breaking, field-defining text, *Doing History* is a timeless, essential, and mindful resource for social studies educators. In this revised edition, Levstik and Barton inspire teachers to confront the diverse realities of a complex and conflicted history by guiding students in the study of history as a multifarious array of choices complicated by social, political, and economic factors deeply rooted in cultural variation, controversy, perplexing dilemmas, and persistent historic issues. Grounded in authentic and research-informed classroom applications, each chapter presents tools to constructively empower students as transformative, agentic beings capable of engaging in historical inquiry that teaches them how to seek justice, learn from diverse people, exercise reasoned deliberation, intelligently participate in community-facing civil action, and live harmoniously in a complex, diverse world.

**Tina L. Heafner, Professor of Social Studies Education,
University of North Carolina-Charlotte, USA, and former President,
National Council for the Social Studies**

A foundational text for teaching history to elementary and middle school students! Through vivid teaching examples, Levstik and Barton show how young students can grapple with the complexities of history. The authors present theory-informed pedagogical practices for inquiry-based instruction, historical research, deliberation, and arts integration while also providing varied ways to assess students' historical thinking and disciplinary skills and methods to support English language learners. This new edition includes updated classroom examples and the latest scholarship to guide educators in teaching controversy and inclusive histories. All social studies educators need a copy in their professional library!

**Sara B. Demoiny, Assistant Professor of Elementary
Education, Auburn University, USA**

# Doing History

## Investigating with Children in Elementary and Middle Schools

*Sixth Edition*

Linda S. Levstik

Keith C. Barton

Routledge
Taylor & Francis Group

NEW YORK AND LONDON

Cover image: Ailime / Getty images

Sixth edition published 2023
by Routledge
605 Third Avenue, New York, NY 10158

and by Routledge
4 Park Square, Milton Park, Abingdon, Oxon, OX14 4RN

*Routledge is an imprint of the Taylor & Francis Group, an informa business*

First edition published by Laurence Erlbaum Associates 1997
Fifth edition published by Routledge 2015

*Library of Congress Cataloging-in-Publication Data*
Names: Levstik, Linda S., author. | Barton, Keith C., author.
Title: Doing history: investigating with children in elementary and middle schools/Linda S. Levstik, Keith C. Barton.
Description: Sixth edition. | New York, NY: Routledge, 2023. | Includes bibliographical references and index.
Identifiers: LCCN 2022009436 (print) | LCCN 2022009437 (ebook) | ISBN 9781032016948 (hardback) | ISBN 9781032016931 (paperback) | ISBN 9781003179658 (ebook)
Subjects: LCSH: History–Study and teaching (Elementary)–United States. | History–Study and teaching (Middle school)–United States.
Classification: LCC LB1582.U6 L49 2023 (print) | LCC LB1582.U6 (ebook) | DDC 372.89–dc23/eng/20220224
LC record available at https://lccn.loc.gov/2022009436
LC ebook record available at https://lccn.loc.gov/2022009437

ISBN: 978-1-032-01694-8 (hbk)
ISBN: 978-1-032-01693-1 (pbk)
ISBN: 978-1-003-17965-8 (ebk)

DOI: 10.4324/9781003179658

Typeset in Garamond
by Deanta Global Publishing Services, Chennai, India

*To our spouses,*
*Frank Levstik and Shaunna Scott*

# CONTENTS

# PREFACE

As we did in previous editions of *Doing History*, we invite you to take a mental journey with us—to picture primary students debating whether Christopher Columbus should be considered a hero or eighth-grade students producing a video to examine whether a historic document—the Bill of Rights—speaks to current issues. We ask you to further imagine classrooms where students regularly, and actively, do history—frame questions, gather data from primary and secondary sources, organize and interpret that data, and share their work with different audiences. Finally, we ask you to imagine a history curriculum that reflects the rich diversity of people in the United States and around the world.

We have been fortunate to spend a number of years working with teachers and students in just such classrooms, both in the United States and in other countries, particularly Ghana, New Zealand, and Northern Ireland. We have seen powerful historical study in classes where many of the children were recent immigrants as well as in classes where children's families have lived in the same area for generations. Some classes are full inclusion programs where the special education and "regular" teachers collaborate; most include students with special needs, at least for social studies. The classrooms range from urban and suburban to rural settings. But despite their many differences, these communities of inquiry have several things in common. In each one, even the youngest children describe historical study as interesting and important. Moreover, historical study in each of these classrooms deals with important content and engages students in authentic inquiry. *All* students are invited to be historical participants. Throughout the book, we draw on these classrooms to provide models of instructionally sound, thoughtful, and thought-provoking history teaching with students from a wide variety of backgrounds. Most chapters also begin with a vignette from one of these classrooms.

Many of the teachers cited in this book worked with us on research related to the development of historical thinking. Some continue to do so. We met others through our work with teacher education programs and professional development grants, or through professional meetings. All of them generously shared their time, ideas, and classrooms. Although we would prefer honoring each of them by using their real names, confidentiality agreements sometimes preclude that possibility. Many appear under their own names—Rhoda Coleman, LeeAnn Fitzpatrick, Jeanette Groth, Amy Leigh, Grace Maggard, Tina Reynolds, Kim Sergent, Renee Shipman, Stephanie Sexton, Dehea Smith, Rebecca Valbuena, Linda Cargile, and Ruby Yessin—whereas others are identified by pseudonyms. Similarly, all children's names are pseudonyms except where we had permission to credit a child for a specific piece of work. Again, we wish we could identify all the students who so generously indulged our curiosity and answered questions that often must have seemed foolish, who lent us their work, and who shared their time and ideas. Our experience has been that children enjoy discussing their ideas about history and that they want to find out more about how things have changed over time. In addition, our conversations with children and adolescents in other parts of the world remind us of how tightly our conceptions of the past are linked to national contexts—to our sense of national agency, of the possibility for change, and of hope or hopelessness as we face the future.

As you read the vignettes, think of them as snapshots of history in action—including some of the obstacles even good teachers face. As with a snapshot, each vignette is a glimpse of a particular experience teaching and learning history. The rest of each chapter puts the vignette in perspective, explaining why it is sound instruction and sound history and providing examples of activities ranging from the first years of primary school through the end of the middle grades. Although we have not tried to present a complete set of activities or recommend a specific curriculum, we have tried to suggest a framework for rethinking history instruction in elementary and middle schools. Our goal is to stimulate your thinking so that you can decide how to apply these ideas to your own classrooms and with your own students. One way to begin thinking about how to adapt these ideas is to refer to children's literature mentioned throughout the book. These suggestions are by no means exhaustive. Rather, selections are specifically intended to represent diversity of perspectives and different levels of difficulty.

Continuous and constructive assessment takes on a special role in teaching history. By *continuous* and *constructive* assessment, we mean that evaluation occurs throughout instruction, not just at the end of a unit or grading period, and that the effects of assessment on teaching and learning are positive. Moreover, assessment in history attends to specifically *historical* aspects of students' work. Against what criteria, for instance, do we assess students' progress in perspective recognition or building supportable interpretations? How do we use assessment to help students think more carefully about evidence or about cause-and-effect relationships? Rather than locating assessment in a separate chapter, then, you will find this topic woven throughout the book. We introduce the principles of constructive assessment in Chapter 2 so that you have a basis for evaluating the assessment techniques that follow. In subsequent chapters, you will find examples of rubrics for assessing students' progress in both perspective recognition and developing historical interpretations. Other chapters provide a variety of techniques for evaluating students' history presentations—from position papers and history museums to oral performances. Each of these techniques is embedded in actual classroom practice so that you can see how real teachers work to make assessment not only continuous and more constructive but also an authentic part of teaching and learning in history.

## NEW IN THIS EDITION

As with any approach to teaching, ideas change and grow over time. So it is with this book. Some of the changes are relatively minor—we have updated the bibliographies, incorporating new scholarship on historical thinking and learning, and have suggested new children's literature to support good teaching. Other changes are more substantial.

This edition includes expanded attention to teaching about oppressed groups in history, especially racialized minorities. Although addressing the experience of diverse groups in history has always been a point of emphasis for us, new times and new perspectives have deepened our understanding of how to approach some topics—including what can go wrong. Much of the traditional content of school history, for example, has prioritized perspectives of White settlers and, in so doing, has tacitly legitimized dispossession of Indigenous peoples. In this edition, we have sought to further problematize such assumptions by expanding attention to Native viewpoints and reframing (and sometimes omitting) topics once known as "Westward Expansion" or "Pioneers." In addition, when dealing with conflict between groups, we have sought to recognize more clearly that conflict does not arise simply from "differing viewpoints" but, more often, reflects intentional and systematic violence and oppression. Finally, we have provided extensive guidance for when it is—and is not—appropriate to engage children in activities related to the history of oppressed people. Although having students take the perspective of those in the past is a basic instructional technique emphasized throughout this book, in some situations this approach can traumatize children or trivialize historical experiences. We hope our treatment of perspective-taking will help teachers think clearly about how to frame such activities in ways that center the agency of those who have fought for justice—and when they should be avoided altogether.

The teachers in this book—and others like them in the United States and abroad—continue to renew our conviction that history *is* relevant to the lives of even the youngest school children and that disciplined, reflective historical inquiry *is not* the sole province of university historians but, rather, the obligation of all of us who seek a more inclusive and responsive common good. We hope this edition continues to do justice to the lives and work of these teachers and to the students in their classes. We also have been gratified, since the publication of previous editions, to find ideas from the book used successfully by other teachers, in other schools, and in other parts of the country and the world. We hope that their example supports you and your students as you build communities of historical inquiry in pursuit of the common good.

# ACKNOWLEDGMENTS

This book grew out of a series of collaborations—with teachers and students, with each other, and with the many colleagues with whom we have discussed and debated the issues surrounding the teaching and learning of history. The teachers and students with whom we work have been incredibly generous, giving us feedback on many sections of the book and always providing a reality check on our theorizing. We want to thank the administrators who let us observe in their schools, supported our research, welcomed our university students into their schools, and invited us to participate in professional development workshops with teachers in their schools. We also appreciate the U.S. Department of Education's "Teaching American History" grant program for the opportunity to work with teachers from a wide variety of settings in our own region and across the country.

In earlier editions of *Doing History*, we thanked a number of people who read and responded to portions of the original manuscript, and we do so again. Earlier editions profited from encouragement, insightful reviews, and useful suggestions offered by Corinna Hasback, Kathryn Engebretson, Terrie Epstein, Raymond H. Muessig, Noralee Frankel, Rob Kunzman, and Lynne Smith. Sadly, we acknowledge the loss of Frank Levstik, whose support helped make this book, and so much else, possible. In addition to locating a variety of sources, he and Jennifer Levstik read, listened to, and commented on numerous drafts of our first edition. Lauren MacArthur Harris shared her valuable insights into the teaching of world history. Jennie Smith, Elaine Conradi, Melissa Simonds, Spencer Clark, Paula Bayer, and Heather Hagan provided indispensable help in finding good children's literature. Leslie King allowed us to investigate the impact of some of our ideas in new settings, as did the teachers who participated in the "American Legacies" and "Documenting American Democracy" programs.

Each new edition benefits from contacts with teachers and university educators from around the world. We wish we could acknowledge all those colleagues who have so generously shared their insights and their hospitality. In addition to growing through our work with innumerable colleagues in North America, we continue to learn from the invigorating international conversations that have developed around history education.

# AUTHOR BIOGRAPHIES

**Linda S. Levstik** is Professor Emerita, Department of Curriculum and Instruction, at the University of Kentucky, USA. Her research and writing focus on students' historical thinking, including the impact of national context, archaeological experiences, and gender-equitable instruction on learning history. She has conducted studies in the U.S., New Zealand, and Ghana and co-led three Teaching American History grants in Kentucky and Tennessee as well as CiviConnections, a three-year nationwide program funded by the National Council for the Social Studies and Learn for America designed to enhance civic participation in K–12 settings. She is the recipient of the 2007 Jean Dresden Grambs Distinguished Career Research Award from the National Council for the Social Studies and co-editor with Cynthia Tyson of the *Handbook of Research on Social Studies* (Routledge, 2004). Her work has appeared in national and international journals for teachers, teacher educators, and researchers. Prior to earning a Ph.D. from the Ohio State University, she taught in public and private elementary and middle schools in Ohio.

**Keith C. Barton** is Professor in the Department of Curriculum and Instruction and Adjunct Professor of History at Indiana University, USA. His research investigates students' understanding of history, human rights, and civic participation; classroom contexts of teaching and learning; and the history of the social studies curriculum. He has conducted studies in the United States, Northern Ireland, New Zealand, and Singapore, and he has served as a visiting professor at the National Institute of Education (Singapore), Victoria University (New Zealand), Uppsala University (Sweden), and the UNESCO Centre for Education in Pluralism, Human Rights, and Democracy at the University of Ulster (Northern Ireland). Prior to earning a doctorate from the University of Kentucky, he taught elementary and middle school in Los Angeles and near San Francisco, where he also served as president of his teachers' union and as a teacher-consultant for the Bay Area Writing Project. His work has appeared in national and international journals for researchers, teacher educators, and practitioners, and he edited *Research Methods in Social Studies Education: Contemporary Issues and Perspectives* (Information Age Publishing, 2006). He is also co-author, with Li-Ching Ho, of *Curriculum for Justice and Harmony: Deliberation, Knowledge, and Action in Social and Civic Education* (Routledge, 2022).

**Linda S. Levstik and Keith C. Barton** have published together in journals such as *American Educational Research Journal, Journal of Curriculum Studies*, and *Teachers College Record*. That work, along with their reflections on designing and conducting research, has been collected in *Researching History Education: Theory, Method, and Context* (Routledge, 2008). They have written about the role of history in preparing students for participation in pluralist democracies in *Teaching History for the Common Good* (Routledge, 2004) and have reviewed research on the relationship between history and citizenship for the *Handbook of Education for Citizenship and Democracy* (Sage, 2008).

# 1

# PAST, PRESENT, AND FUTURE

## The Sociocultural Context for Studying History

We learn [in history]…how people's views change over time. A lot of people's views change, but not everybody. We still have things like the KKK around…so obviously their views haven't changed since like the Civil War and stuff, but I think most people's have. Not necessarily everybody… There's definitely still prejudice around, not necessarily just about Blacks and Hispanics, either.

—Caitlyn, sixth-grade student

You may remember a very different history from the one Caitlyn describes. Too often, history instruction is simply a march through time that never quite connects to the present. History becomes, as one second-grader explains, "a main date." The dates may mark interesting stories, but the stories are finished—beginnings and middles established, climaxes identified, and endings predictable. Figures from a pantheon of heroes and villains step forward briefly, take their bows in stories that often fail to distinguish between myth and history, and disappear back into the pictures displayed above whiteboards. George Washington was the first president, had wooden teeth, and chopped down a cherry tree. Abraham Lincoln was honest, read by firelight, and walked a mile to return a nickel. It is little wonder that children sometimes ask what the point in all this storytelling might be.

Consider the kind of history Caitlyn's comments suggest. She clearly struggles to make sense of the prejudice she sees around her—both to explain how it is that prejudice exists and to separate herself from it. She uses her study of history to identify prejudice as an enduring human dilemma and to understand that "a lot of people's views change, but not everybody…There's definitely still prejudice around." In other words, we are still in the middle of the story. The ending isn't predictable, and the story unfolds in our own time and in our own lives. The point of history is that this is, after all, an enormous family drama. Each of us develops the plot twists with which future generations will have to cope. From this perspective, history forces us to consider what it means to be a participant in this human drama.

## HISTORY INVOLVES MULTIPLE ACTIVITIES AND PURPOSES

As Caitlyn's comment indicates, the past is complex. There are many ways of making sense of history, and no single purpose takes precedence as the sole reason for studying the subject. History involves a number of different activities, each of which can be used for

History is used for multiple purposes. *Barton & Levstik (2004), Levstik & Thornton (2018)*

DOI: 10.4324/9781003179658-1

a variety of ends, and these combinations of activity and purpose constitute four distinct "stances" toward the past. One of the most familiar is the *identification stance*, in which we look for connections between ourselves and people in the past. "You have Aunt Eliza's laugh," a father in New York tells his daughter, "and a stubborn streak just like your grandmother!" In a classroom in East Los Angeles, a girl explains that her mother has told her about leaving school as a child in El Salvador to help support her family; a classmate has learned that his uncle was once "the greatest truck driver in all Mexico," able to make it through flooded roads when no one else could; and yet another has heard her grandparents recall the homes and businesses they owned before leaving Vietnam. And throughout the United States, students learn how "we" became a nation or how "our" ethnic group has struggled to achieve its dreams. In recognizing family characteristics, sharing family stories, and locating ourselves within a larger community, children (and adults) are expected to affirm connections between their own lives and those of people in the past.

Moral responses to history involve judgments about the people and events of the past. *Barton & Levstik (2004)*

Other times, we take an explicitly judgmental attitude toward the people and events of history. This is the *moral response stance*. Sometimes we remember the sacrifices and hardships of those involved in tragic events, such as the Irish Famine, the world wars, or racist violence. Other times, we hold up events for condemnation (enslavement, the Holocaust, the storming of the U.S. capitol) or celebration (the Women's Suffrage and Civil Rights Movements, the end of apartheid). And still other times we single out people we regard as heroes or role models—George Washington, Harriet Tubman, Rosa Parks. Judging the past as good or bad—or simply deserving of reverence—is another fundamental way in which people relate to history, both in school and out.

Historical analysis involves identifying patterns, examining causes and consequences of events, and constructing historical accounts from evidence. *Barton & Levstik (2004), Kitson & Husbands (2011), Lévesque (2008)*

Two other approaches are less personal and less emotional. The first is the *analytic stance*. Students engage in historical analysis when they look for historical patterns or examine the causes and consequences of events in the past—how life has changed over time, the causes of the American Revolution, the effect of World War II on daily life, and so on. Sometimes, this kind of analysis is aimed at understanding the growth of contemporary society, as when students study the origin and development of their country's legal and political structure. Other times, the past may serve as a source of lessons or analogies; notice, for example, how often historical examples are used in discussions of the possible consequences of foreign policy decisions. Students also take part in analysis when they learn how historical accounts are constructed. Working with primary sources, comparing conflicting accounts, and reaching conclusions based on evidence are all part of the analytic stance.

Exhibition involves the display of historical information, whether in school or out. *Barton & Levstik (2004)*

Finally, one of the most common approaches to history in schools involves the *exhibition stance*. Here, students are expected to display what they know about the past by answering questions at the end of a textbook chapter, responding to teachers' questions in class, or taking achievement tests. This is the kind of history people seem to have in mind when they decry how little students these days know about history or how standards have fallen. The exhibition stance is also the easiest to dismiss, in part, because it is driven more by demands for accountability than by a concern with developing deep understanding of history and, in part, because it reminds most of us of our own worst encounters with the subject. Yet exhibition is an important part of how history is used in society, and knowledge of the past is often displayed in museums and historical re-enactments as well as through hobbies such as genealogy or antique collecting. All these stances—identification, moral response, analysis, and exhibition—influence the teaching and learning of history, and we must keep each of them in mind as we think about how to develop students' understanding of the subject.

## HISTORY HELPS US PICTURE POSSIBLE FUTURES

Any approach to history is as much about the present and future as it is about the past. When we identify with groups in history, we stake out identities in the present; when we look at where the world has been, we hope we will understand where it is going; when we judge the decisions of the past, we promise to make better ones next time. In order for history to fulfill such roles, though, students need a broad and inclusive exposure to the subject. By marking out particular paths to the present, history also points to some possible roads to the future and forecloses others.

History points to some possible paths to the future and forecloses others. *Holt (1990)*

Students who do not see themselves as members of groups who had agency in the past or power in the present, who are invisible in history, lack viable models for the future. Consider, for instance, the impact of traditional history instruction that emphasizes the agency of some men—conquering the wilderness, establishing governments, leading social movements—while presenting most women as acted on—following husbands to new lands, invisible in government, silent on public issues. Particularly when such instruction matches school practice, in which girls are often taught to be passive and boys active, there is little modeling of alternatives for the future. Not only is this problematic for girls, but it also limits all students' access to the full range of choices open to human beings across time and among places. Ignoring the complexities and controversies inherent in the gendered interplay of public and private life leaves stereotyped ideas about gender unexamined. Unmediated by careful curricular attention, stereotypes and their accompanying misunderstandings lead some students to limit their aspirations as well as their classroom participation and may encourage others to view information about and from some of their peers as insignificant. Of course, similar examples could be used for other groups who have been less visible in traditional history. When history is silent about these sorts of issues, it is often perceived as separate from ordinary life, divorced from the puzzles of culture and change that absorb us on a daily basis.

*Schmeichel (2011), Sheppard & Mayo (2013), Crocco (2018)*

Shifting the focus of the history curriculum to a pluralist perspective presents a more inclusive and authentic vision of the futures available to all students. Studying a range of perspectives helps students understand discrimination, marginalization, and opposition as well as power and privilege. It opens up a broader range of possible ways of acting in the world—and acting in the future. To help students envision such a history, teachers should:

Exploring significant themes and questions is a basic activity of history. *Evans (1988), National Council for the Social Studies (2021), Levstik & Thornton (2018)*

- Focus on enduring human dilemmas. Emphasize that the dilemmas of the present have their roots in the past. Untangling those roots can be both freeing and empowering.
- Focus on human agency. Emphasize the ways in which people have acquiesced to, ignored, or acted against oppression and injustice as well as the ways in which people have worked to build the futures they desired.
- Focus on subjecting interpretations to scrutiny and skepticism. Emphasize the "authored" nature of historical interpretation. Whose voice is heard? Whose is left out? How else might the story be told?
- Connect to the microlevel. Emphasize bringing historical perspective to bear on current issues both in the classroom and the larger society.
- Connect to the macrolevel. Study discrimination, marginalization, and opposition as global phenomena that require global as well as local and national responses.

## HISTORY IS ABOUT SIGNIFICANT THEMES AND QUESTIONS

If history helps us think about who we are and picture possible futures, we cannot afford a history curriculum mired in trivia and limited to a chronological recounting of events. Instead, we need a vibrant history that engages children in investigating significant themes and questions and that involves them with people, their values, and the choices they make. In the past, we have assumed that students needed "basic skills" before they could engage with big issues. The trouble with this is that time lines, names, and memorized "facts" are not history, and they certainly are not compelling. The enduring themes and questions that humans have struggled with over time are, however, more captivating history (see Table 1.1). In the past, we have reserved these for historians and then wondered why children too often found history insignificant. By shifting the instructional focus from hearing about one historical story to asking questions worth pursuing, children have an opportunity to engage in the real "basics" of history.

---

Table 1.1

Significant Themes and Questions in History

*Three Essential Questions in History*

Humans and the Environment: How has the changing relationship between human beings and the physical and natural environment affected human life from early times to the present?

Humans Interacting with Other Humans: Why have relations among humans become so complex since early times?

Humans and Ideas: How have human views of the world, nature, and the cosmos changed?

Source: *World History for Us All* (https://whfua.history.ucla.edu/)

*Seven Key Themes in History*

Patterns of Population: The distribution of populations and patterns of human migration have had a significant impact on human history.

Economic Networks and Exchanges: How people have exchanged ideas and goods over time and distance has provided the basic framework for present-day economies.

Uses and Abuses of Power: Changing power relations has been one of the central themes of history.

Haves and Have-Nots: The uneven distribution of wealth is one of the most important problems humans have faced across history.

Expressing Identity: Over the course of human history, expressing identity has contributed to and challenged people's sense of well-being, self-respect, and their interactions with others.

Science, Technology, and the Environment: Over time, humans have used science and technology to exploit their physical and natural surroundings.

Spiritual Life and Moral Codes: Over time, different communities have expressed (and often fought over) myriad ideas about a spiritual realm and about rules for right and wrong.

Source: Adapted from *World History for Us All* (https://whfua.history.ucla.edu/)

---

Table 1.1 provides one set of suggested themes and questions. You would, of course, have to adjust the questions to fit particular grade levels. For instance, a primary school class might begin with a question such as, "Why do people move from one place to another?" rather than, "How has human movement been encouraged and inhibited?" Their study might begin with the students' own experiences and then expand to consideration of community patterns over time. In contrast, a middle school class might consider the question, "How have our decisions about the environment changed other communities?" Again, students might begin by analyzing local conditions, then trace them back in time, and finally study the impact of local conditions on the larger community, nationally and internationally. As you look over the three questions and seven themes in Table 1.1, consider how you might adapt them to engage students in thinking about who they are, where they came from, and where they might go in the future.

Most of us probably don't remember this kind of history. At worst, we may remember a string of isolated dates and questions at the end of a deadly dull textbook chapter. At best, we may remember a teacher who told impassioned stories about times long ago. But even at its best, we heard a single story, we already knew how it would come out—and some of us weren't in it. In fact, history always stopped long before it got to us. Therefore, we had no role in history. Always excluded in time, often excluded because we were the "wrong" gender, class, race, ethnicity, nationality, language, or sexual identity, we weren't invited into the story—unless we were willing to identify with the main characters. And we were rarely encouraged to think about why the story was being told that way, or how it might have looked from a different perspective. In other words, we were unlikely to see history as either authored or interpretive.

> Many students have been excluded from the story of history.

## HISTORY IS INTERPRETIVE

No historical account can be entirely objective because historical knowledge always involves interpretation. At the most basic level, anyone interested in knowing what happened in the past faces a problem peculiar to history: The events are already over with and cannot be directly observed or repeated. As a result, finding out what happened always

> All history is interpretive.

**4**

involves indirect methods (such as using primary sources and artifacts), and indirect methods require interpretation: The historian has to decide which sources to use, how reliable they are, and what to do when they contradict each other. We all know the same event can be explained differently by different people, and anyone who has listened to family stories grow and change over time knows that interpretation shifts with the teller. When Uncle Christopher tells the story of Scottish emigration, for example, it is a tale of brave ancestors wrapped in their clan tartans. In Aunt Kathryn's rendering, the tartans are more tattered and the family roots more humble. As one group of historians notes, "History is never either a neutral force or a complete world view; history is always *someone's history.*" All of us, then, start with our own diverse social histories—the stories of who we are as interpreted through the experiences of daily living, family stories, pictures, and artifacts.

*Appleby et al. (1994, p. 11), Ehrenhalt (2019)*

People in the past were also influenced by their backgrounds and biases. There are dozens of firsthand accounts of the Battle at Lexington Green, for example, and no two of them are alike. Faced with conflicting sources, the historian must decide which descriptions seem most plausible, and such decisions necessarily involve judgment and interpretation. The historical record is more often incomplete than contradictory, though, so we must piece together fragments of information to construct a complete description. This inevitably involves speculation because some facts can never be recovered. Consider, for example, the assassination of U.S. President John Kennedy. No single source contains enough information to know exactly what happened at the scene, so historians have to pull together evidence from films, recordings, firsthand accounts, and medical reports. The fact that this event has generated decades of controversy indicates just how impossible it is to establish what happened: There will always be gaps in the record, and people will disagree over the most reasonable way of filling in those gaps. For many historical events, it is impossible to separate description from interpretation.

The historical record is incomplete. *Bennett (1967)*

School history, however, has usually been limited to a narrow range of interpretations. Often, it begins with the assumption of a unified society and has told a story that deemphasizes racial, ethnic, gender, and class distinctions. As a result, many of us have become invisible in history. If our students are to be visible—able to see themselves as participants in the ongoing drama of history—then we have to rethink the ways we conceive of history. Specifically, we should:

History instruction has traditionally deemphasized diversity. *Epstein (1994), Kendi (2016), Wilkerson (2020)*

- Begin with the assumption of a pluralist society. All of us belong to many groups that are intricately related to each other. Some of us have exercised more power than others; others have more often been excluded from power.
- Recognize that no single story can possibly be our story. Instead, our multiple stories, braided together, constantly speak to and against each other. Each of us is a strand but not the whole.
- Remember that history is alive. All our stories are only partially known, always unfinished, and constantly changing as we speak and act.

*Lerner (1998), Blain & Kendi (2021)*

## HISTORY IS EXPLAINED THROUGH NARRATIVES

Historical accounts also involve a more important kind of interpretation—not just in establishing what happened but also in showing how events relate to each other. A simple list of events from the past is usually referred to as a *chronicle. History*, however, is something more: Historical explanations frequently explain events in a narrative form. A historical account, then, often is a story about the past—with a beginning, middle, and end and a setting, characters, problem (or problems), and resolution. Think, for example, about accounts of the American Revolution. The story begins at the end of the French and Indian War, as Britain imposes taxes to pay for the defense of the colonies. As the colonists become increasingly upset about the unfairness of taxation without representation, they begin a series of protests, which England meets with increasingly repressive responses. The colonists eventually declare their independence, a war results, and the colonists are victorious. This historical episode has a structure similar to any narrative, fictitious or

Historical narratives explain how events are causally related. *Barton & Levstik (2004), M. White (1965)*

otherwise—a setting, characters, a problem, and a resolution. Several historians have argued that this kind of narrative structure is the basis of all historical explanation.

But whenever history is told as a narrative, someone has to decide when the story begins and ends, what is included or left out, and which events appear as problems or solutions. As a result, historical narratives always involve interpretation: Someone decides *how* to tell the story. To take a simple example, it would be impossible to tell everything that happened during the American Revolution (even if complete records survived). That would mean explaining how Thomas Jefferson sharpened his quill pen each time he sat down to write, how Crispus Attucks buckled his shoes each morning, how Abigail Adams lit candles in her home—and millions of other details about every person in the colonies and in England, every minute of every day for decades. No historian tries to write such a "complete" account, and no one would have time to read one. Instead, every historical account is selective—someone decides which events are important enough to include in the story. Deciding which events to include and which to leave out forms one of the most basic aspects of historical interpretation.

At an even more significant level, however, historical interpretation involves deciding not just what events to include but also how they relate to each other. Explaining that "taxation without representation" caused the American Revolution, for example, is an example of interpretation: One reason is selected as the most important. Some historians, however, have pointed to other reasons as crucial, including the desire of colonial elites to maintain their economic position, protect the institution of enslavement, or profit from westward expansion. The facts alone cannot explain why the war took place; explaining the war's cause is a matter of interpretation. To take an even more familiar example: What was the nature of U.S. involvement in the Vietnam War? Some would tell the story of a military hampered by weak politicians and ungrateful protesters, whereas others would tell of the triumph of the Vietnamese people over a brutal dictatorship and a vicious superpower. What appears as failure from one perspective appears as victory to another. The events of the war remain the same, but their meaning changes depending on the story being told. Even when the factual events of history can be firmly established, their meaning—their arrangement in a narrative—is always a matter of interpretation.

Historians engage in interpretation, then, whenever they shape the events of the past into a story. Because no account of the past is ever complete, and because any event can be told as part of more than one possible story, interpretations vary from one historian to another. One may see progress, where another sees decline, one may find the importance of events that others ignore, and so on. Far from being avoided, debates over interpretation are at the very heart of the historical profession. Historians know that more than one story can be told about the same events and that interpretations will change over time; there simply is no single, unchanging story of history. Such ambiguity is regarded as an inevitable, productive, and desirable part of the search for historical knowledge. That is not to say, however, that any interpretation is as good as any other. Any story about the past must, for example, account for the available evidence. A narrative of the World War II era that denies that the Holocaust occurred will not garner much respect, because the facts of the Holocaust can be conclusively established.

## HISTORY IS MORE THAN POLITICS

Unfortunately, the range of interpretations traditionally found in textbooks and school curricula has been extremely small. The historical narratives that students encounter at school, for example, focus almost exclusively on the legal, political, and diplomatic history of the United States—laws, presidents, wars, and foreign relations. Information that does not fit into these categories is rarely afforded much (if any) importance. As a result, those who traditionally have had little access to politics—such as women and minoritized groups—have largely been excluded from the narrative interpretations of history offered in school.

Historical narratives are authored.

No historical account is complete.

Hannah-Jones (2019), Holton (1999)

Historical interpretations vary from one historian to another. Foner (2002), Gaddis (2002), LePore (2018)

Not all historical narratives are equally valid. Kansteiner (1993), Kendi (2016), H. White (1992), Wilkerson (2020)

School history has usually focused on law, politics, and diplomacy.

Busey (2017), Elshtain (1981), Hinojosa (2020), Kimmerer (2013), L. King (2016), Lerner (1998), Santiago (2019), Wilkerson (2020)

Women, especially when part of minoritized communities, appear infrequently in the curriculum because, for much of the nation's history, they have had only indirect access to politics—and as long as politics remains the focus of history, women will appear only when they influence that predominantly male realm (as, for example, during the abolition or women's rights movements). There is no objective reason, however, for history to concern itself so exclusively with the public political arena. Historians long ago began turning their attention to other areas of life—such as family relations, domestic labor, and religion—and, not surprisingly, found women to be significant historical actors. More recently, historians have explored connections between spheres previously regarded as public and private, and again, they have found that gender, in all its variety, has played a more significant role than was long recognized. As long as these topics remain absent from the study of history, however, so will far too many women.

Deciding to limit one's attention to politics, then, amounts to excluding large portions of the population from U.S. history; it is one way of deciding what is left in and out of the story. Not only women, of course, but many other segments of the population have suffered from this exclusion. Too often, for instance, Blacks only appear as important historical actors in relation to White politics, and the political, economic, and cultural developments within Black society have not been considered a part of the country's story (and still less have Asian Americans, Pacific Islanders, Indigenous peoples, or those of Mexican, Central American, or Caribbean ancestry been accorded a prominent place within that story). Historians have been devoting attention to such issues for decades, but as long as this more inclusive interpretation of U.S. history remains outside the school curriculum, so will the opportunity to make sense out of huge swaths of the country's history.

The traditional stories of history have been particularly severe in their treatment of Indigenous people. For many years, the history of the United States was roughly equivalent to the triumph of White settlement. In that story, the presence of Indigenous people appeared as an obvious problem to be solved through their removal or relocation. Indigenous people saw the story very differently: From their perspective, the problem was the forced surrender of their land (and often their way of life), and armed resistance, peaceful settlement, and collaboration all represented attempts at solutions. A historical map showing the expansion of White settlement, then, has precisely the opposite meaning for Indigenous people: It shows the contraction of their own territory. Again, the facts of the encounter between Indigenous and European populations in North America can be established in most cases, but their significance changes greatly depending on the story being told.

Put simply, there is not a single story of history but many stories. Indigenous–White relations, the American Revolution, enslavement, changes in domestic labor, immigration, military involvement in other parts of the world—all these will look different from varying perspectives. Each point of view will regard some events as more important, others as less so; each will include some details while omitting others; what appears as progress in one story will seem like decline in another; and solutions in one will be regarded as problems in others. Each story will invariably contain the kind of interpretation that is an inseparable part of historical understanding.

## HISTORY IS CONTROVERSIAL

The combination of interpretation and importance makes for a volatile mix. If historical truth were handed down to us on a stone tablet, the meaning and significance of the past would be certain and unchanging, and there would be no room for controversy. Not only would we know what happened in the past, but we would also know just what story to tell about it; anyone who suggested alternative explanations could be dismissed as an unenlightened crank. And if history were unimportant, if it were not so central to our individual and collective identities, its interpretive nature would hardly matter. Historians and others could be relegated to the remote confines of archives and libraries where they

Women have often been omitted from the history curriculum. Gordon (1990), Hahn et al. (2007), Lerner (1998)

Understanding U.S. history requires attention to Black, Indigenous, Asian, Mexican, and other populations. Busey (2017), L. King (2016), N. Rodriguez & Kim (2018), Santiago (2019)

Sabzalian (2019)

Deloria (2004), Hundorf (2001)

On the use of terms for Indigenous populations of North America, see Sabzalian (2019)

Interpretation is an inseparable part of historical understanding.

**7**

History is one of the most controversial areas of knowledge. *Hinojosa (2020), Kendi (2016), LePore (2018), Wilkerson, (2020)*

would be free to argue over their conflicting narratives, out of sight and out of mind. But history has a more vital fate: Because many stories can be told about the past and because those stories powerfully influence our understanding of who we are and where we come from, history is destined to be among the most controversial areas of human knowledge.

Historical controversies have been a regular feature of U.S. life. *Kammen (1991), Nash et al. (1997), Kendi (2016), Wilkerson (2020)*

Such controversies are nothing new: They have been a constant feature of the public understanding of history in this country for over a century, as some groups have struggled to become part of the story of U.S. history and others have fought just as hard to keep them out. Regional tensions produced many of the most impassioned historical debates in the first decades of the twentieth century, as Westerners argued that the Eastern United States dominated textbooks and public celebrations, and Southerners maintained that New England received too much attention at the expense of their own section. The legacy of the Civil War lent a particular fervor to debates between North and South, as each strove to establish its own interpretation as the accepted and "correct" one. In 1920, the New Orleans chapter of the United Daughters of the Confederacy warned mothers not to let their children celebrate Lincoln's birthday at school, and other Southerners promoted Robert E. Lee as the country's pre-eminent "man of honor." Today, we see similar controversies involving efforts to remove statues and other memorials to historical figures who support enslavement, eugenics, or other racist institutions and perspectives. Clearly, the symbols of the past have had an important and enduring legacy that still produce serious disagreements.

*Kammen (1991)*

Contemporary concerns lead to controversies over historical interpretations.

Interpretations of the Civil War continue to be a major source of disagreement within the country, with some people (but no historians) believing that enslavement was benevolent or that it was not the primary cause of secession. Other historical controversies are more fleeting. In the 1890s, Anglo Americans protested the proposal to make Columbus Day a legal holiday because only "the Mafia" would be interested in celebrating the life of an Italian; in 1915, prejudice against German Americans forced the removal of a statue of Baron Von Steuben at Valley Forge; and the 1920s saw a movement to condemn U.S. history textbooks as full of pro-British propaganda. These debates, of course, just seem silly today: Historical controversies always result from contemporary concerns, and few people now care about the issues that inspired such strong feelings against Italians, Germans, or the British. It's hard to imagine anyone getting upset about a monument to Baron Von Steuben anymore.

Racial controversies influence our understanding of history.

Attempts to tell a more inclusive story of U.S. history are met with fierce resistance. *Bain & Kendi (2021), Casanova (1995), Cornbleth & Waugh (1995), Evans (2004), Hinojosa (2020), Nash et al. (1997)*

But as we all know, there are other contemporary issues that still inspire fierce passions. Racial tensions, both spoken and unspoken, permeate every sphere of our society and invariably affect our understanding of how the story of U.S. history should be told. Since the beginning of Black History Week in 1926 (and before), teachers, parents, students, and scholars have argued that Blacks deserve a more prominent place in that story. This perspective has grown even more inclusive in recent years, as it becomes apparent that all racial and ethnic groups—as well as women, working people, and others—should be part of the story of U.S. history and that they should be included as full and active participants rather than marginal "contributors." Because issues of race, gender, and class still divide our society, though, every attempt to tell a more inclusive story of U.S. history is met with fierce resistance, as defenders of the status quo argue that these attempts minimize the achievements of traditional White and male historical figures.

## THE GOAL OF HISTORY EDUCATION

Many teachers conform to tradition in their classroom practices. *Barton & Levstik (2004), James (2008)*

Teachers may consider history education a daunting task, with its multiple activities and purposes, its interpretative basis, its controversial nature, and so on. And indeed, it is a complex undertaking, and the best history teachers struggle throughout their careers to get a better handle on this stubborn subject. In the face of such challenges, it may seem easiest to dismiss the issues raised in this chapter and simply conform to tradition. Many teachers do precisely that: They plod through the content of the curriculum, and they spend their time trying to keep students quiet and submissive. But that's no way to teach.

If teachers do no more than cover content and manage behavior, their students will learn little and care less, and teachers themselves will become frustrated and cynical. To avoid such depressing developments, teachers must have clear goals to drive their instruction— goals that focus their work and inspire their students. Teachers who do things differently—who resist the temptation of conformity—have a sense of purpose that extends beyond covering content or controlling students' behavior.

We believe one overarching goal can and should drive history education in the United States: Preparing students for participation in a pluralist democracy. Throughout this chapter, we have outlined aspects of historians' work, as well as the multiple purposes that influence history in school and out. All these perspectives help us better understand historical activity and the influences on students' understanding, yet none can tell us how we should teach history. Schools are not miniature research universities, nor do they simply mirror what goes on in the outside world. Educational decisions must be made on the basis of educational values, and there is a long tradition in the United States of educating students for democracy. This has always been the primary objective of the social studies, and of course, history is part of that broader subject. Yet, although most teachers would accept that students should be prepared for democratic participation, they may not always have a clear image of what that means. In order for the goal of democratic participation to provide the direction that teachers need, we must be clear about what it involves.

First, democracy requires participation, and this means more than voting in elections once in a while. Traditional civics education has focused primarily on the relationship between individuals and the state, and thus, students have learned about political representation, legal rights and responsibilities, and the management of conflict. Yet participatory democracy is characterized as much by collaboration as by competition, and this collaboration takes place in a variety of settings—in unions, churches, neighborhood groups, professional associations, faculties, parent–teacher organizations, political parties, and so forth. In each of these settings, people reason together to take action in pursuit of a better future. This points to a second characteristic of participatory democracy: Concern for the common good. We cannot simply pursue our own private interests or attempt to impose our will on others; we must be concerned with what is best for all the communities of which we are a part. Without such concern, people are little more than members of a loose association of selfish individuals, and they can hardly consider themselves part of a community at all. Moreover, in a pluralist society such as the United States, we must take account of multiple perspectives on what constitutes the common good and how to get there. This emphasis on pluralism is the third characteristic of democratic participation and perhaps the hardest to achieve. There is no pre-existing consensus that tells us what to strive for or how we should live together; these are issues that must be worked out by carefully listening to each other, even when we disagree. Especially when we disagree.

History education cannot single-handedly produce a democratic society, nor can it guarantee that students will reason together, care for the common good, or listen to each other. However, the subject should be able to contribute to each of these. It can do so, first, by giving students the chance to take part in reasoned judgment. Members of a democracy must look at evidence together and decide on the best course of action, and this strategy is precisely what is involved in analyzing historical information: We have to make choices about what information is reliable and how it can be used to reach conclusions about the past. Second, history can engage students in consideration of the common good, an activity that depends on identification with larger communities—ethnic, national, global, or all these at once—and on a sense of right and wrong. By considering historical events that affected their communities, and by considering the justice of these events, students should be better prepared and, perhaps, better motivated to engage with such issues today. Finally, history can play a critical role in helping students understand perspectives that are different than their own. Whenever we consider the actions of people in the past, we have to come to grips with ideas, attitudes, and beliefs that are no longer prevalent. We cannot simply dismiss such differences, or we would be unable to understand anything that happened in history. To make sense of the subject, we must strive to see the logic of ways of

*History teachers need clear goals to guide their instruction.*

*The purpose of history education should be to prepare students for participation in a pluralist democracy. Barton & Levstik (2004)*

*Educational decisions must be made on the basis of educational values. Thornton (2005)*

*Education for democracy has always been a primary objective of the social studies.*

*Democratic participation involves collaboration in multiple spheres of public life. Barber (1992), Barton & Ho (2022), Parker (2003), Putnam (2000)*

*Participatory democracy requires that we move beyond individual interests and toward a concern with the common good. Barton & Levstik (2004), Barber (1992)*

*The study of history can give students experience reaching conclusions based on evidence.*

*The study of history can engage students in deliberations over the common good.*

*History can help students understand perspectives different than their own.*

life different than our own—and this should have some payoff in understanding diverse perspectives in the present. At the very least, it's worth a try.

## CONCLUSIONS

*Lerner (1998)*

From our perspective, the desire to avoid controversy leads to one of the most serious weaknesses in the discussion of history—the refusal to admit that all history is interpretive. Those who defend the status quo portray their version as the "real" story (because it's already in the textbooks) and condemn all other interpretations as somehow weakening the "truth" of U.S. history. Given that these arguments are usually made by precisely those people who benefit most from ignoring issues of race, class, and gender, that position is hardly surprising. But if schools are to prepare students for active participation in a democracy, they can neither ignore controversy nor teach students to passively accept someone else's historical interpretations. Being part of a democratic society means much more than that. Education for democratic participation requires that students learn to take part in meaningful and productive discussion with people of diverse viewpoints. Consequently, throughout this book, we portray history as a subject in which students learn how people create accounts of the past and how those accounts could be told differently. Far from being limited to some select group of students, we think this kind of instruction is practical for all children in the elementary and middle grades, and in the next chapter, we explain the principles of teaching and learning that guide our approach.

*Lerner (1998)*

# 2

# IT'S NOT JUST A MISHAP

## The Theory behind Historical Inquiry

Understanding theory to me was like "Ah ha!" Teachers hear so much about theory, and when they go to a workshop or an in-service, they usually say, "Skip the theory, just get to the practical stuff." And so much of what I used to do I just did by instinct—I knew what worked, what would bring results, but I never knew why. Theory helped me understand why it worked, why A plus B equals C. I understood how cooperative learning and integrated instruction and sheltered English all went together; it was like the pieces of a puzzle—they all made sense together. I realized the things I was doing weren't just disconnected pieces, but were part of a design. I found out all these practical ideas I was using had a theoretical foundation behind them.

Knowing theory makes my teaching better. I can pick and choose better—I have a better sense of what will work and what won't. A lot of what I used to do was hit-or-miss; I would try something, and I would never use it again. Now, when I consider a new teaching idea, I can filter it through what I know about theory: I can decide whether it adds to my program or whether it's just busy work. When I go to a conference, I can say, "Oh, that helps build schema," or "That's integrated language"—versus some program that's just a hundred questions or something, where I say, "That wouldn't work, it's not authentic." And theory helps me make sure I'm not doing something just because it looks cute, like, "Oh, gee, I'll have them make a scrapbook." Now I might have students make a scrapbook from the point of a view of a character in a novel, because I know it helps them pick out main ideas, develops their ability to understand characters, provides an authentic assessment—it actually teaches something, it isn't just a cute idea. I don't think, "Oh, isn't that cute! Oh, a bear!" I understand why teaching thematically isn't just having a heart or a bear on every handout.

—Rhoda Coleman, fifth-grade teacher

Rhoda is right: Sometimes teachers hear a lot of theory, and usually it doesn't seem as important as the practical ideas—the good stuff. And some theory really isn't very useful: We've all heard or read theories that obviously came about in a laboratory or office, developed by people who didn't seem to have any idea what real children do in real classrooms. But theory, like teaching, can be good, bad, or somewhere in between. From our perspective, good theory helps teachers make sense of their own experience: It provides them with a clearer understanding of what they see in their classrooms every day—the "Ah ha!" Rhoda mentions. Good theory also helps teachers plan more effective and meaningful lessons for their students: Just as Rhoda explains, theory allows teachers to separate ideas that teach something important from those that are simply cute, novel, or well packaged. Rather than devoting years to trial-and-error attempts to find the best lesson ideas, a teacher who understands the theory behind how students learn can more consistently develop effective plans.

> Useful theory helps teachers make sense of their own experiences.

In this chapter, we lay out the basic principles that guide our understanding of how to teach history. On the one hand, these represent our reading of sociocultural theories of learning, along with research on teaching and learning, particularly in history and social studies. On the other, they also reflect key aspects of the best history teaching we've seen. Rather than being removed from the realities of the classroom, the theory described in this chapter draws on what we know from our experience with teachers and students. We find these ideas useful in understanding what makes for good teaching, and we think they will help teachers plan their own instruction. Without these principles, the activities we describe in the rest of the book are good but isolated lessons, and teachers may or may not be able to use them in their own classrooms. But by understanding the theory that guides this approach, teachers can apply and adapt these suggestions to meet the needs of their students.

*For reviews of research, see Aitken & Sinnema (2008), Barton & Avery (2016), Hicks et al. (2012)*

## STUDENTS LEARN WHEN THEY CONSTRUCT MEANING

You have to start with what the kids already know. Just reading the text and answering the questions at the end of the chapter doesn't work for my English learners, and I really don't think it works for any students. You can't just let them go in and read a chapter cold. If you can't build on something they already know, they can't learn it. They can't understand it if they have no background; they don't get a thing out of it, and you're wasting your time. Students need to put themselves in the place of someone at the time, or read a diary entry—something more personal. A lot of times, history is "untouchable," and if I can say, "This is what an 11-year-old girl really wrote," they're like, "Wow!" That really makes it come alive. They like to read about everyday people who lived a long time ago, even more than famous people, because they can compare it more to their own lives.

—Rebecca Valbuena, fifth-grade teacher

For many of us growing up, our image of *learning*—at least in schools—revolved around *remembering*: Mathematical procedures, details of stories or novels, facts about history or geography or science. Recalling information, though, has little significance if students don't know what it *means*. Students may memorize multiplication tables, for example, but have no idea how to solve real-life math problems; they may learn all the state capitals without understanding what a capital is or what goes on there. In history, we have seen students "learn" that the cause of the American Revolution was taxation without representation but fail to comprehend what taxes are or how government works. Without understanding, storing items in memory is pointless. Even the memory itself usually doesn't last long, and application to new problems is limited or non-existent. Every teacher has had the experience of thinking that students have learned something new, only to discover that they had forgotten it a week later or couldn't apply it in a new situation. This kind of superficial learning occurs precisely because students have only memorized information rather than having constructed an understanding of it.

*Remembering information does not lead to understanding.*

In order for learning to be something more than preparation for *Jeopardy!*, it must involve the construction of meaning. Learning takes place when students engage with information—from teachers, classmates, materials, experiences, and sources outside the classroom—to develop their own understanding of the content. They do not simply "acquire" or "master" knowledge but rather *construct* it based on these interactions. Through reading, writing, watching, listening, talking, and performing, students gradually come to understand the meaning of ideas that are new to them. When their experiences are rich enough, these understandings stay with them and provide the basis for later learning. Not all students, though, will have the same ideas, because they are not simply parroting someone else's thoughts. The very fact that they're constructing their own understanding means they'll make sense of information in varied ways, at differing levels of complexity. This is not just true for children, but for everyone. Ask adults what *patriarchy* means, or *racism*, or *terrorism*, or *religion*, or *justice* and you'll hear widely varied ideas, because each of us has developed our own understanding of social and political concepts such as these. These are

*Learning involves construction of meaning.*

*Göncü & Gauvain (2012), O'Donnell (2012), Schunk (2012)*

*Students' understandings will differ.*

the kinds of ideas that are central to history, and we can't expect every student to understand them in the same ways.

Part of the reason that understandings differ is not just that students are beginners at history (and other subjects), but that their *new* ideas depend on their *old* ideas. Students come to school with prior knowledge, and this knowledge profoundly shapes how they make sense of the curriculum. Building on this prior knowledge is a central task for all history education. Students may not know much about specific people and events, but they will know some things about more general concepts. For example, children may not have heard of Rosa Parks or civil rights (although some will have, especially after the primary grades), but even the youngest will have ideas about fairness and courage, and these are the basis for making sense of new information. Some students may also have learned about life in the past from family photographs or artifacts, television and other media, or visits to museums or other historical sites. This knowledge may be spotty and will certainly vary from one student to another, but it is the foundation for learning history in school. When students cannot connect what they're supposed to learn to what they already know, their understanding is superficial and fleeting.

To help students make these connections, teachers must design instruction to build on students' prior knowledge. This means seeking out students' ideas through questions, interest surveys, and careful observation of participation in learning tasks. It also means becoming familiar with students' communities, so that teachers can tap into the broader funds of knowledge that students have access to. In a farming community, for example, teachers may be able to build on local knowledge of plants, animals, and other aspects of the environment, as well as of agricultural technology; in a setting with more industrial jobs, students' families may have insights into other kinds of technology, into unions and labor relations, and into the impact of the national economy on local production. The purpose of becoming familiar with the knowledge of students and their communities is not to pigeonhole them into narrow stereotypes, because every setting—and every student—will incorporate a range of background knowledge about a variety of topics. However, by becoming more familiar with both individual students and community patterns, teachers can help ensure that they are making as many connections to prior knowledge as possible.

Another important way to connect history to what students already know is by focusing on the everyday lives of people in the past. People are what children understand best; even from a very young age, they can reason about the beliefs and intentions of others. For something to make sense to young children, it must make human sense, because children understand situations in terms of how they involve people. Historians also focus on the human sense of situations: Much of their work involves studying the beliefs and intentions of people in the past. When the race is on to make it through the textbook, though, the human element is first to get pushed aside, and students wind up studying the things they know the least about, such as politics, diplomacy, and government. The absence of people in the study of history may account for the lack of enthusiasm that has been attributed to the subject. By focusing on people, teachers can not only build on what students know best but also help them understand what history is about.

In addition to planning lessons that build on prior knowledge, teachers must also make sure that they *activate* students' knowledge, particularly at the beginning of lessons and units. Even when students have relevant background knowledge, they may not make connections without reminders of what they know. This can be as simple as asking students what they know—for example, "We're going to be learning about immigrants—people who have moved to the United States. What do you know about why people move from one place to another?" Teachers can also ask students to make predictions about texts or images, such as, "This book will be about a woman who lived almost 200 years ago. How do you think her life might be different than a woman's life today?" Most teachers are also familiar with KWL charts, in which the class begins their study of a topic by listing what they already know about it. Even better, teachers can activate students' knowledge by having them contribute to a joint web or concept map (on the board or a sheet of chart paper). This not only activates students' knowledge but also helps them make connections as the

*Students' understanding is shaped by prior knowledge. O'Donnell (2012)*

*Students have learned about the past from family, media, and other sources. Barton (2008), Levstik & Barton (2008)*

*Students must be able to connect new learning to what they already know.*

*Teachers must become familiar with the knowledge of students and their communities. Gonzalez et al. (2005), Salinas et al. (2006)*

*Focusing on everyday life builds on students' prior knowledge. Barton (2008), Levstik & Barton (2008)*

*Children strive to make human sense of the world. Donaldson (1978), Wellman & Gelman (1992)*

*Teachers must activate students' prior knowledge.*

*Alvermann (1991), Ogle (1986)*

**13**

class returns to the web throughout the lesson or unit to identify information that was accurate, to correct mistakes, and to add new information. It is important to keep in mind that the usefulness of discussions, predictions, webs, and K charts in linking new knowledge to old depends on teachers' attention to integrating them into instruction throughout a lesson or unit, rather than simply introducing them at the beginning of a topic and then dropping them.

It is also important to remember that students' prior knowledge is the starting point for learning, not its end point. Sometimes students' ideas are inaccurate. Many, for example, have picked up the impression that Rosa Parks was an old woman at the time of the Montgomery bus boycott. or that she refused to give up her seat because she was physically tired. In some parts of the country, students may believe that Native peoples only lived long ago. and that there are no more Native communities or individuals. In cases such as these, teachers need to make sure they address students' misconceptions by providing sources that counter their ideas, and by calling attention to those differences—otherwise, students' mistaken beliefs may continue despite new learning. More often, students' ideas are simplistic, naïve, or incomplete. They may, for example, overgeneralize their knowledge of a given time in the past and believe that all people during that period shared the same values or ways of life. Similarly, sometimes students understand one aspect of a period but miss the bigger picture; they may know that racist attitudes toward Blacks were even more common in the past than they are today, but this may lead them to think that the Civil Rights Movement was about changing attitudes rather than changing laws and institutions. Teachers must start with these ideas, but the purpose of education is to expand students' understanding so that their knowledge becomes deeper, richer, and more varied.

## PURPOSEFUL SOCIAL ACTIVITY PROMOTES MEANING

There's the synergistic effect of minds working together, hearing what others are doing—it gets *my* neurons sparking, it multiplies what everybody can do. Then there's also the democratic process: Everybody having a say, everybody participating, not just the teacher standing up and lecturing. It also gives them a chance to discover instead of just *telling* them; they get to hear different points of view and discuss outcomes on their own rather than just you connecting the dots for them.

—Rhoda Coleman

How does this construction of meaning take place? That is, how do students go about taking their prior knowledge and combining it with new information? Although teachers can activate students' prior knowledge and call attention to how those ideas relate to new experiences, they cannot directly teach understanding—they cannot do the mental work for their students. Both research on human learning and our own experience as teachers directly contradict the "transmission" model of learning, which assumes knowledge goes directly from one source (whether a teacher or textbook) to another (the student). We cannot simply fill children up with information, no matter how elaborate our system of rewards and punishments; we can't "connect the dots" for them.

Individual students construct their own knowledge, but the process is not a solitary one. Meaning results from, and is motivated by, participation in social activities. Knowledge, that is, comes about as students take part in a community of learners and gradually internalize ways of talking and behaving that characterize that community. Such communities are not only the setting for learning but also the mechanism by which knowledge is constructed—by talking to a partner, working in a small group, discussing with the whole class. Even though students develop their own individual understandings, their ideas come about through the discussion and negotiation that takes place in joint activity. Such activity is not just incidentally social, though—that is, it's not just a group version of something that could be done completely independently. A community of learners shapes ideas about what knowledge is worth having, how to acquire it, and how to use it. In any field, knowledge has meaning only in the context of the questions, procedures, and

*Margin notes:*

Students' prior ideas should be integrated into instruction.

Sometimes teachers must address students' misconceptions.

Teaching should expand students' understanding.

Learning takes place within a sociocultural context. *Lave & Wenger (1991), Resnick (1987), Rogoff (1990), Vygotsky (1978), Wertsch (1998)*

*Göncü & Gauvain (2012), O'Donnell (2012), Schunk (2012)*

debates in which it develops. Scientists, for example, do not pursue their investigations in isolation: The questions they ask, the standards they apply, and the way they report their results are the product of ongoing debate and discussion among a community of scholars (and the concerns and values of the wider society also influence that community). Nor does any single community have a monopoly on producing knowledge. Understanding the environment, for example, may come about very differently depending on whether one is a farmer, research scientist, or environmentalist. Meaningful learning involves not just mastering the content of a subject (no matter how deeply) but also understanding the diverse ways of thinking and acting mathematically, historically, or scientifically in our society.

A critical component of the kind of social activity that leads to learning is that it is *purposeful*. Students—and adults—take seriously the kinds of activities that are valued in their society, including in its many sub-groups. This means that for activities to be meaningful—to allow for the construction of meaning—they must be authentic: Students must take part in the kinds of activities that have value in the wider society, not just in tasks created for the purpose of schooling. From their earliest years, children willingly engage in a wide array of learning experiences, many of them quite challenging. As they grow up, they practice for hours to qualify for a team, try out for a play, or perform in a band—at school or in a garage. A child may struggle to read a school text but manage a complicated digital maneuver with ease. What makes the difference? Certainly, children learn some things solely for a grade and with little or no expectation that they will ever use what they have learned outside school, but as we can all attest, a good deal of the knowledge acquired in this manner quickly fades. Developing expertise with a computer program or app, or practicing for a play, team, or band, on the other hand, serve a variety of meaningful purposes for students. This sense of purpose motivates study, but it also aids memory. Unfortunately, few children experience school history as useful in these ways. Instead, as one fifth grader we know explained, school history is "usually something you're supposed to *know, not do*." History, at least as children experience it in school, is too rarely connected to any important purpose and too often simply something to know for a test.

Students learn when they take part in activities valued in society. *Göncü & Gauvain (2012), Lave & Wenger (1991), O'Donnell (2012)*

Asked to reflect on why history might be worth learning, children may explain that it helps us know "who we are" or "how we got here," by developing a deeper understanding of self and others. In some settings, older students link this kind of learning to contemporary concerns. In Northern Ireland, for example, history at school focuses on the use of evidence to build supportable interpretations, and students engage with the perspectives of competing groups in the region's past. Many students come to believe that this kind of balanced and evidence-based history can serve as an antidote to the sectarian and divisive accounts they otherwise hear, and that history can contribute to easing tensions among differing communities. Similarly, Ghana's national curriculum explicitly aims to promote interdependence and peaceful coexistence among different ethnic and religious groups by teaching about connections among their differing political, economic, and social realities. As a result, students come to see history as preparing them to help develop and strengthen the nation's democracy. By learning the history of each other's ethnic groups, one girl explained, "perhaps we will not have the troubles [interethnic warfare] of other countries in Africa."

*Barton (2002), Barton & McCully (2005)*

*Levstik & Groth (2005)*

As we explained in Chapter 1, we share these students' hopes that history education can support informed democratic participation. The Ghanaian experience suggests that when this goal is adopted by teachers and shared with students, students are more likely to see historical study as purposeful and significant—and worth learning. Similar purposes in the United States might direct us to more fully explore race, class, gender, ethnicity, language, and sexual orientation, and to more fully address individual and group agency—spending time on how people have resisted oppression, worked to build coalitions to solve problems, and lived rich and full lives. An investigation of the Civil Rights Movement, for instance, could call students' attention to courts and legislation but also to the power of collective action—sit-ins, boycotts, marches, voter registration, and

History education should support informed democratic participation.

other strategies. Students might also investigate and make comparisons with current examples of collective action: Black Lives Matter; #MeToo; climate activism; or local, community-based efforts to improve education, economic opportunities, and health and nutrition, or provide safe and affirming spaces for members of marginalized communities. This kind of purposeful history teaching provides some of the background necessary for thoughtful and informed civic participation. It also supplies evidence that even difficult struggles can have positive outcomes. Good teaching focuses on helping students connect what they are learning to this kind of overarching purpose—a purpose that guides questions for investigation, provides reasons for in-depth understanding, and suggests uses for the results of those investigations, thereby supporting intellectual growth as well as civic competence.

*Students should learn how people organize to address social issues. Barton & Ho (2022)*

*Purpose directs content selection, encourages a sense of agency, and supports intellectual growth.*

## LEARNING HISTORY INVOLVES INQUIRY

You have to go into a topic in depth, not just see who can get to the American Revolution by May; otherwise, they won't remember it. I may be slow because I'm just on Jamestown, but my students still remember what they learned about Native Americans. It's important that they're actually *doing* history, not just memorizing information.

—Rebecca Valbuena

I don't remember very much about the Revolution, but it doesn't matter. We'll get it again in junior high.

—Fifth-grade student (one month after studying the topic)

What *is* purposeful social activity in history? Obviously, it's not answering questions on a worksheet or at the end of a textbook chapter, or learning a few isolated (and often incorrect) facts about famous people connected to major holidays. No one does these things outside school. The central activity of historical learning, instead, is *inquiry*: Asking meaningful questions, finding information, drawing conclusions, and reflecting on possible solutions. People learn any subject when they seek answers to the questions that matter to them, and this is particularly true in history. As we pointed out in Chapter 1, outside school, people really do want to know what life was like in the past and how their community developed; they want to know about tragedies and triumphs, heroes and villains; and they want to use that knowledge to make sense of the present. They are willing to investigate these questions by reading, talking to people, watching movies and television shows, and visiting historic places—even if it's only driving by old buildings in their cities and towns. Their inquiries may not be very detailed or comprehensive, but in school, students should be engaging in more careful and systematic inquiries of the kind that people recognize are important in the wider society.

*The central activity of historical learning is inquiry.*

*Inquiry involves asking meaningful questions, finding information, drawing conclusions, and reflecting on possible solutions.*

*People learn when they seek answers to questions that matter to them. Dewey (1933, 1990/1900 & 1902)*

*Children are naturally inquisitive learners.*

*Students should engage in authentic historical activities.*

*Students develop questions when they are immersed in rich historical resources.*

Fortunately, children are naturally inquisitive learners who strive to make sense of their world. Anyone with young children knows the challenge of keeping up with their urge to explore and their ever-present question, "Why?" Teachers can capitalize on children's natural enthusiasm by making their classrooms places where students explore important and meaningful questions. Immersed in historical literature, photographs, documents, and artifacts, students will begin to develop new interests and questions, ones that they are willing to investigate because they *matter* to them. These investigations will involve talking to people, making observations, taking notes, and other activities designed to collect evidence needed to reach conclusions about the past. Students can present these conclusions in many different formats: Making posters, designing displays, creating skits, writing short essays, composing artwork, or just talking with each other. To become truly meaningful, these presentations should also include reflection on the importance of what was learned. Why should we care about changes in technology, about women's suffrage, about the Trail of Tears, or any of the many other topics students can investigate? These are the elements of historical inquiry.

Notably, inquiry takes time. Although some small-scale inquiries can be conducted in a lesson or two, many of the most productive inquiries extend over weeks. Instead of moving through the major events of world history chronologically, for example, a teacher might devote a two-month unit to the history of human interaction with the environment. A unit like that would not mean identifying every time people and the environment have interacted—obviously impossible!—but developing students' understanding of the variety of ways people throughout time have adapted to the environment, changed it to meet their needs, competed for resources, and so on. This kind of study, however, must begin with the concerns and interests of students and must help them find answers to questions that grow out of those motivations. This means that students have to learn what it is to ask and answer historical questions—how to find information, how to evaluate sources, how to reconcile conflicting accounts, how to create an interpretive account.

Some educators think this is an unproductive and inefficient use of time; they argue that students could learn the material more easily through direct instruction or carefully structured readings. That perspective, though, shows a fundamental misunderstanding of what it means to learn "the material" of history. First, it ignores the fact that people learn best when they explore issues that matter to them and when they understand the purpose of such learning. In history, students usually have not had the chance to investigate questions they consider relevant. Their experiences most often have been determined by curriculum guides, textbooks, or packaged materials rather than the pursuit of meaningful knowledge. As a result, they may have no idea why they are expected to study the subject, because they rarely see what it means to *use* history in authentic ways. Although students may sometimes be admonished that they will "need this later," this provides little motivation to take part in artificial exercises removed from useful application. And for students from historically marginalized communities, being expected to learn about the exploits of their oppressors can be demeaning and offensive, no matter how "efficiently" that information is packaged.

Focusing on "efficient delivery" of historical content also ignores the fact that, in order to understand any subject, students need insight into important organizing ideas rather than simply a list of factual information. Understanding history depends on complex ideas such as evidence, perspective, agency, and causality, as well as substantive concepts such as colonialism, revolution, protest, racism, political representation, gender, exploitation, religion, and many others. This requires sustained study. Conceptual learning does not involve the same all-or-nothing mastery as remembering isolated facts: Either you know the capital of Minnesota or you don't, but students' understanding of concepts related to aspects of culture, environment, and society develop gradually over time and continue into adulthood. It might be nice to imagine that students could learn why people oppress each other in a few short lessons, or how technological and economic changes have affected differing social groups, but historical understanding simply doesn't work like that. Students have to study topics in enough depth to understand them and reflect on the meaning and significance of what they've studied, and they have to recognize that this is part of a life-long quest to make sense of the world. Although it's certainly possible to "cover" a great deal of information by plowing through a textbook or set of worksheets, this leads to a "race to get to the American Revolution by May," in Rebecca's words. Students are unlikely to learn anything important from doing so.

Perhaps most importantly, the idea that inquiry is an inefficient means of learning ignores the fact that inquiry is, in itself, one of the most important objectives of history education. Students should be learning to engage in inquiry not just as a means to an end—a way of mastering facts—but also because inquiry has inherent value. To understand what the subject is all about, students must be *doing* history, as Rebecca suggests—questioning, collecting data, interpreting, explaining. In English language arts, if students learned spelling and punctuation but not how to communicate, we would consider that a failure; if they learned algorithms in mathematics but not how to solve problems, that too would be a waste of time. History is no different. If students learned a wealth of information about the past but did not understand how that knowledge had been produced—through

Inquiry often requires in-depth and sustained study. M. King et al. (2015), Wells & Chang-Wells (1992)

Inquiry begins with the concerns and interests of students.

People learn best when they explore issues that matter to them and when they understand the purpose of learning.

Students from historically marginalized communities may see little purpose in learning the history of their oppressors.

Effective teaching helps students learn important organizing ideas. *Prawat (1989a, 1989b)*

Inquiry itself is one of the most important objectives of history education.

Students must learn how knowledge is produced, and how to produce it themselves.

the use of historical inquiry—or how to go about constructing new knowledge about new questions, then their study would have been pointless. Lack of experience in the process of inquiry also would leave students susceptible to myths, distortions, and flat-out lies—all of which they will encounter throughout their lives, from those who seek to manipulate them. Resisting such manipulation requires experience with the process of inquiry, not a storehouse of information.

One final point needs to be made about inquiry. Many educators confuse inquiry with "source analysis." They recognize that authentic engagement in history includes the use of original sources—documents, photographs, artifacts, and so on—but they mistakenly believe that the principal task of doing history is "analyzing" those sources. You'll find countless lesson plans, articles, and other resources in which students are provided with a document and directed to identify who wrote it, what purpose it was created for, and so on. Some states even test students on their ability to engage in such analysis. This is a caricature of historical inquiry—or maybe more like a travesty. In historical inquiry, students *use* sources (especially collections of sources) to learn about the past, because those sources can provide evidence to answer the questions they have. This does require knowing what a particular source is and why it was created (although many things can be learned about a source regardless of why it was produced). However, this kind of analysis cannot be the focus of inquiry; the purpose of inquiry is to *use* sources to reach conclusions about the past. In inquiry, students will usually know about a source before using it—the teacher or materials will identify it as "a memoir written for a magazine" or "a posed photograph of a middle-class family" or "a census record of the people in each family in this town in 1840." Analyzing sources as an end in itself would be a waste of time. Historians certainly are never handed a source and told, "Analyze this," and students should not be either. Historians—and all those interested in the past—collect evidence from a variety of sources to develop conclusions in answer to their questions. This is what inquiry is and what students should be doing.

## TEACHING MEANS SCAFFOLDING

You have to provide them with structure. You don't just say, "Write a paragraph"; you introduce them to some vocabulary, brainstorm about the topic, make comparison charts and graphic organizers, and then help them use those to write a paragraph. If you want them to produce something, you have to provide structure; you have to take them where they are and move them one step further.

—Rebecca Valbuena

Outside school, learning almost always involves ongoing collaboration among the members of a community, as more knowledgeable members help beginners become full-fledged participants in activities they both consider worthwhile. Consider, for example, how young children learn to talk. The process extends over many years and involves countless interactions, as children try to communicate, and adults accept and encourage their attempts while also modeling more fluent ways of expressing what they want to say. Although the precise kinds of interaction may vary from one culture (or sub-culture) to the next, children who have no opportunity at all to interact will not learn to talk; they construct their understanding of language through interaction with fluent speakers.

To take a somewhat different example, professional schools require prospective practitioners—doctors, teachers, and so on—to engage in extensive field experiences in which experts help them learn to deal with real-life situations. No one would trust a doctor who had learned medicine only from a book; to treat patients, doctors must undergo a lengthy period of practical training. During this time, experienced practitioners model the practical use of medical knowledge, and novices are gradually given more responsibility for treating patients on their own. Most learning outside the classroom follows a similar pattern involving a kind of *apprenticeship*, in which those who are more knowledgeable

---

*Understanding the process of inquiry can help students resist myths, distortions, and lies.*

*Inquiry is not the same as analyzing sources.*

*In inquiry, sources are used to provide evidence, not as objects to be analyzed in isolation.*

*People learn through interaction with more knowledgeable members of a community. Göncü & Gauvain (2012), Lave & Wenger (1991), Rogoff (1990), Vygotsky (1978), Wertsch (1998)*

*In apprenticeships, those who are more knowledgeable help novices develop expertise.*

gradually help novices develop expertise. They provide them with the structure Rebecca mentions.

Unfortunately, children rarely have the chance to take part in this kind of sustained interaction in history. Most often, they are expected to listen while teachers transmit information to them, or to read from worksheets or other materials. Participation is usually limited to the common *initiation-response-evaluation* pattern: The teacher asks questions, students respond, and the teacher tells them whether the answers were right. Other times, students may be given independent assignments or expected to "do research," but they aren't taught how to go about the process of learning. As every teacher knows, few students have the skills necessary to conduct research on their own. Although inquiry is essential to education, simply assigning such tasks won't guarantee meaningful results. Most students need help to make the most of their experiences, and teachers' most important responsibility is to provide them with the structure and assistance they need to learn—a process known as *scaffolding*. Just as scaffolding on a construction project supports people as they work, scaffolding in the classroom supports students as they learn. Children learn best when they take part in joint activities with teachers (and more knowledgeable peers) who help them go about their inquiries. Such scaffolding is especially necessary for complex and ambitious tasks such as inquiry.

Scaffolding takes many forms. First, teachers have to encourage students' interest in accomplishing tasks; although children are naturally inquisitive, they are more likely to follow through with their investigations when teachers help them develop and maintain interest. Second, teachers must actively support and encourage students as they continue to work through their inquiries. This support often involves breaking down a task into manageable components. This doesn't mean teaching skills in isolation but, rather, helping students see how they can complete portions of a project without becoming overwhelmed. As Rebecca explains, students can write a better paragraph when they become familiar with vocabulary, engage in brainstorming, and plan their compositions rather than simply being told, "Write a paragraph." Similarly, students learn more from inquiry when teachers give them experience developing questions, identifying resources, and planning presentations than when they are just sent to the internet and told to "do research." Graphic organizers often play a key role in providing the structure for these tasks because, as Rebecca says, if you want students to produce something, you have to provide them with structure.

Another crucial element of this scaffolding is the teacher's modeling of procedures. As suggested earlier, teachers must demonstrate what it looks like to do history; just as students need to see their teachers reading and writing, they need to see them grappling with historical questions, collecting information, drawing conclusions, and so on. Teachers must show students what it looks like to accomplish a task successfully; if they don't see examples, they won't know what they are supposed to do. In addition, teachers have to work closely with students as they try out these procedures; this involves constantly using probing questions to help students discover how to apply historical skills in their own work. Finally, teachers have to give students critical feedback on their performances: They must help them understand how their work compares to ideal versions. Without such feedback, many students will not know whether they are accomplishing a task successfully. The ultimate goal of all these forms of scaffolding is to transfer control from teacher to student by enabling students to plan their learning and monitor their own progress—abilities sometimes referred to as *metacognition*.

## ASSESSMENT MUST BE CONSTRUCTIVE

*Assessment, evaluation, testing,* and worst of all, *grading*—for many educators, these are three of the most unpleasant words in their professional vocabulary. They conjure up a host of negative associations—from scaled scores and percentiles to long evenings spent poring over countless versions of the same assignment, correcting errors and pleading for insight

*Cazden (1988)*

Students need help engaging in inquiry.

Scaffolding supports students as they learn. *Glazewski & Hmelo-Silver (2019), Rogoff (1990), Saye & Brush (2004), Wood et al. (1976)*

Teachers have to develop and maintain students' interest.

Students need tasks broken down into manageable parts.

Graphic organizers help structure tasks.

Teachers' modeling of procedures is a crucial element of scaffolding. *Schunk (2012)*

Probing questions help students apply historical skills.

Feedback is one of the most effective ways of supporting students' learning. *Hattie & Timperley (2007), Schunk (2012)*

Assessment and evaluation are used interchangeably throughout this chapter.

**19**

into why students just don't get it. Considering how much importance schools attach to grades and other forms of evaluation, students are usually shocked to discover that their teachers don't enjoy the process and would just as soon jettison the whole enterprise. For most of us, it's not evaluating but instructing—the scaffolding we discuss throughout this book—that provides our image of what teaching is all about. Evaluation seems, at best, a necessary evil to be tacked onto the end of units so we can come up with a grade for report cards. At worst, it can ruin a perfectly good relationship between a teacher and her students.

But it doesn't have to be that way. Instead of an unpleasant add-on, evaluation can be a meaningful and sometimes—believe it or not—enjoyable task, a set of practices at the very heart of teaching and learning. To fulfill such lofty expectations, however, evaluation must play a different role than we usually imagine. If the primary purpose of classroom evaluation is to produce a set of grades, then neither students nor teachers are likely to see much benefit in the practice. When grade books, rather than students' needs, determine the form of assessment, assignments become little more than an attempt to trip students up—to force them into revealing what they don't know, so the grades will resemble a normal distribution. This obsession with sorting students virtually guarantees that evaluation will be a negative experience, one designed to uncover deficiencies in students' knowledge and understanding.

In the kinds of classrooms described in this book, the primary characteristic of evaluation is its *constructive* character. By constructive evaluation, we mean, first and foremost, that it serves a constructive purpose—it has beneficial effects on teaching and learning. For students, this means that evaluation tasks allow them to show what they know rather than what they don't know. The teacher is not an adversary who tries to ferret out what they have failed to accomplish but an advocate who helps students demonstrate their achievements. Most teachers, at one time or another, worry that students' performance doesn't accurately reflect what they have learned; they believe (or hope) that students know more than they have been able to show on tests or other assignments. Constructive assessment confronts this problem head-on by giving students as many ways of showing what they know as possible—through formal and informal measures, through tasks chosen both by teacher and student, through speaking, writing, and other forms of presentation. When students and teachers work together like this—looking for the best means of demonstrating what's been learned—students' self-esteem benefits because they have every chance to live up to their potential. The teacher's instruction is better, meanwhile, because she gains more complete insight into what students know and what they still need to learn.

To gain this kind of insight, teachers need more than one way of tapping into students' achievement. By combining several means of assessment, they can be more confident of finding out what students know and can do. Three of the most useful ways of finding out about students are through their discussion, their writing, and their performances or presentations. No one of these tasks provides a complete picture of learning: Some students may remain silent during discussions but write fine essays, some may give insightful presentations but never finish their writing, and so on. Relying on just one measure means that students who do well in that medium—writing, speaking, drawing, or whatever—will do well, but those whose strengths lie elsewhere will seem deficient. Using multiple means of assessment gives all students the chance to show what they know. This approach also frequently involves giving students choices. In some cases, students may choose the form their assessment takes—a student might be allowed to decide, for example, whether an inquiry project will result in an essay, a poster, a videotape, or a presentation to the class. Other times, it may be the topic of study that students choose; within a broader unit chosen by the teacher (such as the Women's Suffrage Movement or the Great Migration), each student might decide which specific questions to investigate and be evaluated on. When given choices, students are more likely to capitalize on their opportunities for learning than if they are simply answering questions posed by the teacher, using methods assigned by him or her.

Evaluation can be meaningful and even enjoyable.

Hart (1994), Johnston (1992), Shepard (1991)

In constructive assessment, teachers are advocates for students.

Multiple forms of assessment provide a more complete picture of students' progress.

Giving students choices of format and topic can help them demonstrate their learning.

Assessment activities should also be authentic—they should be similar to the tasks people do in their communities, businesses, or scholarly disciplines. This often involves preparation for an audience beyond that of the teacher. When the teacher is the only audience for a task, students have little motivation to show what they know. When children retell a story they have heard to someone who doesn't know the story, for example, their explanations are more complete than when they know the listener has heard it as well. Similarly, when students communicate for a real audience, they perform at a higher level than when they complete an assignment only to turn it in to the teacher; students are motivated to show what they know because of the necessity of getting their audience to understand them. This use of authentic activities highlights another characteristic of constructive evaluation—its continuity with teaching and learning. Traditionally, teachers think of assessment as what comes after learning: You teach students about something (or they read about it on their own), and then you test them to see if they learned it. In most classrooms, it's easy to tell the difference between learning and assessment. In fact, schools often go to great lengths to make the two situations as different as possible: When students are being tested, they don't talk, they don't move around, they don't work together, they don't get help from the teacher. But in the kinds of classrooms described in this book, there is no such split between learning and assessment. An observer walking into one of these classes would not be able to tell whether it was a "teaching" day or a "testing" day, because they're one and the same thing. Teachers take notes while students are talking, observe their presentations, review their projects, and read their written reports; all these are part of the ongoing assessment of learning. There are few separate times set aside for assessment because assessment is always taking place.

> Assessment should mirror the authentic tasks people engage in outside schools. *Wiggins (1992)*

> Assessment should not be separated from teaching and learning.

Perhaps the most important principle to keep in mind in assessing students' historical understanding is that constructive evaluation must be consistent with a constructivist perspective on teaching and learning. People learn new information by linking it to what they already know; their understanding, then, is never a simple reproduction of the information they encounter but always an interpretation in light of prior understanding. Students' understanding at any given time represents interaction between external sources of information and their prior knowledge. As a result, no two students' understanding will be identical, nor will a child's understanding be the same as an adult's. As we already have mentioned, learning history is not an all-or-nothing process in which you either "know" a topic or you don't, but a lifelong process of knowledge construction that involves not only amassing more information but also increasingly sophisticated insight into the connections and relations among concepts. Constructive evaluation seeks to provide teachers and students a picture of how this development of understanding is progressing, rather than assessing whether students have "caught" discrete pieces of information.

> Constructive assessment provides information on the development of understanding, not retention of information.

## CONCLUSIONS

In this chapter, we have identified the aspects of learning that we think provide the best guidance for teaching history. Based on contemporary research and our own experience, we have argued:

- Learning involves construction of meaning, which results from interaction of prior knowledge and new information.
- Learners construct meaning by participating in purposeful, socially valued activities.
- The principal activity of history is inquiry, in which students ask meaningful questions, collect evidence, reach conclusions, and reflect on what they've learned.
- Teachers must scaffold students' participation in inquiry (and in all learning) by providing structure, assistance, and feedback.
- Assessment should be constructive—it should contribute to teaching and learning by providing insight into students' construction of meaning.

Although we have described these principles separately, they have little meaning in isolation. Teachers will not succeed if they engage students in inquiry but don't build on their prior knowledge, if they scaffold students' participation but don't allow them to construct their own ideas, or if they engage them in purposeful activity but test them on memory of facts. Teachers must implement these principles in an integrated way, and by doing so, they can promote meaningful and lasting learning for students—including those from a variety of backgrounds and in a variety of circumstances. As Rebecca Valbuena explains, understanding this theoretical background ensures that good teaching isn't just a mishap:

> I can't tell you how much [knowing about theory] has changed me; it all makes sense. Being a good teacher means you know what to do, and you have a purpose for what you're doing. Everything you do has to have a theoretical base, from classroom management on. I think a lot of teachers do things naturally, but if you know the theory beforehand, it's so much more satisfying. It's not just a mishap; you're doing it on purpose. Knowing the theory takes you to a level beyond.

# 3

# THERE AREN'T A LOT OF "FOR SURE" FACTS

## Building Communities of Historical Inquiry

It is 11:10 on a cool October morning, and 26 7- and 8-year-old children are gathered around their teacher, Ruby Yessin, listening to a story about Johnny Appleseed. At one point, Ruby stops to talk about what is known about the historical Johnny Appleseed:

| | |
|---|---|
| *Teacher:* | What kind of a story is this? Remember we said that some stories were tall tales? |
| *Jennie:* | And folktales! |
| *Teacher:* | Right, some are folktales. And Johnny Appleseed is a le…? le…? |
| *Choral:* | Legend! |
| *Teacher:* | Legend. That means some parts of the story are? |
| *Ryan:* | True. |
| *CeCe:* | But some are just made up. |

At this point, the children engage in a general conversation about why parts of stories might be made up. One boy suggests that the real story probably wasn't exciting; others think that people probably didn't know "the real facts," so they simply made them up.

| | |
|---|---|
| *Teacher:* | What parts of this story do we *think* are true? |
| *Gabriel:* | Well, there *was* a man who planted apple trees. It said so in that other book. |
| *Avram:* | Yeah, but his real name wasn't Appleseed, remember! |

Several of the children recall that John Chapman was the "real" Johnny Appleseed. Ruby draws them back to the original question: Which parts of the story do we think are true? Again, she puts the emphasis on *think*, and the students begin to discuss "facts" versus "exaggerations." The conversation bogs down as some children repeat suggestions others have already made. Lucy and Gabriel appear to be having an argument over whether "Appleseed" can be a "real" name because it was a nickname used by Chapman's contemporaries.

| | |
|---|---|
| *Lucy:* | See, it says here [in the encyclopedia entry] that he was "popularly known as Johnny Appleseed." I think that's what people called him then. |
| *Gabriel:* | Uh-uh. That's what's popular *now*. |
| *Teacher:* | I'm getting mixed up. Is there some way we can keep track of our ideas here? |
| *Lucy:* | We could make a list! [Two children get the large pad of chart paper that hangs in the front of the room. Another grabs the plastic cup of magic markers.] |
| *Avram:* | Let's take the story in pieces! We can put each fact we find under "facts" and have exaggerations on another paper. |

For the next 20 minutes, the children analyze the story, event by event. They use two other books about Johnny Appleseed along with a brief encyclopedia entry, but there are several places where they aren't sure whether something is a fact. At Ruby's suggestion, they use red markers to circle

DOI: 10.4324/9781003179658-3

**23**

these items. Someone else suggests underlining "for sure" facts in green and "for sure" exaggerations in black.

> *CeCe:* There sure aren't a lot of "for sure" facts!
>
> *Teacher:* No, there aren't. We seem to have a lot of questions about this story. What would it look like if we wrote it so that it didn't have any exaggerations? Could we write it so that it only said what we are pretty sure happened?
>
> *CeCe:* That would be a short story!

Aitken & Sinnema (2008), M. King et al. (2015), Wells & Chang-Wells (1992), Wertsch (1998), Levstik (2013)

The students in the previous vignette are members of the kind of community of reflective, historical inquiry described in Chapter 2. Such a community encourages participation with others in goal-directed activity, engagement with intellectual problems that cannot be resolved through the routine application of previously learned knowledge, and understanding and resolving problems with the aid of a variety of intellectual tools. Establishing a community of inquiry in a classroom that provides a meaningful, integrative, challenging, and active context for learning history, as Rebecca Valbuena notes in Chapter 2, is not just a mishap. Whether primary school children are investigating the facts and exaggerations of a historical legend, fourth graders are writing the history of their school, or middle schoolers are debating the merits of nonviolent protest as a response to colonialism in India, communities of inquiry have certain things in common:

Characteristics of communities of inquiry.

- There is lively conversation and intellectual negotiation among participants who each have varying degrees of expertise in the topic at hand.
- Conversation focuses on questions and tasks worthy of sustained discussion and in-depth study.
- Students use both prior knowledge and newly gathered data to "master perplexity"—to make sense out of what seemed not to make sense when their study began.
- Teachers model and students practice "classroom thoughtfulness"—taking the time necessary to think carefully and thoroughly before responding to questions or attempting to resolve problems.
- Students *do history*—they pose, investigate, and at least tentatively answer historical questions and develop historical explanations and interpretations—they don't just memorize the history others have done.

This chapter introduces the ways in which language—speaking, reading, and writing—sustain communities of historical inquiry. Consider how the teacher in the opening vignette structures her primary school students' engagement with historical inquiry. First, because the Johnny Appleseed legend is a common children's story and an example of the kind of historical mythologizing that frequently appears in the elementary curriculum, it provides an appropriate forum for *talking historically*—communally analyzing the legend's historical roots. Second, the teacher scaffolds the historical talk so that it becomes a conversation not a recitation. She calls children's attention to the genre—a legend—with which they are dealing and reminds them that legends have particular characteristics that are important for readers to know. Note, too, that the teacher does not ask which parts of the story are "known to be true"—known by someone else. Rather, she asks her students to call on their prior knowledge of literary genres and the historical Johnny Appleseed and consider what parts they "think are true."

"Talking historically" is conversation not recitation.

Scaffolding is necessary for in-depth inquiry.

The choice of language is important here. By asking students what they think, the teacher models a more tentative language that invites speculation rather than final answers. She also encourages students to take intellectual risks that keep conversations alive and engaging. Who is Johnny Appleseed anyway? Is this fiction or history? How can we distinguish between facts and exaggerations? What makes us think that one part of a story is true but not another? As they participate in the conversation, these children not only think about what counts as history but also consider why people might exaggerate beyond the historical data and how different genres use historical information—important questions about the ways in which history is used in the larger world. They also learn that some of the most interesting questions don't have single, or easy, answers. Such questions are central to

**24**

reflective, historical inquiry, and so is the language students use to conduct, present, and reflect on their inquiries. In this chapter, several teachers are introduced who carefully consider how reading, writing, and talking support reflective historical inquiry.

## TALKING HISTORICALLY

As already mentioned in Chapter 2, all of us learn how to "mean" in a variety of social contexts. In addition, we learn how to express what we mean through various symbolic forms—literature, art, music, dance, drama, writing, and conversation, among others. Symbolic forms are not, however, simply windows through which meaning shines clearly. Instead, symbolic form both expresses and shapes meaning. A photograph of a family standing beside a covered wagon (Figure 3.1) shows us how small a space early White settlers had for all their possessions. We can analyze other details as well: The military uniform that one man wears, the seemingly empty prairie stretching behind the family. But the photograph also freezes what would otherwise have been a fleeting moment, giving it weight and meaning it might not otherwise have had. The frown on the woman's face comes to represent more than simple weariness with posing or a response to bright sun; instead, we read in her face the rigors of the overland journey. The empty prairie suggests that this was uninhabited land ripe for the taking rather than contested space whose settlement resulted in mass displacement of its original inhabitants. Much like photographs, written texts store, shape, and transmit information, but they use words rather than visual images. The use of imagery and analogy, the choice and arrangement of words, and the expectations we have for a particular genre shape how we interpret written texts.

Conversations are similarly complex and important undertakings. Sometimes we take them for granted. Talk seems so common that we forget how intricate a really engaging conversation can be. First, the style of talk implies meaning beyond words. Something as simple as a form of address or tone of voice can imply social status as well as feelings not easily conveyed by words. Conversations about history may range from explanations, arguments, and justifications to narratives and dialogue about moral and ethical issues. Such talk offers an important opportunity for students to test out their ideas about the past and especially about its relation to the present and future. The primary school

*Lemke (1991), Van Oers & Wardukker (1999), Wells (1999), Bernstein (2013), Arias-Ferrer & Egea-Vivancos (2019)*

*Levstik & Barton (2008), Sabzalian (2019)*

*Arnheim (1981), Purves (1990)*

*Conversations are intricate social interactions. Oyler (1996), Nokes (2012)*

**FIGURE 3.1   On the prairie: Family with covered wagon, 1886.**

Bakhtin (1986), Leinhardt (1994)

students' enthusiastic participation in deconstructing the Johnny Appleseed legend combines elements of literary and historical discourses. It is the kind of rich and interesting conversation that often grows up around good children's literature in classrooms that value multiple perspectives.

Kayla Jackson's classroom is another such place. Kayla had not always been enthusiastic about her district's emphasis on English/language arts standards. In her 3 years as a teacher, Kayla structured her social studies curriculum around building a peaceful, caring classroom community, and she wanted to sustain that program. A conversation with a colleague convinced her that she might make the new standards meet her needs, and the lesson she designed using Henry Cole's *Unspoken* was a first step in that direction.

Cole (2012)

This wordless picture book addressed Kayla's peace and caring goals for social studies—it focuses on a family helping with the Underground Railroad—but it also presented some challenges. Her second graders had little content background regarding the Underground Railroad, and their vocabulary for talking about the past was limited. What they did have, though, was the peace and care vocabulary Kayla had already introduced, and they loved good mysteries. Kayla found that mysteries helped her students interpret cause and effect and anticipate consequences. The wordless picture book combined the cause and effect of mysteries with the emotional resonance of caring for someone in danger. This was something her students could understand! Further, having students carefully observe illustrations in *Unspoken* in order to describe characters, settings, and events and identify key details in a text met the language arts standards while fitting well with the kind of conversations she wanted students to have about the past.

*Focusing on issues of social justice addresses history education's civic goals. Levstik (2013)*

*Careful observation scaffolds students' inferences about historical chronology.*

Serendipitously, the day Kayla introduced *Unspoken* was dark and stormy, with window-rattling thunder. "This is perfect weather for a history mystery," Kayla announced. "And I have just the right one for us today." Holding up *Unspoken*, Kayla covered the subtitle that identified the historical connection with the Underground Railroad. She explained that she would need the children's help with this book because it had hardly any words. Explaining, too, that they would need a really big version of the book to solve the history mystery, she used the document reader so that everyone could see details in each illustration. The students' first task, Kayla explained, was to figure out what was going on by imagining questions the people in the story might be asking. Kayla expected that her students would draw on everyday experiences to develop initial questions for each character, but she also anticipated that the illustrations would generate questions about time and place. When Jaden asked if this story happened "a long time ago" because of the main character's "clothes look long ago," Kayla focused students on time clues. They decided the story took place "long ago" because "soldiers don't ride on horses like that now" and "people don't wear those kinds of shoes anymore." Soon, another student asked if *Unspoken* is a true story, and Kayla explained that it was historical fiction, a story that put "made-up characters" in situations that happened in the past.

*Discussion helps students distinguish between fact and fiction.*

"Here's *another* mystery," she said, pointing to another illustration. "What real situation is going on here?" Students leaned forward, searching for clues. Aaron was the first to notice a single eye staring from a pile of unshucked corn. His observation provoked so many questions that Kayla drew possible "plot lines" on the board. Students dictated story events in "time order," and Kayla drew lines emanating from the last event. The class suggested different paths or plot lines the story might take. No one guessed that at the end of *Unspoken* the stranger hiding in the corn might simply vanish. Where had s/he gone? The mystery remained. Kayla promised more clues the next day.

*Graphic organizers help students keep events in order and anticipate upcoming events.*

## RECOGNIZING PERSPECTIVE AND AGENCY

*Diversity is valued in communities of inquiry. Epstein (2009), Darling-Hammond (2010), Levstik (1997, 2013)*

Because *Unspoken* focuses on the perspectives of a family of White "conductors" on the Underground Railroad, and the young boy escaping enslavement appears only as an eye looking out from the corn and, later, as a sketch on a wanted poster, Kayla introduced a second book, *Underground*, that presents the perspectives of those escaping enslavement.

"One of the characters in this book," she explained, "could have been the stranger hiding in *Unspoken*. Let's see if we can find out what might have happened to the person who disappeared from *Unspoken*."

The illustrations and minimal text in *Underground* focus on shadowy figures who slip past a sleeping guard; find shelter in a farmhouse, much like the one in *Unspoken*; and eventually find themselves in a place where they can be free. Kayla emphasized the emotions represented in this story and asked students to help her "read with expression." "Imagine you are all trying to sneak by the guard. How should we read this page that says, 'We were quiet'?" The students' whispered words swept through the room. Eventually, they outlined the perspectives of different characters and began to discuss what power a character might have had to influence events. What choices could these people have made?

*Levstik (2000), Levstik & Barton (2008), Arias-Ferrer & Egea-Vivancos (2019)*

"Why are there so many secrets in both these stories?" Kayla asked. Students suggested that mysteries sometimes happened when people were afraid. They listed the kinds of things people could do, especially when they were afraid, and Kayla linked both stories to the importance of building peaceful, caring places where people could be less afraid and kinder to each other. She also introduced a more historical vocabulary appropriate to students' ongoing observations. The class added the terms abolitionist, Underground Railroad, overseer, corncrib, Confederate, Union, and reward poster to their Word Wall and then used the new vocabulary as they retold each story. Finally, Kayla read a short excerpt from a story set in Buxton, Canada, a final destination on the Underground Railroad—perhaps the new home of some of the people students met in the books they had just read.

*Introducing historical vocabulary supports deeper conversation.*

Making sense in history requires opportunities for discussion—for testing out ideas, listening to other possibilities, asking questions, and challenging interpretations—and the availability of images, oral interviews, fiction, and non-fiction enrich that discussion. Although the conversations in the opening vignette and in Kayla's classroom include some elements that would be familiar to historians, elementary and middle school children are not—and need not be—full participants in historian's professional discourse. Instead, they employ meaning-making practices that work in their multiple communities. In Kayla's classroom, for instance, they begin with language familiar in their discussions of peace and caring. In both of these primary school classrooms, students combine elements of literary, historical, and moral discourses as well as classroom protocols. This is rich and interesting talk. It is also the kind of talk that is unlikely to occur if the only experience children have with history is filling in blanks on a worksheet or memorizing presidents in chronological order. Nor is it likely to occur where children are silenced because either what they have to say or the way in which they say it isn't valued. This is particularly important in classrooms where the children come from diverse linguistic or cultural backgrounds. Talking historically is more likely to occur where teachers and students value the multiple perspectives that diversity can provide, where conversation is supported by in-depth study, and where conversation revolves around questions worthy of sustained discussion.

*In discussion, children jointly make sense out of history. Wells (1999), James & McVay (2009), Nokes (2012), Levstik & Thornton (2018), Henderson & Levstik (2016)*

*Levstik (1997), Barton & Ho (2022)*

## THE IMPORTANCE OF QUESTIONS

Anything that may be called knowledge, or a known object, marks a question answered, a difficulty disposed of, a conclusion cleared up, an inconsistency reduced to coherence, a perplexity mastered.
—John Dewey, *The Quest for Certainty* (1929, pp. 226–227)

If children are to enthusiastically engage in sustained conversation about history, four things are required:

- Questions that are worth discussing.
- Questions that do not have simple or single answers.
- Sufficient and appropriate data sources so that students can attempt to answer the questions.
- Imaginative entry into the past.

*Penyak & Duray (1999), Parker & Hess (2001)*

## There Aren't a Lot of "For Sure" Facts

Questions are at the heart of inquiry. *National Council for the Social Studies (2013)*

Obviously, questions are at the heart of this approach to history. But we are talking about very different questions than the ones many of us are familiar with from textbooks and workbooks. The point of these questions is not to see whether students have read a particular text; rather, it is to provide direction and motivation for the rigorous work of doing history. An example of this kind of direction and motivation can be seen in a sixth-grade classroom in which the students are studying India. The class has just completed working with an artifact kit using a variety of resources to compare life in a modern Indian city with life in the students' hometown. A guest speaker previously told them that, to understand some of the differences between India and the United States, it is necessary to understand each country's history.

CE (Common Era) and BCE (Before the Common Era) are used instead of AD (Anno Domini) and BC (Before Christ) by historians and archaeologists.

Jeanette Groth, the teacher, now asks the sixth graders to use their textbooks to identify eight events in Indian history that they consider pivotal. While the students read and take notes, Jeanette places on the board a large time line that runs from 2500 BCE to 1948 CE She then asks students to suggest items for the time line. There is debate about whether farming in the Indus valley was pivotal and whether it could legitimately be considered to have a "main date." Soon, however, students move on to the establishment of the British East India Company, colonization by the British, and the eventual British withdrawal. They use time lines developed by the eighth-grade U.S. history class to compare what was happening in each country during each time period. Jason points out that the colonization periods for both India and the North American colonies overlap, "but our Revolution came sooner."

Some inquiries are teacher-initiated.

On the surface, this may not look terribly different than a good, traditional history class. In fact, however, this activity is crucial for several reasons. First, it asks students to think about what is historically significant. Second, it makes clear that neither U.S. nor Indian history exists in a vacuum. Finally, it establishes the historical background—prior knowledge—needed to raise the next, teacher-initiated, question: Were there any similarities in the ways in which the people of India and the people of the 13 colonies rid themselves of British rule? Iman exclaims, "Well, we kicked their butts!" Ainslie chimes in, "We tried to get the British mad, to get them started in a war, but the Indians tried compromise." The students draw on their fifth-grade experience in re-enacting a trial of the participants in the Boston Massacre, they talk about the techniques the rebels used to end British rule, and they check dates on the time line to see what was happening in India during the same period. At this point, different groups are asked to develop comparative time lines showing British colonial rule and the independence movements in each country. By the next class, students are ready to compare colonialism and rebellion in India and North America. Their discussion is lively, requiring them to select relevant information, combine pieces of information—even though some of those pieces might, at first, have seemed unrelated—compare the problem under investigation with problems previously encountered, and use skills and concepts previously employed. In other words, their inquiry requires both prior knowledge in history—their fifth-grade study of the American Revolution—and in-depth study—their investigation of British colonial rule in India.

Inquiry requires prior knowledge and in-depth study.

## PRIOR KNOWLEDGE

History has intersecting discourse communities.

Students bring background knowledge to their study of school subjects.

History is interpreted publicly and personally, as well as by historians. *Seixas (1993), Levstik & Barton (2008), Epstein (2009), VanSledright (2010)*

We know that new knowledge builds on the learner's prior knowledge base. This seems self-evident, but it is certainly not simple, particularly in history. First of all, history might be more adequately described as a set of intersecting fields rather than as a unitary discipline. Thus, social historians, military historians, archivists, public historians, interpreters at historic sites, archaeologists, and genealogists, to name just a few, all deal with history, but their various fields are marked by sometimes disparate modes of inquiry, styles of communication, and perceived purposes. In addition, students bring much more background knowledge to the study of history than we sometimes credit them with. History is, after all, not confined to historians. Families construct histories as they interpret events through the lens of family involvement. The media also interpret historic events.

They create documentaries and news programs that purport to explain—and sometimes make—history, but they also present fictionalized versions of the past. There are also persistent historical myths and legends held dear by parts of the larger culture—Betsy Ross sewing the first flag, Columbus "discovering a new world," and so forth. For some students these images are comforting; others may feel excluded by the popular culture's mythologies. In any case, these myths and legends are often part of the historical knowledge base that children bring to school. Once in school, students acquire historical information (and misinformation) from instruction. The sixth graders studying India, for instance, were able to think more clearly about resistance to British colonialism because they could draw on their prior study of the American Revolution. Notice, however, that their teacher did not rely on unassisted recall. Instead, there were prompts to trigger prior knowledge, most notably the U.S. history time lines constructed by her eight-grade class.

Because reflective historical inquiry is rooted in what students already know and can do and gradually moves beyond the known, savvy teachers take into account the conceptions and misconceptions held by students and supported by popular culture, as well as the knowledge base provided by the fields of history. Historical inquiry develops most easily when the creation or discovery of a problem challenges prior knowledge, providing opportunities for students to outgrow what they already know. As they create and test hypotheses, explore variations on initial problems, and reflect on the consequences of answers as well as the processes of and purposes for their study, students engage in authentic historical work, building on prior knowledge to *produce* rather than *reproduce* knowledge. Although their interpretations may be naïve and are rarely new to the discipline of history, students are not simply reproducing knowledge that others have produced. Instead, they attempt to construct a coherent explanation for a set of historic events. The sixth graders' comparison of Indian and American independence movements, for instance, obviously owes much to prior studies in U.S. history as well as to some of the facts, concepts, theories, and discourse that mark history as a field. In addition, students' attempts to construct this comparison should make them more interested in and thoughtful about other independence movements as well as other historical interpretations of the events they have just analyzed. Clearly, this approach emphasizes in-depth understanding both of history and historical methods.

*Levstik & Barton (2008), VanSledright (2010)*

*Inquiry can begin with challenges to prior knowledge.*

*Students produce rather than reproduce knowledge. Wells & Chang-Wells (1992), Newmann & Associates (1996), Segall (1999)*

## IMAGINATIVE ENTRY

In a fifth-grade classroom, Tessa discusses the outcome of a class trial based on the events surrounding the Boston Massacre:

> The British won [in our class], but in the real trial the British didn't win. …But I'm a colonist. I'm a patriot. She [the teacher] showed us all the evidence, and she showed us everything that happened and we studied it, but she didn't tell us anything that happened after that, and she said all right, are you for the British, because the British, on one hand were taxing the colonists and the colonists had no way of representing. They could not vote for people who were running in England and they had no say in their taxes. They were going to do it upon them so that was on the colonists' side, but the British on the other hand, they were being thrown rocks at. My name was Archibald, and I didn't know that I had already broken my wrist on a British officer, so when I got on the stand and they said have you ever assaulted a British officer, then he said we have evidence you broke your wrists off a British officer, and I went OOH! I didn't know, but I shouldn't have said that, because in the book it said, "Bleep, you Yankee bloopers."

From Tessa's comments, we can see that she finds history neither boring nor irrelevant. Her interest in the different perspectives of British soldiers and colonial rebels is generated and supported by the opportunity to act historically—to take on the perspective of a participant in the historic drama. While in-depth understanding in history comes as students assess, organize, and interpret historical data in the ways already described, it is also grounded in the kind of imaginative entry into the past that is part of Tessa's experience.

*Newmann et al. (2015)*

Students might, for instance, participate in simulations and role plays or re-create biographies or historical stories that require imaginative entry into a historical era or event. (See Chapter 11 for discussion of when simulations and role plays are appropriate.) In doing so, they use historical information to help them either assume the role of historical actors or vividly describe historical events or people. We are not suggesting fanciful retellings of history. Rather, students must speculate on the motives, values, and choices of historical actors in order to build supportable, *evidence-based* accounts that explain events. In doing so, they must imagine the perspective of participants from another time and place without imagining beyond their data. Tessa, for instance, is well aware of the need for historical evidence. The fact that she missed an important piece of evidence altered the outcome of the trial. If this had been a test, she might have missed the item, taken her grade, and forgotten all about it. Because this was part of a simulation, her error was corrected in a context that made the correction important and memorable. Tessa's experience also pointed out how easily misinformation can alter interpretations—and how important it is to hold conclusions as tentative and to re-evaluate ideas. Finally, Tessa's experience points up another feature of effective group inquiry. Although Tessa's study was done in community with other students, it was not a matter of each student investigating what every other student investigated, searching for a single right answer. Rather, each student's research provided one piece of a larger puzzle and served as at least a partial check against inaccurate or unsupportable interpretations.

Imagining the lives and perspectives of people distant in time and place can be challenging for students. Sometimes they assume that people thought differently or lived differently simply because they weren't intelligent enough to do otherwise. Simulations, such as Tessa experienced, rely on primary source documents and images to help students imagine themselves into earlier lives. Sometimes, though, we ask students to travel so deep into the past that documentary sources can't follow them. Instead, elements of material culture in context provide the primary evidence of ancient people's intelligence and ingenuity. Sadly, popular culture doesn't help us much here. Media presentations of "cave men" don't usually emphasize their intelligence and often make our ancient ancestors the subject of mockery rather than inquiry. On the other hand, archaeology has a great deal of appeal to elementary and middle school children (and adults) and, with appropriate scaffolding, can generate just the kind of imaginative entry that led one student in Young-do Lee's fifth-grade class to exclaim that ancient people "were the great, great, great, great grandfathers" of many modern tools and technologies. Indeed, Young-do's fifth graders changed their minds about ancient people, declaring that "they had to be very smart"… "like Albert Einstein." They identified sophisticated mental operations involved in innovation, noting that ancient people might be "trying something that makes them think of something else. Like fire! They get close and feel warmth and get an idea." This, one girl suggested, led people to "experiment and they think, 'How did I make that happen?' so they can change a material and try that." These fifth graders described ancient people's agency—their choices, ideas, and inventions—as making later innovation possible. One boy also noted that ancient people made many decisions regarding using, adapting, or resisting new technologies. They imagined that some women might want to go hunting but that their society might not allow that to happen. They might be limited to more domestic tasks. They also identified the need for teachers to spread skills or develop talents, and they considered the role of curiosity in technological innovation.

What happened to make them compare an ancient toolmaker to Albert Einstein or imagine the combination of determination and curiosity that might inspire innovation? The intellectual tipping point turned out to be two-fold. First, students had a chance to observe and try out some ancient technologies. The opportunity to try a pump drill made it very clear that these tools required considerable skill. Second, they created a *chaine operatoire*, or sequence of operations, for a technology they investigated. This involved identifying the resources, skills, and inventions that led up to a particular tool. Just imagine for a moment what it would take for ancient people to cook a meal—the natural resources, technologies for hunting, gathering, carrying, storing, and preparing food, as

Historical accounts are based on evidence. *Levstik & Barton* (2008), *VanSledright (2010)*

M. King et al. (2015)

well as opportunities to learn those skills, determination to do so, and so on. Analyzing something as seemingly straightforward as this elevated students' respect for their ancient forebears.

*Levstik et al. (2014), Arias-Ferrer & Egea-Vivancos (2019)*

Another feature of in-depth study is the application of new learning beyond the classroom. In other words, historical inquiry has value and meaning beyond success in school. Remember that we already said that history presents us with both stories of origins and possible destinations. These are not just school stories left behind when children exit the classroom. Instead, these are stories that have the power to transform students' understandings of themselves and their possible futures. The writer James Baldwin expressed his sense that historical stories could help children

*History can be transformative.*

> know that just as American history is longer, larger, more various, more beautiful, and more terrible than anything anyone has ever said about it, so is the world larger, more daring, more beautiful and more terrible, but principally larger—and that it belongs to [the children].
>
> (Baldwin 1963/1998, pp. 685–686)

In one sense, our lives become more meaningful when we see ourselves as actors within the context of a historical story—we look for the connections among past and current events, the lives of those around us, and our own lives. We begin to recognize that no society or group of people is wholly wise or virtuous, that all of us have the capacity for good and ill. Wisdom develops as much from stories about human failure as from stories of success. In short, to see ourselves in historical perspective, we need stories about the range of human experience, and we have to learn to evaluate the meaning of those experiences from many perspectives.

*Griffin (1992), Epstein (2009), Henderson & Levstik (2016)*

## TAKING ACTION

Asked to explain the purpose of history, students in the U.S. often say that knowing history helps people avoid the mistakes of the past. When asked how history might help *them* make decisions in the present, however, they aren't quite sure. Traditional history instruction doesn't help them much, here. Yet we cannot fully realize the civic purposes of historical study if we don't invite students to think about the connections between *historical agency* and their own civic engagement.

*Agency* is about power—how groups, individuals, and institutions establish, maintain, constrain, expand, resist, or lose power. In the nineteenth century, for instance, women faced legal, economic, and social restrictions, yet some women petitioned Congress for equal rights and worked for other social causes. Other women lived comfortably within existing legal and social restrictions, while some resisted within the confines of home and family. Still others were forced to conform, sometimes with tragic results. Race, class, ethnicity, and individual experiences influenced the types of agency available to different people. So did various social and political institutions. Think of how Andrew Jackson's decision to violate a Supreme Court decision upholding Cherokee land claims or Franklin Roosevelt's decision to intern Japanese Americans dramatically altered the options available to women (and men and children) in both groups.

*Levstik (2007), Levstik et al. (2014), LePore (2018), Arias-Ferrer & Egea-Vivancos (2019)*

*Agency is a powerful concept to help students think about civic decision-making.*

Investigating the agency available to and chosen by historical actors illuminates the complexities of people's decision making. No one has unlimited options, and no matter how much any group has in common, there are still differences within as well as between groups in this regard. Understanding these differences helps students make better sense of historical people, ideas, and events. There is little evidence, however, that investigating historical agency inevitably leads students to consider their own expressions of agency. Generally, this requires explicit instruction. One way to approach this is through historically informed service learning.

*P. Levine (2013), Wade (2007)*

Gracie Maggard, Kim Sergent, and Stephanie Sexton discovered just how powerful service learning could be when they decided to involve their students in a historically

*Historically informed civic action connects past and present.*

**31**

rich community issue. Each year, their small community in eastern Kentucky holds a program to commemorate Dr. Martin Luther King, Jr.'s birthday. Over the years, however, enthusiasm for the event waned. Gracie, Kim, and Stephanie noticed, too, that their students knew little about King beyond his "I Have a Dream" speech. Both Gracie and Stephanie planned to teach units on the broader civil rights movement to their fifth- and eighth-grade students and thought that their units might culminate in a joint presentation to the community about King and the civil rights movement. Kim, a high school teacher, decided that this project might be an interesting challenge for her Future Teachers club members, too. How could her students help their younger peers learn more about the civil rights movement and, perhaps, raise community awareness about the significance of the movement?

As each class focused on investigating aspects of civil rights, Kim's students concentrated on developing a project with the fifth graders. Gracie had introduced a picture book, *Martin's Big Words*, to her class. The book's format—pairing images and words to trace influences on King's social activism—suggested an interesting possibility. Perhaps the fifth graders could develop a *digital documentary* along similar lines. All three teachers had just completed a workshop on digital documentaries and were interested in introducing this technique. They knew from their own experience that documentaries required considerable scaffolding but thought this joint project might be able to provide just that. The fifth graders would have older students as partners who could help with technological challenges (accessing and uploading images, laying in text and sound, planning transitions and the like) as well as interpretive ones (checking for accuracy, avoiding sound-bite interpretations, citing evidence). Kim and her students began planning. With input from Gracie, they decided to organize a single documentary around King's words. Each fifth grader selected a quote from King, collected pictures that they thought illustrated the quote, and then wrote a description of what was going on in King's life at the time. Rather than work with the moviemaking technology during the drafting stage, students first prepared presentation slides, organized (and reorganized) these into a storyboard, and then practiced reading the accompanying narration aloud. This turned out to be one of the more challenging aspects of the production. Students read too quickly or with too little expression, and Gracie, Kim, and the high school students found themselves working on expressive reading along with historical thinking. Finally, students uploaded their pictures and recorded the narration. Gracie also video recorded students as they worked so that they would have a history of the whole process.

Meanwhile, Stephanie's students decided that they wanted to create a gallery display representing their investigations. They created posters combining images, text, and primary sources, similar to History Day presentations. Stephanie had wanted to emphasize the careful use of primary sources, and the posters reflected this while emphasizing local as well as national activity related to civil rights. Stephanie could have used digital documentaries, too, but she decided to focus on the technology that best supported her goals in regard to historical evidence. Drawing on digital repositories, she created *portable archives*—folders containing materials she downloaded to represent different perspectives and highlight different types of agency. This allowed her to maximize time students spent working with sources rather than time spent searching for them.

Similarly, Gracie used digital documentaries because she had sufficient help to manage this labor-intensive activity. She also limited the frustration factor by building a single documentary. All students contributed, but they could problem-solve the technical aspects of the project jointly, rather than wait for individual assistance. Further, she provided a template—*Martin's Big Words*—for students' first attempt at a documentary. Left to their own devices, students tend to follow some of the same patterns of one-fact-after-another in documentaries that they do in reports. The template supported a more interpretive stance, and the final product reflected this more interesting and historically sound approach. Indeed, when the high school hosted a display of the eighth-grade posters and fifth graders' digital documentaries, response was so positive that organizers of the community Martin Luther King Day commemoration invited them to be featured presenters.

*Rappaport & Collier (2007)*

Digital documentaries allow students to combine text, sound, and image in a historical interpretation. *Swan & Hofer (2013)*

*National History Day* http://www.nhd.org/

The breakfast quickly sold out. As people gathered for the event, they passed through a gallery of student work highlighting the significance of civil rights in their community and nation. The digital documentary played during the breakfast to enthusiastic reviews and an invitation to come back the next year. Perhaps more important, students noted the connection between civil rights activism in the past and their own ability to engage their community in commemorating those events.

Not all historical inquiry lends itself to service projects. Teachers who engage their students in this kind of agency make sure that the historical inquiry is central to decisions about service, and the service rendered not only deepens students' understanding of the connections between past and present but actually alleviates a real problem. Because Kim, Gracie, and Stephanie are deeply involved in their community, they can connect their students with appropriate groups and individuals to ensure that student input is needed and wanted. Further, they make good use of the technologies available to them to ensure that students' work makes as broad an impact as possible. Other students, the larger community at the breakfast, and, later, the school board responded to the students' work. As a result of teachers' and students' efforts, many more people participated in learning about and publicly discussing civil rights than had been the case in the community's recent past.

*See Anand et al. (2002) for another approach to community history.*

## REFLECTION AND ASSESSMENT

The rich communities of historical discourse described in this chapter and throughout the book provide teachers an ideal opportunity for the kinds of constructive assessment described in Chapter 2. First, these classrooms produce a wide array of data about students' developing historical understanding that give teachers insight into how students are progressing along the road to increasingly mature historical thinking. Second, this insight into students' thinking comes about in the context of historical inquiry and interpretation. Teachers learn what students can do historically by engaging them in authentic and purposeful historical activities; students' talk, question setting, research, and interpretations all offer insights into what they know, what they still need to learn, and what progress they are making toward the goals of historical study. Finally, classrooms like Ruby's and Jeanette's provide multiple pathways for assessing students' historical understanding. As we describe in the following chapters, constructive assessment in history can involve peer and teacher review, self-assessment, anecdotal records, formal scoring rubrics, checklists, and other formats for gaining insight into students' thinking. Teachers' "kid-watching" skills and a willingness to document their observations are the best tools they have for assessing this process.

*Alleman & Brophy (1999), Shemilt, (2018), Shepard (2000), Yell (1999)*

One challenge for teachers is organizing this array of data so that it provides useful information not just to the teacher but also to students and their parents and guardians. This need not be as burdensome as some teachers fear, but it does require planning. Some of the teachers with whom we work accomplish this complex task by using portfolios as a means of organizing assessment data. This involves not only collecting pieces of student work but also helping students learn to monitor their own progress by involving them in the task of assessment. Students, for instance, can manage much of their own organization if they understand the established protocols—such as knowing what records must be kept, where they are kept, and how they will be used. By simply taking time weekly (or daily if needed) to make sure the system is working, teachers can obtain a wealth of data without running themselves ragged. At one point, some schools required portfolio assessment. Although requiring portfolios is less common now, teacher-implemented portfolios have a number of advantages that suggest bringing them back in inquiry-based instruction. The teachers with whom we work find them very useful in several ways.

*Portfolios help organize assessment data.*

Some teachers, for instance, use portfolios to organize student assessment. Using a *learning portfolio*, teachers and students jointly decide what should be included in an ongoing collection representing student work either across the curriculum (usually in elementary classrooms) or for one content area (more common at the middle school level). These

*Learning portfolios are ongoing collections of student work. Hart (1999), Milson & Brantley (1999), Pappas et al. (2005)*

**33**

portfolios are organized to correspond to the categories used in reporting student progress. Documenting historical thinking within a learning portfolio might include audio and video recordings, samples of different genres of historical work, self-assessments, and the like. In some classrooms, students, in cooperation with their teacher, select work for a weekly or monthly portfolio to share with parents and guardians. Although not all teachers require the return of these materials, most ask that parents respond to the portfolios and that students return them on the next school day. Using this technique might require a discussion with students about how to share their work with their families.

Ruby, for instance, sends a *Friday Portfolio* home each week. She describes one experience helping her first graders decide what to include. It had been a busy week, and she wanted to make sure they would share something about the Russian dance company performance at a school assembly, learning Russian folk dances, or perhaps the maps they had worked on that showed some of the geography of Russia. She asked her students, "What will you say when your parents ask you what happened this week?" Almost as one, her students responded, "The Russian kissed Melissa."

In response, Ruby and her students developed some conversation starters to help students share their Friday Portfolios. They decided they might want to start with, "Something I am proud of because…," "Something I did for the first time…," or "Something I didn't know before…" In addition, because not all the adults in her students' lives could read, and it was good practice for her students in any case, Ruby asked students to read one piece of their writing to someone else. In this way, the Friday Portfolios became a source of communication between home and school, and the students had a way to share what they were learning.

An *assessment portfolio*, like the Friday Portfolio, is jointly constructed by the students and the teacher. Students have an opportunity to include what they consider to be their best work in different categories and then to explain why they selected each piece. In addition, the teacher requires the inclusion of certain items—perhaps a sample of a particular genre of historical writing, a self-assessment of a project, or an annotated bibliography of sources used in developing an interpretation. Jeanette, for instance, might require students to include an argument for the importance of one of the events on the time line they developed, while Ruby might ask her students to include their pictures of "for sure" facts about Johnny Appleseed.

Assessment portfolios provide a good opportunity for teachers to conduct conferences with students about their work. Abby Mott, one of the teachers you will meet again later in this book, goes over the assessment portfolio with each child, discussing strengths and areas that need to be worked on in the coming weeks. Her students write up a set of goals for the upcoming grading period; the goals are then put in their portfolios as a way to organize for the next grading period. Besides the obvious advantage of emphasizing evaluation as an opportunity to plan for the future, these conferences allay student fears about report cards. By the time the report cards are distributed, there are rarely surprises. The students have a pretty clear understanding of their progress to that point and what they can do in the upcoming term. Abby has found that these conferences not only reassure students and promote more accurate self-assessment, they provide another opportunity for children to engage in historical talk—to return to ideas introduced earlier in a study and to discuss them one-on-one with an interested and informed adult.

## CONCLUSIONS

Although each encounter with history may not transform every child in quite the ways James Baldwin suggests, cumulatively, in-depth historical study is more likely to encourage children to recognize themselves as historical participants rather than passive recipients of the past and unwitting victims of the present. As have others before them, they can change both the present and future. Simply telling students the same myths and stories over and over again will not have this effect. As Oscar Wilde once noted, "The one duty

*Portfolios help structure reporting to parents and guardians.*

*Friday Portfolios and assessment portfolios are useful organizing tools for assessment and communicating with families and guardians.*

*Portfolios help structure student–teacher conferences.*

*When students help develop their own portfolios, they have a clearer understanding of their own performance.*

*Baldwin (1988)*

*Wilde (1982)*

we owe to history is to rewrite it." In-depth study invites students to critique the myths, rewrite the stories, and tell multiple stories. It asks them not just to memorize someone else's interpretations but to develop their own; not just to accumulate information but to ask themselves and each other, "So what?" What difference does this information make in the world? What does it say about what it means to be human in other times and places and right now in our world? If students cannot enter imaginatively into the past, if they lack in-depth information about the world around them and its myriad possibilities, they are also less likely to understand the people next door.

*Darling-Hammond (2010)*

History organized around imaginative entry into the past, in-depth studies of enduring themes and questions, focused on tasks that have relevance beyond the classroom and tied to students' prior knowledge may seem an overwhelming task. Certainly, communities of historical inquiry don't just happen; they require careful planning on teachers' parts, time to build a foundation of mutual trust and respect, and freedom from some of the constraints of "coverage." The following chapters provide specific research-based suggestions involving a variety of classrooms in neighborhood schools and magnet schools; urban, suburban, and rural schools; schools in which many children are bilingual (or becoming so)—where doing history is intellectually invigorating for both teachers and students.

# 4

## TO FIND OUT THINGS WE DIDN'T KNOW ABOUT OURSELVES

## Personal Histories

On the first day of school, Tina Reynolds asks her fourth graders to complete the sentence, "History is…" on slips of paper and to discuss their answers. At least half the class writes, "I don't know," while others give short answers like "long ago," "antiques and old stuff," or "presidents and other famous people." Tina asks if they have ever learned about history; a few recall that parents or other relatives have told them about the past, while others can't remember having learned anything about the topic.

She then asks if a *person* can have a history: "Could there be a 'History of Christy,' for example?" Some think yes, some no, but none can explain why. Tina says that she has a history of herself to show them and asks what they think it might look like. Again, students aren't sure. She shows the class a poster she has made with a time line of important events in her life, and students' interest begins to pick up; they eagerly volunteer to read out loud each of the milestones in Tina's life—when she was born, started school, got married, and so on. She then tells students they are going to make their own time lines to show the most important things that have happened to them, and that they will use these to create a "History of Me" to share with the class.

After a discussion of what they might include, students begin working on a list of the five most important things that have happened in their lives. Although they are excited about the topic, writing is difficult for many; making a list like this takes a while. Seated at tables of four and five, though, they continually share their experiences as they write—telling each other about siblings being born, vacations their family has taken, or starting a new sport. Tina, meanwhile, talks to students as they work, asking them to explain why they chose the items they have or helping those who are having trouble. After completing their lists, students fill in dates of each event on a blank time line of the last ten years. Because most have no idea when each thing happened, they take these home to complete with their parents' help. Tina also asks them to add any new events they discover in talking with their parents.

The next day, it is obvious that students have not only recorded a set of dates but have learned an entirely new set of stories from their parents. They are eager to share these in class—the time Martin rolled down the stairs on his tricycle, the time Lisa "almost drowned," and so on. Afterward, students begin creating their personal histories. All have to write narrative essays about their lives, but they can present these to the rest of the class in different ways—by recording a video or audio recording, making a poster with photographs (or drawings) and captions, or simply reading their essay. One student even acts as a "museum guide" to the important events of his life. The next several days are devoted to this assignment, as students write essays, design posters, and plan scripts for recordings. When the time comes to share these products with their classmates, even the shyest are proud to present, and students listen with careful attention to the stories of each other's lives.

DOI: 10.4324/9781003179658-4

In our interviews with children from first grade through middle school, we have found that all of them know something about how things were different in the past. Less often do they have a clear idea what *history* means. Because students usually don't encounter the subject at school before fourth grade, they sometimes don't even clearly recognize the word; those who have heard it may link it with the past generally ("antiques and old stuff") or may associate it with famous people or events. But rarely do they realize that they are part of history, or that they have a history of their own. A seventh grader trying to explain the difference between science and history observed that he and the other students were *part of* science, because it was about them and the world around them—"We're *in* science," he pointed out, "but we're not *in* history." Because too many students do not see themselves as being "in history," developing a sense of what the subject is all about and how it relates to them must be one of the teacher's first and most important goals.

*Levstik & Barton (2008), Levstik & Pappas (1987); see also Brophy and VanSledright (1997)*

Students do not always see themselves as part of history.

## ASKING HISTORICAL QUESTIONS

Beginning with students' own lives is an obvious way to develop an understanding of their place in history, and it also introduces them to key elements of historical inquiry. In the earlier passage, Tina engaged her students in the most basic of historical questions: How has my own past affected my life today? She did this by asking students to think about their past in terms of significance: She didn't want them to try to remember everything that had ever happened to them, but to select the five most important things—those that had the greatest influence on their lives today. This seemingly simple assignment, thus, introduced students to what it means to ask historical questions. Moreover, this was a highly authentic question. As we have already noted, history is concerned with explaining how we got to be where we are, and knowing the story of one's own life is the most basic form of historical understanding. Note also that students became most interested once they moved away from a general and abstract discussion of history and began talking about specific people they knew.

Understanding history begins with students' own pasts.

History examines the effect of the past on the present.

Students are interested in history that focuses on people. *Barton & Levstik (2004)*

Making a list of important events, however, was not something that came easily; it didn't seem to be the kind of question students had ever been asked. Many had trouble deciding what to include on their lists, and a major part of Tina's responsibility was to help them think about how to answer the question; she stayed busy asking students how events in the past had affected their lives today and how their lives would be different if those events hadn't happened. Some students stared at blank pieces of paper until she came around to their desks and asked probing questions to help them think about the events that had been important to them; afterward, they were more prepared to commit their ideas to paper. The collaborative nature of Tina's classroom also helped students consider the question. Although they worked individually, students shared their ideas constantly and heard others explaining their experiences. Many weren't sure what was important until they heard their classmates sharing what was important to *them*.

Students benefit from collaboration among themselves and with their teacher. *Darling-Hammond (2008)*

## COLLECTING HISTORICAL INFORMATION

This exercise also introduced students to the collection of historical data. They began with the most basic source of information—their own memories. By developing a list of events that they remembered, they saw how they could serve as a source of data themselves. They also began to notice the limitations of relying on memory: Although they remembered many of the things that had happened to them, few knew when they happened—either the dates or how old they were at the time. By having to combine their own memories with information from relatives, they learned that using multiple sources can lead to a fuller picture of the past than relying on any single source—one of the most basic principles of historical research.

Historical inquiry can help students see the need for multiple sources of information.

Even the idea of consulting resources in order to learn can be a new concept for children; they sometimes claim they couldn't possibly know anything they haven't directly experienced. In helping students develop a list of important events in their lives, for example, Tina asked one group to think about the milestones that excite parents when their children experience them for the first time. One girl suggested getting a new tooth, another mentioned learning to talk, and both added these to their list of events to find out more about. Exasperated at these suggestions, one boy exclaimed, "How would *I* know any of those things happened!?"—he refused to write these down because (he believed) he had no way of knowing that he had ever gotten his first tooth or learned to talk. He couldn't remember it, he reasoned, so how could he know that it ever happened? Although it seems obvious to adults that a person can know something about the past without directly remembering it, this is an understanding that has to be developed in children through exercises like these.

Many students are unfamiliar with how people learn about the past. *Barton (2008)*

Collecting information from relatives obviously gives students a comfortable and accessible way to move beyond their own experience. Even such familiar sources, though, begin to acquaint them with fundamental issues of historical interpretation. Students quickly learned that their sources might disagree and that they had to make judgments about reliability. Several found that relatives remembered events differently, and in explaining why they believed some sources rather than others, many noted that parents were more reliable because they probably saw the events firsthand, and more distant relatives would have heard about them later. Other students found that "baby books" were a useful source of information when people disagreed, and one student found that both his parents had been wrong about when he lost his first tooth. His baby book, he explained, was the most reliable source because events were written down in it at the time, but people trying to remember events years later might forget exactly how they happened. In this simple assignment, then, students dealt with fundamental historical issues—how to reconcile conflicting accounts and how to judge sources' reliability.

Relatives provide a comfortable and accessible way for students to move beyond their own experiences.

Students must learn to deal with conflicting sources.

Just as students needed Tina's help to develop a list of events, they needed some structure in collecting information about dates. This was their first exposure to time lines and to collecting chronological data, so Tina did not simply tell them to go home and find out when events had happened. With those instructions, students probably would have brought back papers with a random collection of words and numbers and little idea how they were connected. Instead, she gave each student a time line of the last ten years and explained how to record the information they collected, and she used her own life as an example. As a result, students appeared to have little trouble keeping track of their information, and the next day they could easily use their time lines to answer questions about when things had happened (see Figure 4.1). Collecting data is a fundamental part of all research, yet it is enormously difficult for young children. Providing them with the structure necessary—in this case, in the form of a printed time line—is crucial to ensuring their success. The importance of this help became apparent when students made their presentations. Many of those who created posters of their lives developed larger and more elaborate time lines for them, and several remarked that making them—spacing the years evenly and so on—was the most difficult part of the entire assignment. Without the help of a printed version to begin with, many students would never have been able to keep their information organized. Because they had that help, they not only completed the assignment successfully but tackled the more challenging task of making new time lines for their presentations.

Students need experience evaluating sources as evidence for historical interpretations. *Ashby & Lee (1998), VanSledright (2002)*

Teachers can provide the structure students need to collect information.

## DRAWING CONCLUSIONS AND REFLECTING ON LEARNING

As we noted in Chapter 2, learning activities should be *authentic*; if students complete assignments only to please their teachers or get a grade, they're unlikely to understand the purpose of what they're doing or be able to apply it in new situations. In their "History of Me" assignments, students were not simply collecting information about themselves and filling it in on a time line; that would have been more or less a typical school experience

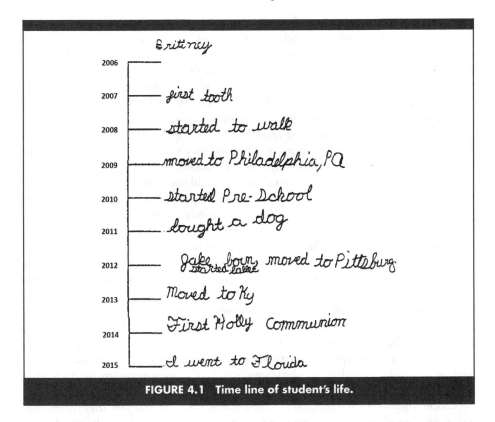

**FIGURE 4.1   Time line of student's life.**

(even if a more interesting one than answering questions on a worksheet). Tina, however, required her students to go further and use this information to create a narrative of their lives for an audience of classmates—and the creation of narratives is one authentic use of historical information in our society. Like the students in Chapter 3, Tina's were not just learning skills or content but were also using what they learned to create new knowledge.

Producing this kind of knowledge, though, was no simple matter. After completing their initial time lines and discussing their results in class, students began creating written narratives and presentations about their lives. Because they were learning more about writing during other times of the day, they were familiar with the elements necessary for an effective narrative—putting events in order, including details, and so on. But when it came to taking the information from their time lines and putting it into a new form, many had great difficulty. Several didn't realize that their time lines contained the information they needed to begin, and they displayed an attitude teachers will quickly recognize: They acted as if they were supposed to pluck ideas out of thin air on a completely unexpected topic. The look and sound of "I don't know what to write" came from several students around the room, despite the fact that Tina had just spent two days engaging them in prewriting activities. Most did indeed see the connection to their previous work and used their time lines to plan their essays. But others needed more explicit help: They needed someone to show them how to use what they had already learned. As Tina (and their classmates) helped them make this connection, the expectant sound of "Oh! Now I get it!" replaced the desultory "I don't know what to write." As always, scaffolding was critical. Teachers cannot simply throw an assignment at students and expect them to learn from it; at one time or another, most will need help figuring out how to use their knowledge and skills in their work.

An even more significant problem for some students was deciding which information from their time lines was important enough to include in their narratives. Although Tina led the class in a discussion of how to choose what to write and modeled the process using her own time line, many still weren't sure how to go about it. Because many elementary school students learn only about creative, fictional writing, they often have little understanding of how to use written language in other ways. Tina's students knew they

Creating narratives is an authentic use of historical information.

History depends on integration with other subjects.

Teachers need to help students apply their knowledge and skills.

Students have difficulty putting what they have learned into new forms.

shouldn't just rewrite everything from their time lines, but they didn't know what was important enough to include in their narratives. Just as she did when they first began the assignment, Tina had to help students (individually and in small groups) think about how to choose from among a list of events to include those that were most significant. In essence, she was scaffolding their understanding of historical significance.

Of course, students' understanding of significance will not be the same as an adult's. Many chose the events they had enjoyed the most (a favorite vacation, for example) rather than those an adult might think were actually the most important. Given that they hadn't run into this kind of question before, and because they were only nine years old, that's hardly surprising. But Tina consistently kept their attention focused on the issue of significance rather than simple storytelling. She never told any student, "Don't include that, that's not important," but she always asked, "Why did you include that—what impact has that had on your life?" As a result of this constant probing, students learned that history is a matter of significance: By the end of the assignment, they could be counted on to explain their choices by beginning, "This has had an impact on me because…" Although not all their explanations were equally convincing, they knew that any justification for including an event had to refer to why it was important in the present—and they learned to use the word *impact* along the way.

Students also began to learn about the relationship between presenting conclusions and using sources that are available. Some found that they didn't have photographs of many of the events they wanted to include in their presentations. As a result, they had to make choices about how to represent their lives. Some included whatever pictures they had and then revised their judgments about significance: The most important events in their lives turned out to be chosen from the photographs they had. Others took a different approach: They used the pictures that were available but explained how they represented other events in their lives—a photograph of a vacation, for example, might actually represent the birth of a sister because she was still a baby in the picture. Again, that is exactly what historians do: They decide how the available resources can be used to tell a story. For years, historians based much of their work on letters, diaries, and diplomatic papers; as a result, they had to omit people who didn't leave behind these kinds of documents. In recent years, many historians have attempted to find other sources to represent the lives of people in the past—wills, court proceedings, tax records, and the like. Similarly, some of Tina's students based their ideas about importance on the sources that were readily available, whereas some used other criteria and the sources as indirect representations.

Authentic tasks also ask students to reflect on their purpose. Tina avoided telling students what they were supposed to think and, instead, let them develop their own ideas about the assignment's purpose. Rather than telling them what she thought the purpose was, she periodically asked students to reflect on what *they* thought. Several times, for example, she began the history portion of the day by reading books such as *In My Family/ En Mi Familia* and *Grandfather's Story Cloth/Yawg Daim Paj Ntaub Dab Neeg*, in which adults reflect on the events of their youth, and she asked students why they thought the characters found stories about their past so important. She also asked students why they thought they were doing this project. Their answers reflected a range of understanding: "To find out what year we did things and what we did," "To find out things we didn't know about ourselves," and "To find out what history is," for example.

Other teachers might justifiably take a more directive approach and explain how a "History of Me" relates to personal identity, the impact of the past on the present, or the gathering and interpretation of data. Tina's approach, though, has the distinct advantage of allowing children to draw their own conclusions from school experiences. One of the things about this project that most interested students—and surprised Tina—was their realization that each had his or her own unique history, different than everyone else's. Tina hadn't considered that they wouldn't already realize that, and she hadn't thought about emphasizing that as a goal of the assignment—yet, for students, it turned out to be, perhaps, its most important purpose. By placing responsibility for creating meaning with the students themselves, Tina allowed them to come away with the understanding

**40**

they found appropriate. Her approach also lays the foundation for developing truly critical thinking: Instead of waiting to be told why something is important, Tina constantly teaches students to ask themselves, "So what?" This kind of reflection is a crucial—but frequently neglected—component of meaningful historical inquiry.

*Reflection gives students responsibility for creating meaning and engages them in critical thinking.*

## ENGLISH LEARNERS, NEWCOMERS, AND HISTORY

History can seem a difficult and distant subject for English learners, particularly those whose families are newcomers to the United States. These students often struggle when learning history: The language is tough, the topics unfamiliar, the purposes unclear. They may have trouble understanding teachers, texts, and classmates; they may not know how to complete assignments; and perhaps most important, they just may not care. And why should they? Why would they be motivated to learn about events hundreds of years ago in a country they're new to, especially when they're not proficient in the language? Studying history can be especially alienating when students don't have a chance to learn about people they identify with. When this happens, students may become "lost" to history in school, cut off from the benefits of learning about people and events of the past. They will still learn history in their homes and communities, and from the media, but they will miss out on the chance to systematically compare different historical periods and experiences, to examine historical narratives critically, and to collect, evaluate, and synthesize evidence.

*Traditional history classes can be alienating for English learners and newcomers to the United States.*

Although Tina's class didn't include any newcomers or English learners, her approach to introducing history involved precisely the elements necessary for them to become engaged in the subject. First, she related history to students' own lives and backgrounds. They already knew many things about themselves, of course, and they could draw on familiar sources—relatives and objects in their homes—to learn more. This makes content more comprehensible, but it also helps students see that their identities are considered important; they and people they care about *matter*. This tells them that their own lives are worth studying and that their families have expertise that is valued at school. Relying on familiar sources also reduces the language demands of history; although students may have to report on what they have learned in English, the learning itself will most likely take place in their native language, as they ask relatives for information. This provides a firmer foundation of knowledge before students take on the difficult task of writing and speaking in English. Think about how much more accessible this is than traditional history: Would students beginning to learn English get more out of talking to their parents and reporting on a familiar topic, or reading a difficult textbook account of the state's first governors? Which would be more interesting, and which would be more comprehensible? And keep in mind: The first approach is actually about the fundamentals of history; the textbook is just about a few famous people and events, not about the nature of historical knowledge.

*Teachers should connect history to students' lives and backgrounds. Cruz & Thornton (2013), Goldenberg & Coleman (2010), H. Rodríguez et al. (2005), Salinas et al. (2006).*

*Incorporating sources from students' lives is a more authentic form of history than relying on textbooks or packaged materials.*

The "History of Me" project also included the kind of differentiation necessary to help English learners succeed. Some approaches to differentiated instruction emphasize developing separate plans for each student and basing these on a careful diagnosis of each student's needs and abilities. We find this advice impractical and even counter-productive. Few teachers will be able to adapt instruction to the needs of 35 individual learners, and expecting them to do so sets up unrealistic expectations. Moreover, there is no evidence that students' cognitive abilities or affective interests can be "diagnosed" in such precise terms. Anyone who knows children knows that their interests and accomplishments vary from day to day and even moment to moment. Confining students to a particular "style" or "strength," based on imprecise methods of assessment, limits their exposure to the range of procedures and materials necessary to understand history. Although some students may be more visual, others more tactile, and so on, all students learn better when they have access to different modes of understanding and the chance to combine these in ways that make sense to them.

*Differentiation benefits English learners. Cruz & Thornton (2013)*

*Goodwin (2011), Willingham (2009)*

*Students need access to a range of historical materials and approaches.*

**41**

Tina's approach to differentiation was both more realistic and more productive than individualized instruction. She didn't assume that writing was the only way to display knowledge or that those who didn't write well couldn't learn history. But rather than trying to supply each student with a unique curriculum, she provided choices, and she worked with students to help them make decisions about which were best. For example, she allowed them to decide on formats for their presentations—they could make posters, use photographs, record audio or video, and so on. Most students chose to create posters with photographs, captions, and time lines, and to describe their work out loud to the class. This required oral and written language, as well as visual and mathematical understanding, but there was no single "right" way to complete the task. This is especially important for English learners, because it allows them to use language in ways they are comfortable with rather than expecting them to engage in a single way of responding that may be beyond their current abilities. Giving students a choice of forms for presentation also made the assignment more authentic. Although written sources are an important format for history, so too are museums, documentaries, and oral accounts. The forms available to students for their presentations introduced them to the different ways of presenting historical knowledge and to some of the unique features of each.

Another aspect of the "History of Me" project is important for English learners: Focusing on personal stories. This affirms students' backgrounds and experiences, but it also serves a second purpose. For many students beginning to learn English, it is easier to use language appropriate for narrating stories about oneself than the formal language of academic subjects. The vocabulary is more familiar, the grammar more straightforward, the purpose clearer. Nearly all students will be accustomed to storytelling from their own cultural and linguistic backgrounds, so they will be taking part in a familiar practice. This helps reduce the demands they face when simultaneously trying to learn new content, new tasks, and a new language. Here, the task is already familiar, and they can focus on language and content. Moreover, the narrative language of personal stories is an important part of the history they will encounter later—stories with settings, characters, problems, and so on. Telling stories about their personal past naturally leads students into accounts of other times and places.

## ASSESSING STUDENTS' LEARNING

One of a teacher's most important tasks is assessing students' learning—not simply so she can establish accountability to administrators, shake loose a set of grades for the report card, or even to reward students for a job well done. The purpose of assessment is to improve teaching and learning. Assessment fulfills that goal when teachers establish clear standards and criteria for achievement, when they help students understand the meaning of those standards, and when they provide feedback on how well students have mastered the goals of the class—including how far they still have to go. This kind of critical feedback is a key element of the instructional scaffolding mentioned in Chapter 2, and the assessment strategies described in Chapter 3 depend on such feedback. Letting students know what they have accomplished, and making them aware of the criteria for improvement, enables them to learn far more than if they are only given summative evaluations of their assignments.

In a world of multiple-choice tests and percentage grades, assessment may appear easy: Make out a test, see how many answers each student gets right, and assign grades. But no such simple procedures are available for the complex, real-world tasks found in classrooms where meaningful historical inquiry is taking place. A "History of Me" produces no single list of factual items that could be used on a test for the whole class. Not only will students have used a variety of sources and investigated a diverse set of experiences, but they also may have learned different things about history: Some may have come to understand how past events affect people's lives in the present, some may have learned about the reliability of sources, while others may have increased their understanding of dates

### Margin notes

Productive differentiation involves giving students choices.

English learners need chances to use language with which they are comfortable. *Fránquiz & Salinas (2011), H. Rodríguez et al. (2005)*

Telling personal stories is an authentic and accessible historical genre for English learners. *Cruz & Thornton (2013), H. Rodríguez et al. (2005)*

The purpose of assessment is to improve teaching and learning.

*Alleman & Brophy (1998)*

and sequencing. All of these are valid and worthwhile achievements, yet no single test will be valid for all students in the classroom. Complicated and authentic tasks call for complicated and authentic forms of assessment, and these must take multiple forms. For the project described in this chapter, for example, Tina relied on both anecdotal records and rubrics, and she gave students the chance to represent their learning in different formats.

Tina used anecdotal records throughout this project and, indeed, during all her teaching. She always has a pencil and a notepad at hand, and her observations of students as they work independently, discuss assignments in a group, or interact with her one-on-one provide rich insights into their understanding of the demands of the task. During the "History of Me" project, for example, when a student was able to explain how past events influenced her life in the present, Tina wrote that down on a slip of paper to add to the assessment folder she kept for the student. When another student appeared to understand the influence of past events but had trouble expressing it clearly, Tina provided scaffolding ("Try saying, 'If this hadn't happened, I would…'"), and noted in her records that he was able to provide an explanation when she helped with the wording. And for a few students, she observed that they were unable to give any examples of how the past had affected their lives. Similarly, Tina took note of students who had consulted multiple sources and those who had relied on only one, and she noted students who were easily able to match dates with events on their time lines and those who needed help from herself or their peers. All these observations arose naturally during students' completion of classroom activities.

Anecdotal records like these did not result in a grade; they resulted in information on students' learning. They helped Tina see what help each student needed and provided a basis for deciding what kinds of ongoing instruction and assistance she should provide. Based on her anecdotal records, Tina knew that some students needed no more help with explaining the connection of past and present and that the next time she talked to them (during this project or the next) she could move on to other aspects of historical significance, such as multiple causation or the interaction of past events. Similarly, she knew that students who had only consulted a single source would need to be reminded to use more in the future and that they might need additional assistance in doing so. Anecdotal records thus provided Tina a means of individually tracking students' progress on a variety of important historical skills, and she used this information in planning instruction, reviewing students' achievements with them, and completing the narrative section of their report cards. Although she did not include the anecdotal records themselves as part of students' portfolios, she used them as a basis for discussion while reviewing the contents of the portfolios with students.

Some aspects of the "History of Me" project also lent themselves to assessment through more formal scoring guidelines. All students, for example, had to write narrative essays about their lives (remember that Tina did not have any English learners), and these were an important part of their portfolios. Scoring guidelines known as *rubrics* have become increasingly common as a way to assess complex student performances, especially written compositions. Rubrics are typically formatted as grids, with evaluative criteria (e.g., organization, detail, word choice, mechanics) along one side, and performance categories (e.g., novice, proficient, advanced) along the other. Each cell identifies one or more specific criteria used to assess students' performance, such as *effective use of a variety of transitions* for "advanced organization," or *occasional use of examples* for "beginning detail." Many states or districts have developed such rubrics as part of their assessment programs, while others have adopted those developed by educational consulting services. Search the internet for *written composition rubrics* and you'll see just how many of these there are and how they vary in length and detail—from those that fit on a single sheet to others that contain copious detail and extend over several pages. Many teachers are expected to use these standardized rubrics in preparing students for high-stakes tests, but our concern here is not with systems of accountability but with using assessment to improve teaching and learning.

When used well, rubrics can support teaching and learning by helping students understand the skills they are learning, clarify what performances should look like, and provide feedback on what they have done well and areas that need improvement. Rubrics can also

Authentic tasks require multiple forms of assessment.

Anecdotal records allow teachers to track individual students' progress. *Bates et al. (2019)*

Assessment helps teachers plan for ongoing instruction and assistance.

Anecdotal records provide the opportunity for ongoing assessment. *Bates et al. (2019)*

Scoring guidelines or *rubrics* provide criteria for assessing complex student performances. *Afflerbach (2017), Popham (1997)*

Rubrics should not just evaluate but also *teach. Stiggins (2001)*

Rubrics can help students improve their performances. *H. G. Andrade (2000)*

**43**

benefit teachers by helping them reflect on their expectations and providing guidance for teaching and reteaching. If most students score at the beginning level in using details, for example, a teacher will know that she needs to devote more attention to that skill—and if she finds it difficult to decide which level students have achieved, she may see that she needs to be more specific in her own ideas about what constitutes details. Unfortunately, rubrics are not always used well. Some may be so detailed that teachers fail to use them, while others are too vague to be useful. Sometimes, teachers use rubrics only for summative assessment rather than as an opportunity to help students reflect on and improve their writing, so students may not understand what the criteria call for or how to achieve them. Adhering too closely to the strict form of rubrics also can lead to unimaginative and ineffective writing, designed to achieve a high score but without any attempt to communicate meaningfully.

Tina's use of rubrics was more constructive and productive. She used her state's written composition rubric for this assignment, and she devoted a substantial amount of time to helping students understand the meaning of each component. The English language arts portion of the day usually began with mini-lessons on components such as effective introductions, use of details, sentence structure, and various aspects of punctuation. A critical part of these lessons was what are sometimes called anchor papers or anchor examples—models of good writing produced by previous students. Explanation alone will almost never help students understand what they are supposed to do; they must see models of those performances. Students followed up on these mini-lessons, not by completing worksheets on isolated skills, but by engaging in meaningful writing.

To ensure that students were applying the skills called for in the rubric, Tina conferred with them individually on a daily basis. During these conferences, she used the rubrics to help students evaluate their own work. She talked to them about how many details they used; whether they used connecting words such as *because*, *after*, and *then*; how they captured their readers' attention; and so on. A key goal in the use of rubrics is for students to internalize the standards of achievement, and Tina accomplished this through a combination of explanation, modeling, meaningful writing, and individual conferences featuring self-assessment and feedback. In addition, to improve her own teaching, Tina met regularly with her grade-level partner to review sample papers, discuss how they could apply the rubric to students' work, and develop ideas for feedback and reteaching. These discussions are foundational for using rubrics constructively rather than simply for grading or test preparation. In order to be effective, though, such meetings require a spirit of reflection, collaboration, and self-awareness. When teachers are simply required to hold grade-level assessment meetings—as they often are—discussion often focuses on sharing without analysis, or attention to superficial details or technical procedures that do little to improve their work.

## THE "HISTORY OF ME" AND FAMILY DIVERSITY

Interestingly, the students who can most easily describe how their own pasts have affected the present often are those whose parents have divorced and remarried; they are usually quite ready to explain how changing houses, being adopted, or getting new siblings has influenced their lives. Presenting a "History of Me" can be an enormously fulfilling experience for such students; we have been impressed with the way they can use this activity to affirm their backgrounds and proudly present their lives to their classmates. We have been just as impressed with their classmates' readiness to hear about and appreciate differences in family life.

As with academic skills, developing these values depends in large part on how well they are modeled by the teacher. Teachers who accept and show interest in diverse families—stepfamilies, blended families, and those with one parent, same sex or gender non-conforming parents, caregivers who are grandparents or other relatives, and so on—will find that their students do the same. When teachers develop supportive and caring environments

*Rubrics often fail to improve teaching and learning. Popham (1997), Wilson (2006)*

*Models of good work help students improve their writing. H. L. Andrade et al. (2008)*

*Self-assessment and feedback are critical for helping students use rubrics. H. L. Andrade et al. (2008), Goodrich (1996/1997)*

*Personal histories allow students to take pride in their own lives.*

*Teachers can model and promote appreciation of diverse families. Tschida & Buchanan (2017), Turner-Vorbeck & Marsh (2007)*

in their classroom, "celebrating diversity" becomes more than a slogan, and investigating personal histories helps children see how their backgrounds both converge and differ.

Nevertheless, the purpose of an assignment like this is not to pry into children's personal lives. Most students and their families will readily answer questions about important events in their lives, but others will decline to participate. Students will not want to share some events that have had an impact on them—abuse by a family member, for example, or the loss of a loved one. In other cases, parents will resent participating in this assignment. Many people believe schools should not ask questions about children's lives outside school, and undocumented residents often fear that personal questions will lead to deportation or denial of services for their family. The solution to these dilemmas—we don't call them "problems" because we recognize and accept the reasons for them—is not to avoid assignments about personal histories, nor is it to exempt some students and, thus, highlight what they may think of as an inadequacy. Rather, teachers must make such assignments flexible enough to accommodate differences among students and their families in our extraordinarily diverse society.

*Some families decline to reveal personal information.*

*Assignments must be flexible to accommodate diversity.*

To do this, teachers should never require students to share (with them or the class) anything they don't want to. In essence, a "History of Me" should include the most significant events children *want to share*, not those most significant in any kind of absolute sense. In addition, teachers always should give students the option of investigating someone's life other than their own; the purpose of the assignment, after all, is to find out how the past affects the present, not to force students into putting themselves on display. Those who don't want to call attention to themselves should have the option of doing a history of a friend in another classroom, a teacher at the school, or someone else in the community. Rather than being forced to take part in an unpleasant assignment, they then have the enriching experience of learning about someone else's life—and classmates invariably are more attentive to these presentations than any other. However, it is important to keep in mind that all students must be given these options, not just those whom the teacher thinks may need them. Otherwise, the mere presence of an alternative may seem just as unpleasant as the original assignment.

*Students should not be required to share personal information.*

*All students need choices in assignments.*

The diversity of family backgrounds also requires that schools provide material resources for students who may not have them at home. Tina's class included students from a wide range of economic backgrounds; some had access to high-speed internet and the latest electronic devices at home, but for others, just buying the materials to make posters may have been difficult. Rather than allowing students' schoolwork to mirror their families' economic status, the school supplied the equipment they needed. We recognize that not all schools have the technology or supplies that students need to do their best work, but providing students access to appropriate resources is an essential part of equitable and effective education.

*All students should be given the time and support to engage in a variety of assignments.*

## EXTENSIONS

A project like the "History of Me" can be extended in several ways to develop experience with asking and answering historical questions. An obvious follow-up is for students to use historical biographies to investigate the impact of an individual's past on his or her life. These include books appropriate for young children and those more suitable for the middle grades—for example, *The Harvey Milk Story*; *Claudette Colvin: Twice Toward Justice*; *Malcolm Little: The Boy Who Grew Up to Become Malcolm X*; and *Side by Side: The Story of Dolores Huerta and Cesar Chavez/Lado a lado: La Historia de Dolores Huerta y Cesar Chavez*. Using literature like this allows students to move beyond their own experiences and gives them the chance to examine the lives of people whose race, ethnicity, gender, sexual identity, socioeconomic class, or physical abilities may be different than their own.

*Krakow (2002), Hoose (2009), Shabazz (2014), M. Brown (2020)*

*Biographies allow students to move beyond their own experiences.*

Teachers often assign students to read biographies and then "do a report"—but as a colleague of ours once noted, it's been a long time since most of us sat down and wrote a report on a book we've read. Book reports are not an authentic genre in our society;

*Book responses, like all assignments, need a clear purpose and audience.*

**45**

they're just a traditionally assigned (and traditionally despised) means to assess whether students have done their work. Outside school, people may discuss a book with others who have read it, or they may recommend it to those who haven't, and many teachers pattern their classrooms on these more authentic tasks—assigning students to take part in literature response groups, for example, or to make advertisements or other recommendations for the books they've read. Such assignments develop children's language skills in a more authentic way than writing a report, which has no clear purpose or audience.

In literature response groups, students meet to analyze works they read. *Certo et al. (2010), McIntyre (2007)*

How can students use biographies in a way that models the use of inquiry in a more specifically historical way? Certainly, there's nothing wrong with using them in connection with discussion groups or other such assignments, in the same way any piece of literature would be used; people do read historical biographies for pleasure, they do discuss them, and they do recommend them to others. But in addition, using biographies along with projects like those in this chapter can focus students' attention on the historical nature of the genre. Historians do not read biographies and then write reports on them; rather, they do one of two things—either they write such works themselves or they evaluate those that others have written. Both tasks are well within the abilities of students in the elementary and middle grades.

Students can use multiple sources of information to create biographies.

Students can write their own accounts, for example, by using published biographies, videos and internet sources, and oral memories to make a time line of important events in a famous person's life and then construct these into written narratives or other kinds of presentations. Just as they did with their own histories, the emphasis would be on establishing the impact of events on the person's life and explaining what might been different if those events had never happened. A 6-year-old would produce a much different work than a 14-year-old, yet both would be engaged in a more purposeful assignment than "doing a report": They would be asking historical questions, collecting and interpreting information, and reflecting on what they found. Using multiple sources to create a historical account in this way is an important step in moving students beyond the simple recall of historical narratives toward a more critical and interpretive encounter with historical evidence. In addition, instead of making the teacher the sole audience for these student-created biographies, the class could compile and compare their findings. For example, they might discuss which of the figures they investigated has had the greatest impact on contemporary society—thus extending their understanding of the influence of events on individuals to the influence of individuals on society.

Students can critically evaluate published biographies.

Students can critically evaluate published biographies or other accounts by examining the basis for authors' claims, just as the children in Chapter 3 did with Johnny Appleseed. What statements are based on evidence? How good is the evidence? Which simply derive from unconfirmed folklore? We mentioned earlier that, in doing a "History of Me," students should only be asked to share what they want to share, not everything that has happened to them. At first glance, that may have seemed distinctly inauthentic: Surely history is about the truth, not about covering things up. But as we explained in Chapter 1, any history leaves some things out—that's the very essence of historical explanation. Students who have had to decide what to include and what not to include in their own biographies may then recognize (with teachers' help) that books about famous people do the same thing, and they can try to explain why some biographies of George Washington note that he owned hundreds of slaves while others ignore the topic. Students can compare different biographies of the same person and rank their authenticity and believability, just as historians do.

## CONCLUSIONS

From the upper elementary grades through college, history is one of the most securely established subjects in the curriculum, and most U. S. students will take the same survey of U.S. history at least three times—in fifth, eighth, and eleventh grades, usually—and a fourth time if they go to college. Yet the amount of information they retain from these courses is shockingly small, as national tests and surveys have shown for many years. How can there be such a mismatch between what students study and what they learn? Tina suggests that part of the problem lies in the inappropriateness of content such as when the state was admitted to the union, who the first governor was, and so on. As she points out, "It's ridiculous to go through a book reading about the founding of the state when students don't even have a sense of what history is, of what it means. Without knowing what history is all about, the rest of it will just go over their heads." We agree. At some point in their school career—hopefully in the primary grades, but later if necessary—students have to learn what history is all about, that they themselves have a history, and that they are *in* history just as much as they are in the natural world. The activities in this chapter may seem simple, but they initiate students into an understanding of history and their role within it.

Moreover, these activities help lay the groundwork for students' participation in a pluralist democracy. Although they involve no discussion of grand social and political issues, no debates over public policy and the common good, personal biographies do introduce students to important elements of such participation. As we have emphasized throughout the chapter, developing biographies requires selection, interpretation, and presentation of evidence, and these are indispensable for public deliberation. By learning how to find information and what to do with it, students should be better prepared to use evidence as they consider a variety of social issues, not only in school but also throughout their lives. In addition, they should become more aware of how others have used evidence and of the choices that have led to particular selections, interpretations, and representations. One set of lessons in fourth grade won't accomplish that, of course, but if teachers consistently build on such beginnings, students' understanding of history—and democracy—should increase enormously.

# 5

# TELL ME ABOUT YOURSELF

## Linking Children to the Past through Family Histories

Faruqi (2015), Williams & Mohammed (2009)

Flournoy (1985)

Rebecca Valbuena begins a unit on immigration by portraying her grandfather, a Latvian rabbi who immigrated to New York as a 10-year-old in the early twentieth century. She places photographs of him around the room, streams traditional Latvian music, and explains why he came to the United States and what he found here. After answering questions about his life, she asks students why their own families—almost all of whom have immigrated—came to the United States. They quickly produce a list with a variety of reasons—to find work, to be with relatives, for political freedom, to get away from war, and (the most common) "for a better life." This discussion leads into the first assignment of the unit: Interview someone who has immigrated to the United States. Working together as a class, students develop a list of questions that would be important to ask: What country did you come from? Why did you come here? What difficulties did you have when you first arrived? Was the United States what you expected? And, at students' insistence, how much did it cost? Over the next few days, students develop written and oral reports based on their interviews, and then they compare their findings to the experience of immigrants in other periods of history—such as the Irish on the East coast in the mid-1800s and the Chinese on the West coast in the late 1800s. At the end of each day's lesson, Rebecca reads aloud a different book about children who have immigrated to the United States, such as Reem Faruqi's *Lailah's Lunchbox: A Ramadan Story* and Karen William's and Khadra Mohammed's *My Name is Sangoel*, and students discuss the feelings and experiences of the characters in the books.

After students have completed their personal history projects, Tina Reynolds begins a unit on family history by reading *The Patchwork Quilt*, in which a girl and her mother discover meaning in the way a grandmother's quilt "tells stories" about the family's past. Tina asks students whether their relatives have ever told them about the past, and nearly every hand is raised: One boy talks about his uncle who was in "the war"; a girl relates how her grandmother likes to talk about the old things she owns; another student explains that his great-grandmother's World War II factory badge is in an exhibit at a nearby museum. The rest of the lesson focuses on the concept of "generation"—which relatives are in their own generation, which in their parents', and so on. The next day, Tina introduces students to a new assignment: Creating a family history based on interviews with their grandparents. Although students can do a "Family History Chart" as an optional assignment, their primary task is to give a presentation that focuses on the differences between their grandparents' lives and their own. Tina assigns several questions for students to ask in their interviews and works with them to develop several more of their own. She also spends an entire lesson modeling how to conduct an interview, as well as how to take notes. Sharing the results of these interviews takes several days, as students feel compelled to share as many of the things they've learned as possible.

An important challenge in teaching history lies in linking the subject to students' prior knowledge. As we discussed in Chapter 2, people can make sense of new experiences only

DOI: 10.4324/9781003179658-5

when they compare them to what they already know. Without such connection, children are unlikely to understand the history they encounter at school. Yet it's not always obvious how to make those links; certainly, many of the topics traditionally covered in history have no clear relation to students' own experiences, and most materials do little to suggest how such topics might be relevant. The challenge for teachers, then, lies in deciding what aspects of important historical content match up with elements of students' lives. Finding that link is the key to broadening students' understanding of history beyond their own experience, and family histories provide one of the most useful ways to do that. Tina's and Rebecca's classes show how the lives of students' families can introduce them to important and meaningful topics in history.

*Teachers must decide how to connect students' experiences with important historical content.*

## CONNECTING STUDENTS TO IMPORTANT HISTORICAL THEMES

Sometimes classrooms are described as being either "teacher-centered" or "student-centered," but we find that most focus on the interests of neither students nor teachers but on whatever is in textbooks or other curriculum materials. To link important historical content to children's backgrounds, however, teachers have to make their own decisions about what to teach. Even when working within the framework of required standards, teachers must make countless decisions about the specific content they will teach, as well as about how to present it to students. From our perspective, it is up to teachers to determine what historical content is worth teaching and what aspects of students' experiences provide the best avenue for doing that.

*Pappas et al. (2005)*

*Thornton (1991)*

Rebecca's classroom provides a clear example of such an approach. Her school's textbooks don't start with a comparison of contemporary immigration to that of the Irish and Chinese in the 1800s; like most texts, they start with Native American life and early European explorers and proceed through time in strict chronological order, up to the time of the Civil War. Limiting history to events hundreds of years in the past, however, practically guarantees that students will have few opportunities to make connections to their own experiences, so Rebecca begins by considering how this content can relate to her students' lives.

*Barton (2009)*

*Instruction must begin with students' interests and experiences.*

*Authentic history focuses on important themes.*

Rebecca knew that the movement of people is one of the most important themes throughout both U.S. and world history (see Table 1.1, Chapter 1), and that students would return to it throughout the year—when they studied European settlers' displacement of Native Americans, for example, or when they studied the enslavement of Africans. Moreover, Rebecca focused not just on the bare facts of immigration but also on issues that would allow students to compare these different movements of people—questions such as, "What motivated people to migrate?" and "Did they find what they expected?" By beginning the year with the study of an important theme, students were better able to see how the year's topics were related than if they simply proceeded through a series of chronological events.

*A thematic approach to history encourages students to make connections across time and place.*

Rebecca also chose the topic of migration because of the obvious ways it allowed children to make connections with their families. Nearly all her students had recently come to the United States—some from Mexico, some from Central America, some from Southeast Asia—so they and their families were directly familiar with motivations for moving and the consequences of doing so. (In other classrooms, students may not be newcomers from another country, but their families may still have moved from one place to another and for some of the same reasons—to find a job, to be with relatives, and so on.) But this is not to say that all teachers should begin with the topic of immigration and interview their relatives about why they have moved; our intent is not to replace the traditional beginning of elementary history (Early Explorers) with a new one (Immigration). Teaching history does not mean relying on a cookbook in which someone else has decided which sequence of topics is appropriate for children in all classrooms. Only teachers can do this, and they can do it only by knowing both history and their students.

*Teachers must know both history and their students.*

Tina, for example, also followed her "History of Me" projects (see Chapter 4) with family histories, but hers were not related to immigration. Tina's students lived in a stable residential neighborhood, and some of their families had been in the same town for generations. Interviewing their relatives would yield little or no information on why people move or what they find when they do. (Although her students did study immigration, it came later in the school year and was based primarily on children's literature.) Instead, Tina's students conducted interviews on a different topic: To find out how life was different in the past. They found out what chores their grandparents did when they were young, what they did for fun, and so on. In Tina's class, this provided students with an introduction not to immigration in U.S. history but to the study of how material and social life has changed over the last 75 years. Despite the differing focus, Tina and Rebecca developed their curriculum in identical ways: They chose important themes and helped students broaden their understanding through family histories.

*Family histories can link students' backgrounds to important historical themes.*

## IMAGINATIVE ENTRY: PERSONALIZING HISTORY

As we discussed in Chapter 2, children strive to make human sense of the world around them. Rebecca emphasized the importance of personalizing history, of helping them see how the subject involves real human beings. Her introduction to the immigration unit is a perfect example: Just as Tina's students were excited about reading her personal time line in Chapter 4, Rebecca's students listened with rapt attention as she took on the appearance of her grandfather and described his experiences for students. In such a presentation, history is not about anonymous groups of immigrants who moved for some vague reason at a distant point in history; it's about the teacher's grandfather who came to the United States when he was a child like them.

*Students are interested in the personal, human elements of history.*

The multisensory aspect of Rebecca's presentation was also critical. Students did not just hear about or read about an immigrant, they saw photographs of him, saw the way he dressed, and even heard the kind of music he listened to. (Even for teachers who do not have information from their own families, photographs of immigrants are easy to obtain, because this is a richly documented topic in U.S. history.) Students can also take part in acting out the experience of immigrants. Tina's, for example, planned and acted out an encounter between immigrant families and government officials after reading *Ellis Island: Coming to the Land of Liberty* and *At Ellis Island: A History in Many Voices*. Visual images, music, artifacts, and role-playing are second nature to any teacher whose students do not speak English as a first language, but in teaching history, these strategies should become part of every teacher's repertoire. The more avenues to the past available to students, the more likely they are to make connections to what they already know.

*Bial (2007), Peacock (2007)*

*Teachers can provide many avenues of entry into history.*

One of the most important ways to personalize history lies in helping students make connections with their own families. Simply assigning them to find out how life has changed since the 1960s, for example, is unlikely to inspire much interest. By having them interview their grandparents, however, Tina could be more confident that they would find the topic of change over time personally relevant. Indeed, students came back from these interviews with pages of notes and eager to share their stories with the rest of the class. It quickly became obvious that they had not limited themselves to the list of questions they developed in class but had conducted a much more personal and wide-ranging discussion of their families' pasts. Students also took an interest in their classmates' presentations because they were hearing not just about history but about each other's grandparents.

*Students are usually interested in learning about their families' histories.*

*Students can study history by beginning with the recent past and working backward. Misco & Patterson (2009)*

Similarly, Rebecca's primary purpose was to develop her students' understanding of the motivations for and consequences of immigration, but instead of starting with experiences remote in time and place and working forward, she began with what students already knew—why their families immigrated—and these reasons were much the same as those that have motivated people throughout history. By making a list of the motivations found within their classroom, students had a starting point that *they already understood* to compare with the motivations of others throughout history. Similarly, when they interviewed family members, they found out what kinds of problems they had when they first came to the United States—finding a job, finding a place to live, not being able to speak the language—and this gave them yet another basis for comparison with the experiences of others who have immigrated.

Literature also provides a highly effective way to help students make personal connections to history. Unfortunately, picture books and other works for reading aloud sometimes fall by the wayside after the primary school years, perhaps because they seem too easy or because reading aloud doesn't always involve students in the production of a tangible product. Yet nearly all children love to be read to; when the time for reading aloud arrived, the sounds of "Yes!" and "All right!" filled Rebecca's room. (Even eighth-grade teachers can be pleasantly surprised by students' positive reactions when they begin reading aloud.) As an adult, Rebecca could read with much more expression than her students, and she tried to make the voices and dialects in the books as authentic as possible; as a result, her students heard what it sounds like to read fluently in English, and they experienced her appreciation of global and regional forms of English. For Tina's students, meanwhile, literature was essential for studying immigration. With little personal experience related to the topic, her students relied on books—short works like *The Color of Home* and *From North to South/Del Norte al Sur*, and longer works such as *Return to Sender*—to provide them with an understanding of the personal dimensions of immigration.

Finally, both Tina and Rebecca made history personal by attending to what children know best—daily life. Having fourth graders ask their grandparents directly about abstract topics such as economics or society would not be effective, because children have only a rudimentary understanding of those concepts. But by asking about chores, entertainment, school, and the like, students developed their understanding of social and economic changes by linking them to their own experiences. Similarly, when Tina's students studied immigration, they wanted to know about practical matters; discussion often focused on questions of what people ate while on immigrant ships, how they went to the bathroom, and so on. Rebecca's students were also interested in these seemingly routine details—witness their concern with the monetary cost of immigration—although they could readily identify with the hardships of immigration that Tina's students only wondered about.

## COLLECTING AND INTERPRETING INFORMATION

Conducting historical research with family members has many of the same advantages we discussed in Chapter 4. Interviewing relatives is an accessible and comfortable way for students to move beyond their own experiences, yet it allows them to see how accounts may differ, how sources can vary in reliability, and how conflicting accounts can be reconciled. Tina found that one of the most striking benefits of this project was that students saw that not everything they learned had to come from a book, and that people were a valuable resource for historical inquiry. Her students were amazed that they could get so much information from people.

As we emphasized before and will emphasize again, however, students need help in learning how to collect and interpret information—no matter how familiar the source may be. Both Rebecca and Tina spent entire lessons teaching students how to conduct interviews. Tina, for example, talked to students about how some topics might be personally sensitive and how their grandparents either might not want to talk about them or might get emotional when they do. Even more important, she gave students a chance to practice interviewing: She had them ask her questions, and she responded as if she were the grandparent being interviewed while they took notes on her responses. Note-taking turned out to be challenging: Students wanted to write down every word she said, and she had to explain how to focus on only the most important points and how to record words and phrases that would help them reconstruct the interview later. That lesson was particularly eye-opening for students: They were shocked that they were allowed to write something other than complete sentences and paragraphs! Although as adults we

Family histories help students build on their background knowledge.

Literature helps students make personal connections to history. *O'Brien (1998)*

Elementary and middle-grade students enjoy being read to.

*Hoffman (2002), Lainez (2010), Alvarez (2009)*

Learning about abstract concepts begins with concrete examples.

Family histories introduce students to important aspects of historical inquiry. *Hickey (2006)*

Teachers must help students learn to collect information.

Students need to learn to use language for a variety of purposes.

**51**

recognize that different uses of language call for different conventions, children need explicit instruction in when to use these.

A significant part of teaching students to collect and interpret information is providing them with ways to keep track of what they learn, and graphic organizers played an important role in both Tina's and Rebecca's classrooms. Sometimes graphic organizers help individual students organize information—for example, the time lines Tina provided for personal histories in Chapter 4. Other times, graphic organizers are useful in calling students' attention to themes that emerge from information they collect. As students reported what they learned from their grandparents, for example, Tina recorded the information on chart paper with headings like *technology*, *work*, *leisure*, and *fashion*. By seeing the information recorded in this way, students not only gained more insight into the meaning of concepts like *leisure* and *technology*, but they could also more readily identify the patterns that began to emerge from the interviews (see Figure 5.1). Similarly, as Rebecca's students studied immigration throughout history, they recorded what they learned on a chart that identified the motivations of each group and the consequences of their migration (see Figure 5.2). Again, by seeing the information displayed in a visually organized way, students could more easily discern the similarities and differences in the experiences they learned about. Finally, leaving charts like these on the wall throughout the year allowed students to add new information whenever they encountered it, and thus to see the topics as issues of ongoing importance rather than isolated units of study.

In both classrooms, students also did more than collect information: They used what they had learned to create authentic historical presentations. Tina, for example, set aside time each day for students to share what they were finding out about their grandparents, and Rebecca's students developed formal presentations based on their interviews with people who have immigrated. Both teachers also assigned written compositions: Students in Tina's class wrote simulated diaries from the perspective of their grandparents when they were children, and those in Rebecca's class turned their interview notes into written essays.

Graphic organizers are a means of visually organizing information. *Gallavan & Kottler (2007)*

Wall charts help students keep track of information collected during ongoing units of study.

Students can use information to create authentic historical presentations.

| Leisure | Work |
|---|---|
| Board games | Washing dishes |
| Baseball | Mowing grass |
| Barbies | Emptying trash |
| Comic books | Feeding animals |
| Riding bikes | Washing the car |

| Fashion | Technology |
|---|---|
| Blue jeans | Transistor radios |
| Sweatshirts | No internet |
| Keds | Walkie-talkies |
| Paisley | Record players |
| Go-Go boots | Color TV |

**FIGURE 5.1  Wall charts based on grandparent interviews.**

| Migration Motivations and Experiences | | | |
|---|---|---|---|
| Group and time period | Motivations for migrating | Experiences during migration | Experiences after migration |
| Irish, mid-1800s | | | |
| Chinese, late 1800s | | | |
| Newcomers today | | | |

**FIGURE 5.2  Migration comparison wall chart.**

Historical inquiry in these classrooms provided an important opportunity for students to develop their ability to communicate through speech and writing, both of which are central to the use of historical information. Authentic performances, after all, are not radical educational innovations; learning how to speak in public and write for an audience are among the most traditional goals of learning and are likely to be important for a very long time to come.

*Authentic tasks include writing and speaking for an audience.*

## SUPPORTING LANGUAGE DEVELOPMENT

With so many students who were English learners, Rebecca spent a great deal of time focusing on language development. Obviously, the activities in this chapter built on students' own experiences and affirmed their cultural and linguistic backgrounds, just as those in the last chapter did. But Rebecca also attended directly to the specific language needs of her students. This involved supporting two separate, but equally important, processes: Students' comprehension of English and their production of it.

When Rebecca spoke with students—either individually or as a whole class—she was careful to provide *comprehensible input*: Language that her students could understand. This did not mean that she simplified the content, but rather that she spoke clearly and slowly, paused often, used short sentences and simple grammar, and limited the number of pronouns in her speech. She also used visual and other resources to support students' understanding of history whenever possible. For example, in introducing the topic of immigration, she dressed up as her grandfather, showed photographs of him, and played music from the time. As she explained the story of his life, she also called students' attention to vocabulary cards containing words for the unit—*immigrant, emigrate, motivation,* and so on. Rebecca's use of these practices improved students' ability to understand the content of the unit. Providing comprehensible input in this way is an important part of a larger approach to teaching English learners known as *sheltered instruction*. The goal of sheltered instruction is to maintain the complexity of content while enhancing students' ability to understand the language being used.

*Teachers have to provide comprehensible input for English learners. Krashen (2003)*

*In sheltered instruction, teachers maintain content complexity while helping students understand English. Echevarria et al. (2017)*

In addition to helping students understand language used in the classroom, Rebecca also facilitated their own production of English speech. One way she did this was by giving them opportunities to notice their errors and correct them. Feedback is critical to this effort, and Rebecca used several common strategies for helping students reflect on how they used English and how the language works. These strategies were:

*English learners need opportunities to notice and correct their errors. Cruz & Thornton (2013), Lyster (2007)*

- *Repetition and recasting.* One of the most basic ways of providing feedback to English learners is to repeat incorrect statements in the correct form and to stress the change. When one student said, "My mother did no want to come," for example, Rebecca added, "That's interesting!... Did *not* want to come." When another student explained, "He no have enough monies," she added, "Aah, he *did not* have enough *money*." Sometimes these corrections simply become part

**53**

of the conversation, with the teacher modeling the correct form as she expresses interest in students' explanations. When a student explained, "I will call to my abuela and ask to her," she responded, "You're going to *call* your abuela and ask her the questions?" Responses such as these model proper forms while maintaining the flow of communication.

- *Requesting clarification and eliciting responses.* When students make statements that are unclear or difficult to understand, a logical and effective response is for the teacher to ask for clarification. For example, when one student said, "My mother didn't take," Rebecca asked him to explain: "What do you mean when you say, 'She didn't take?'" This lets the student know that she is interested in what he has to say, but that he hasn't communicated it clearly yet. She could also elicit a response by beginning the sentence and asking him to "fill in the blank," so that it's clear exactly what needs to be supplied: "Your mother didn't…take what?" Similarly, when a student struggled to explain who traveled with her when she moved from Mexico, Rebecca said, "So one of the people who came was your…who?"
- *Explicit correction and metalinguistic cues.* When students made specific mistakes, such as saying "My grandfather comed to Los Angeles," Rebecca sometimes corrected them: "You mean, 'My grandfather *came* to Los Angeles.'" Similarly, when students used Spanish words, she sometimes simply asked them to use the English word instead: "*Hermano*—what do we say in English?" For students who are more experienced with English, teachers can also ask them to reflect on whether a construction sounds like English without directly pointing out their mistake. For example, if a student says, "My father told to me about his job," the teacher could ask, "'Told to me'—can you think of a better way to say that in English?"

Language learning is most effective when teachers encourage and support students' efforts.

To develop students' language, teachers must engage in meaningful conversations with them.

Trying to correct every mistake does not help English learners improve fluency.

Many teachers are hesitant to correct students' language errors or to call attention to their difficulties with English, but this is an important way of helping them learn the language. As with so many aspects of teaching, however, the overall context of the classroom is critical. Teachers must show genuine interest in their students' ideas and give them a chance to engage in meaningful conversation. They also have to be selective in correcting students' errors, so that students receive feedback that will help them become more proficient; correcting every mistake—for an English learner or a native speaker—would slow down communication so drastically that no one would ever want to say anything. When teachers create an environment that encourages students' attempts at English, however, and when they respond to students in a supportive way, selective language corrections do not have to seem negative or critical.

A final note about supporting English learners is crucial: Although developing English skills is important, becoming fluent in English is not the only role for language development in the classroom. Teachers must encourage all students to use language in ways they find comfortable, so that communication and content learning are mutually supportive, and so that they maintain other languages while also practicing English. This often means allowing them to use varied forms of English as they engage with historical tasks and assignments. It also means that in classrooms with multiple speakers of the same language, students are encouraged to talk with each other in those languages as well—Spanish, Bengali, Mandarin, and so on—as they take part in historical inquiry. As teachers circulate to work with groups, they may ask students to explain their ideas in English, but without making it an exercise in grammar. Language is a primary medium through which students learn content, and if teachers focus too narrowly on practicing English, students' other language resources will be diminished, and their learning of history will suffer.

## ASSESSMENT AND FEEDBACK

Both Tina and Rebecca evaluated students in these lessons somewhat differently than in the way described in Chapter 4. Anecdotal records were a continuing part of Tina's assessment, but, in this case, she did not use a formal rubric to judge their achievement at the end of the unit. Scoring guidelines like those discussed in Chapter 4 are useful for evaluating skills that apply across a variety of tasks or performances. Attempting to create a full-scale rubric for every task students engage in would be unnecessarily time-consuming and, in many cases, would result in guidelines so task-specific that they would contribute

Formal scoring guidelines are most useful for evaluating skills that apply to a variety of tasks. *Popham (1997)*

little toward helping students develop important skills or understandings. The usefulness of most rubrics lies in the fact that students will encounter them again and again, in a variety of settings, and over time, they become increasingly adept at applying those standards to their own writing. When teachers want to tie their assessment to the more specific demands of a particular project, a scoring guide like the one in Figure 5.3 can be a more useful evaluation instrument.

Scoring guides can take a number of different forms, but the one in Figure 5.3 shows one way to evaluate students by assessing their performance on the specifically historical aspects of assignments. During their presentations, students in Rebecca's class were expected to do four things—explain three conclusions they had reached about the experiences of the person who had been interviewed; back up each conclusion with evidence from the interviews; represent the person through authentic (and not stereotypical) clothing, artifacts, props, and so on; and speak loudly and clearly. Just as in a rubric, the different components of the assignment are listed along the left side of the evaluation form, but instead of specifying levels of performance for each, the form allows teachers to assign a

*Scoring guides can guide evaluation of the specifically historical aspects of assignments.*

| Name ___Mercedes___ | | | Points ___35/40___ |
|---|---|---|---|
| | Points possible | Points awarded | Comments |
| Speaks in clear voice, makes eye contact | 5 | 3 | *You're getting better, but remember to look at your audience and speak loudly and clearly. We're all on your side!* |
| Uses props or artifacts to represent the person interviewed | 5 | 5 | *Nice use of your aunt's scarf and jewelry—very authentic!* |
| Explains three conclusions about the experience of the person interviewed | 15 | 15 | *Your explanations of why your aunt immigrated and what she found made us feel like we understood her experiences. I can tell you spent a long time talking to her. Using phrases like "The first thing I learned..." was a good way of helping us follow along.* |
| Supports conclusions with quotes or other information from interviews | 15 | 12 | *You used lots of details in your presentation, and that helped us understand how you reached your conclusions. I wasn't always sure whether you were mentioning things that your aunt told you or things you already knew about before the assignment—be sure to make it clear where you learned the information.* |

**FIGURE 5.3  Scoring guide for evaluation of "Immigration Interview" presentation.**

range of points based on how well students have achieved the objectives. The differing number of points possible for each component makes it easy for teachers to specify the relative importance of each. Although rubrics can also be weighted in this way, the use of varying point values helps students see more clearly which aspects of the task are most important and where they should focus their efforts.

Note that the scoring guide in Figure 5.3 includes room for the teacher to write her comments on students' performance. A "Comments" section is an indispensable feature of evaluation formats like this; it provides space for the teacher to identify exactly which characteristics of a student's performance were well done and which needed improvement. As we noted in Chapter 4, this kind of critical feedback—letting students know what they have done well and what they still need to improve on—is an important form of scaffolding. If students simply receive a number or letter grade with no comments—or with only vague notes like "Great job!" or "Try to do better"— they will not know what to continue doing and what to change. Teachers frequently come across a list of "100 Ways to Say *Good work*" ("All right!" "Wonderful!" "Tremendous!"), but none of the 100 ways is likely to improve performance, because such global praise provides no useful information to students except that the teacher approves of them. For feedback to be effective, it must specify the relevant aspects of achievement. Rebecca's use of comments such as "Using phrases like 'The first thing I learned…' was a good way of helping the audience follow your presentation" is likely to result in more student learning than a thousand ambiguous exclamations of "Stupendous!" Including these scoring guides in portfolios gives teachers, students, and parents a concrete way to talk about students' achievements and progress.

Note also that the scoring guide in Figure 5.3 introduces students to the evaluation of specifically historical skills, rather than only generic aspects of written language or oral presentations. During these projects, both Rebecca and Tina emphasized drawing different pieces of evidence together to reach more general conclusions, and they also noted the importance of clearly specifying where the evidence for these conclusions originated. These are critical components of historical understanding: Synthesis and interpretation of different pieces of evidence are what give historical accounts their meaning, and clear citations are necessary to judge the validity of conclusions. Yet few teachers evaluate such aspects of historical thinking among students; although they can be very perceptive in assessing students' understanding of reading skills, mathematical reasoning, or written composition, most teachers limit their evaluations in history and social studies either to the retention of factual information or measures of comprehension. These are not enough; if teachers are to help students do history, they must pay attention to students' use of historical skills, not merely to their memory or their ability to answer questions on a reading passage. Rebecca's evaluation of how well students drew conclusions and used evidence to back them up represented an initial attempt to address these issues.

## HOW DID WE GET HERE? LINKING STUDENTS TO LARGER NARRATIVES

Why use family histories to introduce students to these topics? Is it simply because they provide a way to personalize the past and give students an easy way to learn how to collect historical information? These are important considerations, but family histories serve a larger purpose as well. We have argued that a central role of history lies in its ability to explain how the past produced the present. The personal histories discussed in Chapter 4 may help students understand that they themselves have histories, but those histories become more meaningful when they are linked to other stories—when students begin to see themselves as participants in larger narratives than those of their own lives.

The stories families tell about the past are one of the most important ways to introduce children to history. Many families tell these stories. Across race, ethnicity, class, and geographic region, children often learn about what has gone on before in their families and where they fit into that picture. Consider the eagerness of Tina's students to explain what they had learned about the past and the readiness of Rebecca's to share the reasons their

*Effective feedback specifies the relevant aspects of achievement. Hattie & Timperley (2007), Wiggins (2012)*

*Historical accounts involve the synthesis and interpretation of multiple pieces of evidence.*

*Teachers need to evaluate students' historical thinking in addition to more general skills.*

*History helps students see themselves as part of narratives larger than their own lives.*

families had immigrated. These were hardly new topics: Students had talked about these things with their families before. Passing on family history of one kind or another is a basic part of many cultural traditions. Using family histories as a part of instruction, then, represents the height of authenticity: It engages students in precisely the kind of historical practice that exists outside of school.

L. King (2019), Levstik & Barton (2008), Levy (2014), Sánchez & Sáenz (2017)

As with most topics, students in the same classroom will develop different levels of understanding and awareness of this purpose. In Tina's class, for example, some students saw little more than that they had it easier than their grandparents, so they should appreciate what they had. Others, however, recognized that the way they lived was directly dependent on what came before; for example, one student explained that he found history interesting because "I'm always curious, and history just answers zillions of questions, like 'How did we get here?'" Similarly, Rebecca found that her unit on immigration helped students understand their place within a diverse nation and how they were fundamentally like others. That wasn't always obvious to them: In a culture that often denigrates diversity, some students may think of themselves or others as falling short of an assumed U.S. ideal. Rebecca notes, for example, that students at her school often pick up on the general prejudice toward immigrants and refer to other students with pejorative racial terms—names they themselves may have been called only a few years earlier. In a basically intolerant culture, students cannot be expected to spontaneously understand the personal and political effects of such prejudice. She found, however, that after studying immigration and comparing the experiences of people throughout history, students were more likely to understand how they and their classmates were alike. History provided them an expanded perspective on their place—and the place of others—in U.S. society.

History helps explain, "How did we get here?"

History can provide students an expanded perspective on the place of all people in society.

## FAMILY HISTORY AND DIVERSITY

Keep in mind that the purpose of family histories is for students to learn historical content in a meaningful way, not to put themselves or their families on display. Tina, for example, allowed students to interview anyone about the same age as their grandparents if they preferred. Similarly, Rebecca simply required students to interview someone who had immigrated; although most chose their parents, some interviewed other relatives or neighbors instead. Just as important, both teachers approached these assignments with an acceptance of, and respect for, diversity. During their discussion of what constituted a "generation," for example, Tina's students became interested in learning exactly how they were related to people in their families; many were just starting to see what made someone an uncle, cousin, and the like. This discussion naturally turned to questions of biological and step relations—what they were, how to refer to them, and so on. Tina emphasized that family diversity was completely normal; she explained that there had always been plenty of people who didn't live with two biological parents but that, in the past, people sometimes regarded that as shameful. The "Family History Chart" she used (see Figure 5.4) is a good example of this approach: Rather than taking the form of a traditional lineage chart, in which each person has two and only two parents, it divides families into generations—thus allowing students to include only one parent if they want, or two or three or four. Because Tina modeled respect for the diversity of family relations that characterizes our society, her students felt free to discuss their own families without fear of shame or ridicule. Of course, some children still didn't want to share such topics openly, and she didn't require them to.

Students need to be given the choice of collecting information from people other than family members.

Family history charts can allow for a diversity of family structures.

Teachers who respect the diversity of families do not treat differences as deficiencies.

Rebecca modeled a similar respect for her students' family backgrounds. About half of her students' families were undocumented, yet Rebecca made no distinction between their experiences and those of families that had official permission for immigration. Certainly, no students were made to feel ashamed of their backgrounds; as a result, they openly discussed and wrote about their experience hiding under a blanket in the back of a car, using a friend's passport, running across "the line," or paying a *coyote* $300, only to be caught anyway. As in Tina's class, though, no student was required to share such personal details.

## Generations

| Yours<br>(you, siblings, cousins) | Your parents'<br>(parents, aunts, uncles) | Your grandparents'<br>(grandparents, great<br>aunts/uncles) |
|---|---|---|
| Name_____ | Name_____ | Name_____ |
| Place of Birth_____ | Place of Birth_____ | Place of Birth_____ |
| Date of Birth_____ | Date of Birth_____ | Date of Birth_____ |
| | | |
| Name_____ | Name_____ | Name_____ |
| Place of Birth_____ | Place of Birth_____ | Place of Birth_____ |
| Date of Birth_____ | Date of Birth_____ | Date of Birth_____ |
| | | |
| Name_____ | Name_____ | Name_____ |
| Place of Birth_____ | Place of Birth_____ | Place of Birth_____ |
| Date of Birth_____ | Date of Birth_____ | Date of Birth_____ |
| | | |
| Name_____ | Name_____ | Name_____ |
| Place of Birth_____ | Place of Birth_____ | Place of Birth_____ |
| Date of Birth_____ | Date of Birth_____ | Date of Birth_____ |

**FIGURE 5.4  Family history chart.**

## EXTENSIONS

Because migration is such an important theme in history, there are many possibilities for extending the topic. Historical examples of voluntary immigration could be expanded beyond the experiences of Irish, Chinese, and contemporary immigrants (as in Rebecca's class) to include those from Germany, Japan, Italy, Russia, Poland, or any number of other countries. In addition to studying voluntary migrations to the United States, students could examine migrations that have been coerced. Examples in U.S. history include enslavement of Africans, forced removal of Native peoples during the Trail or Tears, Japanese American internment during World War II, and repeated deportations of Mexican Americans in the twentieth century. Students also could study migrations that have been means of escape, such as the Underground Railroad or the movement of political and economic refugees here and throughout the world.

*Focusing on important themes in history makes the study of state and local history more meaningful.*

Such investigations can provide a meaningful connection to local history. For example, students near Cincinnati could examine the violence and discrimination faced by people of German ancestry during World War I; students in California could learn about the extradition of Mexican Americans during the Depression or prejudice against Japanese and Chinese workers in the nineteenth century; and those in Southern states could study the forced removal of Blacks in their communities in the early part of the twentieth century.

These are only a few examples; the power of family histories lies in the way they can be adapted to local circumstances. Most students are required to study their state's history at some point (often in fourth grade), but unfortunately, the topic usually amounts to little more than temporarily memorizing the names of early political leaders or other "heroes." (And from other perspectives—such as those of Native peoples—these leaders are often anything but heroes.) Moreover, the study of state history generally reinforces the misconception that history is synonymous with progress—that the past has been marked by consensus and increasing prosperity. Rarely does state history acquaint students with the conflicts that have had a lasting impact on them. The topic would be much more vital, interesting, and meaningful if it focused on topics—such as immigration and its consequences—that help explain the present.

Similarly, a topic such as *communities* in third grade will be more meaningful than learning about "Anytown, U.S.A." if it involves students in investigations of migration in their own communities. Not every community is fortunate enough to have as high a proportion of newcomers as Rebecca's, but people everywhere move. Students could collect information on the moves they, their parents, and their grandparents have made in their lifetimes and use the data to answer a variety of questions: Have most people lived in one place all their lives? Have more people moved from one city to another, one state to another, or one country to another? Why have people moved? Rather than an exercise on how to find the post office on a generic map, the study of community could help students develop an understanding of how communities have developed over time. (For a more detailed description of community study, see Chapter 9.)

Using family members to learn about history, as Tina's students did, also has unlimited possibilities for extensions. Although her students focused on aspects of everyday life and rarely made connections to larger political or economic issues, teachers in the middle grades can help students learn about national and world events through the experience of their relatives, who often prove to be rich resources. One eighth grader in a class studying changing patterns of labor and unionization in the twentieth century, for example, had assumed her family would have little insight into the topic. To her surprise, they knew a great deal: Her father had been president of a teachers' union; her great-grandmother had left her family's farm during World War II to work in a chemical factory and had saved pro- and anti-union pamphlets from the 1940s in her scrapbook; and a great-uncle had been president of an AFL-CIO local—a fact no one had ever mentioned to her because no one thought it would be interesting. Students in another middle-school class interviewed community members to create a desegregation time line comparing events nationally to those in their own school and community. In both projects, personal insights of relatives and community members, and the further research they inspired, led to a level of involvement that no textbook or worksheet could have stimulated.

Collecting this kind of information can also help students better understand the evidentiary and interpretive nature of history. We noted in the last chapter that when children ask their parents questions, they quickly see that people disagree about the past. Students investigating truly significant issues (rather than when someone first learned to ride a bike) will encounter even more fundamental disagreements. Those in the middle grades, then, could compare the perspectives of family members on the Iraq war, struggles for LGBTQ+ acceptance, or expanding and contracting reproductive rights for women, and contrast these to accounts found in textbooks or the media. When students see historical interpretations on television or in movies, they may either uncritically accept or uncritically reject what they see—but when they have a chance to compare these interpretations to those of family members, they gain a better understanding of just how complicated history is. Students come away not only knowing more history but also coming closer to understanding how history is interpreted and presented.

Students in the middle grades can also use their families to learn about historical evidence other than oral accounts. In one eighth-grade class, for example, some students documented their families' involvement in the Vietnam Era with draft notices, transfer orders, newspaper clippings, and political buttons and posters that their relatives had saved. By combining these with the interviews they conducted, they put together a wide-ranging collection of historical evidence. Other students in the class used report cards, school yearbooks, and newspaper clippings to create histories of their parents' school careers. In both cases, students learned about the variety of sources on which historical accounts can be based.

As with any topic involving families, teachers must provide choices. Rather than expecting that every family will have experience with a war, social activism, or any other single

State and local history should include the conflicts that have influenced the present.

Community study should include attention to the historical development of specific locales.

Family histories can link students to national and world events.

Oral history and the experiences of families provide motivation for learning about modern history. *Crocco (1998), L. King (2019), Sánchez & Sáenz (2017)*

Family disagreements help students see history as controversial and interpretive.

Families may have a wealth of historical source materials.

Families have different historical experiences.

topic, teachers must recognize that each family's experience will differ. Some students may be able to investigate their relatives' involvement in the political events found in textbooks, but many others will benefit from looking at topics more closely related to social history. The point of involving family members is not simply to provide some gimmick by which students learn more about textbook content but for them to understand how history is written and interpreted.

## CONCLUSIONS

At first glance, history appears to be more remote from students' experiences than subjects such as language, math, and science. Even young children are familiar with talking, counting, and nature, but the world of the past seems inherently more abstract and distant. Some educators have even argued that the subject is so far removed from children's experiences that they are not ready to study history until high school! Family histories, though, help students make concrete connections to topics that would be less accessible if they were introduced only through readings in a textbook. By learning about their families' experiences moving or the way their grandparents lived when they were children, students both build on the mental schemas they already have and begin to move outward to people further removed in time and place. Tina points to this as one of the most important benefits of the activities described in this chapter: "Students start to get interested in something other than themselves, other than their friends, their clothes, their bubble gum."

As we noted in Chapter 1, one of the ways in which history contributes to democratic participation is by encouraging students to think about ways of life other than their own. By studying immigration, Rebecca's students had to consider the lives of people who came from different countries, whose circumstances were different than theirs, and who had different ideas, attitudes, and beliefs. They began by noting similarities between past and present, but they increasingly explored differences as well. Similarly, Tina's students knew that their relatives were like themselves in many ways, but their family history projects also helped them understand how they differed—the fashions they wore, the games they played, the technology they used. Although we will discuss more complicated forms of perspective recognition in later chapters, the activities described here introduced students to a basic element of historical understanding and democratic participation—the recognition that we are both similar to and different from other people and that both are crucial to understanding each other.

Students need to understand both similarities and differences across time and space.

Focusing on families is also tremendously motivating for students and relatives alike. Tina's students were excited about getting to interview their grandparents and to tell their stories in class; as one girl pointed out, "I learned things that my grandma did that I didn't know. You know what you have now, but you don't know what they had before." In Rebecca's room as well, students shared countless artifacts from their families' backgrounds, and parents sent in photograph after photograph for students to include in their presentations and papers. Successful schools recognize the importance of students' families and try to make them feel comfortable at school; family history projects take this recognition one step further by making family experiences a part of instruction. As Rhoda Coleman points out, "Parents love it, they love the interaction between the school and home. For once, this 10-year-old is asking them about their lives. Their child is asking them, 'Tell me about yourself.'"

# 6

# "I THINK COLUMBUS WENT TO HELL!"

## Connections and Controversies in World History

Christopher Columbus rode on a sail boat called the Santa Maria. He was standing on the ship when a wave splashed over the boat. The ship sinked and he swam to land. He gave the Indians fake jewelry and they gave him real gold. He took the Indians back with him to Spain across the ocean to castel. The king and queen gave him money to make other trips. He brought food like corn, potatoes, beans and tobacco. He also brought back gold. He was famous.

—Donte Morgan, age 6

Twenty-two kindergartners and first graders excitedly share their homework assignment—interviews with family members, neighbors, and friends about how people become famous. Some of them wrote their responses independently; others had an adult help them. They report that interviewees thought fame came when you were rich or when you did "something real cool," "headturning," or "something out of the ordinary." People identified presidents, athletes, and Miss America as well as local historical figures and celebrities as famous. But, students concluded, staying famous was not a certainty. "Sometimes," Gayle declared, "you can really blow it."

In part, the children had in mind the controversy over Columbus Day celebrations, which had been in the news around the time of this project. Columbus was certainly famous, but not everyone seemed to agree that it was "good fame." Their teacher, LeeAnn Fitzpatrick, brought in a newspaper article and a cartoon pointing out that some Native Americans (the term used in the article) saw Columbus as a villain, while other people, including some Italian Americans, viewed him as a hero. What was going on here? Why were people arguing over a day honoring an explorer students knew largely from a song, a few cartoons, and holiday sales?

LeeAnn saw the controversy about Columbus as an interesting beginning for inquiry with her young students. The controversy was authentic—real, important, and public—as well as accessible to children. Abundant resources at appropriate levels made further inquiry possible, and the students found the whole question of fame an interesting one. They enthusiastically set out to learn more about Columbus's world, to consider why his voyages continued to generate controversy, and to write about his place in history. Should Columbus be considered famous? A hero? Here were questions that connected LeeAnn's primary school students to world history.

### WORLD HISTORY: COMPARISONS, INTERACTIONS, PATTERNS

In the wake of Columbus' explorations, culture contact between people from the Americas, Europe, and Africa altered the continents on which they met and from which they came. We sometimes think of globalization as a modern phenomenon, but as LeeAnn's students

DOI: 10.4324/9781003179658-6

were about to discover, humans have been "globalizing" for centuries. Modern technologies simplify some aspects of the process—we can cross an ocean in only a few hours, explore another country on term break, or see and speak in real time with people around the globe—while complicating others—weapons, exploitation, and disease travel as easily as people. But these are merely modern incarnations of a long-standing process. Some members of the earliest hunting and gathering societies journeyed far from their home territories, establishing (or coercing) economic and cultural ties between communities, merging (or warring) with other groups, and learning about, introducing, and sometimes coercing the use of new technologies. Archaeological investigations continually unearth evidence of early contact among quite distant peoples, from desert people buried with shells from a distant ocean to tools and art forms that reflect cultural exchange across wide swaths of the planet. We may never know the names of the people who engaged in these exchanges, but we know that humans are a curious, inventive species, perpetually crossing borders and connecting in a variety of ways with others of their kind. Inquiry into world history encourages students to gaze across national borders and look for those broader patterns of interaction and disruption that connect human beings across the globe.

*Hodder (2009, 2012), LaMotta & Schiffer (2001), Sabzalian, (2019), P. Smith (2009), Trigger (2006)*

This may not be what most people think of when they hear the term *world history*. Perhaps you studied the "roots of democracy" in ancient Greece or the rise and fall of the Roman Republic as part of a "Western Civilization" course focused on Europe and the West. Or you might have learned about a variety of world civilizations—Egyptian, Chinese, Mayan, Venetian, and so on—by studying each one individually, with little attention to connections, interactions, disruptions, or comparisons. Some of the teachers in this book had the same experience but wanted to try a more global approach. Initially, the enormity of the task frustrated them. Which countries should they include? Which could be left out? A region-based march through time seemed little more than another example of a "mile-wide and inch-deep" curriculum. How about periodizations? Could the whole world be enmeshed in a "medieval period" or "enlightenment" at the same moment in time? Surely not. As these teachers searched for alternative approaches, they shifted scale to focus on connections, interactions, disruptions, and patterns that cut across national boundaries. In doing so, they found common purpose with others interested in *collective learning*—the capacity of human beings to learn from each other, pass on what they have learned, and apply that knowledge (for good and ill) to global as well as local challenges. By emphasizing the fluidity of human societies and the connections among them, some of the teachers you will meet in this book hoped to broaden as well as deepen the possibilities for collective learning.

*Bernstein (2013), Dunn (2012), Greenblatt (2011), Manning (2003), McNeill & McNeill (2003)*

*Collective learning draws on the broad range of human experience.*

*Hughes et al. (2007), Kilgore (1999)*

## MAKING CONNECTIONS

Making connections across broad reaches of time and space can be challenging. For one thing, concrete examples are always more interesting than abstract patterns—the story of Gutenberg's invention of the printing press, for example, is more appealing than "technological development" in general, and the challenges for merchants along the Silk Road are more interesting than "international trade." The further away we get from living, breathing individuals, the harder it is to motivate students or to build on their knowledge and interests. Moreover, at the upper elementary and middle school level, state and local curricula may organize history (and geography) around world regions and civilizations, and textbooks usually follow the same approach. As a result, teachers can fall into the trap of proceeding from one unit to the next with little attention to the connections that are the heart of world history. As one teacher pointed out to us, it's all too easy to develop wonderful units on Ancient Mali and Great Zimbabwe and give the impression at the end, "Now we're done with Africa!" So how can teachers keep the specific topics that are interesting (and required) without losing sight of the bigger patterns that they're part of?

One solution is for teachers to organize their instruction around broad themes but to illustrate those with specific case studies. One middle school teacher we know, for example, teaches a 3-month unit on "border encounters." The overall purpose of this unit is for students to better understand what happens when cultures clash, either when an established civilization is challenged by those on the margins of empire or an empire expands through conquest and colonization. Rather than lead students through a list of abstract principles, however, he has them develop their own conclusions by studying a variety of rich examples of encounters such as Visigoths and the Roman Empire; the Xiongnu and Chinese along the Great Wall; Maori and British in New Zealand; Native nations, Mexicanos, and White settlers in the American West; and so on. Each case study is interesting in itself but by seeing them grouped together, students can better recognize similarities and differences in world history. If they studied these examples in widely separated units on the Roman Empire, Ancient China, British imperialism, and nineteenth-century United States expansion, students would be much less likely to develop a comparative understanding of such encounters. Other such themes might include *human movement*, focusing on worldwide patterns of migration, or *home and family*, focusing on kinship patterns in different times and places.

Not all teachers will have the time, resources, or freedom to organize their teaching like this. However, there are ways to reap the benefits of a thematic approach to world history within the confines of a curriculum more closely tied to covering specific time periods and regions. Renee Shipman and Linda Cargile, who teach at the same middle school in southern California, do this by emphasizing connections across time and place. As outlined in California's state curriculum guidelines, Linda's sixth-grade class covers ancient civilizations, and Renee's seventh graders learn about medieval and early modern times; both have a list of specific regions, cultures, and civilizations they are expected to include. As they teach about these topics, though, they systematically draw students' attention to linkages to other topics and to the broader patterns they are meant to illustrate.

Renee, for example, begins the school year with a brief overview of the seven key themes of world history that are found in the *World History for Us All* model curriculum:

https://whfua.history.ucla.edu, Metro (2020)

- Patterns of population
- Economic networks and exchange
- Uses and abuses of power
- Haves and have-nots
- Expressing identity
- Science, technology, and the environment
- Spiritual life and moral codes

This is not an extended teaching unit—just a brief overview during the course of several days in order to introduce students to these themes and help them develop a conceptual understanding of their meaning. But as students study more specific topics during the year, Renee continually asks them to look for examples of these themes. When studying European colonization of the Americas, for example, she calls students' attention to the exchange networks within Central and South America and how these become integrated into a world economic system; when studying the Renaissance, students examine how spiritual life and moral codes were affected by exploration, technology, and the rediscovery of classical scholarship; in learning about medieval Islam students consider how new religious beliefs and languages become part of local and distinct identities in Africa, Asia, and Europe.

Making connections from past to present is also critical. Linda's sixth graders, for example, choose aspects of Greek society to investigate for class reports. In their presentations, they have to identify how their topics impacted life today by explaining how Greek innovations are still visible in modern forms of art, government, philosophy, warfare, and religion. For Linda, understanding the impact of ancient civilizations on later time periods is a crucial reason for including them in the curriculum. After all, no historical topic is important in itself; we study particular periods and events in order to learn how they affected the present, or how they illustrate broader themes.

*Making connections between past and present is critical.*

## START GLOBALLY, CONNECT LOCALLY

Making connections across time periods, or from past to present, are two effective ways of linking the topics of world history to broader patterns. Another way of making explicit the connections between local and global events is to start with contemporary issues that engage students' interest. Consider, for instance, Walt Keet's seventh grade class. When he was a relatively new teacher, Walt introduced the class to South Africa's ongoing transition from apartheid to a multiracial democracy. He thought that a topic so deeply rooted in historic issues of colonialism and human rights could be connected to patterns of conflict, segregation, and attempts at renewal in other parts of the world, including the United States.

Initially, Walt focused on Nelson Mandela, South Africa's coalition government, and the creation of a Truth and Reconciliation Commission to investigate that country's difficult and often horrific history. As events "on the ground" changed in South Africa, Walt shifted focus, emphasizing expanding and contracting conceptions of citizenship in the new South Africa and elsewhere, making use of a computer network to connect his students with other parts of the world. Walt introduced video conferencing technology that met the school's security requirements and allowed Walt to monitor comments, images, or text before they were sent out on the network. Better yet, from Walt's perspective, his students could actually interview people about the questions they were investigating, whether the people were somewhere else in the United States or around the world.

When Barack Obama was running for a second term as president, Walt wanted to make connections between his students who had witnessed the election for a second term of a Black president in the United States and South African students who experienced post-apartheid presidential elections after the death of Nelson Mandela. He was especially interested in engaging students in conversation about how countries deal with past inequities. There were obvious links between the United States and South Africa, from colonialism and de facto and de jure segregation to civil war, civil rights, and the eventual elections of Nelson Mandela and Barack Obama. Not surprisingly, Walt's students had stronger and more varied opinions about the U.S. election than the one in South Africa. Walt decided to put post-apartheid, post-Mandela South Africa in perspective by first discussing the impact of iconic figures in civil rights movements in both the U.S. and South Africa. In previous years, he had shown the movie *Cry Freedom*. That film follows anti-apartheid activist Steven Biko through the perspective of the White newspaper publisher who befriended him and who, from exile, wrote about Biko's murder at the hands of the White South African government. This time, Walt used *The Twelve Disciples of Nelson Mandela*, a documentary film that follows a group of South Africans as they leave their homeland and set out to build support for Mandela and the African National Congress. Walt thought the film did a good job of putting the protagonists' experiences in the larger global context of people's struggles for freedom and better connected U.S. and South African histories. He also drew on two books. The first, *Somehow Tenderness Survives,* offered a collection of short stories dealing with how, despite apartheid invading all aspects of South Africans' lives, people were able to hang on to both tenderness and hope. The second, a young readers' version of Trevor Noah's *Born a Crime*, describes the author's experiences as a biracial child in a place where his very existence was illegal.

Despite less public attention in the United States to changes in South Africa, Walt continued to find students were very interested in these "border areas" of human experience. As you will see with other teachers in this book, Walt found his students most disturbed that people could let such things happen. Why, for instance, had a majority Black population not kicked their oppressors out? Walt expected that his students would also point out similarities with U.S. enslavement especially given continued tensions in the surrounding community, but several students suggested that a better comparison was the colonizing of North American lands already inhabited by Native peoples. In response, Walt decided to introduce a geographic explanation for Europeans' world conquests by showing a portion of National Geographic's *Guns, Germs, and Steel*. Careful not to leave the impression

*Harris (2006)*

*Rochman (1990), Noah (2020)*

*Harrison et al. (2005), P. Smith (2009), Wolf (2006)*

that guns, germs, and steel were the *only* explanation for European imperialism, apartheid, or genocides, he also organized a time line activity comparing race- and ethnicity-based segregation and genocides at different times and places. This was yet another way of connecting one particular time and place—South Africa under apartheid—to one of the most troubling patterns of human interaction in world history.

To help students see this link, Walt attached a long Velcro tape around the perimeter of the room. Velcro-backed, dry-erase cards allowed him and students to rearrange the time line to highlight centuries, decades, or years. In this case, Walt marked off the time line in centuries beginning in 1500. He then organized the class into small groups and gave each group a set of color-coded, captioned images representing humans' general communal as well as state-sponsored responses to perceived differences. First, each group placed the pictures where they thought they belonged on the time line, discussed their placements, then checked for accuracy and rearranged the time line accordingly. Different groups searched the time line for patterns regarding oppression, resistance, reconciliation, and reparation, as well as for patterns of forced separations (e.g., enslavement, apartheid, reservations), voluntary ones (e.g., separatist groups such as the Amish), and related genocides (e.g., Armenian and Cherokee "removals"). Following a whole class debriefing, groups posted images and commentary on their video conference. Walt checked their work and posted it for comment, having invited students in a global issues course in another state to comment. The global issues students provided additional historical examples, and Walt's seventh graders became even more excited about the possibilities of connecting with peers across the network.

*Perdue & Green (2005)*

At about this point each year, Walt asked his students to consider related questions. "Is it possible to learn about a difficult past," he asked, "without making it impossible for people in the present to live together?" He then asked if students could "find any examples in other parts of the world to help us think about these questions?" These questions concern many people facing the present consequences of past oppression, violence, and inequity. Think about something as seemingly simple as a name. What difference does it make if people call a mountain Denali or Mt. McKinley? If a country in the Balkans is Macedonia or North Macedonia? If the capital city of South Africa is Pretoria or Tshwane? What does *naming* have to do with people's identity, and how, over time and place, have humans managed overlapping identities? Walt used these questions to initiate inquiry into how human societies alter their responses to difference.

## START LOCALLY, CONNECT GLOBALLY

Unlike Walt Keet, who started globally but connected to students' more local concerns, LeeAnn Fitzpatrick—the teacher in the vignette that begins this chapter—started with the persistent controversy over Columbus Day, which periodically erupted locally, to connect her students globally. Traditionally, world history receives little attention with young children. To some extent, this is related to assumptions that young children can learn best those things directly experienced and closest in time and place (see Chapter 2). As we mentioned earlier, research on human cognition suggests that these assumptions are not well-founded; understanding is not so much a matter of physical proximity as it is the degree to which children can make human sense out of whatever history they are studying. Certainly Donte, in his story at the beginning of this chapter, makes interesting human sense out of Columbus's interactions with Indigenous peoples. As were several of his peers, Donte was convinced that Columbus violated basic rules of fairness—he traded fake jewelry for real gold, and he took human beings away from their families just to show them to a foreign king and queen. The class had discussed this part of their study with LeeAnn asking what would happen if she declared that she was going to need "sample school children" to take home with her because her neighbors didn't understand what she did all day. She asked the children how they would feel if she just decided to keep a couple of them. They couldn't go back home, they'd have to be out on display for other people

*R. King (2012)*

For cautions regarding teaching about such subjects as the so-called "Columbian Exchange," see Sabzalian (2019)

to watch, and maybe they couldn't understand any of the language or customs of this new place. This was an issue that made clear human sense to the children. It made no difference that the setting was distant in time and place; people should never be souvenirs nor be taken unwillingly from their homes. Columbus had committed a historic wrong. As 5-year-old James declared, "I think Columbus went to Hell!"

Even before the children found out that Columbus had, in their view, behaved unfairly, their study was grounded in a familiar concept: Fame. First, the survey asked children to find out how other people in their environment viewed fame. These questions generated interest and discussion at home as well as in the classroom. Students compared their own responses to survey questions with those they received when they conducted the interviews and discussed the differences. Why, for instance, when asked to identify famous people, did so many men mention athletes, women name politicians, and children mention singers and actors? And no one had mentioned Christopher Columbus, despite all the newspaper coverage! Did that mean he wasn't famous? Or maybe he just wasn't very important? Discussion lasted a good 30 minutes, and when LeeAnn suggested that, perhaps, they could study more about Columbus and answer these questions, the students were enthusiastic. At this point, she introduced a set of questions that encouraged children to consider how a voyage that began in Spain more than 500 years ago touched their lives today:

- Why do some people celebrate Columbus Day?
- Is Christopher Columbus famous?
- Would we be here today in America if there had never been a Christopher Columbus?
- What do you think it was like living 500 years ago? How did people travel in those days?
- What would a person need in those days to travel across such a large body of water?
- How long ago was October 12, 1492?
- How long did it take Columbus to make his voyage to America?

Levstik (2013), Pappas et al. (2005), Wells (1999)

Organize inquiry so that all students can be challenged as well as successful.

Because LeeAnn's students had little prior experience with inquiry, and a number of them were not yet independent readers, she organized activities that would help students select information from sources she provided as well as organize and communicate their findings in ways that their peers could use. LeeAnn's integrated approach to curriculum design also led her to look for ways to incorporate other content areas such as mathematics and English/language arts into her instruction. She divided the class into five groups based, in part, on what tasks seemed within reach for each group:

*Group One: A Global Perspective.* LeeAnn provided a large blank map of the world, globes, and flat maps. Students referred to the comparison charts they had already developed, used the globes and flat maps to answer the following questions, and transferred information to the blank map. Their map was then hung up in the classroom as a reference for further discussion. Questions included locating the following on a world map:

1. The countries the kings lived in who turned Columbus down when he asked for financial assistance (England, France, Portugal).
2. The country that gave Columbus the money to finance the voyage (Spain).
3. The places that Columbus wanted to travel to (India, China, the East Indies, and Japan).
4. The route Columbus followed to get to the Americas.

*Group Two: Life in a Small Place.* LeeAnn provided a large cross-section drawing of a ship, string, rulers, and the like. After measuring the size of Columbus's ship and cutting string to the appropriate length (90 ft), the children used books, illustrations, and the comparison chart they had worked on earlier to identify cargo (food, firewood, water, wine, clothes, ropes, sails). On the cross section of the ship (see Figure 6.1), they then drew the cargo that they thought Columbus would need. Later, LeeAnn marked out an outline of the ship on the playground so the children could try to fit into the ship. Children were

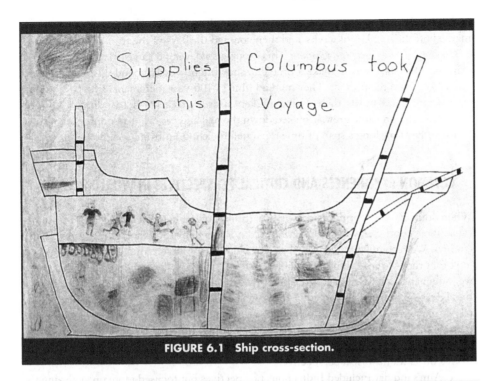

**FIGURE 6.1   Ship cross-section.**

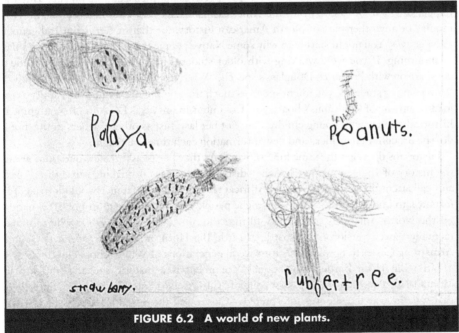

**FIGURE 6.2   A world of new plants.**

asked to think about what it was like living on the ships, with so many people, in such a small space, for such a long time.

*Group Three: Seeds of Change.* The task for this group was to find out what kinds of new plants—unfamiliar to Europeans—were found in the Americas. Again, LeeAnn provided appropriate books along with a chart where the children categorized the plants as fruits, vegetables, and non-edible plants. Children drew pictures of the plants in each category and then labeled their illustrations (see Figure 6.2).

*Group Four: Counting the Days.* Groups 4 and 5 had some of the youngest children, for whom the concept of time needed considerable support and visual reinforcement. Group 4 was tasked with making a time line showing how long Columbus's voyage lasted. They took calendars from August until October, cut them apart, put them on a time line, marked off the number of weeks, and then counted the days of the trip.

*Group Five: How Long Is a Century?* This group also developed a visual representation of time, but their task was to make a time line showing how many hundreds of years separated 1492 from the present. They marked time in 100-year increments by first grouping interlocking cubes in 10s, then placing markers after 10 groups of 10 to indicate a 100-year period. As the time line grew, it snaked down the hall and provided an impressive visualization of just how long a span of time separated the children from Columbus.

## COMMON EXPERIENCES AND CRITICAL PERSPECTIVES IN WORLD HISTORY

When students are writing things like "I think Columbus went to Hell!" it's going to cause some controversy. All of us think we know some history, especially about our own country. We recognize, of course, that we could always learn more, but we don't usually look for proof of those things we think we already know. It is troubling, then, when what we thought we knew is challenged. Sometimes we reject the challenge—the new information is wrong! Sometimes we want proof—what evidence is there for this challenge? And sometimes we seek out more information—what did I miss before? Challenges to what we thought we knew happen all the time in history. Sometimes they come as the result of new information. More often, they come because we are suddenly asked to look at something from a different historical perspective.

LeeAnn's inquiry included Indigenous perspectives but focused more on analyzing the impact of Columbus's entry into the Americas. Consider how you might reimagine this inquiry or any other part of North American history, for that matter, from Indigenous perspectives. You might start with why some Native people consider Columbus Day a day of mourning. If you were working with older students, that discussion might include a

*Douglass (1852)*

comparison with Frederick Douglass's speech, "What to the Slave is the Fourth of July?" With younger students, you might spend as much time on life in a Taino community as on loading up one of Columbus's boats. The Columbus inquiry was LeeAnn's first attempt at historical inquiry with young children but not her last. Just as other teachers in this book do, she brought in new ideas and new information each time she taught.

Historians do much the same kind of work. As they began asking new questions about the history of Indigenous peoples, they discover new ways of making sense of the past and call attention to silences in the historical record. What difference would it make, for

*Appleby et al. (1994)*

instance, to understand that the Comanche people constituted the most powerful nation on the North American continent well into the nineteenth century? Or why a fundamentally flawed version of the battle at Little Big Horn, nonetheless, elevated George Armstrong Custer to heroic status for several generations of White school children.

*Linenthal (1994), Gwynne (2010), Welch (2007)*

Little Big Horn Battlefield National Monument is a historic site and museum in Montana. You may remember it as the site of "Custer's Last Stand." From 1876 until 1976, that was the way the site was interpreted—Custer and the Seventh Cavalry made a last desperate stand against Indigenous peoples who threatened settlement in the U.S. West. The visitor center at the site was located close to where Custer died, and visitors viewed the battlefield from the perspective of the cavalry. Few visitors went to the site of the Native village or were introduced to Indigenous views of the battle. Beginning in the 1960s, however, the U.S. Park Service began to change its interpretation. What happened? Well, Indigenous people's protests, along with changing ideas about a more inclusive history, made people "see" Little Big Horn differently. This new view challenged old ideas

*Reinterpretations often challenge old assumptions and stereotypes.*

so that Little Big Horn became less massacre and more battle, less triumphant march of civilization westward, and more fight for survival on Native lands. Much of the information had been there all along, but its meaning changed dramatically as some scholars asked different questions, sought out different sources, and found new information. Between

*Fox (1993), Sabzalian (2019), Scott et al. (2000), P. Smith (2009)*

1983 and 1994, for instance, archaeologists working at Little Big Horn began comparing physical evidence—artifacts—with eyewitness reports from various combatants. Overall, they found that Indigenous people's reports closely matched the physical evidence. In consequence, any current history of the site must take this new information into account.

As you can see, challenging the "known" is not just cognitively sound instruction; it is also an authentic disciplinary model for doing history. As we already noted, children's schemas develop through generating questions and testing hypotheses. The same is true of historians; without challenges to existing schemas, they would have nothing to do. If the story of Little Big Horn were finished in 1876, there would be no need to rethink how the site is interpreted or for current historians to attempt to reconcile conflicting accounts to create a richer, more authentic interpretation. But the story is not finished, nor can it ever be; even if there were not conflicting accounts of what happened, historians would continue to interpret why it happened. Sometimes this interpretive restructuring involves minor tinkering—enriching but not significantly altering current schemas. Other times, it generates major restructuring of schemas, as when we stop telling the story of Columbus "discovering" a new world and start talking about culture contact and attempts at cultural erasure, exchange, resistance, imperialism, settler colonialism, and oppression. Children's and historians' mental models of the past are constantly restructured—not just by learning more historical information but by regularly reflecting on what that information means, on what other points of view are possible, and on what light new historical knowledge throws on current world events.

Each of the teachers in this chapter asks students to reflect on how perspective or point of view influences historical interpretation and leads to controversy. Renee, for example, regularly asks students to reflect on the assumptions that underlie the subject matter of the curriculum and even the wording they encounter. In a unit on exploration, she asked students to consider why textbooks use the phrase "New World," and why the Aztecs were unlikely to have thought of their home that way. She also had them compare the relative costs and benefits of exploration for Europeans and Indigenous people and even went so far as to point out, "We're not going to hear much about Native Americans in the textbooks because they were the losers, and we don't write much about losers in our textbooks." Having students compare perspectives, and assess which perspectives the curriculum most closely reflects, is a crucial part of developing historical understanding.

Similarly, when Walt explained to students that, after conquering southern Africa, Europeans renamed rivers, cities, mountains, and villages, he noted that they also Europeanized Black Africans' names. Students read sources that explained how some South Africans now want to peel away European names as part of an attempt to reclaim histories, including patterns of life in precolonial Africa, hidden behind European names. He also included a link to an article about controversial histories represented in museums, historic sites, memorials, and place names. Students used the video conferencing "doodling" feature to respond to Walt's comments and the article. This allowed all students to comment, a feature lacking in many classroom discussions.

Walt also engaged students in considering multiple perspectives by presenting them with the African National Congress (ANC) and Nationalist positions and then asking them to go backward in time to uncover the roots of dissension. In order to better help his students recognize the powerful emotions and perspectives behind the historic events, he used a concept map (Figure 6.3).

By symbolically representing perspectives, this concept map helped students think about what points of view needed to be researched in order to understand the dilemma the early coalition government, and succeeding governments, faced. It also served as a way to organize inquiry groups. One group was assigned to each of the South African perspectives represented on the graph. A slightly larger group was assigned to provide a world perspective, with pairs of students given the task of investigating how the United States, Chile, and Argentina handled the issues of human rights violations and the national memory of these events. The class had already studied the aftermath of World War II and the Nuremberg Trials, so they had some historical precedent on which to base their current study. Chile and Argentina's history provided more recent examples of countries faced

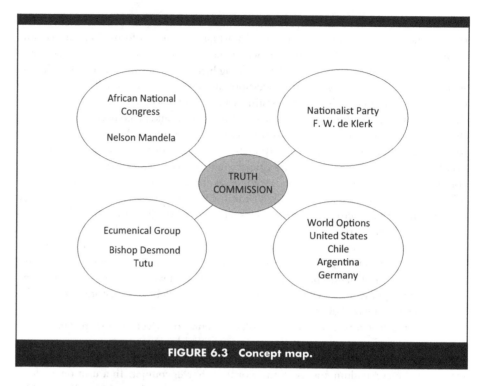

**FIGURE 6.3 Concept map.**

with major political changes following massive human rights violations, while a U.S. comparison encouraged students to think about what their own country faced in the aftermath of Civil War, in the midst of ongoing concerns over civil rights and more recently, in the aftermath of domestic terrorism. Finally, Walt introduced a brief article, *Mything Mandela*, as a way to explore how turning historical figures such as Mandela or Martin Luther King, Jr., into icons tends to over-simplify complex people and ignore the larger movements of which they were a part. In assessing this discussion, Walt decided it was important enough to consider expanding it in the future.

*Menkart (2014)*

Because Walt's students had more experience with selecting sources, note taking, citing sources appropriately, and the like, but less with researching multiple perspectives, he used three techniques to focus students on the cultural and historical roots of the different perspectives they might encounter in their study:

*Barton & Levstik (2004)*

*Portable Archives.* Because he wanted students to learn to use some sources that were new to them—demographic data, political cartoons, and film—Walt put together sets of primary and secondary source material along with background information on South Africa and the other countries students would be investigating. Each archive or set of sources contained demographic charts (age, ethnicity, education, and the like), digital newspaper articles and photographs, and trade books chosen for the way they represented different perspectives. He also attached a short set of questions to guide their analysis of each source.

*Pappas et al. (2005)*

*Double Entry Journals.* As each group began using the source packets to gather data on the point of view they were researching, Walt asked them to keep a double entry journal. At the top of each entry, students listed the source for the information. In the first column, they listed a position or argument along with supporting data. Opposite that position, in the second column, students made notes on what they thought the counter-arguments might be. So, for instance, the student citing de Klerk's position that a truth commission would lead to revenge and a possible coup noted in the first column that some people were already calling for public trials of the notorious state police and that military leaders had threatened to overturn the coalition government if that happened. In the second column, he speculated that Mandela and the ANC might not be able to maintain their standing with people who had been victims of the state police if past atrocities were swept under the rug. Using this technique, Walt hoped to help the students think about what support they would need to make their position more clear and/or compelling. "After all,"

*Atwell (1987)*

Journals help organize research and support positions.

**70**

he reminded his students, "people organized governments, arrested and executed other people, went into exile, and sacrificed their lives for these beliefs."

*Charting Key People and Events.* Walt also asked students to record significant names in the graphic organizer categories as a way to keep track of people representing the different perspectives. Other students could then note where they might look for opposing viewpoints. A class time line helped students organize information chronologically and made it easier to think about cause-and-effect relationships.

*Boner (1995), Cuthberston (1995)*

In order to help students connect individual pieces of information to the larger framework of South African history, Walt provided regular whole-group experiences. He invited a guest speaker to talk about South Africa's current government. He also required that each student select and read one novel set in South Africa, conducted small-group discussions of the novels, and had students read background material on the colonization of South Africa, the Boer War, and the origins of apartheid. During one class, he provided political and resource maps of South Africa and led a discussion of regional differences in the country. Students were expected to draw on their research as they participated in the discussions.

It is important to note that, although some assignments in each class were done outside of class—conducting surveys or reading books—most of the research was conducted in class. This is an equity issue as much as it is an opportunity to teach students specific research skills. Conducting research in class means that students with fewer resources to draw on at home are not at a disadvantage. In addition, it does not place the instructional burden for teaching students how to research on the home. Finally, conducting research in the classroom allows the teacher to help students think about appropriate forms for communicating what they are learning with different audiences.

It is crucial to conduct research in class rather than as homework.

Some teachers might consider multiple interpretations only appropriate for older students, such as Walt Keet's seventh graders, but LeeAnn thought that even Kindergartners and first graders could understand that there are different versions of the Columbus story. She selected three picture books and she, a teacher aide, and a student teacher divided the class so that each of the three groups listened to a different book about Columbus. In the class discussion that followed, the students recorded information on a comparison chart. As you can see by reading Figure 6.4, there were several places where the books did not agree or where one book gave information that another did not, and these differences were reflected in the students' answers to the questions of whether Columbus was (or should be) famous.

*James (2009)*

| Book title and Author | Why did Columbus go on the ocean voyage? | What did people think the world was like? | What happened to the people who already lived in America? | What did Columbus accomplish? |
|---|---|---|---|---|
| *Where Do You Think You're Going, Christopher Columbus?* By Jean Fritz | Short route to the Indies (Japan & China) Wanted gold Wanted to make people Christians | Agreed that the earth was "found like a ball" Disagreed about how big the Earth was Thought that there were gold, jewels, and spices in the Indies | Traded beads and bells for gold and parrots Indians were friendly Took 6 back to Spain on first trip Took 500 to sell as slaves Killed Indians for gold | Proved the sea was big Did not find Japan or China Did not know he was lost Found some gold Famous in Spain Named islands |
| *Christopher Columbus* by Ann McGovern | Wanted to reach "the east" by going west Wanted gold for Spain | Most people thought the Earth was flat A few people thought the Earth was round | Traded glass beads Indians were "gentle and friendly" Took 10 back to Spain on first trip | He was a hero in Spain He did not know he was lost He did not want to find a new world |
| *The Columbus Story* by Alice Dalgliesh | Wanted gold for Spain | Far away was the "Sea of Darkness" | Indians thought Columbus came from heaven Traded bells, beads, and caps for gold Indians were "gentle and friendly" Took "some" Indians back to Spain | He said all the land belonged to Spain He crossed the sea first |

**FIGURE 6.4  Book comparisons.**

## CONTROVERSY AND INQUIRY

*Hess (2009), K. Young (1994)*

Approaching history as these teachers do is not without its problems. Encouraging cross-cultural inquiry challenges traditional interpretations and brings enduring myths into question. Other teachers may object to this approach. New interpretations may be thought to threaten national pride. Some parents, too, may find it disconcerting to learn from their 5-year-olds that Columbus did not discover America, that Europeans did not treat Indigenous people well, and that resistance continues, while others may not want explicit comparisons made between U.S. racial problems and those in other parts of the world. As a teacher, you cannot ignore these potential problems, but you can plan ahead so that you respond intelligently to challenges. Present issues in as balanced a way as possible, emphasizing what is supportable given the available evidence and what is representative of current scholarship. Moreover, if you are presenting history as a process of interpretation, rather than as a single version of the "truth," you should be able to explain the grounds for that approach to concerned colleagues or parents. It often helps to explain that you are trying to help students develop supportable interpretations rather than requiring that they hold any single explanation to be the end product of historical thinking. In polarized political environments, though, even this approach may be challenged.

*Plan ahead to respond to concerns about controversial issues.*

*When students are fully engaged and enthusiastic about their studies, parents often are, too.*

Most of the teachers with whom we work have found that when their students are excited and interested in historical study, most colleagues and parents are pleased and supportive. These teachers more often report that their most significant problem in challenging historical myths is the persistence of those myths in the larger culture. It is hard to challenge the myths surrounding Pocahontas, for instance, when they are enshrined in a popular animated film and reproduced in toys and commercial messages or used to satirize a political opponent. The same is true for the persistence of the myth that Columbus proved the earth was round. (That the earth was round was, of course, a piece of information known to just about all educated people of the period.)

*Dennis (2002)*

## ASSESSING HISTORY OUTCOMES

### Reporting Out

*Erekson (2014), Pappas et al. (2005)*

As communities of inquiry, such as those developing in Walt's and LeeAnn's classrooms, grow, they need to develop strategies for sharing and assessing work. Students who have done substantial inquiry require more than a final grade to bring their study to closure; they need an opportunity to make public sense out of what they have learned. "Going public" means students organize what they have learned during their investigations in order to present their findings to others. You will recognize the importance of this part of inquiry when you think about how much you learn when you teach a subject, as opposed to when you simply study it for a test. As you will recall from Tina's experience in Chapter 4, students often have difficulty sorting out what is important about their studies and then organizing that information for particular audiences. Such "presentational talk" takes practice and substantial support from the teacher. Because LeeAnn's students had little experience in presentational talk, she incorporated a number of small in-class presentations in which students were able to use the different graphic organizers their groups had worked with. Thus, two groups referred to charts, the map provided a focus for a third group, and the time lines were used by the last two groups. After each group explained what they had learned, LeeAnn opened the discussion for questions and comments from peers. In a follow-up discussion, she also helped students further synthesize the results of their studies across groups. "Now that we have seen all the group projects" she said, "let's go back to our comparison chart and see if we still have conflicting information." In discussion, then, students noted where information from different sources agreed or disagreed. They found that some sources still claimed that Columbus's voyage proved that the earth is round, other sources differed on whether Queen Isabella really sold her jewelry to finance Columbus's voyage, and not all the sources mentioned taking Indigenous people back to Europe.

With plenty of discussion and debate as foregrounding, LeeAnn then drew the students back to their first questions: Was Christopher Columbus famous, and if he was, why was he famous? "Now each of you will have a chance to be a historian and answer the questions we've asked," she told them, asking them, too, if they remembered how historians told people about the past. Students gave several suggestions—books, movies, speeches—and finally decided to write books about Columbus. "Remember that historians can have different ideas about the past, but they have to use the facts," LeeAnn explained. "Historians also think about who might read their books and explain things so their readers will understand them. Who might read our books?" Students decided that because their parents and friends had helped them do the original survey, they might be interested in reading what the students had learned. The class decided to share their books with parents at a special "Christopher Columbus Presentation" at the end of October. With an audience in mind, a written genre—biography—selected, and the results of their study displayed throughout the classroom, the students were ready to write. During writers' workshop, a time set aside each day for student writing, editing, and publishing, those children who were independent writers began biographies of Christopher Columbus that would answer the question, "Was Columbus a hero?" Other students dictated their stories to an adult. Over about a two-week period, children wrote, conferenced with an adult or peer, edited, illustrated, and then published their books. As editor-in-chief, LeeAnn made one suggestion about medium (mechanics) and one about message (content) components of each child's story prior to publication. At the Columbus presentation, children shared their biographies, presented their projects, and discussed what they had learned, including:

*Students can select appropriate historical genres.*

"Books on the same subject can give you different information."

"Different maps can use different colors to tell you things. Oceans are usually blue, but could be brown, and Italy can be yellow or pink."

"We learned where France, Portugal, Spain, England, Italy, India, China, and Japan are. Also Africa, the Atlantic Ocean, the Pacific Ocean, Indian Ocean, and the Mediterranean Sea. And the United States and the Caribbean Islands."

"You need to take many of the same supplies on an ocean voyage today as you did 500 years ago."

"We learned that living today is more convenient compared to Columbus."

"Different countries grow different kinds of foods."

"It is easier to count to 500 if you count by 10s until you get to 100."

"Columbus did not treat the Indians fairly, so why was he considered a hero and named 'Admiral of the Ocean Sea?' He was famous."

As you can see, by the time the Columbus presentation concluded, LeeAnn had accumulated considerable data regarding student performance. But not every assessment of student inquiry requires an outside audience in quite the way that LeeAnn arranged for her class. In Walt's case, his state's assessment system required individual, assessable products for social studies assessment. As a result, he organized "reporting out" through round-table negotiations and a position paper.

*Assessment can match both state requirements and an inquiry perspective.*

*Round-table Negotiations.* Walt held a class training session on consensus building as students completed their research into the different positions regarding a South African "truth commission." He then selected one student arbitrator and one student representing each of the different points of view on the issue for each round table. Arbitrators were to keep negotiations on track and serve as time keepers. Once all students had been assigned to a round table, they were given the remainder of the class period to lay out the major arguments for each position. During the next class session, negotiations began. Students were to see if they could reach some consensus in their groups regarding the establishment and functioning of a truth commission. As a homework assignment, students were asked to write a brief statement outlining their understanding of their group's results. What points of agreement were there? Of disagreement? In the next class, positions were again diagrammed on the board and areas of agreement and disagreement discussed.

*McGinnis (1991)*

**73**

*Position Papers.* Finally, Walt asked students to step back from their studies and reflect on how their own ideas had changed from the beginning of the study. He asked them to look over their research notes and dialogue journals and to think about what their study of South Africa told them about the kind of history people needed to learn. After a brief discussion, Walt passed out two articles. One criticized school history for dwelling on problems such as race relations and another complained that school history too often ignored problems in the past. "Now it's your turn to take a stand on this issue in your own country," he explained. "Use what you have learned about South Africa to help you respond to the critics in these two articles. What should American students know about the problems in our past?" In the criteria for this task, Walt emphasized that the quality of support for each position was the basis for assessment rather than the particular position a student might take.

## Focusing on History Outcomes

As you can tell by now, by the time students conclude the kinds of inquiry described in this chapter, their teachers possess a wide variety of information on their inquiry and interpretive skills. Because so much of students' work in history involves reading, writing, and speaking, however, attention to assessing the specifically historical purposes of students' work sometimes gets diverted. The historical aspects of students' inquiry into world history include working with different data sources, recognizing different perspectives, making connections between local and global history, and identifying patterns and connections between places and across time. As soon as LeeAnn's students completed a map of Columbus's world, for instance, she noticed that they could accurately identify the countries that turned Columbus away, where he finally received help, and where he hoped to end up, but they confused "the Americas" with the United States, coloring in the present-day United States, including Alaska, to indicate where Columbus actually landed. In response, LeeAnn spent time discussing what the Americas were like in 1492, what Europeans might have thought they looked like, and how many Indigenous nations already existed there. Later, when students filled in the comparison chart, LeeAnn assessed what they were learning from different data sources—the three different books on Columbus.

Walt uses a rubric—a written set of criteria—to help students understand his expectations for different tasks from small-group discussions to written position papers. Early in the year, he writes the criteria himself and gives them to the students, but as time goes by, he turns more and more of this task over to the class. Figure 6.5 shows the jointly created

*Assessment helps teachers plan more effective experiences for students.*

*Yell (1999)*

*Teachers need to assess specific historical aspects of inquiry.*

*Written criteria help students understand the standards for their work. Monte-Sano (2008)*

---

Question at Issue:
What Should U.S. Students Learn about Problems in Their Country's Past?

Turn in a 5-10 page position paper. This paper may contain a combination of words, pictures, graphs, and any other types of illustrations that make a persuasive case for a position on this question. The paper will be evaluated on the following criteria:

- The author clearly explains what he/she/they consider to be the purposes of learning history.
- The author clearly shows an understanding of the similarities and differences in the historical situations in South Africa, Chile, Argentina, and the United States and makes the differences clear to the reader through the use of words and illustrations (charts, pictures, etc.).
- The author clearly connects what is happening in the rest of the world to what is happening in the United States.
- The author takes a position and supports it with accurate information from at least 4 different sources used during our study and gives bibliographic information for each one.
- The author describes and counters major arguments against her/his/their position.

**FIGURE 6.5  Position paper.**

**74**

Name of student _____     Date _____

### South Africa/Apartheid Study

The student completes the left side of this evaluation and then the teacher will complete the right side. Afterwards we will discuss your work, identify areas of strength, and decide on the areas that need to be improved.

| O = Outstanding | S = Satisfactory | N = Needs Improvement |
|---|---|---|

| Student Evaluation | | Teacher Evaluation |
|---|---|---|
| _____ | I used a variety of relevant and challenging resources to learn about my subject | _____ |
| _____ | I gained confidence in my ability to evaluate historical sources | _____ |
| _____ | I used both primary and secondary sources to learn about my subject | _____ |
| _____ | I improved in my ability to construct a persuasive historical argument | _____ |
| _____ | I improved in my ability to identify different historical perspectives | _____ |
| _____ | I improved in my ability to discuss ideas with which I disagree | _____ |

The most important thing I learned from my study was:

**FIGURE 6.6  Student/teacher evaluation.**

criteria for a position paper, and Figure 6.6 shows a similarly created evaluation sheet used at the end of the unit. Such joint evaluations provide an opportunity for Walt to discuss specific aspects of the study with each student. When he first developed this type of evaluation, he hoped it would elicit important information from his students. He wanted to know, for instance, how adept they were with the language of historical study used in the class—perspective recognition, archives, primary and secondary sources, and pattern and connection. Walt soon discovered that joint evaluation also provided important information to his students, especially about their teacher's goals and expectations. Over time, joint evaluations also helped his students become more self-reflective about their own learning. Because this is a time-consuming process, however, Walt found that it was not practical to conduct joint evaluations after every unit of instruction. Instead, he decided to use them as a periodic gauge of student progress and especially as an opportunity to debrief more contentious topics with his students.

Joint evaluations help debrief controversial topics.

The assessment procedures used by the teachers in this chapter evolved over time. They tried some techniques, adjusted them to suit their circumstances and students, and evaluated their effectiveness in use. Fundamental to this process is each teacher's desire to establish a particular kind of learning community. It is not just that they want students to learn world history, although this is certainly a primary goal of instruction, but that they also want assessment to contribute to inquiry, not interrupt it. Traditional test questions—questions that allow only one possible right answer or focus on reporting on what

Monte-Sano (2012), Wertsch (1998), Yell (1999)

someone else thinks or has said—are less likely to foster this sort of community of inquiry. Constructive assessment—questions and problems with multiple acceptable responses—invite students to contribute something new or change or modify an inquiry while also providing data on how students are progressing in that inquiry. Constructive assessment also signals to students that what and how they think and know is important. Teachers model powerful ways of knowing and doing history by differentiating tasks—offering choices in terms of tasks as well as how tasks are approached and reported on—and scaffolding tasks—providing appropriate structure to help student master the complexities of a task.

## CONCLUSIONS

Too often, world history is virtually invisible in U.S. elementary schools and receives scant attention thereafter. This need not be the case. Inquiries into world history make an important contribution to students' developing historical understanding. Walt's class study of South Africa, for instance, had a profound impact on students' views about race-based discrimination, not just in South Africa but also in other parts of the world, including the United States. Renee's introduction to organizing themes—from patterns of population to expressions of identity—also encouraged students to consider worldwide connections.

Gaddis (2002)

Perhaps most significantly, studying world history makes clearer the profound historical effect of people's differing beliefs, values, experiences, and knowledge. Recognizing some of these differences challenges students' assumptions about the growth and development of human societies, laying a foundation for countering stereotypical thinking and enhancing cross-cultural communication. In addition, studying world history puts national history—and national identity—in a broader context, suggesting alternatives to current local and national practice. To the extent that such study makes explicit students' connections to other parts of the globe, it better prepares them to participate in the kind of decision-making required of inhabitants of an increasingly interconnected world.

National Council for the Social Studies (2010), Peace Corps World Wise Schools (1998)

# 7

# Camel Dies, Lose Three Turns

## Scaffolding Inquiry into World History

It's easy to identify Linda Cargile's classroom, because music is drifting into the hallway—and not the intellectually stimulating sounds of Mozart or Yo-Yo Ma but the more raucous strains of Steve Martin's "King Tut." Walking into the classroom, a visitor sees 37 sixth graders focused on a YouTube video of Martin and the "Toot Uncommons" performing his 1978 novelty song. As the Tutankhamen exhibit toured the United States that year, Martin's lyrics about the boy king reached number 17 on the charts—surely one of the few songs about ancient Egypt ever to become so popular. After the video finishes, Linda plays similar compositions created by last year's class of sixth graders.

This is the opening of a project in which students will create their own historical songs. Working as individuals, in pairs, or in small groups, students will select a god or goddess from one of the ancient civilizations they've studied and develop original compositions and recordings. Over the next several days, students identify at least 10 pieces of information about the figure they've chosen and begin writing lyrics. As Linda points out, their compositions can be—and should be—funny, interesting, and engaging, but they also have to be historically accurate...unlike Steve Martin, who sang that King Tut was born in Arizona before moving to Babylonia!

After drafting their lyrics, students move to the computer lab for a week and set their songs to music using a digital audio workstation. At the end of the project, students play their songs for each other in class and save them in a compilation folder, "Music for the Gods." This includes such classics as "Hades Could Kill You in Your Sleep," "Bast, Lady of the Past," and "Big Zeus Might Zap You."

This project, as well as student-created digital videos on "makers and shakers" from world history, is always one of students' favorites, and they often come back to Linda the next year to ask if she's played their songs for the new class of sixth graders. One of Linda's students, when asked what advice she had for future teachers, pointed out that assignments should always be creative like this and should involve variety and choice: "Think about what the students want to do," she advised, "and put yourself in their shoes: When you were in school would you have done this project?"

We pointed out in the last chapter that world history can be a challenging subject to teach to young students. Transnational patterns of trade, comparative civilizations, the development of world religions—these are abstract topics whose appeal may not always be obvious. Moreover, students in the United States grow up on a steady diet of U.S. history, but they usually have little exposure to that of the rest of the world, which they may regard with apathy or even suspicion. Introducing these topics requires that teachers carefully consider how they can best motivate and engage their students. In the last chapter, we emphasized the importance of selecting compelling case studies, such as the Columbian

DOI: 10.4324/9781003179658-7

Exchange or apartheid in South Africa, to illustrate broader patterns in the global past. In this chapter, we focus on the kinds of activities that students find interesting—especially those involving creativity, choice, and variety. We also examine how teachers can support students' learning by using a variety of media and through their scaffolding of students' performance.

## CREATIVITY AND THE CONSTRUCTION OF MEANING

Creative teachers get lots of attention. Everyone is impressed by teachers who know how to engage students in exciting activities that keep them interested in school. When teachers move away from textbooks and worksheets and start using art, drama, digital technology, and the like, everyone takes notice—students, parents, administrators, and other teachers. It's even more impressive when teachers allow children themselves to demonstrate their creativity. Any of us would rather walk into a classroom filled with original student artwork, or one in which students are composing a historical song, making their own documentary, or constructing elaborate displays, than to watch students mindlessly scribbling down information. After seeing the spark that creativity brings to learning, it's hard to watch anything else. Silent classrooms where children endlessly answer written questions just don't seem worthwhile anymore.

Linda is certainly the kind of creative teacher we all love to meet. Her cavernous classroom is filled with student-produced artwork: Mobiles on Confucianism, Buddhism, and Daoism; construction-paper mosaics on Roman life; posters on "the paradox of civilization"; and museum exhibits on Ancient Egypt (originally displayed during an open house for parents, with both students and teachers dressed in period costume). Other creative activities that her students take part in throughout the year—in addition to developing digital audio and video productions, as mentioned earlier—include designing slides on individuals from ancient civilizations, making their own history word searches and crosswords, designing brochures on world religions, producing "cybermagazines" on early humans, and even taking part in a "Surreal History Art Explosion." In this last project, students use graphic design software to create surrealist art that displays findings from their research into Ancient Egypt—a project whose theme, as Linda suggests, is "from antiquity to postmodernism and beyond."

In the previous chapter, we also introduced you to Renee Shipman. Although her world history classroom may not be as flashy as her colleague Linda's, it's just as creative. Among the projects displayed on the walls are a series of "Newspapers of the Reformation," with titles such as *European Daily*, *Renaissance Weekly*, and *The Reformation Information*. Students worked in groups to create these, and each paper had to include articles on philosophy, social life, conflict in the Catholic Church and the Counter Reformation, and advertisements for new technology. Students also used folding display boards to create "century projects" in which each group chose a different century and summarized art, ethics, political changes, technological contributions, and significant people or events during the time period.

Some students don't become interested in history until they can take part in creative activities.

All these projects are time-consuming; Linda even refers to art as a "time-eater." Nonetheless, she says, it's worth it. Some students, she points out, aren't interested in anything *but* art, and they demonstrate no interest or achievement in history until they begin to work on something creative. Many of them come back to her each year to ask if she's still doing the same projects with her class. For Linda, creating this spark and developing an interest in history—even a *love* of history—is crucial. Students have to connect with the subject, she says, before they can become analytical about it. Moreover, she knows that they're not going to learn every fact they encounter, especially for topics as broad as world history, but she believes that she can create an enthusiasm that will endure, so that even if they find themselves sitting in a boring history class someday, they'll know it doesn't have to be that way. This, she says, is why she does so many engaging projects: "That's who I am. If I'm not having fun or enjoying it, neither are they."

But is developing enthusiasm the only reason for creativity in the history classroom? Some beginning teachers think that having fun is an end in itself. It's clear that students are more engaged in creative activities, so they mistakenly conclude that fun is all that matters—a fun activity, they think, is, by definition, a good one. The problem with this perspective, as any experienced teacher will tell you, is that having fun doesn't necessarily mean that students are learning anything. Unfortunately, as teachers realize the need for students to understand the content of the curriculum, many of them abandon their focus on fun and creativity and revert to textbook-centered instruction—a practice that not only isn't fun but also isn't likely to help students understand the material in any meaningful way. Too few teachers take on the challenge that motivates Linda's teaching: Engaging students in creative activities that ensure meaningful learning.

*Activities should lead to meaningful learning.*

To meet this challenge, it's important to understand the purpose for having activities in the first place: Activities provide the means by which students construct knowledge, so they are an indispensable part of lesson structure. In any lesson, information has to come from somewhere—books, digital media, lectures, artwork, a guest speaker, students' own experience, and so on. A large portion of the teacher's job is to make sure that students can access those resources meaningfully, and so they select sources carefully and scaffold students' comprehension of them. But after students have read, listened to, watched, or experienced the information in well-chosen resources, they still have to *do something* with that content in order to understand and remember it. This is the purpose of activities.

*Smagorinsky (2001)*

Activities require students to take information and process it—to turn it around, manipulate it, make sense of it. It's during activities that students have to think about content more deeply so that they can use and apply the information. We've all had the experience of listening to a lecture or watching a documentary and feeling that we understood it completely, only to be flummoxed when we tried to explain it to someone else. We had absorbed the information, but we still needed to do more in order to understand it meaningfully. This is where activities come in. Activities give students the chance to think through content and make it their own—to construct meaning from it.

*Activities give students the chance to construct meaning through active processing of information.*

The best activities are those that require genuine engagement on the part of students, so that they really do have to make sense of content rather than merely reproducing it. This almost always involves taking information they've encountered in one form and transforming it into another—for example, by turning the content of trade books or reference works into songs, movies, artwork, or pieces of creative writing. It's during this transformation that the construction of meaning takes place, and that's one reason that answering worksheets and textbook questions isn't effective: It's not just that they're not fun, but that they require minimal manipulation of information. Students can usually just find the answers in another piece of text and copy it more or less the way it was originally written. There is so little cognitive processing involved that students don't have to understand much in order to do well. Creative projects like those in Linda's and Renee's classes, though, require a much higher level of involvement. Students can't write an effective advertisement for a Renaissance invention without understanding the place of that technology in society at the time. They can't just "find the answer" to a task like this by looking it up as they can when they answer a question from a text.

*A. Miller (2007), Smagorinsky (2001)*

This means, however, that students have to be held to standards of historical accuracy. Linda stresses, for example, that students' lyrics—while they can and should be funny and creative—have to be accurate; they can't make up facts about the figures or time periods they're writing on. When one group of students creates a board game to show what they've learned about the experiences of travelers on the Silk Route, they have to make sure that the game really does reflect the challenges faced by people at the time—climate, terrain, thieves, and so on. When a player draws a card that says, "Camel dies, lose three turns," it's because students have learned about the importance of camels as a form of transportation on the route, not just because it sounded clever.

*Creative activities must also be historically accurate.*

One final point about these creative connections: Teachers need variety from lesson to lesson. This doesn't mean that every day has to be new and unpredictable, but it does mean that, over the course of weeks and months, students should engage in more than one kind

---

Table 7.1

Activities for Constructing Knowledge

| | | |
|---|---|---|
| Advertisement | Digital Documentary | Poem |
| Board game | Hot seat | Presentation slide |
| Broadside | Historical marker | Role play |
| Character web | Letter | Script |
| Comparison chart | Memoir | Simulated journal |
| Debate | Museum display | Song |
| Decision chart | Newscast | Source collection |
| Dialogue | Newspaper article | Venn diagram |

---

*Varying activities helps students remember content. Aitken & Sinnema (2008)*

of activity. Even the most engaging project will get boring with repetition; students don't want to write song lyrics about every topic they study! There are also important cognitive reasons for instructional variety. Research has shown that when students try to recall information from class, they don't just think about the content itself; they also think about the way in which they learned it. That is, if students try to remember how Roman government worked, they will access that information, at least in part, by recalling the activity they did; they'll think something like, "Roman government…that's where we did a role play of a meeting of the Assembly…" Instructional variety, then, gives students a second route—beyond the content itself—of remembering what they have learned. If every lesson is the same, they don't have this alternative.

Beginning teachers, though, sometimes are daunted by the prospect of developing so many different, creative activities. When they see a classroom like Linda's, they think, "I could never come up with all those great ideas!" What they don't realize is the secret that sets such teachers apart from their less-exciting colleagues. Teachers with the greatest reputation for creativity actually may not be particularly imaginative at all. What makes them who they are (apart from their desire to keep students motivated and intellectually engaged) isn't creativity; it's a list. That's right: A list. Teachers like Renee and Linda have a list of about 20 activities—either in their heads or written down somewhere—that they can use with lots of different topics, and each year they simply decide which activity should go with which topic.

*Teachers need a list of creative activities.*

Last year Linda's students wrote lyrics about emperors; this year it's gods and goddesses. Renee's students do character webs on cultural figures from the Renaissance—Machiavelli, Shakespeare, Gutenberg—but next year, the character webs may be on explorers. If they suddenly found themselves teaching U.S. history, they'd still be using the same set of activities, but with new content. Moreover, they may not have come up with any of these ideas on their own. The best teachers are relentless in collecting ideas from lots of different sources—workshops, professional journals, university courses, and, most of all, from other teachers. Whenever they hear an idea that has potential, they add it to their repertoire, and they pass it on to others. So, if you haven't begun your list yet, now is the time. Table 7.1, which lists many of the activities found in this book, is a start.

## CHOICES, CONNECTIONS, COMPARISONS

Many of the activities in Linda's and Renee's classrooms involve choices. In some cases, students have choices about the medium they use, just as Tina's students did in Chapter 4. In their reports on Roman art and architecture, for example, Linda's students could choose to present information in the form of a presentation slide, a mosaic, a poster, or other media. This gave students the chance to use their strengths; they weren't limited by being required to use a form they had little experience or facility with. On the other hand, the variety of products that come out of these choices also gave students the opportunity to see what accomplishments in other formats might look like. Students who had never designed a presentation slide learned from their classmates' creations, and for the next project, some chose to do one themselves. Expanding students' repertoire of learning strategies is an important part of any teacher's job.

Students in these classrooms also frequently chose the specific content of their projects. Every student in Linda's class had to write a song about an ancient god or goddess, but they could choose any such figure, from any of the cultures they had studied during the year. Similarly, Renee's students could select any piece of technology from the Renaissance as a basis for their advertisements. This gives students a sense of ownership. Renee says that her philosophy is that students have to take responsibility for their learning, so they do a lot of independent projects in which they select what they want to study; part of her goal, she says, is for students to learn how to learn, and to learn what works best for them.

*Students benefit from having choices about the content and format of their assignments.*

Providing students with choices can help them make connections to their own backgrounds or to the interests they have. Both Linda and Renee have students who identify as Black, as White, or as natives of various countries in Asia, the Pacific, or Central and South America (or some combination of these identities), and they deserve to see themselves reflected in the curriculum. When teachers can make connections between the content of the curriculum and students' interests, experiences, and backgrounds, students become more engaged in their learning. One of Renee's students, for example, noted that he liked studying Central America "because most of my ancestors were Aztec or Maya." Giving students choices in project topics helps increase the likelihood that they will be able to find these connections.

*Choices allow students to make connections to their interests and background knowledge.*

*Aitken & Sinnema (2008)*

Many teachers worry, though, that giving students so many choices, or trying too hard to connect the curriculum to their background, will fail to push them beyond what they already know. If they only study what they're already familiar with, how will they ever learn anything new? This is one of the reasons that comparison is so important; whenever possible, students need to compare the topics they've chosen to other content. In describing their mobiles on the religion they've chosen to report on, for example, Linda's students have to make comparisons with other religions. When students compare topics this way, it ensures that they will have to move beyond what they already know best or feel most comfortable with. Such comparison is important not only for students' self-selected topics but throughout the history curriculum. In the previous chapter, we talked about making connections between past and present, and between local issues and global ones, but world history is replete with opportunities for comparison, and indeed, this is at the very heart of what world historians study. Students can compare practices of different religions, the social structure of different civilizations, the goods exchanged along different trade routes, the causes of changes in different civilizations, and so on.

*Stearns (2008)*

One type of comparison that can cause particular problems, however, involves religions; in fact, any instruction on religion can pose challenges for teachers. Linda says that whenever she comes to the topic of religion, she can expect calls from parents who, at the least, want to know why their children are learning about other religions—and at worst, want to complain that teachers have no business mentioning religion in the classroom. As with any potentially controversial topic, Linda responds to such questions with a clear rationale for her practices, a rationale that reflects her knowledge of legal, civic, and historical arguments for why and how to include religion in the curriculum.

*Barton & James (2010)*

Of course, public school teachers in the United States cannot promote religion in their teaching, but social studies teachers can (and must) teach *about* religion—a practice that is fully supported not only by major professional and religious organizations but also by Supreme Court decisions. When we say that teachers cannot "promote religion," we mean that they cannot indoctrinate students: They cannot present a set of religious beliefs as being true or correct. Nor, indeed, can teachers suggest that *any* religious beliefs are better than *no* belief, because government can no more promote religion in general than it can favor any particular religion. This separation of church and state is established in the First Amendment of the U.S. Constitution, and it reflects the founders' recognition— based on their own understanding of European history—of the potentially disastrous

*Teachers can and must teach about religion. Haynes & Thomas (2007), National Council for the Social Studies (2014)*

**81**

consequences of state-sponsored religion. Given the country's long-standing religious diversity, the principal of religious freedom continues to serve us well.

Teaching *about* religion, on the other hand, is absolutely necessary in history and social studies classrooms, because it is impossible to understand numerous aspects of human society—past or present—without understanding religion. Religion is a principal means by which people in many times and places have understood and made sense of the world around them—the origins of the universe, their reasons for living, and the proper way of conducting themselves. Religion often has had a significant impact on art, architecture, literature, politics, and social movements—not to mention on war, conflict, and violence, each of which frequently has been grounded in (or justified by) religious differences. In studying ancient and medieval history, for example, students have to understand a variety of religions, including both those that are still practiced and those that are no longer current. It's also important to recognize, as Renee points out, that even though students usually understand the basic beliefs of their own church, they don't necessarily understand the larger complexity or variation found within their religion, much less in other systems of belief, and they tend to over-generalize their characterizations of religions. Studying religions at school, then, deepens and enriches their understanding of a vitally important aspect of human society.

We noted above that comparison is one of the best methods for helping students understand content, and the study of world religions lends itself particularly well to a comparative approach. During many periods of history, two or more major religions were prevalent in the same region, so it's only natural to study each of them and to note their similarities and differences. However, teachers need to be aware of at least two important drawbacks to this approach. First, studying religions only in connection to historic civilizations can give the misleading impression that they have not changed over time—an idea that some religious adherents may like to promote, but one that is historically inaccurate. In order to more fully understand the role of religion in society, students need to learn about a variety of religions in the contemporary world and not only while studying the past. Second, comparing religions can give the misleading impression that all have similar characteristics—founders, holy books, key beliefs, and so on. That approach works relatively well when studying Judaism, Christianity, and Islam, but it falls apart when looking at religions outside the Abrahamic tradition. Some religions have no single "founder"; written texts may be non-existent or have a very different status than the Tanakh, Bible, or Koran; and identifying central tenets can be an over-simplification of religions that have developed over millennia and incorporated a range of cultural traditions. In addition, boundaries among some religions—such as Confucianism, Daoism, and Chinese folk religion—are not as distinct as in other traditions. When comparing religions, then, it is important not to view them through a single lens but to help students understand the fundamentally different ways they have developed and the diverse roles they play in society.

Learning about a variety of religious traditions also serves motivational and civic purposes. From a motivational standpoint, many students enjoy learning about the role of religions of which they themselves are a part. Linda's Buddhist students, she points out, are happy whenever their religion comes up in class, because it helps validate them—it makes them feel that their backgrounds are valued enough to be a part of the curriculum. Having herself grown up Jewish in a Christian world, Linda says that she knows what it feels like to come from a community that doesn't always "fit" the image found in school. Some teachers who avoid teaching about other religions, however, point out that they live in more homogeneous communities, so there's no need to bother learning about such differences. Although this tends to be over-stated—even the smallest town will have a variety of Christian denominations, for example, as well as non-believers—it's certainly true that not all teachers are fortunate enough to have students from Muslim, Buddhist, Christian, and other traditions all in the same classroom. But students' communities are not limited to their own schools or towns—students are also part of national and global communities, and they have responsibilities to other people throughout the nation and world. Even if they do not often meet people from significantly different backgrounds, their social, political, and economic decisions affect members of other religious

*Religion is an important part of how many people make sense of the world.*

*Students need to learn about religion in the present as well as the past.*

*Comparing religions on similar elements can be misleading. Barton (2015)*

*Students need to learn about the diverse nature of religious beliefs and practices. Barton (2015)*

*Students must understand religious diversity regardless of the nature of their local communities.*

communities every day, and thus, it is important to understand the perspectives of those with different beliefs. As Linda notes, we live in a multicultural world, and we have to show respect to our peers—wherever they may live.

## MULTIPLE FORMS OF MEDIA IN THE HISTORY CLASSROOM

One of the most striking characteristics of Linda's and Renee's classrooms is the variety of media found in them. Not only do students use art and technology as a way of constructing understanding, their teachers also make sure that students can access content through media other than print. One of the chief problems that teachers face is that not all their students read equally well. The higher the grade level, the wider the span of reading achievement, and of course, in communities with large numbers of children who have not grown up speaking English, the disparity within classrooms becomes even greater. This can be a particular problem in teaching history, because even the best students may have difficulty reading archaic language in primary sources, and when it comes to world history, many written primary sources aren't in English anyway. However, this doesn't mean that teachers have to revert to textbook narratives in teaching world history or when teaching students who are not highly accomplished readers. Visual and tactile sources can provide an alternative means of learning about the past.

*Students need access to multiple forms of media.*

*Visual and tactile sources provide alternative ways of learning history.*

As Linda points out, art can help us understand people and their ideas. A single work of art, for example, can act as a "snapshot" of a society at a particular time and place by showing us what people looked like, how they worshiped, the ideas they valued, and what they considered beautiful. (More on this in Chapter 14.) We can learn about their clothing, technology, social roles, and other aspects of daily life. During the year, her students study ancient civilizations by using tomb paintings and papyrus images from Egypt, seals from India, paintings from China, and other forms of artistic expression.

*Art helps students understand people and their ideas. Wohlman (n.d.)*

In teaching about Ancient Rome, for example, Linda devotes a week to the analysis of Roman art and architecture. The unit follows several weeks of studying Roman society, and Linda begins by asking students some warm-up questions to activate their prior knowledge:

*Linda's unit can be downloaded from https://whfua.history.ucla.edu/eras/era4.php*

- What is art?
- What is architecture?
- Why do you think people create art?
- What can historians learn about different societies by examining their art?
- What do you already know about art in ancient times?

These questions help students begin to think about the different places art can be found, as well as the variety of purposes it can be used for, and they quickly come to discuss whether only the paintings found in museums count as art, or whether music videos, graphic novels, and even graffiti can be considered art—issues that will set the stage for studying Roman glassware and portraits on Roman coins. Linda also discovers that their specific knowledge of art in the ancient world is somewhat limited and seems to be dominated by images of people in togas, along with the stylized, sideways postures found in Egyptian art (and parodied by Steve Martin). Asking students whether they think Egyptians really walked like that gives students a chance to think about how images have to be "read" through lenses of artistic convention.

This discussion is followed by a brief reading on the Greek, Etruscan, and Egyptian influences on Roman art, the significance of Pompeii and Herculaneum, and the enduring importance of Roman art and architecture. This reading contains a lot of information, but its purpose is not for students to memorize the content but to expose them to some of the ideas they will encounter in the unit, as well as to familiarize them with relevant vocabulary—*aqueduct, patron, glassware*, and so on. Students do not copy definitions of these words, though; copying definitions does little to help students develop understanding of unfamiliar concepts. Instead, definitions are supplied in the reading, and students have to summarize the definition in their own words, and then draw a picture that summarizes each of the terms. These are further examples of the kind of activities that lead students to transform information from one form into another, and in doing so, to construct their own understanding of it.

Over the next two days, students work in groups to complete a series of more specific activities—on realistic portraits, cameos, coinage, glassware, mosaics, mummy paintings, the Coliseum, the Pantheon, and public baths. Using a variety of print and visual sources, each group completes a graphic organizer that again asks them to draw a picture of the art form, as well as to identify the social context in which the form was produced, its enduring significance, and any other interesting details that they come across. This focus on social context and significance points to the fact that history should never simply involve learning content about the past; memorizing information is precisely the kind of thing that can give history such a bad reputation. Instead, Linda's readings call attention to aspects of content that are at the core of why we learn history in the first place—so that we can better understand how societies operate, how people in other times and places viewed their world, and how the past has impacted the present. During this unit, for example, students often encounter ways that art was used as a source of propaganda or to demonstrate power—a link between art and politics that will be important as they study many different time periods.

The final activity is more extensive and provides the principal means of assessment for the unit. In this, students work in groups to synthesize the unit's main ideas by creating one of the following:

- A booklet, brochure, poster, or slide presentation on Roman art.
- A booklet, brochure, poster, or slide presentation on Roman architecture.
- A board game about Roman art and architecture.
- An original mosaic on a theme in ancient Rome.
- A slide presentation using digital photographs of Roman influences in the local environment.

## DEVELOPING LANGUAGE THROUGH ACTIVE ENGAGEMENT

English learners need many opportunities to take part in language activities—reading, writing, listening, and speaking. Proficiency in a second language doesn't develop passively; learners have to be actively engaged in using language (both its reception and its production) to become better at it. Although learning a second language isn't exactly like learning the first one, one thing is similar: The need for active involvement. A second language isn't something "out there" that students somehow capture. Language is a practice (or a set of practices, really), and students improve only when they have many chances to engage in these. Just as young children need to listen and talk at home, so, too, do English learners need to take part in a variety of language activities at school. This is particularly important in content areas such as history, because many students have limited opportunities to use historical language outside school.

The classrooms in this chapter provide rich contexts for language development. Linda fills her room with books—lots and lots of them. These are mainly trade books on the world history topics students are studying, and on topics they might use in their independent projects. There is no shortage of suitable books on world history and ancient civilizations—works such as *Atlas of Ancient Worlds*, *Barbarians!*, *Pharaoh's Boat*, *Chinese History Stories*, and many others. Books on world religions are also abundant: *Confucius: The Golden Rule*, *The Genius of Islam: How Muslims Made the Modern World*, and visually rich reference works such as *Christianity* and *Buddhism*. Just as important, Linda exposes her students to further uses of language through songs and other artistic media produced by both professionals and peers.

Linda's students also have countless chances to express themselves through language. Most of the activities in her class take place between partners or in small groups, and

History helps us understand how societies operate, how people in other times and places viewed the world, and how the past has impacted the present.

English learners need to use language actively. *Cruz & Thornton (2013), Goldberg & Coleman (2010)*

*Chrisp (2009), Kroll (2009), Weitzman (2009), Ting (2009)*

*Freedman (2002), Barnard (2011), Wilkinson (2006), Wilkinson & Margan (2006)*

this requires constant language use, as students negotiate meaning and plan assignments. The assignments themselves obviously go far beyond the "fill in the blank" activities that are common in many classrooms. Students have to create original song lyrics, for example, and these have to be both accurate and engaging. This requires thinking through how ideas can be expressed in multiple ways, and how varied wording leads to different effects. Students have to make similar decisions about how to use language effectively when they narrate documentaries, plan slide presentations, design brochures, create zines, and construct board games. In Renee's classroom, poster projects and "Newspapers of the Reformation" also demand careful reflection on how to use language in specific contexts and for particular purposes.

The most common uses of language in social studies—textbooks, teacher lectures, and whole-class questioning of students—play limited roles in these classrooms, because each of these presents particular challenges for English learners. Yet each of these has a place in students' developing understanding of social studies, and they can be adapted in ways that make them more accessible for students with limited English proficiency. When speaking to the whole class, for example, teachers should avoid idioms, slow down their speech, and pay attention to the clarity of their pronunciation. In questioning students, teachers should provide a generous amount of wait time, because English learners often need to formulate answers mentally (and even practice them) before beginning to speak. Teachers can also let students know ahead of time which questions they will have to answer in class, so they will have even more time to prepare.

> Teacher talk can be adapted for English learners. *Cruz & Thornton (2013)*

Textbooks are among the most difficult sources for English learners to understand, because of their complex sentences, passive voice, and extensive use of pronouns. When English learners (and others) must read textbook passages—and especially when they have to do so independently—it is important to provide the following supports:

> Reading textbooks independently requires extensive support. *Cruz & Thornton (2013), Short (1998)*

- *Pre-reading discussions*, so that students can connect the content of upcoming passages to their background knowledge and experiences.
- *Vocabulary overviews*, so that students are alerted to potentially unfamiliar words and phrases that they will encounter.
- *Predictive guides*, so that students can use visual clues and headings to predict the content and organization of textbook passages.
- *Sectioned readings*, so that students can be responsible for particular sections rather than being overwhelmed by lengthy chapters.
- *Graphic organizers*, so that students see visual layouts of how information is presented in a passage.
- *Note-taking practice*, so that students better understand how to record and synthesize the content in textbooks.

Even with adaptation, textbooks and teacher talk should not dominate social studies classrooms. Imagine how difficult it is for English learners to develop their abilities when most words they read are in textbooks, most words they hear come from the teacher, and most words they use result from answering questions. Not only is this boring, but it is far too narrow a set of experiences to become proficient in a language. Linda and Renee, like all the teachers in this book, give students rich and varied chances to take part in the language of history by exposing them to a variety of sources and having them express themselves in a range of ways—not just occasionally but all the time. Students are surrounded by meaningful and authentic language use, both written and spoken, and they delight in the chance to become part of it.

> English learners need rich and varied experiences with language.

## WHEN OBJECTS ARE THE PRIMARY SOURCES

Art and architecture can motivate student interest and inquiry, but there is another important reason to help students analyze and interpret material culture: Sometimes objects are the only evidence available for studying past cultures. Before the discovery of the Rosetta

> Sometimes objects are the only evidence for studying past cultures.

Stone (which made it possible to read Egyptian hieroglyphics), art, architecture, and other remnants of material life provided the primary evidence for understanding ancient Egypt. For the earliest human communities, moreover, there can be no Rosetta Stone, because these people left no written records. The only way we can make sense of their lives is through material culture—the objects people left behind, whether ceremonial objects found in burial sites, discarded household goods, or tools left at work sites. When archaeologists unearth the remains of buildings abandoned in the wake of war, famine, migration, or changing fashions, or they collect seeds and animal remains preserved in garbage pits, they help us better describe human migratory and trade patterns, the shift from hunting and gathering societies to settled agriculture, or the spread of artistic and technological innovation and patterns of economic development. And although reading and interpreting material culture is the foundation for studying the most distant past, it also enhances the study of cultures less distant in time and place—including our own.

For several years, fifth-grade teacher Jenny Schlarb focused on material objects as historical sources. After training with *Project Archaeology*, a program that introduces teachers to activities and resources for teaching with and about archaeology, she decided to ask for help from her state's archaeological survey. That office sponsored K–12 students in ongoing archaeological fieldwork, and Jenny was sure her students would love this experience. As had Linda and Renee, Jenny built up a repertoire of tried-and-true activities and continually sought out new ideas. Drawing on *Project Archaeology* suggestions, Jenny asked her students to bring in objects or artifacts that represented their lives—pictures, toys, stuffed animals, video games, favorite books, and so forth. She also shared David Macaulay's *Motel of the Mysteries*, a humorous account of a future archaeological excavation. Her students loved the ways in which archaeologists in the book misinterpreted material objects—deciding a toilet was a "sacred urn," for instance. Macaulay's send-up of archaeology gave the students a good laugh but also pointed out some of the pitfalls of interpreting objects.

Jenny's students also created mobiles to illustrate archaeological concepts (distinguishing between paleontology and archaeology, defining stratigraphy and artifact). While students made good use of the mobiles to remind themselves of common terms, they particularly liked a "mystery box" developed by a student teacher. The locked, glass-topped box displayed a rotating array of objects that students categorized as either artifacts or non-artifacts. When was a rock "just a rock" and when could it be identified as an artifact? As one student explained, you had to be able to tell when someone used a rock to "do work, like kind of regular chips from a stone" from a rock "that was just sitting there, not used by humans."

The most exciting part of their study of archaeology was the "dig." Dig sites changed from year to year, but students' enthusiasm never waned. One class participated in an excavation of possible slave quarters on the site of Henry Clay's nineteenth-century plantation. Interviewed three years later, they recall this experience as one of the most interesting ways to learn about the past. Each group of students worked at one of the excavation units—a series of trenches dug some yards from the restored plantation house. Students examined stratigraphies (the layers of deposits in the units they helped excavate); screened dirt in search of artifacts; and cleaned, sorted, and identified old bottles and buttons, nails, and fragments of china. Archaeologists encouraged them to think about time clues—the evidence of changing technologies for manufacturing the objects they found—as well as context—the location of artifacts in the stratigraphy. At each of these sites, students used the skills they practiced in class. As students shifted from job to job, one of the boys, muddied and grinning, exclaimed that this was "the best day of my life."

By the end of the day when students gathered on the lawn to discuss their experiences, it was clear that some objects were more easily interpreted than others. They could easily conclude that iron tools indicated access to manufactured goods, toys the presence of children, and blacksmithing tools the presence of horses. On the other hand, a long, thin metal rail protruding from the side of an excavation led some students to conclude that they had found part of the Underground Railroad. And even though they had been

*LaMotta & Schiffer (2001)*

*Hodder (2009)*

*Levstik et al. (2005)*

From an archaeological perspective, *artifacts* refer to anything made or used by humans.

*Macaulay (1979)*

excavating slave quarters the majority of the day, some declared that Henry Clay opposed slavery—something a guide had told them during the house tour. Although it required very little discussion before students recognized the inconsistency, the ease with which they accepted the guide's interpretation suggests how important "debriefing" can be.

Debriefing conversations offer teachers opportunities to assess what their students are learning and to address misunderstandings quickly. Jenny realized, for instance, that she hadn't made it clear that the Underground Railroad was a secret escape route, not a subway. She was also surprised by how little transfer there was from one activity (excavating the slave quarters) to another (touring the reconstructed home). This is a common problem with field trips. It is easy to assume that students see and hear what we intend them to. As with so many other aspects of teaching, however, careful observation and a relatively quick *cognitive check* pay enormous dividends. This can be as simple as asking: "What were the most important things you learned?" or, more specifically, "What evidence did you uncover about lives in Henry Clay's house and lives in the slave quarters?"

A *cognitive check* is a quick way of assessing what students have learned from an activity.

As you can see, many of Jenny's (as well as Linda's) activities require students to work in groups—in fact, most of the activities throughout this book require some kind of cooperation. It's important for teachers to understand the difference between structured group work (often known as *cooperative learning*) and simply having students "work together." In order for group tasks to be effective, certain structures and procedures have to be in place. One of the most important is that working together is not an option, but is required by the very nature of the assignment. Sometimes this involves assigning roles to group members (so that each student's contribution is required to complete the task), but another way of requiring cooperation is to have students complete a single task. For example, rather than giving each student a graphic organizer to complete and telling them to work together— which always results in some students working together and some working individually— Linda gives the entire group just one sheet to fill out. Of course, some students could still decline to participate or take over from their classmates, and this requires two further elements of effective groupwork: Individual accountability (in which each student is held responsible for learning the content) and the teaching of group skills (in which students learn and practice the norms and procedures of effective cooperation). Just as effective discussions require that students learn *how to* discuss, effective cooperation requires that students learn *how to* cooperate.

Cooperative learning requires structures that ensure students must work together. *Aitken & Sinnema (2008), Cohen (1986), Johnson et al. (1993)*

Hess (2009)

## COOPERATIVE LEARNING AND TECHNOLOGY

Many of the teachers in this book enjoy using a variety of technological tools to support history learning. They may use digital archives that provide access to photographs, paintings, newspapers, and a wide variety of other historical sources. Two of the most comprehensive collections are those of the Library of Congress and the National Archives, but most museums, universities, and state historical societies, along with many non-profit foundations, have their own archives of digitized sources. Many teachers also teach students how to use programs and applications for creating presentations, artwork, zines, and other media. Not all teachers are as tech-savvy as Linda, a self-professed "technology nerd," but most of them are willing to try something new if it promises to motivate students and enhance history learning.

https://www.loc.gov, https://www.archives.gov

Linda especially likes projects that combine sound, pictures, and video. In the "Makers and Shakers in World History" project, for instance, students create an original digital documentary examining the life of a person who made important contributions to the ancient world. Several programs make it relatively easy to create digital documentaries, and some are likely to be preinstalled on just about any laptop. These programs allow students to upload still images as well as video with or without accompanying text and to lay musical tracks to accompany images and text. Students usually find the technological challenge of creating a documentary highly motivating, but their teachers quickly realize that this can distract students from the historical goals they had in mind. As Linda has discovered, technological distractions can be minimized by "front-loading" the history. First, she challenges students to select a historic figure who made an important contribution to the ancient world: What makes a person historically significant? What evidence would establish historical significance? Next, Linda introduces a variety of sources for student inquiry, from trade and reference books to textbooks, selected internet sites, and hand-outs that she reproduces for them. As they work, students summarize their findings in their own words, and Linda reminds them to include details that reflect the *depth and complexity tools* introduced earlier in the year. These tools (displayed on a large poster in her room) are concepts and questions that focus students' attention on ideas such as *trends* (What are patterns of change over time?), *rules* (What structures underlie this?), and *multiple perspectives* (How would others see this differently?). Ideas like these engage students in the kind of higher order thinking that teachers are familiar with from Bloom's taxonomy, but many teachers find that they are more specific and more applicable to content areas than the general categories of that taxonomy.

Kaplan & Gould (2005)

Just as good teachers keep lists of activities, they also look for tools such as these that help organize students' intellectual engagement with content. By introducing them early in the year or, ideally, using them over several years, students become increasingly confident in applying the depth and complexity tools in different contexts. Just as importantly, teachers can more confidently rely on a common language for academic work. Linda's students, for instance, not only know what she means when she suggests they look for parallel ideas or events, or consider multiple perspectives, they know how to act on her suggestions.

Once they have assessed the significance of a "mover or shaker" in the ancient world, they are ready to draft a script for their digital documentary. Because she knows how easily students ignore their research once they become immersed in the technical aspects of production, Linda checks each narrative before students move to computers. Once the script is checked, students must find all the accompanying visuals, write and the narration and read it out loud, add a soundtrack, and apply visual effects. Some teachers use "storyboards" at this point to help students visualize a narrative sequence based on their scripts. Students plot each screen of their documentary, sketching in images and noting the sounds that might accompany the narration.

One eighth-grade teacher added a peer-review "editing room" component to the storyboard activity. Students reviewed each other's storyboards, asked questions, and made content and design suggestions. By the time his students moved to the computers, they were thoroughly grounded in the content and, he thought, less likely to be carried away by the technological challenges at hand. This final step—turning research into digital documentaries—is highly motivating for students. We have watched teachers as well as students become so absorbed in this work that they barely notice when the bell rings or a workshop ends. They proudly screen their work, discuss the content and technological choices they have made, and appreciate their peers' interest in their work. Linda honors her students' hard work by playing them at the year-end open house, where she presents her own "Oscars" for Best Documentary, Best Film Editing, Best Narration, Best Special Effects, and Best Soundtrack. Perhaps one of the most interesting things she does, however, is create her own documentary, *Behind the Scenes of Making the Movies*. As students work, Linda interviews them and records their activity, documenting what they liked as well as the challenges they faced. Not only does her documentary provide a historical record of this important experience and serve as a good introduction for students the following year, it has turned out to be a good assessment tool. Sometimes, for instance, students report that they got so carried away with technical aspects of editing that they didn't do well on the delivery of historical information or on their analysis of their topic. In other cases, she can see how students struggle with interpreting particular types of sources, finding appropriate visuals, or condensing their research into the digital format without losing the nuance and comprehensiveness that marked their original research.

Schul (2010)

As Linda evaluates student work, she also tries to plan for the future and consider how to deal with some of the obstacles inherent in digital documentaries. The most obvious obstacle is time: Documentaries are time-consuming. Linda finds the intellectual pay-off worth the time, but she "buys" this time by pairing the documentaries with other shorter, high-impact activities. She also provides enough structure to allow students to make the most of the time available and to become more and more independent as they conduct inquiry into distant times and places.

Teachers need to plan to help students become increasingly independent.

## ASSESSMENT IN A MULTIMEDIA ENVIRONMENT

Some teachers worry that when students engage in so many creative activities and have so many choices available to them, assessment will be a nightmare. As the teachers in this book are quick to point out, just the opposite is often the case. It isn't that assessment is less time-consuming but that it is more reliable, because it is more evidence-based. That said, teachers do have to keep up with assessment, or they may find themselves drowning in data at the end of a unit.

Throughout this book, teachers use a number of strategies to manage assessment. Several of the teachers in this chapter find that the depth and complexity tools explained earlier are especially useful. Guidelines such as these help students think about how they conduct their historical studies, establish standards for quality work, and provide a common language for discussing student performance. They find that as students become more experienced with the guidelines they also become more adept at self-assessment. Because teachers and students have been working with the same guidelines all along, students are rarely surprised by their teachers' evaluations. And, when the work is interesting as well as challenging and students exhibit the behaviors the guidelines describe and their teachers encourage, assessment is also more interesting. Depth and complexity tools also save time by eliminating the need for separate guidelines for every historical inquiry. Teachers may add expectations or directions specific to a new task, but the overall standards remain the same, freeing students to engage in the creative and intellectually challenging work characteristic of these classrooms. Students benefit by receiving clear information about their intellectual progress and having multiple opportunities to learn and exhibit what they are learning. Teachers benefit from a surer sense that their assessments of student work accurately reflect student performance and point toward further growth.

*Kaplan & Gould (2005)*

Assessment guidelines provide a common language for discussing student performance.

Depth and complexity guidelines are certainly useful, but they do not focus on some of the more technological aspects of students' work. Although some schools conduct separate assessment of technological literacy, we argue that this, as with other skills, is best understood and assessed in context—and media-rich history classrooms provide just such a context. In classes such as Linda's, for instance, technological literacy is fundamental to historical understanding. Students use digital repositories, and their historical interpretations may be expressed in a digital documentary or as a video. When students' facility with accessing digital sources or combining images, text, sound, and movement in a documentary become important elements in communicating their historical interpretations, they should be assessed.

A separate rubric may be useful for some technological aspects of some historical work. Digital documentaries, for instance, combine a number of processes from laying in sound and images to selecting transitions and timing. The rubric in Figure 7.1 is one example. The teacher who developed this rubric gave it to his students to use as a group self-assessment. Before students were allowed to screen their documentaries, they used the rubric to check and correct technical aspects of their work. Later, their teacher used the same rubric as part of his evaluation of their work.

After watching one too many digital documentaries in which historical figures returned from the dead or gave death-bed testimonials to explain their own historical significance, he also decided to show students portions of documentaries that employed more historically grounded techniques (and were less prone to eerie sound effects). As did Linda, he eventually added a script-check, too. Linda's video of her students at work also helped her

*Manfra & Hammond (2006)*

**89**

| Digital Documentary Technical Aspects | Works Well (write comments below) | Room for Improvement (write comments below) |
|---|---|---|
| Sound: Music is appropriate, adds to documentary without distracting the viewer. | | |
| Sound: Narration is clear, spoken with appropriate emphasis. | | |
| Text: Text is clear, does not clutter the screen, extends the impact of sound and image. | | |
| Image: Images (still and video) are clear, appropriate to time and place, synchronized with sound and text, and strengthen interpretation | | |

**FIGURE 7.1   Rubric for technical aspects of digital documentary.**

assess how well the work went, what problems students encountered, and where she might need to adjust an assignment. The videos also aid student self-assessment by providing a record of progress over time.

Finally, some teachers find learning management programs helpful in keeping track of students' progress on their varied documentaries. This program allows teachers to send students notes on their work, including reminders of requirements or deadlines, suggestions of other sources and, oftentimes, a bit of encouragement when tackling difficult sources or technologies. The notes then provide a record of communication that teachers use in conferencing with their students and in evaluating historical and technological work.

## CONCLUSIONS

Making connections to the present and to students' own lives, providing creative choices, and using a variety of media—it may all seem a bit overwhelming. Surely, it's easier to just explain some ideas out of the textbook, have students look up a few questions, and be done with it. And we all know teachers who do just that. But unimaginative, uninspiring, by-the-book teaching does no one any favors—not students, not society, and not even teachers themselves. The kinds of projects we've described in this book are critical to preparing students for participation in democratic life for one principal reason: *They help students learn*. Each of the elements of good history teaching we've described here—scaffolding, choices, connections, comparisons, and so on—are important because they help students better understand society's past, and thus improve their ability to make reasoned

The purpose of activities and projects is for students to learn content more meaningfully.

judgments in the present and future. Creative multimedia projects are also fun and visually impressive, but we don't choose instructional activities because they're fun and flashy; we choose them because they help students make sense of content.

These projects do take time and effort—by both students and teachers—but even so, they're not as exhausting as some people think. As we've noted in this chapter, teachers don't have to develop every activity from scratch. By becoming familiar with several basic formats for students' investigations and presentations (using both digital and other forms of media), teachers can match each topic with a different activity, and they can vary these pairings from year to year. Although the specific projects may look very different, teachers can soon become familiar with the underlying structure of each, and as a result, they won't need to continually create new ideas. Similarly, although the demands of assessing students' understanding in a variety of formats can seem daunting, by using a consistent underlying structure and clear rubrics, teachers can both reduce the time they spend on assessment and make expectations clear for students. And finally, teachers may feel exhausted after leading students through an extensive project, but it's quite literally a "good tired"—the feeling of accomplishment and success that comes from knowing that you've helped students learn something important, in a way that they find valuable and meaningful. And after all, that's why we become teachers in the first place.

# 8

# RATS IN THE HOSPITAL

## Creating a History Museum

After her fourth graders have completed family history projects, Amy Leigh introduces them to their next investigation—creating displays on how life has changed since the 1800s. On the first day of the unit, she shows them an object she explains was a common tool in the 1800s. Most students quickly identify it as a hand-held drill, and several volunteer to demonstrate how it was used. After discussing how it differs from modern drills, the class gathers on the floor in front of Amy while she reads *Follow Me Down to Nicodemus Town*, which she explains was also set in the 1800s. Amy asks students to point out anything they find in the book that would be different today, and she keeps track of their observations on a sheet of chart paper on the wall. After discussing the book, students work in pairs with historical photographs to make further observations about change over the last century, and at the end of the day, they report on these to their classmates and add new items to the chart.

Over the next several days, students examine physical artifacts Amy has brought in—old watches, purses, tools, clothes, and appliances. Guided by "Artifact Think Sheets," they record ways these differ from similar objects today. After everyone has worked through all the objects, the class meets together again to summarize what they have found and to develop a list of general categories of change—technology, clothes, transportation, etc. Each student then chooses two or three categories to find out more about. After several days of exploration with library and internet resources, students choose partners and pick a single topic to investigate in more depth. Each group develops a set of specific questions they want to answer, and they collect information using not only print and electronic resources but also artifacts, interviews, and photographs. During the research phase of the project, Amy works with each group to help them locate and use information to prepare reports and displays, and afterward, students create exhibits for a "History Museum" in their classroom. They explain their exhibits for other classes who tour their museum and for parents and grandparents during a final performance.

One of the most common suggestions for teaching history and related subjects (at any level) is to have students "do research." Yet as we have noted, simply sending students off on their own to engage in that vague activity rarely results in anything positive or productive. Younger children are unlikely to have any idea what they are supposed to do, while older ones will do what nearly everyone has done in school—copy something out of an encyclopedia or internet source. Many students simply type a query into an internet search engine and hope it results in a site that answers all their needs. Neither of those strategies helps students learn about the past or about conducting inquiry. In contrast, the students in Amy's classroom learned both: They not only investigated how life has changed over time, they also learned to ask questions, collect information, draw conclusions, and present their findings.

*Lipscomb (2002), Milson (2002)*

**92**

DOI: 10.4324/9781003179658-8

Sometimes assignments are difficult, and students dislike doing them. Other times, students enjoy themselves, but the activities are too easy for them really to learn very much. But teachers know they're on to something when students enjoy doing an assignment that does not come easily. The "History Museum" project in Amy's classroom is a perfect example of such an assignment: Students immensely enjoyed it, yet none of it came easily. They spent nearly a month working on the activities, and nearly every minute of that time involved painstaking efforts by Amy to help students use resources to find information, reach conclusions based on their observations, and transform notes into reports and presentations. Having little or no previous experience with the process, students encountered numerous obstacles along the way. As a result, Amy could not just tell them to do research; she had to teach them. In this chapter, we show how she met the challenge of teaching students to ask and answer historical questions.

*Teachers must help students learn how to conduct inquiry.*

## IMAGINATIVE ENTRY

Getting students interested in the topic of change over time was the easiest part of Amy's job. Like Tina's students in Chapter 5, Amy's class had completed family history projects in which they asked their grandparents how life had been different when they were children. As a result, the topic of change over time was fresh in their minds, and they could call on these experiences for specific examples to compare with the information they encountered at school. Moreover, changes in material culture are among the historical topics students know the most about. In our interviews with children from Kindergarten through sixth grade, for example, we have found that even the youngest know that clothes and transportation were different in the past, and older children have an even more complete inventory of generally accurate information about change over time. During the project described earlier, students frequently pointed out having learned about historical changes outside school—seeing an old shaving mug and brush in a local barbershop, for example, or seeing pictures of sod houses in a book. As we noted in Chapter 2, instruction must begin with what students already know; thus, Amy began with the details of everyday life—drills, shaving mugs, purses, and so on—rather than abstract topics such as politics, economics, or society. (She did, however, eventually get to these topics; see Chapter 12.)

*Family histories lead to further historical investigations.*

*Material culture provides entry into historical study. Levstik & Barton (2008)*

The visual aspect of history is also critical in helping students understand what the past was like—particularly any time period before they were born. Amy, then, began the unit (as well as several other lessons throughout the unit) with books such as *Locomotive*, *Fionna's Lace,* and *Washday*. In most cases, she was concerned not with the language or thematic content of the books but with the information the illustrations provided on historical changes. Amy also took care to call students' attention to aspects of the pictures that were vague or ambiguous, and she asked students to consider how they differed from photographs.

*Floca (2013), Polacco (2014), Bunting (2014)*

Using visual images (particularly photographs) is especially important with children because these tap into a much wider range of background knowledge than printed text or oral discussions. In Amy's class, the photographs were a popular part of the unit, as students examined them with great interest and enthusiasm and frequently called their friends over to look at unusual or surprising details. They had no difficulty using the images to develop a list of differences between 100 years ago and today, and they eagerly shared their findings with the rest of the class.

*Visual images can help students learn about the past.*

Just as important as photographs were the physical artifacts Amy brought in. The sight of the old drill in the first lesson was exciting for students, and all of them made sure they touched it and played with it before the day was over. While working on their "Artifact Think Sheets" (Figure 8.1), students constantly played with the objects—rubbing a shaving-cream brush on their skin, flipping the handle of a cherry-pitter back and forth, fiddling with an old camera to see how it worked, using a cuff-maker to create creases in

*Students enjoy manipulating historical artifacts.*

There are many artifacts from the past displayed throughout the room. Please write a paragraph for each of the 5 artifacts. Your paragraphs should address each of the items in this chart.

| | Artifact 1 | Artifact 2 | Artifact 3 | Artifact 4 | Artifact 5 |
|---|---|---|---|---|---|
| Give a name to this artifact that tells its purpose. You may write more than just the name if you'd like to better explain its function. | | | | | |
| Explain what parts of the object gave you clues for its purpose. | | | | | |
| Tell when you think the artifact was used (1800-1849, 1850-1899, 1900-1949, or 1950-Now), and tell how you decided. | | | | | |
| Name the object we now use instead of this artifact. | | | | | |

**FIGURE 8.1  Artifact Think Sheet.**

paper (again and again and again). Because school tasks often rely exclusively on written language, students' preoccupation with physical play can strike an observer as being "off task"; outside school, though, no parent would expect a child to sit still for hours on end. We agree with John Dewey that children's behavior at school frequently appears in need of "management" precisely because they have so little chance to engage in their natural impulse toward activity. By encouraging them to handle and use the objects, Amy built on her students' inclinations rather than attempting to suppress them. As a result, they stayed interested in the objects for several days and developed clear ideas about how they could have been used. Of course, many teachers find themselves evaluated (implicitly or explicitly) on how quiet and physically inactive their students are, and they may need to be ready to explain why playing with a cuff-maker is more appropriate for an 8-year-old than writing quietly at all times. Fortunately, Amy's principal encouraged—even expected— the kinds of hands-on lessons found in her classroom.

Amy's introduction to the "History Museum" project demonstrated several principles that are fundamental to developing students' interest. First, she related the topic to what they already knew, both by focusing on aspects of everyday life and by connecting the topic to their previous family history projects. Rather than being an isolated, "cookie-cutter" plan, it flowed naturally from students' background knowledge and from the issues they had already begun to investigate during the year. Second, Amy made sure that students had a variety of means of entry into the topic, rather than relying solely on oral and written language. Literature, photographs, and physical artifacts gave students a more concrete understanding of life in the past and helped stimulate their interest in the topic. Perhaps most important, this project had a significant element of authenticity. Outside school, people really do take an interest in how life has changed over time: People save artifacts and photographs, and they tell their children and grandchildren how life was different in the past. Understanding historical change is a basic part of each person's life, and that understanding often is passed down through families. Students' excitement about these projects indicates just how much Amy had tapped into the meaning and purpose history has in our society. For several weeks, students rummaged through their homes and

*Dewey (1990/1900 & 1902)*

Administrators can support and encourage inquiry.

Historical inquiry stems from students' interests and experiences.

Teachers can provide a variety of means of entry into historical topics.

*Levstik & Barton (2008)*

**94**

attics (and their grandparents'), looking for their own artifacts to bring in and add to the visual time line in the class. Their interest motivated one girl to work with her parents to make a videotaped tour of the Victorian home she lived in and another to help her grandmother photograph and catalog the family's heirlooms. Even Amy's own grandparents were excited about explaining how to use the various artifacts she brought in for students. When a project stimulates this kind of intergenerational communication, it clearly has a purpose beyond simply pleasing the teacher or getting a grade.

*Authentic projects involve learning beyond school boundaries.*

## TURNING INTEREST INTO RESEARCHABLE QUESTIONS

The first year Amy taught this unit, she proceeded directly from her introductory lesson to having students develop a list of questions they wanted to answer. At first glance, it seems that students who already know something about a topic and are interested and enthusiastic about learning more should have no problem sitting down and deciding what they want to learn. In fact, however, that task was tremendously difficult. Amy had students develop KWL charts on the topics they had chosen, and most encountered a roadblock when they got to the "Want to know" section. Many simply stopped working and apparently had no idea what to write. Others seemed to consider it a convenient time to sharpen their pencil collections, rearrange their desks, or devote their energy to making the physical layout of their charts as attractive as possible. Even with Amy's help and encouragement, most students weren't sure what it was that they wanted to know, and those who wrote anything at all confined themselves to simple questions about dates: When was the car invented? When did people stop wearing hoop skirts? When did milk stop coming in bottles? It seemed that most students didn't really understand the purpose of the questions. They were just eager to get to the library and start copying something down.

*Students are not accustomed to generating questions.*

When it became clear that students weren't getting much out of this question-developing activity, Amy called them back together as a whole class to give them more direction. She wrote the words *Where, What, Why, Who,* and *How* on the board and told students they needed to come up with two questions beginning with each word; she then went on to model how to do that with the topic *schools*—a subject they had discussed in class but that no students had chosen to investigate in their projects. This was a kind of ad hoc solution to the problem, and it gave students enough structure to begin their research. It was clear, however, that students still failed to fully understand the role of questions in conducting research. For example, some tried to copy Amy's questions onto their own charts by simply changing a few key words. When that didn't work, they protested that it couldn't be done and were shocked when Amy explained that the questions would be different for each topic. Others didn't understand why they would come up with questions before doing the research, and one student asked incredulously, "Are we going to answer these questions *ourselves*?" With little prior experience in developing their own questions to investigate, the activity made little sense to students.

*Teacher scaffolding can help students develop more meaningful questions.*

The next year, Amy was better prepared to help with this aspect of the investigation. As you can see in the description at the beginning of this chapter, she did not jump directly from sparking students' interest to expecting them to develop specific questions. Instead, she engaged them in examining artifacts for several days; in the course of making their observations, students found a number of things they wondered about—How did they keep from getting the clothes dirty when they used this kind of iron? How did they keep it hot? Did everybody use this, or just rich people? The experience of observing and discussing the artifacts gave students a chance to come up with specific questions they wanted to know more about and to do so in a natural context. In addition, Amy gave students several days to explore library resources before asking them to specify either their topic or a list of questions. Although she had them narrow their interests to two or three (so their energy wouldn't be completely unfocused), she wanted them to have a chance just to play around with the available resources to find out what they wanted to ask. This turned out to be a popular activity, as students excitedly scurried around the library, talking with

*Observation and discussion of historical artifacts leads to specific questions.*

**95**

Amy and each other about what they were learning. They were often very surprised at the differences they found; one group investigating changes in medicine, for example, was fascinated to find that hospitals were not as sanitary in the past as they are now. They told anyone who would listen, "Did you know that in the 1800s, if you were in the hospital, you might wake up and see a *rat* in your room?! Today you'd probably wake up and just see a spider—*if* you're lucky."

Time for exploration leads to better questions.

This time, there was no shortage of questions students wanted to investigate. When using science or math materials, students require exploration before working with them in a more systematic or teacher-directed way. Similarly, students need time to explore at the beginning of historical investigations. By giving them several days to examine artifacts and then several more days to explore library resources, Amy afforded students a much better chance to recognize what it was that they wanted to know. Once she asked them to come up with a list of questions they wanted to investigate, they didn't become stuck as they had previously. Even during this exploration time, students were learning a great deal about history—not only information about the past but also the process of making observations and drawing conclusions from historical sources.

Teachers can help students develop and refine questions.

That is not to say, however, that developing questions required no further help from Amy. As they moved from exploration to specific questions, Amy called the class together to find out what they wanted to learn in their research. As students suggested questions to investigate, Amy helped them rephrase the questions in such a way that they focused more clearly on "big ideas" (a concept she referred back to often) about changes over time. She asked for a sample question, for example, from students who were investigating the topic *houses*. They suggested, "What did they walk on, dirt, wooden floors, carpets?"—a question that, by itself, would have a fairly simple answer and would probably focus on only one time period. Amy responded, "So, 'How have floor coverings changed since the 1800s?'"—a question that included what students wanted to know but considerably broadened it as well. After several similar examples, one member of a pair of students who had chosen *railroads* suggested, "What happened to James Watt?" Amy asked if he considered that a big question, and his partner said, "No, it would be, 'Why didn't trains run on electricity?' or 'Why did they stop making electric trains?'" Amy broadened it even further by suggesting, "How has the power used for trains changed?" and pointed out that the information they wanted to include about James Watt would be part of their answer to that question.

People often think of education in terms of exclusive opposites: Either students do what the teacher tells them, for example, or they do whatever they want. As we discussed in Chapter 2, we find both those methods indefensible: Students are unlikely to learn anything important from either method. The assistance Amy provided students in developing their questions, on the other hand, was a clear example of scaffolding: She neither told them what to do nor uncritically accepted their first efforts. She knew that their projects had to grow out of their own interests and concerns, and she gave them several days to develop their ideas about what they wanted to do. But she also recognized that not all questions are equally significant: She knew that students would learn more from some questions than others, so she helped them rephrase their inquiries to address what they wanted to know within the context of bigger issues of change over time. In short, she helped them learn more than they would have solely on their own.

Students learn more with teachers' help and support than they would on their own.

## FINDING ANSWERS TO QUESTIONS

For all its pitfalls, helping students develop questions was a simple matter compared with helping them find the answers to those questions. One of the first challenges Amy faced was helping students locate the information that would be useful to them. At the simplest level, this just meant reviewing the kinds of sources they could use. Students immediately recognized the internet as a major source of information, but Amy also emphasized that they could use printed reference works, trade books, and resources outside of school— relatives, other people in the community, and even videos. A more important task was

Information in inquiry projects comes from a variety of sources.

helping students understand *how* to locate information in such resources. For example, many of them returned from their first foray into the library complaining, "There is *nothing* on it!" The reason for students' frustration was quickly apparent: Nearly all of them expected to find books or internet sources with entries entitled "How transportation has changed over time" or "How floor coverings have changed over time." When they found there weren't any such books or that internet sites were too hard to understand, they concluded that there was no suitable information on their topics.

Students' difficulties may have stemmed, in part, from a lack of previous experience with finding information in reference sources, and much of Amy's effort was devoted to teaching them how to really use such sources. In part, this meant working with the whole class and with groups of students to develop lists of words and phrases they might use in finding information. Knowing that one group was investigating *entertainment*, for example, Amy brought in a book called *What did You do When You were a Kid? Pastimes from the Past*. Yet students looked at the index and table of contents and—not finding the word *entertainment* in either—concluded the book had no relevant information. Somewhat surprised, Amy explained that the whole book was about entertainment—that pastimes are entertainment, and students would be able to find information on their topic by looking up other specific kinds of entertainment (movies, television, music, dance) rather than only looking for the word *entertainment*. With each group, Amy had to provide assistance in developing possible alternatives to the main words they were looking for—helping the transportation group come up with *automobiles, railroads, ships, airplanes*; the fashion group come up with *clothing, jewelry, hairstyles* and so on.

Once students found relevant books or internet sites, Amy also had to help them use them efficiently. Most students started reading a source at the beginning and continued through word for word until they got bored (which usually was quickly). One group, for example, looked up *Medicine* on Wikipedia but quickly became bogged down in reading about present-day medicine. Amy used this as an example for the whole class; she explained that the group could skip immediately to the section on *History* in the entry, and then look for the main article identified there (*Timeline of Medicine and Medical Technology*). Although whole-class instruction seemed to make the idea clear in a general way, she still had to work extensively with individuals and groups for them to apply it to their own work. Particularly during the early stages of their research, Amy spent most of her time directing students' attention to this process of evaluating the usefulness of sources— looking together with a student at a source, for example, and asking questions such as, "*Early hospitals*—does that sound like it would have information on how medicine has changed over time?" and "If you want to know if this has anything on railroads, what words are you going to look for when you skim through it?" Without this kind of explicit help in reading print and electronic reference works, it is unlikely that students would ever have gone very far with their research.

Interestingly, sites such as Wikipedia ultimately provided students with only minimal information. In the early stages of their research, many focused almost exclusively on these, but most soon found that other works provided information in a more accessible form. In the end, most students relied on juvenile trade books more heavily than anything else, and the kind of books they found most useful were similar in form. Students rejected any work that contained several pages of uninterrupted text. No matter how much information such a book might have contained, most students simply would not read through it to find what they needed to know. Instead, nearly all students relied on books that contained profuse illustrations on each page and short captions to accompany them. The most commonly used such books were those in the *Eyewitness* series—such as *Money*, *Flight*, and *Invention*—although there are other series with similar formats. The advantage of such books clearly lay both in their visual appeal and the ease with which students could find the information they needed. As one girl remarked, "They get to the point better."

People—relatives and others in the community—also provided important sources of information. Some students decided from the beginning that they would interview people for their projects; one girl investigating changes in homes, for example, planned to talk to

Students often have little experience using reference sources to answer questions.

*Sturner (1973)*

Brainstorming words and phrases can help students locate and use reference sources.

Students need to learn to read selectively for information.

The most useful reference sources have rich visual information and short expository text.

*Cribb (2005), Nahum (2011), Bender (2013)*

People can serve as an important source of historical information.

the interior designer who lived next door to her, and a boy whose project was on transportation knew the retired captain of a local steamboat. They had already interviewed relatives for their family history projects, and Amy reviewed with them how to plan out their questions for interviews. Because some of these were very specific, she also had to help them plan what they would do when people didn't know. For example, one group planned to call a local bank to ask questions about old money; Amy asked them what they would do when the answer was, "I don't know." Most students, on the other hand, had not initially considered humans to be an important source of information on their topics (despite their family history projects!), but once they began planning their displays, they developed a renewed sense of interest in them. Most of them wanted to display objects—old clothes, appliances, money, and so on—and when they started collecting these from people, they learned new information that became important to their papers and presentations.

## REACHING CONCLUSIONS

A basic principle of conducting historical inquiry is that conclusions are based on evidence. Indeed, that simple proposition forms the foundation of the entire field of social studies—not to mention other subjects—and even of democratic participation generally. For students to understand what it means to *know* something, they have to understand that knowledge is fundamentally different from either faith or blind opinion. Although in most cases, different conclusions can be drawn from the same evidence, conclusions that are based on no evidence whatsoever have no place in history, social studies, or public debate. Basing conclusions on evidence, however, came no more easily for Amy's students than asking questions or collecting data.

One of the first challenges Amy faced was confronting students' belief that somewhere, in a single place, lay the answer to each of their questions, and their conviction that if they could only track down that source, they could copy the answer and begin working on their displays. In this, Amy's students no doubt demonstrated the same understanding held by millions of schoolchildren who have developed their perspective from answering questions at the end of textbook chapters. We all know that most such questions can be answered by finding the sentences in the chapter that provide single and direct answers. In fact, most of us probably realized at some point that we could find the answers without ever having read the chapter. Outside the topsy-turvy world of textbook information, however, few questions have such simple and direct answers. Significant historical questions—like those in Table 1.1 and those students developed in this project—require the synthesis of a number of pieces of information. The idea of collecting information from several different places and putting them together in their own way, however, was not what students initially expected they would be doing. It was some time before they realized that they would never stumble on simple answers to their questions but would have to create those answers from the information they did find.

One way that Amy addressed this problem was by having students keep a Venn diagram on their topic throughout their research. She began by demonstrating how to do this with the topic *schools*. She drew a diagram on the board, labeled one side "1800s" and the other "Today," and asked students what kind of information might go in each space. As they conducted their research, students recorded new information on their own diagrams. These proved useful when they moved into creating displays and writing their reports; they had collected information from various sources, and the Venn diagrams allowed them to view the information together in one place. (One drawback to using Venn diagrams was that they called attention only to the differences between two periods of time, rather than the *ongoing process* of change.) Because they weren't used to synthesizing information from different sources, Amy modeled how the diagrams could help them: Using her diagram on *schools* again, she asked what conclusions they could reach—in the 1800s children sat at desks in schools, and now we sit at tables; in the 1800s students dressed up for school, and now we dress casually; and so on. Following class discussion, she worked with each

Conclusions must be based on evidence.

Students often have simplistic ideas about how to find answers to historical questions. Ashby & Lee (1998), Levstik & Barton (2008)

Important questions rarely have simple or direct answers.

Venn diagrams provide a way to organize information on similarities and differences.

Teachers need to model how to draw conclusions from evidence.

group to help them use their own Venn diagrams in this way, and she particularly focused on how they would express those changes over time—composing compound sentences and using words such as *then*, *now*, and *century*.

Perhaps the most surprising challenge that Amy faced in helping students reach conclusions was getting them to see the connection between the research and their displays and reports. Students frequently came to Amy after 10 or 15 minutes of work and said, "We're finished." Because they weren't used to collecting the kind of information that would help them draw conclusions, they had little idea when they had enough and when they didn't. One group investigating *work*, for example, told Amy they had done all the research they needed to do. She looked over their list of questions and found that one of them was, "How has the way they make shoes changed?" In answer, they had written down the word *shoemaker*, and they were now confident that they did not need to collect any further information on the topic. Amy asked if that told them what they needed to know to make their display or write their paper; they could tell by the tone of her voice that she didn't think it was enough, but they weren't sure what else was needed. She called their attention to the scoring guide for the project (see Figure 8.2), particularly the section dealing with "use of details," and asked whether the word *shoemaker* gave them any details they would be able to use in their reports or presentation. They saw that it didn't, and Amy then gave them a way out of their dilemma—"Is this your research," she asked, "or just your brainstorming? I think this is just your brainstorming, and you still need to do more research to find out the details that you'll use." Although they were still somewhat disappointed that they weren't

> Students need help seeing how information relates to their original questions.

| Name _____ | | | Points _____ |
| --- | --- | --- | --- |
| | Points possible | Points awarded | Comments |
| Physical setup: Attractive display, clear labels and captions, includes several historical artifacts or pictures | 25 | | |
| Use of evidence: At least four different sources in display and written report, correctly lists where they came from | 25 | | |
| Use of details: Clear and specific descriptions of historical items and how they were used | 25 | | |
| Oral presentation: Effective explanation of the display; able to engage audience and answer questions | 25 | | |

**FIGURE 8.2  Scoring guide for evaluating "History Museum" display and report.**

**99**

ready to start working on their display, they at least saw they needed more information to complete the assignment.

Similarly, when students finished their research and moved into the next phase of the project, nearly all of them ignored the notes they had taken. They simply began working on their reports without making any reference to what they had learned while doing research. Students in a different group investigating changes in work, for example, discussed the topic among themselves and then wrote, "People who had good jobs would make a dollar a day, and people who didn't have good jobs would make like a penny a day"—a statement that was completely unconnected to what they had found; they just made it up in the course of their discussion. Nearly every group of students repeated the same process: They wrote about how things changed "because it was neater" or "because people just liked it better," making no reference to what they had themselves discovered about changes. Again, Amy had to model for students how to use notes to draw conclusions and how to organize those in a report.

*Teachers need to model the use of notes to draw conclusions and organize reports.*

## INVESTIGATING WITH ENGLISH LEARNERS

Like Tina in Chapters 4 and 5, Amy did not have any English learners in her class, but she taught in a way that would address many of the needs of those whose proficiency with English is not strong. Preparing for the "History Museum," for example, allowed students to draw from their own experiences and background knowledge—by focusing on daily life, bringing in objects from their homes, and talking with people they knew. These features of the project would have both affective and cognitive benefits for English learners. First, they make it clear that students' lives and identities are valued at school; learning is not separated from their home lives but is an extension of it. Like many of the activities throughout this book, the "History Museum" project sends the clear message that students, their families, and their communities have expertise that contributes to their academic achievement. But this isn't just a matter of making students feel proud of their heritage, as important as that is; building on background knowledge is also critical to learning, as we've mentioned more than once. All students need opportunities to make connections between new information and what they already know, in order to develop meaningful and enduring understandings. Otherwise, information may be superficially learned and quickly forgotten. This is even more important for English learners, who may struggle to find links between school history and their own ideas. By focusing on topics related to everyday life, those connections are much more obvious.

*Drawing from students' backgrounds and experiences has cognitive and affective benefits, especially for English learners. Cruz & Thornton (2013), Echevarria et al. (2017), Goldberg & Coleman (2010)*

Amy's classroom featured two other elements crucial for the success of English learners. First, history involved much more than written texts. Students were constantly examining both physical artifacts and visual images (especially photographs) not only as Amy introduced the unit but also as part of their own investigations. For English learners, the burden of constantly being immersed in a new language can be overwhelming. Having a chance to observe images and touch objects is a welcome relief from the steady onslaught of words, and it should be clear that students can learn a great deal from these sources. In many cases, history can be learned just as well from observing and touching as from reading and listening. And some things can be understood much better that way, such as the weight of an old iron, the feel of crinolines, or the look of old buildings; none of these could be communicated as well through words as through objects and images. Working with these sources provides the same academic content and skills that students would be expected to gain through text—learning about change over time, making observations and inferences, drawing conclusions, and so on. But by varying the nature of the sources, teachers make sure that language doesn't become a bottleneck on the development of students' historical understanding.

*Images and artifacts provide alternatives to text for English language learners. Cruz & Thornton (2013), Goldberg & Coleman (2010), Salinas et al. (2006)*

Meanwhile, Amy also modeled the academic language that is critical for success in content areas such as history. Using academic language doesn't just mean learning vocabulary about specific topics, although that is important; it certainly doesn't mean using the stilted language of textbooks rather than everyday patterns of speech. Academic language refers to practices that are useful in communicating information about particular kinds of content. For a project like the "History Museum," this involves:

Academic language involves vocabulary, sentence structures, and rhetorical forms that are used to communicate in a subject. *Short et al. (2011)*

- Vocabulary used to describe and explain historical change: This includes words for time, such as *then, now, century, decade, generation,* and *period,* as well as those for the process of change itself—such as *develop, progress, transform, evolve, emerge,* and *invent.*
- Sentence structures used to express relations: This includes sentences that express relations of time or causation, such as those based on the "Magic Words" discussed in Chapter 13. It also includes simple and compound sentences that describe life in the past ("This object was used to…") or how life was different than it is today ("In the 1800s…, but now…").
- Rhetorical forms that are common in history: This includes forms of speech and writing that connect multiple sentences into longer presentations or compositions. One of the most common rhetorical forms in history is narrative, but many of the activities in Amy's classroom also involved writing paragraphs with main ideas and supporting details, such as when they described what life was like at a particular time.

With each of these aspects of academic language, modeling is critical to students' success. It's not enough to tell students to use words for time or to write sentences or paragraphs that show how life was different in the past. It's not even enough to explain how to do these things. Teachers have to model—frequently—how to do them. As noted earlier, Amy created a Venn diagram on the topic of schools to model the use of drawing conclusions, but she also modeled how to create sentences that expressed these conclusions. At another point during the project, she modeled how to write paragraphs with main ideas and supporting details. This was a challenge for students, and Amy was surprised to find that several thought that they were providing supporting details when they really were just re-writing their topic sentence. ("People in the colonial era looked different than we do today. They did not look the same as us. We look different than people did back then.") Only by writing examples herself and displaying these on the board (and working individually with students) was she able to help them learn how to create their own.

Modeling is key to developing students' use of academic language.

## ASSESSMENT AND SELF-REGULATED LEARNING

As we have noted, one of the goals of assessment is to help students develop an understanding of the standards of achievement so that they can apply them to their own work. Indeed, one of the chief goals of instruction generally is to encourage students to plan and regulate their own learning. Students whose teachers tell them every detail of what to do and how to do it are ill prepared either for later learning or for life outside school. Successful students—and successful citizens—approach the world around them with curiosity, and they take charge of their own learning. They look to teachers not so much to tell them what to do as to provide examples of what successful performances looks like. Assessment can be an important tool in the process of developing such self-motivated and self-regulated learners. When clear standards are established before the beginning of an assignment, teachers and students can work together to reach those goals—and the teacher's role becomes one of supporting students' learning rather than directing it.

Students should learn to plan and regulate their own learning.

This kind of self-directed learning was an important part of the "History Museum" project in Amy's classroom. Our emphasis on the pitfalls that students encountered may give the impression that this was a somewhat tedious or unexciting project, but nothing could be further from the truth. Students consistently stayed on task and made steady progress toward completing their work, and they were always ready to share with visitors and each other what they were finding out. The "feel" of the classroom was consistently open and relaxed despite the many obstacles students faced. One reason students felt comfortable with this process was the emphasis Amy placed on making them responsible for their own learning. At the beginning of the project, she distributed a detailed scoring guide

Scoring guides can make evaluation standards clear to students and help them monitor their own achievement.

(see Figure 8.2), and she expected students to learn how to achieve the standards she had established. When their performance fell short—when, for example, a student thought he had completed his research after writing the word *shoemaker*—Amy responded not by criticizing students or giving them bad grades, but by showing them how to improve their work so that it more closely matched the guide. Throughout the project, she made it clear that they were in charge of their learning, and she was there to help them—thus each day she asked students what stage of their project they were working on, what they were going to do next, and what their alternatives might be if they couldn't do the work they had planned. As we have emphasized, students need to internalize the standards for achievement so that they know what they are trying to accomplish (and why), and Amy was largely successful in helping students make progress in that kind of metacognitive awareness. Near the end of the project, for example, she was reviewing paragraph structure with students and asked what they should do if they found they didn't have enough details to support the main idea of a paragraph. "Do more research," students agreed—a concept that would have been alien to them just two weeks earlier.

It's important to recognize, though, that simply understanding a set of scoring guidelines will not motivate students to learn. Students might clearly fathom the meaning of a set of standards and still have no interest in achieving them; if the task is too hard, too easy, or too meaningless, students will not be likely to engage in any kind of self-regulated learning. Setting clear standards and helping students achieve them makes sense only when those standards relate to meaningful and authentic tasks. In this chapter, for example, one of the most important reasons students stayed interested and involved was that they knew their activities built toward their final performance—displays for their "History Museum." These displays clearly were students' favorite part of their investigations, and they devoted careful attention to creating them—making sure they were visually appealing, easily understood, and full of interesting artifacts. And because they would be explaining their exhibits to other classes and to their parents and grandparents, they knew they had to understand their topics well enough to make these presentations and answer questions. Although teachers often ask students to imagine that they are writing or speaking for a particular audience (usually with mixed success), Amy's students really *were* preparing for an audience. Rather than imagining that someone didn't know anything about their topic, they were preparing their explanations for primary school students who really didn't know anything about them. The authenticity of their expectations led them to plan presentations in which they took clear account of their audience with hands-on demonstrations and questions such as, "Do you know what these were used for?"

Assignments should have authentic purposes and audiences. M. King et al. (2015)

## DEVELOPING AN UNDERSTANDING OF TIME AND CHRONOLOGY

Traditional history instruction is sometimes stereotyped as the incessant memorizing of dates. By this point in the book, we hope it's clear that our way of thinking about the topic is very different. Yet it's hard to deny that understanding time is an integral part of understanding history. In some important ways, the relation between time and history is similar to the relation between spelling and writing. Spelling can hardly be considered as important to writing as purpose, voice, or organization, and few teachers would spend as much time on spelling as on meaning-centered components of composition, yet they also know that students' writing will be more effective if they eventually learn how to spell. Similarly, the importance of time pales in comparison to issues such as historical evidence, interpretation, agency, and significance, yet students' historical understanding will be more complete if they know when things happened. Just as spelling is a small but important part of writing, time is a small but important part of history.

Learning history does not mean memorizing dates.

Understanding time is a small but important part of history.

One drawback to teaching students about time, though, is the temptation to confuse different aspects of the topic. Understanding historical time includes at least two separate components: Being able to order moments in time (sometimes known as chronology) and being able to match moments in time to specific dates. Although, at first, these may seem similar, children are actually much more adept at the first. Our own research indicates that even children in Kindergarten recognize that a picture of a covered wagon refers to a time longer ago than a picture with cars in it. Those in the primary grades can make even more complicated distinctions; as they get older, they become increasingly skilled at ordering historical pictures on the basis of clues in technology, fashion, and social roles. Children's chronological knowledge—their understanding of the order in which aspects of social and material life have changed—represents a very impressive area of prior knowledge.

Despite their knowledge of chronology, children's use of dates and other conventional markers of time—"the Depression," "the Colonial Era," and so on—is much less developed. Primary school children know what dates sound like and usually know what the current year is, but they almost never associate periods in history with any particular years; they can put historical pictures in order, that is, but they don't match them with dates. By fourth grade, many children have begun to use *some* specific dates, such as "the 1960s" and "the 1800s." By fifth and sixth grade, some (but not all) students can identify pictures from the last century to within a decade and match pictures from the 1700s and 1800s with the appropriate century; occasionally students at this age use terms such as "the Victorian era." In general, however, dates and conventional time phrases (e.g., "the Colonial Era") are unlikely to call forth any specific associations on the part of most students before fifth grade (nor for many after that point either). Saying that something happened in "the eighteenth century," "1920," or even "about 30 years" ago doesn't mean anything to most children because those expressions don't match anything they can visualize.

Equating dates with an understanding of time, then, seriously underestimates students' abilities. Because younger children have so little knowledge of specific dates, and because even older ones can't readily identify the dates associated with events usually considered important in school, it's tempting to conclude that they don't understand time; such observations are sometimes used as justification for omitting history from the primary school curriculum. In fact, however, most children have an extensive understanding of historical time—they just haven't learned specific dates yet. Early in the school year, for example, Amy happened to ask students if they thought there were televisions in 1980; most thought there were. She then asked if they thought televisions existed in 1970; the class was evenly split. Finally, she asked if there were any in 1960, and students were unanimous that nothing so modern could have been around so long ago. When students' knowledge of dates is as undeveloped as that, teachers cannot expect that using dates will help students know when something happened.

Instead of assuming that learning a date helps students know when something happened, teachers have to approach dates as concepts to be developed: They have to help students associate their visual images of history with the dates that correspond to them. Although Amy's students didn't think there were televisions in 1960, they could easily place a photograph from the 1960s between those from the 1950s and the 1970s. One of her goals, then, was for students to learn to use dates that went with their images of different time periods. In part, this involved constantly calling students' attention to the dates associated with the topics they were studying and asking them when they thought various developments took place (see, for example, the "Artifact Think Sheet" in Figure 8.1). Even more important was the use of a "visual time line" on the wall of the classroom.

Time lines can be found in any history text and on the walls of many classrooms. However, we believe that most do little to develop students' understanding because they provide no connection with prior knowledge. Time lines typically connect one thing students don't know much about—dates—with something else they don't know much about—wars and politics. For a time line to be effective, it must build on students' prior knowledge—their visual understanding of changes in social and material life. In Amy's room, for example, two walls were taken up with a visual time line; this consisted of signs marking the decades from 1850 to the present with pictures placed at the appropriate points on the wall. As students brought in their own artifacts and photographs throughout the year, they added these to the time line as well. Soon after she put this up (and before she had even explained it to students), a striking phenomenon took place: Whenever Amy mentioned a date, in any

The research base for the following discussion of time can be found in *Barton* (2002, 2008).

Children are better at sequencing historical periods than assigning dates or names to those periods.

Dates generally do not allow students to visualize the time being referred to.

Teachers can help students associate their visual images of history with the corresponding dates.

Most time lines do not allow students to make connections to their prior knowledge.

context, students' heads would swing toward the time line—they were using it to find out what the date meant, to see for themselves how people dressed and what kind of machines they had in 1910 or 1940 or whatever. It was as if students were saying to themselves, "Oh, *that's* when 1940 was!" This visual time line served precisely the purpose we're advocating here: It helped students match dates to what they already knew. Such time lines should be as indispensable to elementary classrooms as world maps or reading corners.

Time lines should also include images that help students compare different regions. A particularly common aspect of children's chronological thinking is their assumption of unilinear historical development. Children in the United States tend to assume that historical developments proceeded in a strict sequence—first one thing happened, then that period in history was over, and everything changed. For example, they think that settlers came before cities, immigrants came before the first president, and so on. They fail to recognize that there were cities in some parts of the country at the same time people were moving onto Native lands in the West, much less that there were Indigenous cities before Europeans first settled in North America. Time lines should help students see what life was like for a variety of people at a given time. When students look at a date on a time line, they should see more than a single image; they should see pictures from several geographic regions and from the experiences of a variety of racial and ethnic groups, of women and men, and of working people as well as the wealthy. Helping students diversify their knowledge of historical time is a crucial but often overlooked purpose of instruction.

# EXTENSIONS

An obvious way to extend these "History Museum" projects is by varying the time period covered to match the curriculum of different grade levels. Students in the middle grades, like those in Chapter 7, often study the ancient world, medieval times, or the early modern era, and developing displays on change over time clearly fits well with such topics, as would comparative time lines in which students compare changing ways of life in civilizations of China, Mali, Zimbabwe, Mesoamerica, Europe, and so on. Similarly, students studying state history (often in fourth grade) would benefit more from creating displays on historic changes in their state than from trying to memorize the details of early political leaders or the adoption of the state flag. For younger children, a teacher could plan the unit around changes over the last 50 years or even less. A primary school teacher we know sets aside time for "History Show and Tell." Each day a student brings in "something old" and describes what he or she has learned about it. The age of the items they bring in varies widely—from a nineteenth-century embroidery sampler to a 5-year-old softball. Although this activity is not as extensive or systematic as the "History Museum," it also develops students' understanding of historical time: By discussing the objects and placing them on an artifact time line in the classroom, students enhance their understanding of life at various times in the past. (One of the first things students realize is that "looking old"—like the beat-up softball—is not a direct indication of age.)

Students, particularly in the middle grades, can also be asked to devote more attention to aspects of historical change that largely were ignored by Amy's students. Most of the presentations in her class focused on aspects of material culture. Students occasionally touched on issues such as social relations—the *work* group, for example, included discussion of child labor, and the *fashion* group talked about changing expectations in women's appearance—but the main focus was always on physical changes as represented in photographs and artifacts. Instead of investigating changes in material culture, though, they could examine the way social relations have changed over time—topics might include changing attitudes toward women, minorities, childhood, the poor, war, family structure, religion, labor, law, or the environment. Middle-grade students also could focus more attention on the *reasons* for change over time, such as broader changes in culture, economy, or society. Just as in Amy's class, any of these topics would involve students in asking questions, collecting information, drawing conclusions, and making decisions about forms of presentation.

Visual time lines are an indispensable part of classrooms.

U.S. children often assume historical developments proceeded in a strictly linear sequence. *Barton (2008), Levstik & Barton (2008)*

Students should develop an understanding of the diverse images that may characterize any given time period.

"History Museum" projects can be extended to other time periods.

In "History Show and Tell," students bring in and describe historical artifacts of varying ages.

*Passe & Whitley (1998)*

Students in the middle grades can focus on changing social relations.

Students can focus on the reasons for historical changes.

## CONCLUSIONS

The projects described in this chapter represent several significant elements of the historical methods and instructional principles laid out in Chapters 1 and 2. First, investigating changes in everyday life builds on the historical topics students usually know the most about: Even young children already have learned about changes in technology, fashion, and social roles from their relatives, the media, and popular culture generally. Investigating those topics further allows students to add depth and nuance to their understanding while dealing with familiar and comfortable content. Second, such projects engage students in genuine historical inquiry. Although young children who are still developing their reading skills will have trouble using some kinds of written primary sources—particularly from more remote time periods—analyzing photographs and artifacts allows them to use important historical materials in an authentic way. The questions that students develop, meanwhile, are not contrived but derive naturally from their investigations and lead them to use a variety of other sources. Finally, directing such projects toward authentic audiences motivates students to develop the in-depth understanding that presentations or displays require. As this chapter has made clear, of course, such authentic, disciplined inquiry is not easy; teachers must guide and support students at every step of the process—stimulating their interest, helping them develop questions, modeling procedures for collecting information, and so on. Yet the fact that teachers and students are so willing to stick with such projects attests to their potential for engaging students in meaningful historical learning.

These projects also prepare students for participatory democracy in two important ways. First, as we have noted throughout the chapter, students could not simply look up the answers to their questions—they had to find relevant information and draw their own conclusions from it. This is one of the most fundamental requirements of democratic participation: People have to be able to develop ideas based on the careful consideration of evidence. In order to deliberate with others, we cannot rely solely on authority, tradition, or unreflective opinion, because others are likely to have their own authorities, traditions, and opinions. Neither can we simply make things up, even though students (and adults) often like to do so. When we deliberate together as members of a group, we must have reasons for our positions, and these reasons must be grounded in evidence, because otherwise, we will have nothing to talk about and no way of bridging the gaps between us. In their "History Museum" projects, students were learning to do exactly that—to base their assertions on evidence and to make it clear how they arrived at those conclusions.

*Barton & Levstik (2004)*

A second contribution of these projects to democratic participation may be less obvious, but it represents an important advance over typical classroom activities. Often, students are asked to display their historical knowledge—by answering questions in class or on a quiz, for example, or by taking achievement tests—but such displays usually are designed only for the purpose of accountability: Did students read the chapter? Can they remember what they learned? Are schools covering the required content? Such displays have few benefits for the teaching of history, and they have no particular benefit for the students who take part in them. Yet in society at large, historical displays are common—at museums and historic sites, in historical re-enactments, and so on—and many people enjoy such exhibitions. Projects such as those described in this chapter are one way in which displays of history in school can become more like such displays outside school. In their "History Museum" projects, students were displaying information for the benefit of others—their classmates, students in other classrooms, and their relatives. This is one of the basic ways in which people in our society participate in history: They pass along information about the past to others who don't already know about it. This gives meaning and purpose to the exhibition of historical knowledge: It is not done just for the purpose of accountability but because it helps other people learn. Sharing information in this way makes democratic participation richer and more complete.

*Barton & Levstik (2004), Levstik & Barton (2008)*

# I HAVE NO EXPERIENCE WITH THIS!

## Historical Inquiry in an Integrated Social Studies Setting

It is 10:00 a.m. on a surprisingly pleasant January day. A bank of windows along one wall lets in the sunshine; when several children complain that the room is too warm, Dehea Smith opens a window, and a breeze moves through the room. The 21 children in Dehea's third-grade classroom are working on a variety of tasks. One group of three works with a set of geography materials, two children work at the computer, typing in their newsletter entry about the stage design they are working on for the school TV news program. Others work on a "Museum of the World" display that will organize some of the artifacts that the class has collected over the first semester of the year. Still others are completing their "Morning Goals"—usually work in math or literature. The classroom is small and crowded. Children sit in groups of three, either at desks turned to face each other or at two round tables in the middle of the room. These are new groups, and the children have hung signs above each table or set of desks with their group name on it: Radical Red Rovers, Chkemy, Brown-eyed Tigers, and so forth. Earlier in the year, students had trouble working cooperatively. Over the first semester, Dehea assigned partners, occasionally moving into larger groups for some tasks. They have begun working in groups of three in the new semester. As the children finish up their work, Dehea passes out booklets entitled "Government is for Kids, Too!"

| | |
|---|---|
| *Dehea:* | We've studied things far away, either in time or location—or both! Can you think of anything we've studied that was far away in location? |
| *Several voices:* | The rainforest! |
| *Dehea:* | Yes, rainforests are far away from here. What about something we've studied that was far away in time? |
| *Lily:* | Native Americans in the old days. |
| *Dehea:* | Right. It's interesting to study things that are far away from us, but it is also important to know something about things a little closer to home. There's also something else that will be different about this study. When we studied the rainforest, I picked many things that we were going to study. And when we studied Native Americans, Ms. Armstrong [student teacher] made a lot of the decisions about what questions we would investigate. But this time, you are going to make most of those decisions. |
| *Kayla:* | So, we're kinda like the teacher? |
| *Dehea:* | Well, you will certainly be doing some of the things that teachers often do. |
| *Justin:* | Alright! |
| *Marshall:* | We get to decide on the questions? |
| *Dehea:* | That's right. But in order to know what questions we want to answer, it's good to find out what we already know. I'm curious to know what you already know about Lexington. For instance, how many of you have ever been to a place that's bigger than Lexington? [General discussion of places that are bigger.] Can you think of a place smaller than Lexington? |

DOI: 10.4324/9781003179658-9

| | |
|---|---|
| *Rena:* | Nicholasville. |
| *Dehea:* | How many have been there? |
| *Justin:* | I've been there, but I don't know if it's smaller. Seems like it, but I don't know for sure. [More discussion about how you can tell if a place is big or small.] |
| *Dehea:* | Hmm. How many of you have walked around downtown? Not just driven through. Really walked around. [About 11 hands go up—although the school is close to downtown, most of the children are bussed in from other parts of the city.] Well, let's brainstorm about what we already know. While I'm getting some paper, just look through—survey—the booklet I just gave you. |
| *Tad:* | Should we write any questions down? |
| *Dehea:* | Ah—good idea! Write down questions. |
| *Amelia:* | Can we use our research folders? |
| *Dehea:* | Another good idea. Use your research folders. [She places a large pad of chart paper on the board and waits a few minutes for students to look through the booklets. She walks through the room monitoring progress until it seems that most of the students have at least glanced through the booklet and written down a question or two.] OK, close your books. [Students turn their chairs to face the charts where Dehea waits to take dictation.] What are some of the places you knew about downtown? |

The children start dictating a list of places: Sports arena, theater, opera house, library, museums, hotels, park, banks, big buildings. Dehea looks over the list and notes that she thinks many of these places have something in common. She asks the students to take a couple of minutes to write what they think these downtown places have in common. As they work, she moves between groups, glancing over students' shoulders, commenting that "several people have seen different things," "Keep thinking along those lines," or "This is exciting! It tells me you're ready to learn what's *behind* all of this." Next, she collects their ideas, explaining that "if somebody says what you have on your list, check it off." Children mention that all except banks and buildings have something to do with entertainment, are popular with kids, and involve action or fun. "Yes," Dehea agrees, "they solicit children to come. They invite you to come. But there are many other places downtown, too. We've got to decide on some questions to help us learn about these places, too." She tells the students that she will use "quick writing" [a term previously introduced to identify a form of note taking] as they dictate their questions. The first questions involve size and number: How many windows are there? What's the tallest building? The oldest building? But soon children move on: "Why do we need a mayor?" "Why are there taxes?" Dehea also intervenes to ask questions. "I was wondering, too, what *are* taxes?" or, after someone asks how big downtown is, she asks, "Why *is there* a downtown?" She then asks students to take five minutes and write down all the questions they can think of, sharing their work with their partner. Next, children categorize their questions, with Dehea transcribing comments, and asking them for key words to describe each category: Government, history, structures, entertainment, people, geography, urban planning, and employment. Anna mentions that some of these categories overlap, and Dehea agrees.

In the past, critics have sometimes argued that schools should teach separate disciplines, such as history, rather than integrated fields such as social studies. In primary school classrooms, however, the question isn't so much which approach might be better as whether the social studies will simply be "integrated" into invisibility in English language arts (ELA) instruction. As we've explained throughout this book, we think reading and language are fundamental to teaching and learning history. There are also sound cognitive and educational reasons for teaching history in the larger context of social studies and cross-disciplinary, thematic units. Because so many of the problems or issues that face people in a pluralist democracy cross disciplinary boundaries, an integrated social studies approach is often a more authentic context for historical study. As we noted in Chapter 1, such contexts support students' sensemaking in history. More authentic contexts provide examples of history-in-action rather than of history separated from action; students can see how historical thinking grows from and contributes to problem solving in the real world. This is very different than decontextualized exercises in reading in the content areas. Instead, students learn to read, speak, listen and write, not to prove that they have a particular skill set, although they certainly develop a variety of skills, but in order to answer compelling questions about the world around them.

This chapter focuses on doing disciplined, reflective inquiry in the context of an integrated social studies unit. We begin with a common third-grade social studies topic,

*Levstik & Thornton (2018), Levstik (2013)*

An integrated social studies approach can provide authentic contexts for studying history.

*National Council for the Social Studies (2010, 2013)*

"communities," which often becomes little more than the "community helpers" you may remember from your elementary years. You probably visited the fire station, learned about doctors and dentists, police officers, and the safety patrol, but rarely went much beyond that. Dehea Smith, the teacher in the vignette that opened this chapter, decided to focus on the concept of community, but in a more substantive way that will involve students in a long-term set of inquiries. Dehea has to align her curriculum with state and local mandates that define the goal of social studies as developing "contributing and knowledgeable citizens" who "understand and apply the content and concepts of the subdisciplines" of the field in their role as citizen.

To meet these goals, instruction and assessment are supposed to focus on democratic principles; the structure and function of political, social, and economic systems; human and geographic interactions; cultural diversity; and historical perspective. Although this may seem overwhelming, if you go back to the vignette, you will see that on the very first day, Dehea's class inquiry touches on almost all of these aspects of social studies. This is especially apparent in the way in which her students organized their initial questions into broader categories. After lengthy discussion and debate, students select labels such as *government*, *history*, *structures*, *geography*, and *employment*. They argue that buildings, for instance, can be categorized as structures, but they also function as places of employment and entertainment, of government and historical interest. As Dehea puts the category headings on separate sheets of chart paper, she suggests that the students provide *key words* to help them remember what they have decided goes into each category. These key words also provide a good deal of information about how students understand each category at this point in their study, and they give Dehea some idea of where to place greater instructional emphasis. The *history* category, for instance, began with only a few questions focusing on finding the oldest building or street. There were no questions about the significance of these things, the sources of current problems, or even more generally how the city had changed over time. On the other hand, there were a number of government and urban planning questions—"What are taxes?" "Why do we need a mayor?" "Who decides on how a city looks?"—that lent themselves to historical as well as current treatment.

## ALL QUESTIONS ARE NOT CREATED EQUAL: MOVING BEYOND THE SUPERFICIAL

If Dehea had stopped with the initial set of questions, students probably could have completed their study in short order. Many of these first questions were superficial. As often happens in classrooms, one type of response can start a domino effect; when Julie asked, "How many windows are downtown," Martin chimed in with "Well, then, how many *bricks* are downtown?" As did Amy in Chapter 8, Dehea reminded her students that good questions often start with "how" or "why," and this helped some, with one student asking, "Why do we need a mayor?" after another suggesting, "Who is the mayor?" This type of approximation seems to be a common response as children struggle to frame substantial questions. Another response typical of this state of question development is the personalization of questions—"Why do *we* need a mayor" rather than "Why does a *community* need a mayor?" Of course, a study of students' own community is more likely to elicit such statements of ownership as opposed to, say, a unit on rainforests.

As we have already noted, question generation is hard intellectual work, and Dehea was not satisfied with how things were going. "We spent all that time gathering facts on the last project, that they are just in that mode," she concluded. She had promised that on this project they could ask their own questions, but she did not want the study limited to mere fact gathering. Instead, she planned on emphasizing continuity and change in the city, how conflicts were resolved, and how even third graders could participate in their urban community. She decided to try another question-generating technique. First, she gave students a homework assignment: Interview people at home and ask them to suggest good questions to ask if someone wanted to learn about Lexington. Students were to decide which of these questions matched categories they had already developed and to identify any new categories they would need.

The next day, Dehea took each of the pieces of chart paper headed with the category labels and descriptions that had already been developed, put one at each work center around the room, divided the class into groups, and assigned each group to a different category. Their task was to edit the list of questions already generated, emphasizing *how* and *why* questions. Next, she told the students to rotate through the centers, adding new questions generated by their homework interviews. Again, they were to check for duplications and not write questions that were already listed. In the end, they created one new category: *Miscellaneous*. As their work period ended, the students recorded the number of questions in each category, estimated the total, and then confirmed their estimation by adding category totals. They had generated 204 questions.

Students edit their own questions, emphasizing *how* and *why* questions.

When students generate this volume of questions, they can easily become bogged down in trivia rather than engaged in substantial inquiry. There are several techniques for narrowing the scope of investigation to a more manageable size, including having children collapse several questions into one or letting students decide on a set of "most important" questions (see Chapter 8 for other ideas). Dehea chose not to limit the number of questions. Instead, she noted that some of the questions could be easily answered; she suggested that students take the rest of that day's research time to see how many questions they could answer using the sources already in the room. She also reminded them to plan their record keeping: "Think about how you want to keep track of your answers first, then share your ideas with your partners."

*Dickinson (1993), Touhill (2012)*

This kind of metacognition—thinking about thinking—was a classroom constant. Dehea set aside time for full-class review of work plans, for individuals to consider how they could best organize their thinking, for students to share their thinking and planning with a peer, and, as you will see later in this chapter, for the development of metaphors to support children's visualization of tasks. After students had planned their work, they began sorting through the questions. Dehea made suggestions for sources they might use: Visitors' guides to find out what kinds of restaurants were downtown, maps to locate major geographic landmarks, and the local *Lexington Answer Book* to find out where the courthouse was located. As the research period drew to a close, one group had answered all but two of the questions on their list, and most of the others had made substantial progress. "This is good information," Dehea told them. "Now, let's see what kinds of questions we have left." In the next few minutes, the class decided that they could eliminate some categories, concentrating more of their efforts on just a few. They also noted that each category contained several different types of questions:

*Garrison & Akyol (2013), Owen & Visa (2017)*

Metaphors help students visualize tasks.

Categorizing questions helps focus research.

- Questions that required a trip to the school library.
- Questions that required both library research and sources from outside the school.
- Questions that were "ridiculous."

*Ridiculous* questions included finding out how many bricks or windows there were downtown. "That would take forever to do!" Jason exclaimed. "It's just ridiculous!" Once they named the category, the students decided that they might answer some of these questions "just for fun," but they were not going to put much effort into them. They also edited a couple of *ridiculous* questions, made them more manageable, and moved them into the history and structures categories. The questions about windows and bricks, for instance, changed from *how many* windows or bricks to *what different styles* of windows and buildings could be found in Lexington. Members of the history group decided that they would see if window styles changed over time; members of the structures group thought they would see if the uses of buildings influenced their styles.

With time, students can identify unproductive questions.

In a relatively short time, then, these third graders had honed their questions to a manageable and substantive list. They were able to quickly dispose of some that seemed initially interesting but had little significance and focus on others that they decided were more important. It took time and patience to get to this point, but in the end, most of the

*Mathis (2015)*

Students may need help thinking about what questions have historical significance. (McTighe & Wiggins (2013), Mathis (2015)

Taking time for question development in the beginning of a study saves time later.

students had a surer sense of what they were investigating and how their questions fit the larger theme of community. Given the opportunity and sufficient scaffolding, these students were able to distinguish between superficial and substantive questions. Dehea supported their efforts by allowing them time to work with the questions, sift and categorize them, debate and discuss their merits, do some initial investigation, and, finally, hammer out their own working definitions of categories. By their next research period, student inquiry was more focused, the theme of change over time began to emerge as a significant issue, and it was time to think about field trips and guest speakers.

## FLEXIBILITY IS ESSENTIAL: BUILDING ON STUDENT DISCOVERIES

As Suling and Jason study maps of Lexington and the surrounding county, trying to locate water sources that might have enticed people to the area, they find two exciting pieces of information. First, they discover that the site of the first White settlement in the area was probably a spring close to their school. "Wow!" Suling exclaims. "That's a trip we need to take!" The librarian helps Jason find an old picture of the spring in a picture history book of Lexington, and Suling and Jason decide that they could make a copy of this "before" picture and then take "after" pictures if they visit the spring. Their second discovery is that a creek runs underneath part of the downtown area. Why would people want to bury a creek? Where did it come out? Who could they ask about this? They list their new questions in their research notebooks and go in search of their teacher.

Flexibility and preplanning facilitate student inquiry. Saye & Brush (2007)

As students conduct their inquiries and make discoveries, they need as many opportunities to pursue sources as possible. Because teachers cannot anticipate all the directions a study will take, flexibility and planning are essential. Before Dehea began the community study, for instance, she made a list of contact people for possible field trips and guest speakers. Obviously, schools do not have unlimited access to field trips or outside experts. Choices must be made and made far enough in advance to ensure access at the necessary time. Dehea called several of her contacts before the unit started so that she knew what arrangements would need to be made. She also decided that the class would use public transportation for any field trips. This accomplished two things. First, transportation was a significant part of the community. It was also part of a community controversy over budget cuts that might eliminate bus routes and services for handicapped passengers. Second, the bus company required only one day's notice to pick up a whole class, whereas school buses had to be scheduled at the beginning of each school year. Dehea, then, was prepared for several possibilities. She felt strongly, however, that planning should be joint work. She wanted her students to be intentional in their thinking. "After all," she explained, "that's the only way they'll learn to do this on their own." One day, she noticed that some of the students seemed anxious to stop researching and pick a construction project—"Let's build a model of Lexington!" Dehea stopped the class and suggested they needed a "metaphor to help us think about our work."

Planning for inquiry should be conducted jointly by teachers and students.

Dehea began by drawing a metaphor on the board: A field of questions and, beneath the soil, information; a researcher digging for information, piling that information into a knapsack, and bringing it back to a "house of knowledge" where it was organized and used to answer questions. "Which part are we working on now?" she asked. The students agreed that they were digging, just beginning to fill their knapsacks. "Do you have enough in your knapsacks to really fill a house of knowledge?" she asked. Again, most of the students agreed that they needed more information before they were ready to build anything. Dehea told them to draw the metaphor in their research notebooks to remind them of their task. At each stage of work, then, she referred students back to this metaphor. Developing the metaphor helped students visualize the multistep task of reflective inquiry.

Albert (1995)

Students need help in deciding how to allocate their research time.

At one point, Dehea asked her students to stop and decide how best to allocate their remaining time and resources. "Make a list of sources you will need," she told them. "If we need to talk to people or visit downtown, we have to plan way ahead of time, and we'll have to make one trip answer a lot of questions. This will take a lot of planning and phone

---

Table 9.1

Class Constructed Work Plan for Part of Community Study

| | |
|---|---|
| Purpose: | 1. Research in Kentucky Collection at the library (collection of newspapers, maps, photographs, and the like related to state and local history) |
| | 2. Walking tour of downtown. Take pictures of structures and historic places |
| April 13: Bus trip to city council work session | |
| Purpose: | 1. See how city government works |
| | 2. Find out what kind of problems the city council has to solve |
| | 3. Tour government buildings |
| Visit from the mayor (to be scheduled) | |
| Visitor from McConnell Springs (to be scheduled) | |

---

calling." As a group, then, the class made the plans listed in Table 9.1 (and recorded in each student's research notebook). Although a field trip to McConnell Springs, the site of the first White settlement in Lexington, would have been nice, the city bus did not go there. Instead, the students decided to ask a representative of the "Save Our Spring" (SOS) group to come to the class, talk about the spring's history, and explain some of the problems encountered in trying to turn the area into a natural and historical park site. Although no speaker was available, the SOS group sent a box full of materials for the students to use. In many ways, this was more productive in terms of Dehea's goals because the unsorted resources in the box made it necessary for students to develop their own interpretations.

Dehea wanted her students to understand some of the ways in which conflict shaped their community. The conflict over what responsibility the local government had in preserving both history and the natural environment seemed one possibility. In addition, several students decided they were interested in crime and weather-related problems in the community—topics that Dehea had not anticipated. In investigating whether crime had increased in Lexington, for instance, one group came upon an article reporting an early public hanging in the city. The article included a gallows speech by the convicted murderer, pleading for other young men to avoid "strong drink and weapons." A second group, curious about why Lexington had few tornadoes or hurricanes, wrote to the regional weather service and discovered, among other things, that their city was on the eastern edge of "tornado alley" and that flooding was a much more common problem historically and currently. A major current conflict involved updating storm sewers, which did not seem particularly interesting until two students found a picture of a 1932 flood that inundated the downtown area. Although there had been heavy rainfall that day, the flooding was largely due to inadequate storm sewers. Both groups added new questions to ask the mayor.

Local history can draw on a rich variety of local sources.

Conflict is an important element in any community's history.

*McGinnis (1991)*

## MAINTAINING FOCUS

Dehea reminds students to take out their research notebooks, and there are a couple of moans.

"If you whine," she says, "there are consequences!"

"Oh, goody," Cheyenne says. "Research!"

There is general laughter as the students retrieve their notebooks. Dehea has noticed some of the groups are losing interest, especially after a week of frequent interruptions. Momentum seems to be lost, and she wants to refocus the class on their research tasks.

"We're going to go back in the past this morning," she tells them. "You will need to take notes. Head your notes *The Quest for McConnell Springs*." Several heads go up in surprise. McConnell Springs is part of their study.

"I know where that is," Jason exclaims.

Dehea smiles, relieved that their interest seems to be reviving. "Now, let's refresh our memories. How do we take notes? Chad, how do you like to take notes?"

**111**

"Don't write down everything they say."

"Just use phrases."

"Use abbreviations."

Dehea interjects a warning to write enough to "trigger your memory," and other students add that pictures can give clues.

"Don't concentrate on just one fact," Kelly adds.

Dehea turns on the video. "If you need me to stop, we can watch it again. Everybody ready? Let me get my notebook, so I can take notes, too."

The video is brief—a seven-minute re-enactment of the discovery and settlement of McConnell Springs. At its conclusion, Dehea asks the students to share their notes.

"Too short!" Karla cries. "I only got two notes."

"Want to see it again?" Dehea asks. The students ask for a replay, and Dehea reminds them to pay attention to the pictures. "Most of my notes came from the pictures!"

After the video has played through a second time, the class begins to discuss what they have learned. This time they have many more notes to share, and Dehea asks them if they could tell from the video what time of year it was. Initially, several of the students are convinced that it must have been fall. They also seem to think that the McConnell brothers are just visiting, not settling here. "Hmm," Dehea murmurs. "We'll need to discuss this!"

In the ensuing discussion, all children participate. If a child is silent too long, Dehea asks their ideas and enforces the rules about not interrupting people when they are trying to formulate an opinion. Finally, Kelly says, "I don't think they're coming back 'cause they're claiming land. They'd come in the spring, so they could clear the land and get their house built before the cold weather."

"Yeah," Jason agrees. "You can't count on luck. You have to be prepared."

Suling adds that "they need time to settle in."

At this point, Dehea introduces a contour map of the area around McConnell Springs along with several overlay maps that show how the area grew and changed, shifting eastward along the Town Branch, the creek that now runs under the city. The children lean forward to see the map, tracing the creek's flow and exclaiming when buildings they recognize from their trip downtown appear on the map.

Frequent interruptions can defuse students' interest.

Because research takes time, and work in classrooms is frequently interrupted, sustaining inquiry can be a problem. Dehea, for instance, lost one week to Spring Break, another to statewide testing, and several days to the science fair, schoolwide assemblies, and similar events. It seemed that each time students became deeply involved, there was another interruption. Some of these interruptions were necessary, even interesting, breaks in routine, but their effect was to extend the community study to the point that students sometimes lost interest. Dehea found that regular whole-group presentations and discussions helped rekindle interest and kept students on task. She focused each of these whole-group experiences around a different aspect of the class study. In the prior excerpt, she focused on the process of note taking, but also on the interaction between the early settlers and their environment. Similarly, a discussion of the role of government preceded an interview with the mayor.

Pappas et al. (2005)

Perhaps one of the most striking aspects of these discussions was the time Dehea took to allow students to build interpretations based on the data they had been accumulating and the information presented in each of these whole-group experiences. It would have been much quicker, for instance, to simply tell the students when the first White settlers came in the spring. Instead, she engaged in a lengthy (30-minute) analysis of evidence that could support student assumptions about season, solicited conclusions—"I think it's early spring"—supporting evidence—"because they are dressed warmly, but there's no snow, and some leaves are on the trees"—and interpretations—"if you get there in the spring you have time to build up food for winter."

Building interpretations based on historical data takes time, especially with younger students.

Note, too, that Dehea worked along with the children, modeling the processes she wanted them to learn and then sharing her work as they did theirs. As the video played, for instance, she stood to the side, clipboard in hand, visibly taking notes. As students shared what they had written down, she would say, "Oh, yes. I wrote that down, too," or "Oh, I missed that. I think I'll add that to my notes, too." At other times, she would write notes to the class on the board—"Does anyone have a book with a picture of an old-fashioned radio?"—and students would respond by writing their name next to her question. By the end of the project, then, the blackboard became a center of communication where teacher and students could write notes without interrupting another group's work.

At the end of a research session, Dehea ran through the notes on the board, making sure inquiries were answered, notes made, or materials returned; then she erased the board. Other teachers use a large sheet of colored paper as a more permanent communications center. In either case, however, having such a system helps keep students focused on their own tasks with relatively few interruptions and gives the teacher a running record of current issues within and between groups.

## NOW, WHAT DOES IT MEAN?

|  |  |
|---|---|
| *Interviewer:* | Hello, I'm Kelly James, here today with William, the famous criminal. Before we go on to your life, let's find out some things about general life in the 1800s. What were some of the places you saw or heard of as a child? |
| *William:* | On Main Street there was a business called Gibney and Cassell. It was run by Gibney and William H. Cassell. |
| *Interviewer:* | Yes, after a long time, it became Parcell's Department store. That was torn down in the late 1970s. |
| *William:* | It was? (acts surprised) |
| *Interviewer:* | Yes. It was made into an office/hotel building. |
| *William:* | One place I REALLY remember was the fourth Fayette County courthouse. I had my trial there. The courthouse was built in 1883 and 1884. It was designed by Thomas W. Boyd. |
| *Interviewer:* | That building was burned down in 1897. Lots of valuable oil paintings and a valuable sculpture by Joel T. Hart were lost in that fire. At this time, Lexington was pretty busy. Let's hear some about your life, William. |
| *William:* | When I was 9 years old and I had to leave my parents was when I began my criminal life. I had to steal just to stay alive! |
| *Interviewer:* | No wonder you did such an awful thing! |
| *William:* | Before I was hung, I made a speech. The speech was a warning for young men to stay away from guns and alcohol. That's how my life got messed up. |
| *Interviewer:* | Since childhood was a bad experience for you, how do you feel it affected your adulthood? |
| *William:* | I felt like I didn't have a future, so it didn't matter what I did. |

At some point, researchers must draw at least tentative conclusions about their work. Dehea's third graders decided that they wanted to share what they had found with their parents through a series of skits. Each group was charged with writing a short script that "shows some of the most interesting things you have learned about Lexington." This turned out to be the most challenging aspect of the research. The students had accumulated lots of "facts" and had found answers to most of their questions but deciding which pieces of information went together and whether any of it would be interesting or important to anyone else was difficult. As it turned out, however, what the students were most intimidated by was writing a script. This was somewhat surprising because they had written scripts for a puppet show about the rainforest earlier in the year and frequently wrote other types of stories and reports. As one of the boys explained, however, "We didn't all write the script for the puppet show. Some people worked on scenery, and some people gathered information and like that. I have no experience with this!" His partner agreed, saying that she had never even been in a play and had no idea of what to put in the script.

At the end of one week of work, most of the children were still struggling. They knew what story they wanted to tell, but they tended to tell it in outline, leaving out all the information they had so painstakingly accumulated. The partners who had found out about the 1832 flood drafted a half-page script that involved waking up, shouting "Flood!" and

*Students need to develop a broad repertoire of ways to share what they have learned.*

*Cope & Kalantzes (1990), Erekson (2014), Arias-Ferrer et al. (2019)*

*First drafts are often only outlines of information.*

**113**

swimming for their lives. Although this was certainly lively, it was short on historical information, the current connection that had captured their initial interest, and accuracy—the flood was only 3 feet deep; its major danger was typhoid rather than drowning. Similarly, the first draft of the group investigating crime in Lexington consisted of an interview with the criminal, William, in which he explained that the "happiest time [in his life] was when I was hung." Although William had actually said this in his gallows speech, the students' script provided no context for the statement. Two other groups wrote more substantial first drafts involving the founding of Lexington and city government.

Sometimes students need to be reminded to include the information they have uncovered in their writing. VanSledright (2002)

Dehea looked over the students' drafts and suggested that they edit their scripts to make sure that each line included important information about their topic. "Oh," Cheyenne said, "We need facts in each line." This notion of anchoring each line of script in facts seemed to make a lot of sense to the students. As you can see from the script at the opening of this section—a third draft—the interview with the murderer took on a whole new dimension, introducing the audience to "general life in the 1880s" and then more specific information "about your life, William." The pair who worked on the flood struggled for some time, finally working with a classroom volunteer to construct the outline and dictate the introduction in Figure 9.1. At this point, the partners took over the writing on their own, explaining why flooding was a more frequent problem than tornadoes, describing what Lexington looked like in 1832, mentioning the deaths due to typhoid fever, and ending with one of the characters going down to City Hall to demand better storm sewers.

Because their grasp of dates was still shaky, another group became frustrated with figuring out the sequence of events. They needed to find out whether their main character would have been alive to witness some of the events they were putting in their script. With

---

Geography:              Flood p. 207

  Town Branch         Main things

  Weather Letter

  Size of city          Side things

  Where was flood

Skit:

  Flood

  Debate about sewers

  How it changed Lexington

Needed:               Fake water

  Story: Someone in the flood

  Radio reporter telling people about the flood

  Script: (Main idea) What reporters sees. Emergency! Flood Warning!

 Still stymied by the thought of what to write, students found it helpful to dictate the following introduction for their script

Narrator:

Where: Here we are in downtown Lexington

What it looks like: There used to be a beautiful creek here called Town Branch. Now, the creek is hidden underground through downtown Lexington under what will one day be Rupp Arena [Show map of Town Branch].

Why we are here: We are here to tell a story about the Town Branch creek and how Lexington finally got storm sewers. Travel back with us to the morning of August 2, 1932. We are in the home of Robert E. Mackenzie and his mother Alice Mackenzie, on Main Street in downtown Lexington.

**FIGURE 9.1** **Outline for script on the 1932 flood in Lexington, Kentucky.**

some urging, they constructed a time line to which they could refer when deciding what things could go in their script. Other groups found that they had not taken careful enough notes to add the details they needed for their scripts. This was particularly apparent when they were deciding on scenery. If a character was supposed to open a door, they wanted to know what the door might look like; if a character was supposed to be in a cabin, they needed to know what furniture and tools were inside. Because it was an authentic assessment, putting together a presentation made it clear to the students which aspects of their research they really understood, where they had holes in their data, and what pieces of information made convincing arguments for a particular perspective.

*Time lines help students visualize the sequence of events.*

*Authentic assessments help students determine what they need to know. Levstik & Groth (2002)*

## TIME FOR REFLECTION AND ASSESSMENT

Third-grader Laine has been interviewing her classmates all week. She has a list of questions on a piece of loose-leaf paper attached to her clipboard.

"Are you ready to be interviewed?" she asks Jason and Suling.
"OK."
"Which of your questions took the most time to answer?"

Laine's interview goes on for some time. She is compiling the responses to use for an article about the research project on Lexington. As she interviews each group, the students pause to decide what things were hard, most interesting, or told them the most about Lexington. "Writing the script was hardest," Jason says. "And I'd never memorized lines before." For others, visiting the mayor and the trip downtown were most memorable. Alana describes how difficult it was for her to work with her partner. "We kept having different opinions about everything!" she says, although their final project is quite ambitious and involves taking the president's family on an imaginary tour of Lexington. Taylor notes that he will make sure he writes down the important dates connected to events "so I can keep track of things better. I had this guy remembering things that happened before he was even born!" Finally, Stuart explains that he learned that "some things changed," but a lot of problems "just seem to be here all along."

*Self-reflection can be built into inquiry projects in different ways. Hart (1999)*

As Laine's interview progresses, it becomes clear that, while her classmates found their recent study challenging, most of them also found it worthwhile and enjoyable. As Laine explains, "Research is learning something. It's not just copying down information." These third graders also recognize that they are beginners, noting that next year they plan to improve in several areas. "I plan to improve on writing so that when I answer questions that need an explanation, I do a detailed explanation," Amara declares. Several of her classmates intend to practice "writing with more excitement" and "writing down what I think." Their comments reflect their struggles with interpretation. As one student notes, "it requires a lot of writing and thinking. You also have to go to a lot of places just to figure one thing out. You have to make a lot of categories and lists." And, of course, once those categories and lists are created, students have to write down what they think it all means. This is a long-term project rather than a one-time event. In addition to considering children's performance in crafting one historical interpretation during one unit of instruction (see, for example, the suggestions in Chapter 10), it also helps to consider their progress over time. Figure 9.2 provides one possible rubric for a more long-term assessment of student progress in developing supportable interpretations. Like the rubric in Chapter 12 (Figure 12.4), this is not intended to evaluate individual assignments. Instead, several examples of student-constructed interpretations—a script for a skit, for instance, along with samples of a student's notes, self-assessment, and video of the final production—might provide evidence for a student's location on the rubric. Not only does this information help Dehea understand how students are progressing individually and collectively, but it also helps her think about what further experiences her students might need as they learn to build supportable historical interpretations. This is part of what we mean by constructive assessment—thinking about teaching and learning as long-term enterprises rather than single events.

*Levstik & Smith (1997), Levstik et al. (2014)*

*Historical interpretation is a long-term project. Gerwin & Zevin (2011), Levstik & Barton (2008)*

| Novice | Developing | Proficient | Distinguished |
|--------|-----------|------------|---------------|
| Student provides a narrative that includes few historical references or may simply provide a chronology of events. Student makes few causal links between events. Narrative may contain anachronisms, or judgments based on present day values. Students may rearrange chronology of events in order to forward a storyline. | Student includes some details that support the interpretation but may include anachronisms or make judgments based on present day values. Facts are not consistently related to each other or to a larger interpretive framework. Cause and effect relationships may be described but not supported by rich, historically grounded, details. | Student's interpretation is clear, coherent, and original (i.e., not copied from another source). It includes details that support the student's interpretation. The interpretation is plausible given the time and place depicted, and credible in terms of the history represented, given available information and level of experience of the student. The text (oral, written, visual) shows how facts are related to the student's larger interpretive framework, connecting a historical "effect" to a possible cause. | Student's interpretation is clear, coherent, and original (i.e., not copied from another source). It is rich in the kinds of details that support student's interpretation. The interpretation is plausible given the time and place depicted, and credible in terms of the history represented. It is grounded in substantial historical data given available information and level of experience of the student. The text (oral, written, visual) shows how facts are related to each other and to the student's larger interpretative framework, connecting a historical "effect" to possible causes. Student acknowledges gaps in the historical record. |

**FIGURE 9.2  Long-term rubric for historical interpretation.**

## CONCLUSIONS

Dehea could have narrowed the focus of her community study to a more traditionally historical approach—the not uncommon "pioneers" unit. Instead, her work reflects a commitment to some of the principles outlined by the National Council for the Social Studies:

*National Council for the Social Studies (2016)*

- Teaching and learning integrate across the curriculum. Besides the integration of social studies disciplines such as history, geography, and political science, students regularly drew on math and language arts and, especially in the reporting out phase, on the arts. As they reflected on their experiences as researchers, these third graders noted that many of their categories overlapped. "It was hard sometimes to decide if something was history, or like government, or maybe structures," commented one girl. Along with scholars from the various disciplines that comprise the social studies, they discovered that in-depth study of authentic issues frequently cuts across disciplinary boundaries and that it is often difficult to mark the place where one discipline begins and another ends.
- Students learn connected networks of knowledge, skills, beliefs, and attitudes that they will find useful both in and outside of school. In addition to learning to access information from print sources, students learned to use interviews, the built environment, and different types of maps. They gained experience in forming connected networks of knowledge and skills in putting together their presentations, as well as in reflecting on the process of inquiry.
- Teachers model seriousness of purpose and a thoughtful approach to inquiry and use instructional strategies designed to elicit and support similar qualities from students. Throughout the unit, Dehea modeled the practices she wanted students to learn and use. She also made sure that there were multiple opportunities for students to put these skills into action. Note taking, for instance, was not an exercise to be used at some future date. It was learned in a context where it was needed.

*Skills are learned in context and through teacher modeling.*

- Teachers show interest in and respect for students' thinking but demand well-reasoned arguments rather than opinions voiced without adequate thought or commitment. A constant refrain throughout the community study was the emphasis on giving "facts and reasons to support your opinions." In addition, students were taught ways to agree and disagree that nurtured discussion rather than attacked individuals.

*Students need to learn to discuss, agree, disagree, and support their ideas.*

Clearly, history was a primary focus of the class's study. In fact, all but one of the group presentations were historical. Unlike studies of one period, however, this study shuttled between past and present. Sometimes this presented problems for children whose time sense was tenuous, but we think the benefits are considerable. First of all, students recognized the continuities in their community as well as the changes. They discovered that certain problems—flooding, for instance—persist over time. They were also able to make comparisons between current and historic issues such as crime and punishment. This helped put currently controversial issues into historical context. The constant comparison between past and present also encouraged students to determine historical significance, at least in part, on the basis of an event's impact on later times. Finally, we think the connections made between controversial issues, both historic and contemporary, and civic action are more likely to encourage students to see themselves and others as having historical agency—the power to make history. The next chapter deals more explicitly with issues of conflict, consensus, and historical agency in the history classroom.

*Historical study does not have to be organized chronologically over the school year.*

*Historical study puts current issues in historical context.*

*Connecting historical and current issues can help students develop a sense of agency.*

# 10

# Why Isn't That in the Textbook?

## Fiction, Non-fiction, and Historical Thinking

As she comes in the door, Jennifer announces that there was team practice in answering social studies questions today. Each child made up a series of questions about the American Revolution, and these were used as part of a five-team contest. Jennifer's team tied for first place. "But this unit wasn't so good. All we did was learn about a few battles and fill in charts. I want to know a whole lot more!" She is particularly annoyed because so much of what she is learning in class either contradicts what she has read on her own or gives only part of the story.

"The text was talking about George Washington and how good he was to his soldiers. There was a part about Martha Washington knitting warm socks for the men, but in one of the books I read, it said Washington had deserters at Valley Forge shot. Why wasn't that in the textbook? They just want you to think he was perfect."

This is not Jennifer's first encounter with the disjuncture between historical narratives and history texts. Earlier in the year, she announced during a small-group discussion that she thought Puritans were "cruel and stupid." Shocked, her classmate, William, called the teacher over and asked, "Do you know what Jennifer thinks?"

"No," Mrs. Bainbridge answered.

"She thinks the Puritans were stupid!" William sputtered.

"Oh?" Mrs. Bainbridge smiled. "That's interesting. What made you decide that, Jennifer?"

Jennifer, having read two novels dealing with witchcraft in the early settlement and colonial periods, explained that Puritans had to be evil if they used religion as an excuse to torture and kill people. "They made their religion as bad as what they were trying to escape. It's wrong because you aren't the person to decide that…just because someone doesn't agree with you doesn't mean you have to kill them. And even if you were a person who didn't believe, you would have to just act like you did, or you'd be in big trouble. They accused innocent people, and even if they were witches, they shouldn't have killed them. These people are supposed to believe in God, you know. Real religious. And God doesn't go around killing people."

Jennifer went on to argue that the textbook told "nothing interesting about the Puritans. They just said that the Puritans were very religious people who wanted to make religion more pure, and they didn't say anything about them, what they did bad…just that they were very organized people."

Barber (1992), Blos (1993), Ehlers (1999), Levstik (1993, 2016), N. Rodríguez (2020), Vickery & Rodríguez (2021)

Levstik & Barton (2008), Levstik (1995, 2016), N. Rodríguez & Kim (2018), VanSledright & Brophy (1992)

As we said earlier, historical stories are powerful cultural forces. They present historical interpretations in a memorable format; they also have a significant impact on children's historical thinking. We continue to hear advocates of history education claim that story, with its emphasis on human response to historical events, is the beginning of historical understanding. Moreover, a number of people argue that teaching history is largely a matter of presenting "a story well told." Clearly, narrative is a more powerful influence on Jennifer's historical thinking than her textbook. In fact, she judges the historical

DOI: 10.4324/9781003179658-10

interpretation in her text and in her class work against the narrative history she reads independently. That she, or anyone else, should do this is not surprising. Stories are, after all, generally more compelling reading than textbooks. For centuries, historians have used narrative and narrative devices to order and assign cause and effect to events in the past. Yet Jennifer's experience indicates that the relationships among narrative, history, and historical understanding are more complex than appreciation of a story well told.

To begin with, defining what is meant by narrative is a challenge. Of course, narratives are created and understood within a particular sociocultural context so that definitions of narrative vary over time and between places and individuals. Generally, however, historical narratives are assumed to share certain elements with fictional stories and such non-fictional accounts as biographies, autobiographies, and traditional histories. They linguistically represent past experience, either real or imagined. Events in these narratives are expected to be connected—to have some point or conclusion. This may seem simple enough, but there is still quite a bit of difference between the grand narratives that present the rise and fall of empires and the narratives of individual agency Jennifer and others find so appealing. Consider, for example, how a fictional narrative shapes and interprets the challenges facing refugees in Jasmine Warga's book, *Other Words for Home.* Warga does not simply lay out the chain of events that led Jude, the book's main character, from war-torn Syria to a new life in Ohio. Instead, she carefully anchors Jude's story in the details of a child's life disrupted by war—saddened by the political estrangement between her father and brother, frightened by increasing violence, then torn from her home, separated from both father and brother, and faced with rebuilding her life in a vastly different country. And, just as she is finding her footing in this new world, the 9/11 terrorist attacks intensify the difficulties for a Muslim girl seeking a home in the United States. This story, beautifully told in verse, offers powerful messages about losing and finding home, finding oneself, and, as Jude explains, "learning how to be sad and happy at the same time" in a complicated world. In contrast, Elise Gravel's non-fiction approach in *What is a Refugee?* Begins with a straightforward definition of the term refugee, then humanizes that definition with first-person narratives from child refugees.

Increasingly, some of the most interesting narrative voices in children's literature can be found in non-fiction. Kadir Nelson's *Heart and Soul*, for instance, offers "the story of America and African Americans" in an engaging and distinctive voice. Nelson's narrator admonishes the reader to "pay attention, honey, because I'm only going to tell you this story but once," then promises that the history to come includes "things that might make you cringe, or feel angry…parts that will make you proud, or even laugh a little." The gorgeous illustrations and personal flavor of the narrative make this a book that begs to be read aloud, used to support student inquiry, and introduced as a model for students' own writing. Compare Kadir Nelson's powerful and engaging non-fiction to Jennifer's experience with her history textbook: "The social studies book doesn't give you a lot of detail. You don't imagine yourself there because they're not doing it as if it were a person." For Jennifer, as for many children with whom we have worked, a narrative acts "as if it were a person" by particularizing and personalizing history. As children's author Eleanor Coerr once noted in relation to her book, *Sadako,* "telling people that 200,000 people have died [at Hiroshima] doesn't have as much impact as the story of one little girl" who experienced it. And because all narratives are created within a particular sociocultural context, no historical narrative (or any other genre for that matter) can possibly tell readers "the way it really was." Instead, narratives shape and interpret lives and events from the past, embedding them in a particular culture and often making direct parallels to the present.

Neither a history textbook nor "battles and filling in charts" have this sense of personal agency. Listen to the depersonalized and law-like voice so often used in textbooks: "*Whenever,* within a feudal system, towns and trade begin to grow…, *then* feudalism gives way to capitalism." This kind of language not only depersonalizes the transition from feudalism to capitalism, but it deproblematizes it as well. History, once again, is presented as the result of inexorable forces seemingly beyond human control. Compare that law-like

For further discussion of this issue, see also A. Anderson (2017), Bruner (1986), Iseke-Barns (2009), Kermode (1980), LePore (2018), Rabinowitz (1987), Sabzalian (2019), H. White (1980)

Warga (2019)

Gravel (2019)

Nelson (2013)

Coerr (1994)

Narratives often make connections between past and present moral and ethical dilemmas. Levstik (1989, 2016), Vickery & Rodríguez (2020)

Bruner (1986), Megill (1989, p. 633), Saul (1994)

Depersonalized language can also deproblematize history.

# Why Isn't That in the Textbook?

*Cushman (1994, p. 7)*

tone to the voice of Karen Cushman's *Catherine, Called Birdy*, describing a medieval manor during the same period:

> Today is quarter-rent day. My greedy father is near muzzle-witted with glee from the geese, silver pennies, and wagon loads of manure our tenants pay him. He guzzles ale and slaps his belly, laughing as he gathers in the rents. I like to sit near the table…and listen to the villagers complain about my father as they pay. I have gotten all my good insults and best swear words that way.

In this passage, the narrative voice is distinctly personal. Cushman touches on universal qualities—greed and gluttony, injustice, resentment, the need for dignity, and the capacity for fear and joy—as well as the economics of a medieval manor but locates them within a framework of human intentions. As *Catherine, Called Birdy* progresses, for instance, you discover that Catherine's father treats her with much the same greedy muzzle-wittedness as he does his tenants: He wants to marry her off like a "cheese sold to the highest bidder." He thinks a merchant would be a good choice because the newly developing towns are better off financially than small manors. Birdy, on the other hand, sets out to foil his attempts to arrange her life for his financial advantage. This small human drama contains many of the elements of the transition from feudalism to capitalism, but the narrative description of a greedy father swilling ale while his tenants suffer and selling his daughter to the highest bidder makes more intuitive sense than the distanced and law-like explanations of the text (and it is much funnier!).

*K. Alexander (2019), Freedman (2006), Hopkinson (2006), Roberts (2019), McClafferty (2018)*

Of course, not all outstanding historical narratives are either fictional or particularly personal. Russell Freedman's book on the Montgomery bus boycott, *Freedom Walkers*, Deborah Hopkinson's *Up Before Daybreak: Cotton and People in America*, David Roberts' *Suffragette: The Battle for Equality*, Kwame Alexander's *The Undefeated*, and Carla McClafferty's *Buried Lives: The Enslaved People of George Washington's Mount Vernon* describe themes and events in U.S. history—but they do not necessarily focus on a specific character in the way that a biography or historical fiction might. Instead, each author personalizes the past by weaving multiple lives into a larger narrative. And because such books are not a new phenomenon, you don't have to ignore older books in your search for a wide variety of good literature. This is particularly important if you are searching for books about topics that received "anniversary" attention, as such moments inspire a spate of related children's books. Looking for something on women's suffrage? You're likely to find good books published around 2019–2020, the centennial of the 19th Amendment. Want alternative perspectives on Christopher Columbus? There's quite a selection if you look to books written around 1992, the quincentenary year. American Revolution? Check out 1976. But don't stop there! There are voices missing in some of these older books—and in some newer ones, for that matter. You can find a book like Nicola Campbell's *Shi-she-etko*, for

*Campbell (2005)*

instance, that does an excellent job of helping young readers understand the damage done to Indigenous children and their communities by the boarding school system. Similar work by authors such as Carol Boston Weatherford document historical figures and events often left out of textbooks, especially for younger readers. The text and illustrations in Weatherford's books, for instance, capture historical moments such as the Tulsa race massacre (*Unspeakable*), and social justice movements (*Voice of Freedom: Fannie Lou Hamer*) in ways that are appropriate for a range of young readers.

*Weatherford, (2018, 2021)*

In addition, search out outstanding authors such as Russell Freedman and Milton Meltzer, who spent many years writing non-fiction narrative history with a passion that continues to capture elementary and middle school level readers' attention today. Meltzer supports his narratives with personal accounts, as when he describes the work of children at Thomas Jefferson's Monticello nail factory. The factory was worked, he reports, by a dozen enslaved youth, ages 10 to 16. "They labored for twelve hours a day, six days a week…When several of the boys in his sweatshop ran off to freedom, Jefferson had them hunted down relentlessly and flogged when caught." Although this is not the story of a single child or even a single family, it certainly "tells it as if it were a person." Each of these authors moves beyond exposition—laying out the facts in order—to story, telling a tale "of common humanity…to help young readers understand the world as it is, and to realize

*Freedman (2006), Meltzer (1994a, 1994b)*

*Meltzer (1994a, p. 24). See Gordon-Reed (2008) for a fuller description of the nail factory and enslaved life at Monticello.*

Well-written non-fictional narratives have voice and passion.

that we need not accept that world as it is given to us." Such narratives can help young readers see that, although the turn of historical events is not inevitable, economic, political, and social forces can sometimes overwhelm individual agency.

Historical events are influenced by more than individual agency. Meltzer (1994b, p. 21)

Part of the appeal of such narratives, as we have said, is that they have a moral. This is probably because the most readily available schema students have to bring to bear in understanding history are "human behavior" schema in which morality, or at least fairness, is often a central concern. In addition to being readily available, these schema are among the most fully developed, especially in young children. Moreover, they are particularly appropriate in understanding historical fiction, biography, and autobiography, based as they are on the particulars of human, and often child, behavior. Unfortunately, they are not equally useful in interpreting history textbooks in which individual human intentions and motivations are often replaced by political and economic analyses and some groups and events ignored altogether. As a result, students may find it more difficult to identify and recall these more analytical historical accounts without considerable assistance.

Bardige (1988)

Barton (2008), Riviére et al. (1998), N. Rodríguez (2020)

Because children have more readily available schema for interpreting some types of historical narrative, however, does not mean that these are the only texts they should read or that children are naturally critical readers of narratives. In fact, narrative is not the only history genre available to students, and the very accessibility of narratives may work against critical reading—if the narrative is intuitively right, its underlying historical interpretation is unlikely to elicit criticism. In addition, the ethical and moral context of the narratives we have described adds enormous weight to an author's historical perspective. Readers of books such as *Other Words for Home* or *Catherine, Called Birdy* may find out how particular people lived their daily lives and that more than one point of view existed, but they are invited to sympathize with or at least understand the protagonist's point of view. When Jennifer read *Sarah Bishop* and *The Witch of Blackbird Pond*, two older novels about witchcraft charges in colonial U.S. history, she clearly identified with Sarah and Kit, the main characters in each book. Although she recognized that another view of the events was possible, she was still convinced that such a view "would be an awful story...They'd probably try and make it seem that the witches [Sarah and Kit are accused of witchcraft] were awful."

See Barton (2022) for an overview of research on students' narrative schema.

Children are not naturally critical of historical narratives.

The moral content of narratives adds weight to their historical perspective.

O'Dell (1980), Speare (1958)

In other words, to the extent that young readers believe a story, they also read it as "telling what really happened." As Jennifer explains, "Even if it weren't all true, it could have been true, and it could have happened like that." This can make it hard to dislodge narrative interpretations, especially if no equally compelling case is made for alternative perspectives. Perhaps if Jennifer had read more recent historical fiction dealing with witchcraft in early American history, she might have altered her perspective a bit. In *Wicked Girls*, for instance, the witchcraft hysteria in Salem is sustained when a group of girls fake satanic afflictions. Interlocking poems reveal motivations that might have struck Jennifer as believable: Frustrations with the restrictions imposed on women as well as the girls' boredom, jealousy, and need for attention.

It can be very difficult to dislodge interpretations drawn from well-written narratives. Levstik (1989, 1995, 2016)

Hemphill (2011)

As she read different novels, Jennifer also encountered a variety of historical perspectives on the American Revolution written over a period of changing interpretations of this period in U.S. history. In the Collier brothers' novel, *My Brother Sam Is Dead*, British and Loyalist sympathizers and the American Rebels commit atrocities, and there is little to choose between them. In Jean Fritz's *Early Thunder*, good and evil exist in both Loyalist and Rebel camps, and people of conscience choose where they think the most good must lie. In the oldest of the books, Esther Forbes' *Johnny Tremain* presents a clear argument for the Rebel cause, while the later *Katie's Trunk* shows the Rebels as disgruntled marauders. It was clear to Jennifer that the textbook version was inadequate. The textbook, she declared, just said that "Americans were right, but it doesn't tell you exactly why they were right, or why the British fought." She expected—and wanted—history to be interpretive and to involve moral issues. She wasn't interested in neutrality so much as in trying to understand why the two sides fought. You may think that the textbook does precisely that. It outlines the events leading up to rebellion and military conflict: Taxation without representation, British control of the colonial economy, ideas about "unalienable rights." But

Collier & Collier (2012), Forbes (1967), Fritz (1967), Turner (1992)

Too often textbooks underestimate children's ability to handle complexity. Ehlers (1999), Mayer (1999)

An outline of events is rarely memorable or persuasive to students.

these reasons, potent as they may be to historians, are not fully explanatory for students. From Jennifer's perspective, such explanations are neither persuasive nor memorable precisely because they ignore the human behavior schema we have already discussed.

Jennifer was angered by what she perceived as the single perspective taken by her textbook—Americans (Rebels) were right. In her reading, she had already encountered other perspectives and expected a more complete story. She wanted to be engaged by history, rather than distanced from it. Unfortunately, expository texts that emphasize greater and greater degrees of abstraction while trying to maintain a neutral or "objective" stance often distance students from history. Well-written, historically sound narratives (fiction as well as non-fiction), on the other hand, can support informed and disciplined imaginative entry into events—and help students make better sense out of expository texts. This is not sugarcoating the bitter pill of academic history or turning history into one big storytelling session. Dealing explicitly with students' ethical sensitivities is, we think, more likely to make history a compelling part of the curriculum. This requires a delicate balance between honoring children's search for historical truth and developing their recognition that other people in other times saw the world differently—not just from us, but from each other. What we are suggesting, then, is that a variety of good literature, combined with careful teacher facilitation, can help students see and understand the complexities that multiple historical perspectives suggest without sacrificing their ethical sensitivities and impulses.

Narrative can support informed and disciplined imaginative entry into history.

Teachers can honor children's search for truth while helping them become more analytical in their response to different historical perspectives.

Bardige (1988)

## SELECTING GOOD NARRATIVE HISTORY

Obviously, any piece of historical narrative is not as good as any other. In fact, if you encountered historical fiction from the first half of the twentieth century, you might well wonder whether historical narratives have *any* relation to "what really happened." Geoffrey Trease, an author of historical fiction, listed just a few of the restrictions that applied to children's historical fiction in the 1950s: No liquor, no supernatural phenomenon, no undermining of authority, no parents with serious weaknesses, no realistic working-class speech (including even the mildest cursing), and no budding love affairs. As if these restrictions were not deadening enough, texts sprinkled with "prithees," "methinks," and the like produced historical caricatures rather than historically authentic characters. More significantly, until relatively recently, historical fiction for children and adolescents simply omitted difficult histories. Today, few authors would avoid discussing the forced evacuation of the Cherokee when writing about Andrew Jackson, and it would be unusual to find books on Columbus that fail to consider the impact of exploration on the inhabitants of the "New World."

Trease (1983)

The teachers throughout this book rely heavily on historical fiction as well as informational books. Initially, most of them felt intimidated by the task of selecting historically accurate, well-written literature. They weren't all history majors and didn't always know the latest scholarship. They also worried about using older books such as *Witch of Blackbird Pond*, fearing that such books would be outdated historically and stylistically. Over the years, however, they developed selection criteria that worked for them. The following guidelines represent the kinds of considerations these teachers have found useful:

Kiefer et al. (2022)

- Does the book tell a good story? Scholarship is not enough to carry historical fiction. If the narrative does not hold up, even the best-documented history will not matter. Ask yourself if the book you are considering tells a story that is interesting in its own right, blending fact and fiction so that the historical background is subordinate, but essential, to the story. In Margaree King Mitchell's *Uncle Jed's Barbershop*, living in the segregated South of the 1920s is the backdrop for a story of commitment to family as well as dreams deferred and realized. Yet the backdrop of segregation and economic collapse are crucial to the story—they are the stage on which the story plays out:

  Even though I was unconscious, the doctors wouldn't look at me until they had finished with all the White patients…My daddy didn't have that kind of money. And the doctors wouldn't do the operation until they had the money.

A book must be good literature *and* good history.

Mitchell (1995)

- Is the story accurate and authentic in its historical detail, including the setting and the known events of history? Again, this attention to accuracy and authenticity must not detract from the story. Instead, the historical details should make the story ring true—not just in the description and use of material culture but also in the values and spirit of the time. As Karen Cushman notes, the differences between past and present run deeper than what people in the past ate, where (or when) they bathed, or who decided to marry whom. Historical people lived "in a place we can never go, made up of what they value, how they think, and what they believe is true and important and possible."

Children's fiction deserves the same attention to historical accuracy as non-fiction.

- Is the language authentic to the times? This is a challenging criterion. For one thing, the language of the past, even if it were English, is not the English spoken anywhere today. Instead of striving for complete authenticity, then, look for language that has the flavor of the times. Idioms, for instance, should be plausible given both the historical period and the characters. One of the delights of *Catherine, Called Birdy* is Birdy's experimentation with cursing. Her brother tells her that the king no longer says "Deus!" or "Corpus Bones!" as "ordinary folk do." Instead, he uses "God's breath!" Her brother adopts "God's feet." Not to be outdone, Birdy tries a different oath each day. First, she tries "God's face," then "God's ears," and finally settles on "God's Thumb," "because thumbs are such important things and handy to use." Note that authentic language may not be grammatically correct; good literature reflects how people speak in real life, not how they are "supposed" to speak. Sometimes this includes language that makes some teachers uncomfortable. A book that deals with racism, for instance, may include racist terms. That should not disqualify the book for classroom use, but it certainly requires careful teacher review to make sure such language is contextualized. The language should be intrinsic to the story and make a clear anti-racist statement.

Completely authentic language is rarely possible in children's historical fiction. Look for the flavor of the times.

Cushman (1994, p. 165), Levstik (2016)

- Is the historical interpretation sound? Overly romanticized, outdated, or stereotyped interpretations may be useful for comparison's sake but not for the core of literature to be used in class. Select several books representing the same topic from different perspectives and make sure that each perspective is supportable given what is currently known about the topic. Make sure characters act in accordance with these interpretations. In Cherokee author Robert Conley's *Nickajack*, the Cherokee nation has split into warring factions, some advocating resistance to the treaty that took away their homelands, others advocating cooperation and relocation. Conley based his story on sound scholarship about the period immediately following the "Trail of Tears." Its impact comes, at least in part, because of the inexorability of the central tragedy—the continuation of vengeance among the divided Cherokee. In the last paragraph of the book, one character lies dying, and his wife sinks to her knees: "The murderer's face was firmly etched in her mind. She would never forget it. This was not the end." Throughout the book, Conley refuses to over-simplify the complexities of this period in Cherokee history, and the different ways people responded to horrific circumstances.

Avoid overly romanticized historical fiction.

Conley (1992)

- Whose voices are missing? Because literature is so powerful, it is important to select as many different, historically sound perspectives as possible. Think about who the participants in an event were and how those participants might have told their story. In studying World War II, for instance, consider investigating the various "home fronts" in different parts of the world. Bernice Hunter's *The Girls They Left Behind* and Richard Peck's *On the Wings of Heroes* focus on "home front" issues as friends and family serve overseas. Ellen Klages's *The Green Glass Sea*, also a home front story, introduces some of the conflicts regarding the use of nuclear weaponry, and Patricia Giff describes life in defense industry towns. Cynthia Kadohata's *Weedflower* and Joanne Oppenheimer's *Dear Miss Breed* draw readers into the world of Japanese internment camps and introduce a largely ignored piece of that history—the experience of Native peoples on whose land some of the camps were located. Stretching overseas, Markus Zusak's *The Book Thief* and Linda Park's *When My Name was Keoko* introduce the experiences of those living in war zones in Germany and Korea.

Giff (2005), Hunter (2005), Kadohata (2009), Klages (2006), Peck (2007), Oppenheimer (2006)

Park (2013), Zusak (2007)

- Does the book provide insight and understanding into current issues as well as those in the past? As we said in the first chapter, history is not just about people in the past but also about the connections between past and present: How did people come to their current circumstances, and how might they shape the future? Well-written historical narratives speak to each of these conditions. It is no accident that as we struggle to come to terms with our collective histories, we rethink many aspects of the past and come to tell new stories about ourselves and others. A recounting of the building of the transcontinental railroad, for instance, is no longer a simple and single story of White Americans conquering the wilderness. Instead, it is also the story of Chinese and Irish immigrants, of displaced Indigenous communities, and of

Well-written historical narratives speak to the present as well as about the past.

**123**

Timberlake (2013), Yep (1994), Yin (2001). See also N. Rodríguez (2020) on the challenges of teaching Japanese internment with children's picture books.

the fear and racism that accompanied expansion. As a result, Lawrence Yep's *Dragon's Gate*, or Yin's *Coolies*, are not just about young Chinese youth's experiences working on the railroad but about the struggle of many immigrants to survive in a new land. Similarly, Timberlake's *One Came Home* isn't just a mystery set in the year of a vast passenger pigeon migration, the Great Chicago Fire and the Midwestern drought of 1871, but a consideration of environmental and gender issues and the moral complications of killing living creatures.

## NON-FICTION AND INFORMATIONAL TEXT

Students need a variety of fiction and non-fiction.

As we emphasize throughout the book, students need experience with multiple historical genres. Fiction is certainly one of these genres, but so is non-fiction. Non-fiction can include the kind of narratives we have been discussing—for example, Weatherford's *Unspeakable*, which explains the Tulsa race massacre in story-like format but without inventing any fictional characters or details. Other non-fiction is referred to as *informational text*—literature that presents information on a topic without emphasizing stories or identifiable characters—such as ...*If You Lived 100 Years Ago* or *Machines in the Home* (about the history of domestic technology). Unlike narrative non-fiction, informational text often has specialized features such as a table of contents, glossary, and index. And some non-fiction, such as biographies, blend narrative and informational text features. Sometimes adults assume that students prefer fictional narratives, but we have not found this to be the case. Students not only hunger for information about their world, they crave expertise. Think about all the classroom experts on athletics, computers, music, cars, and the like. Many students regularly turn to non-fiction sources in support of leisure pursuits. In classrooms where informational text is used in meaningful ways, students select it at least as often as they select fiction. Moreover, where inquiry is the basic approach to history, non-fiction literature is an essential classroom resource.

McGovern (1999), Weaver & Dale (1993)

Jobe & Dayton-Sakari (2003), Duke & Bennett-Armistead (2003), Duke et al. (2012), Kristo & Bamford (2004), Pappas (1991)

Levstik (1993)

Ruby Yessin often starts the school day by reading and discussing non-fiction with her first- grade class. During these times, illustrations are discussed, facts checked, and questions raised about the authenticity of the information. A pop-up book of historical sailing vessels, for instance, fascinates her students and sends them to other books to see if they can find boats familiar in the histories they know of early ocean voyages. In Ruby's class, a child may be called upon to check with the librarian for further information or to use one of the reference books in the classroom to answer questions raised in reading an informational book. Children keep these books at their desks and are allowed to read them during "free reading time." In fact, several students prefer to check out informational books for home reading, too.

When non-fiction receives the kind of attention usually accorded fiction, students respond with enthusiasm.

Extensive and intensive use of fiction and non-fiction builds a "web of meaning" in the classroom.

"Finding out" is a valued activity in inquiry-oriented classrooms.

Many of these informational books are difficult for Ruby's students, but they read as much as they can and allow the teacher, their partners, or other adults to help them understand the rest. It is not unusual in the classroom for a visitor to be asked to read an informational book to a first grader intent on finding out about Shakers, Columbus, Sacajawea, or China. Ruby explains that her extensive use of informational literature is part of the "web of meaning" that she and the children are building. In her class, "finding out" is so highly valued that there is plenty of incentive for making use of non-fiction. Just as with fiction, however, careful selection is important. While Ruby does a lot of book selection on her own, she also relies on recommendations from the school librarian and her colleagues. In general, Ruby uses the following selection criteria:

J. Stanley (1994)

- What are the qualifications of the author? A quick check of the "About the Author" page in a book or on the book's jacket will generally let you know what qualifications an author possesses. Sometimes an author is not an expert on a topic but has consulted with people who are and acknowledges them in the book. Jerry Stanley, for instance, is a history professor who knew a good deal about the background for Japanese internment during World War II, but his book, *I Am an American: A True Story of Japanese Internment*, relies heavily on interviews with Shi Nomura and other former internees. As a result of these firsthand recollections,

Stanley's book has a greater degree of authenticity and sensitivity than he could have provided on his own.

- How accurate and complete are the facts? Some works may present "information" that does not accurately reflect current historical evidence: Prehistoric people following familiar gender roles (there is no evidence that they did), Columbus proving the world was round (people had known that since ancient times), or Betsy Ross designing the first American flag (she didn't). It has been our experience, however, that the most blatant errors in historical non-fiction have more to do with what is left out than with errors of fact. Books on Indigenous peoples, for instance, too often deal only with life on the frontier or lump all Indigenous people into one amorphous group of *Indians* rather than recognizing the diversity of nation and groups that existed in the past or continue into the present. In other instances, books on traditional heroes may present one-sided portraits of such complex people as Abraham Lincoln or Martin Luther King, Jr. One way to guard against errors of either commission or omission is to invite students to compare different versions of historical people and events, noting where sources differ, and researching to find the most supportable facts.

Even when the facts are accurate, check to see whether important information or perspectives are missing.

- Are representations up-to-date? You probably won't come across too many books in schools or libraries that have the kind of blatant and offensive stereotypes that were found in previous generations (although these can still be found in materials for purchase online). However, some books may convey more subtle, but still important, misrepresentations in their text or illustrations. Too many books, for example, continue to portray Indigenous people in subservient positions (for example in images of Thanksgiving), while others give the impression that enslaved people or other oppressed minorities were nothing but passive victims (or worse, were happy to help their oppressors). Checking publication dates is a good place to start, but even recent books may convey outdated interpretations. When you find such books, though, don't toss them out, unless they are blatantly offensive. Even weak books have their uses. Encourage students to bring a critical eye to bear on their reading of all sorts of fact and fiction. Just remember that these books require teacher mediation and should not constitute a large portion of classroom literature. You will have to help students notice the errors, perhaps by contrasting different treatments of a subject as LeeAnn did when her class studied Columbus.

For a thorough examination of Thanksgiving's historical and cultural roots see *Colman (2015)*

- Does the author distinguish between fact and supposition? Two of the best examples of this are books from different eras: Jean Fritz's *The Double Life of Pocahontas* and Joseph Bruchac's *Pocahontas*. Both books go to great lengths to distinguish between the myths that surround Pocahontas and then-available historical, archaeological, and anthropological evidence. In similar fashion, Penny Colman's *The Real Thanksgiving* deconstructs "first Thanksgiving" stories by explaining how the celebration of Thanksgiving has changed over time and why it became so important to Americans' ideas about the past. Some authors provide extensive endnotes that include sources, discussions of different interpretations, and other books students might want to read on the same topic. Amy Timberlake, for instance, provides deep background on her interpretation of the passenger pigeon migrations of 1871. She is particularly good at explaining what is missing from the historical record and how she filled in the gaps. Be especially cautious about books that seem overly romanticized, too-good-to-be-true depictions of the past. Too often this means an author has uncritically accepted tradition rather than critically analyzed sources to write good history.

Think about how the readers will use the non-fiction you select.

Bruchac (2002), Colman (2015), Fritz (1983), Timberlake (2013), Vanderpool (2010)

- How well is the book organized? Generally, an author's sense of purpose and prospective audience helps shape how a book is organized. A good deal of non-fiction will not be read cover to cover, or at least not in front-to-back order. Instead, readers of non-fiction often skip around, searching for a particular piece of information or explanation. Illustrations are very important in this search and should complement and extend the information in the text. Captions should let readers know what they are seeing in clear and vivid language. Increasingly, authors and publishers of informational books include interactive features such as "pull-out" primary sources. Think about how readers might use such books, and check for a useable index and table of contents in any non-fiction.

- What literary distinction does the book have? A good piece of literature reveals the personal style of the author. As Milton Meltzer notes, if a writer is "indifferent, bored, stupid or mechanical" it will show in the work. The facts must be there, of course, but so must the author's voice and vision. The author shapes the facts, and in that shaping makes some facts more significant than others. Meltzer, for instance, could have simply described the tasks given to the young men working in Thomas Jefferson's nail factory and left out the personal

Sheinkin (2013)

cost of those tasks. Instead, his powerful authorial voice makes vivid the desperation of these young men: "The work was so repetitive, boring, mindless, and of course, payless, that they did as little as possible…several of the boys in his sweatshop ran off to freedom." Similarly, Steve Sheinkin could have written a straightforward scientific treatise on the atomic bomb. Instead, he crafts an "edge of your seat" suspense story, *Bomb,* that combines history and science to provoke conversation about the moral dilemmas and long-term effects of scientific inquiry. In a work of literary distinction, the author cares about the topics as, most likely, will the reader.

## FINDING AND USING LITERATURE

This seems like a lot to keep in mind, and if teachers had to be experts on each of these criteria, it could be overwhelming. Fortunately, there are professional resources that make it easier to find and evaluate high-quality children's literature (both fiction and non-fiction). A number of organizations publish regular lists of children's and adolescent literature that can be used for history and other areas of the social studies. One of the most useful is *Notable Social Studies Trade Books for Young Readers*, published annually by the National Council for the Social Studies and the Children's Book Council. This list of recommended books addresses a variety of topics, such as U.S. history and culture, world history and culture, social issues, the environment, and other subjects that may vary from year to year. *Publisher's Weekly* also provides "best books" lists on a range of social studies topics, such as anti-racist books or books for Asian American and Pacific Islander readers. More specialized lists include:

https://www.socialstudies.org/publications/notables

https://www.publishersweekly.com/pw/by-topic/childrens/index.html

- *Notable Books for a Global Society,* focusing on books with international themes (https://www.clrsig.org/notable-books-for-a-global-society-nbgs.htm)
- *Amelia Bloomer Project,* highlighting books on gender equality and inequality (https://amelia-bloomer.wordpress.com/)
- *Carter G. Woodson Award and Honor Books,* emphasizing books on race and ethnicity (https://www.socialstudies.org/awards/woodson)
- *Latinxs in Kidlit,* highlighting books about, for, and/or by Latinxs (https://latinosinkidlit.com/)
- *American Indians in Children's Literature,* critically analyzing children's and young adult books that feature Indigenous peoples (https://americanindiansinchildrensliterature.blogspot.com/)
- *We are Kid Lit Cooperative,* recognizing the humanity of Indigenous and People of Color in youth literature (https://wtpsite.com/)

Because educators have already reviewed books in these lists (to make sure they're "notable"), some of the work of evaluating them has already been done. At the least, these recommended books are unlikely to include obvious stereotypes or misrepresentations.

These lists provide an important starting point, but often, the descriptions are so brief that it can be difficult to tell whether the books will be useful for specific classroom purposes. To find out more about a book, teachers can turn to publications and websites that publish critical reviews of children's literature. These include *School Library Journal, Publishers Weekly, The Bulletin of the Center for Children's Books, Booklist Online, Children's Literature in Education, The Horn Book Magazine* and *The Horn Book Guide, Learning for Justice, Bookbird,* and *Kirkus Reviews.* These reviews can be relatively short, but they often provide information not only on a book's accuracy but also on its literary qualities, the effectiveness of its illustrations, and its age appropriateness. Don't reject a book just because it isn't perfect, though, because every book has limitations. Your goal should be to engage students with a *collection* of generally high-quality literature not to search for perfection.

Selection of good books is not enough; organizing their use is crucial.

Book sets help organize students' reading. L. Smith & Barton (1997), Tschida & Buchanan (2015)

Selecting good books is, of course, just the beginning. Organizing their use is crucial to helping students appreciate the books they read as literature and as historical interpretations. Several teachers find *book sets* help students move beyond an attachment to a single perspective. A *book set* usually includes paired selections of fiction—Cushman's *Catherine, Called Birdy* and Fleischman's *The Whipping Boy* for a medieval study—and several informational books at different levels of difficulty—perhaps Aliki's *Medieval Wedding*, Macaulay's *Castle*, McDonalds's *How Would You Survive in the Middle Ages*, and Schlitz & Byrd's *Good Masters! Sweet Ladies! Voices from a Medieval Village*. In Abby Mott's sixth grade classroom, she combines book sets that the students read with at least one read-aloud book. For the medieval unit, for instance, she chose Osborne and Howell's *Favorite Medieval Tales* to call attention to the development of the English language as seen through medieval literature. Sometimes students only read one of the paired books and the selection that Abby reads aloud serves as a contrast.

Abby discovered early on that simply assigning reading is not always motivating. After a couple of years of trying different techniques, she settled on several things that seemed to engage her students in discussing historical perspective. First, she found that dialogue journals provided an important opportunity for students to discuss their personal responses to readings. In the dialogue journals, Abby and her students carry on a written conversation about the books they read or hear. Sometimes Abby asks students to respond to a specific question such as, "What do you think are the most important differences between your life and Birdy's?" This question might require little beyond reading *Catherine, Called Birdy* and thinking about how an adolescent's life has changed over time (or not). In other cases, she asks questions such as, "How accurate do you think Cushman's and Fleischman's depictions of the Middle Ages are?" and "What sources helped you answer this question?" These require more attention to the construction of a historical interpretation and encourages students to draw on the non-fiction sources in the book. Abby also found that peer discussion helped students move beyond their first impressions of a book. Because not all students necessarily read the same books at the same time, she arranges two types of response groups of three to five students each. The first is a discussion opportunity for students who are reading the same book. Abby may start the group with a couple of questions or a problem that will require their reference to the book they are reading and will focus on both the literary and historical aspects of the book. In one group, for example, she asks students to select three passages that show how Birdy changes over the course of the book. In another, students search for passages that capture the differences between life in the manor and in the village. A third group selects historical descriptions from Birdy that can be supported by evidence from one of the informational books. Notice that the groups are not duplicating each other. Instead, each group is organized so that it will have something specific to contribute to a follow-up discussion among response groups.

A second type of response group mixes students who have read different books. The tasks for such a group might involve creating a list of medieval rules for child rearing, writing a description of medieval wedding customs that have current counterparts, making a comparison chart of the roles of different levels of medieval society, or creating a story map that locates each of the places described in the books. In one class, a group discussing child rearing practices was appalled at the level of violence directed against children. They collected current information about child abuse, found other books on child labor, and ended up making a chart of requirements for a "child-friendly world." Abby then gave them a copy of the U.N. Convention on the Rights of the Child and asked them to compare it to their own recommendations.

As you can see, some of these activities were relatively short term—writing a dialogue journal entry—whereas others became in-depth studies—the child rearing practices, for instance. Students had opportunities to share what they were thinking with their teacher and with small groups of their peers. In the small groups, most of that sharing happened in conversation. But not all students find this the most effective way to share what they know, and even in the most supportive environment, not all students participate equally in conversation. Honoring students' different ways of "authoring"—or sharing what they know and understand—is as important in history as in any other intellectual activity.

Abby discovered early in her teaching career that creating opportunities for students to respond to their reading using a variety of media resulted in richer historical thinking. During their medieval study, her seventh graders presented a reader's theater production, *Rent Day*,

*Aliki (1983), Cushman (1994), Flieschman (1992), Macaulay (1977), McDonald (1997), Schlitz & Bird (2008), Osborne (2002)*

Focusing student attention on the historical substance of literature requires careful teacher planning.

Good questions facilitate response group discussions.

*Bickford (2018), Bolgatz (2005), McTigue et al. (2012)*

When students read different books, discussions focus on comparison and contrast, as well as supportable arguments.

See *Tennant & Boyne (2016)*

*Rowe (2003)*

Encourage a variety of ways to respond to history.

**127**

Aliki (1983), Cushman (1994), Sancha (1983)

based in part on Aliki's *Medieval Wedding*, in which the lives of a noble and his tenants are juxtaposed, and drawing on *Catherine, Called Birdy*, *The Luttrell Village*, and students' research in other books. In *Rent Day*, different characters living on a medieval manor describe their feelings about their lives, the people with whom they live, and the practice of paying rent to the lord of the manor. Another group created a mural styled after the Bayeux tapestry, except that, instead of depicting the Norman conquest, their tapestry contrasted life on the feudal manor with life in the newly created merchant towns. With help from their music teacher, another group put on a concert of recorder music that might have been heard in a medieval castle. One of the more interesting presentations involved the sale of papal indulgences. Several students had focused on Birdy's brother, Edward, a monk working in a scriptorium; on her description of Jews forced to leave England; and on the religious activities at village fairs and in Birdy's home. In their research, they discovered that monks and priests sometimes sold indulgences—papal forgiveness for mortal and venial sins committed for a set period of time. The students created illuminated "indulgences" for the characters in each book, including pictures of the torments of hell and the delights of heaven (authentic to illuminated manuscripts of the time) as well as descriptions of the sins each character needed to have forgiven (based on the students' analysis of the books they were reading).

Bickmore (1999), Levstik & Smith (1996), McTighe et al. (2012), Rowe (2003)

As students worked on these projects, questions arose that sent them back to their reading. Sometimes debates would reignite as new information came to light. By arranging opportunities to encounter and re-encounter a topic, Abby provided a context for communal construction of meaning. Students adjusted their ideas not just in response to the text or teacher comment but also on the basis of interactions with their peers. In addition, Abby encouraged reference to other sources of information. When a dispute over the accuracy of historical information arose, she arbitrated first by having students check each author's credentials and then by sending students to the library to look for confirming or disconfirming information. In doing so, she directed them to other history genres—art, primary sources, and their social studies textbook.

Levstik (1993), Rowe (2003)

Finally, Abby used literature as a springboard to more in-depth inquiry. Based on their reading, students selected other topics to investigate. They were very interested in child rearing, general feudal practices, and the kinds of jobs people might do as adults, in addition to the usual fascination with knights, armour, King Arthur, and Robin Hood. These became individual and group projects that were presented at a medieval fair attended by parents and students from other grades. Notice that, although children began with a personal response to narrative—"It made me frustrated for Birdy" or "I thought that she should just run away with Perkin!"—they were also encouraged (indeed, required) to move beyond narrative. Their interest might be captured by a well-written story, but their responses were educated by a wide variety of genres.

Literature is not the end of historical study; it is one source among many.

## "I DID NOT PANIC": CREATING HISTORICAL NARRATIVES

April 6, 1862

"Boom!" The cannon thundered across the sky. That's what happened on this bloody day. Even now the gunboats' cannon flash across the sky. I can hear the cry of wounded but nobody dares help them. I've heard the tales about bloody battles but none could be as bad as this! Men were falling all around me but I did not panic! The situation is grim but we'll hang on although General Sherman was wrong before, he's pulling us through.

So we Yanks ain't licked yet!

—Hugh B. McKay

Fleischman (2013), Bradbury (2013)

Every piece of writing stands on the shoulders of all the literature that came before it. This is as true of your students' writing as it is of a published author's. Consider the sources for the prior diary entry. The fifth grader who wrote this heard *Bull Run* and *The Drummer Boy of Shiloh* and read actual diaries from the period. Relying largely on primary sources and historical narratives, he and his classmates reconstructed the life of a Union soldier injured at the Battle of Shiloh. Although this student is also in a classroom that overflows with books and in which he expects to write in a variety of genres, he has had little prior experience with primary sources. Nevertheless, narrative devices, including the use of dialect and first-person narration, are familiar and comfortable literary tools for him. Writing is an important way in which he and his classmates construct their own historical interpretations. Students who have not been similarly immersed in literature may be less likely to produce as literate a narrative, but all students can benefit from the opportunity to create historical narratives.

All children can benefit from creating their own historical narratives. *Arias-Ferrer et al. (2019)*

Pamela Vachon's fifth-grade students eagerly anticipated their upcoming study of the Civil War. In previous years, the study had included a re-enactment of the Battle of Shiloh. A storage closet contained a tempting collection of military paraphernalia, including hats and flags that Pamela's predecessor had acquired as he visited historic sites. Unfortunately, as far as Pamela was concerned, the main thing that the students seemed to anticipate was the romance of feather cockades, gold tassels, and cardboard bayonets. She was especially surprised at how many of the students wanted to be Confederates. They were, after all, in a Union state and in an area that had sent many men to fight for the Union. As it turned out, the appeal of the Confederacy had little to do with sympathy for the "lost cause." Instead, as Jacob, one of her students, explained, "The Confederate uniforms are better. Those big feathers are great!" Although there was no way to avoid re-enacting the battle—it was a tradition started long before her entry into the school and involved all the fifth grades in the district—Pamela decided that she could better prepare her students to understand the historical context and the costs of war.

Pamela's students loved historical fiction, especially when she read aloud to them; they were also used to vigorous discussions of literature. When she introduced Ray Bradbury's *The Drummer Boy of Shiloh*, they settled in their seats expectantly. As she finished the story and the students discussed their responses, Pamela called their attention to the list of questions they had previously developed for historical fiction:

Read aloud to students of all ages.

*Bradbury (2013)*

- What would you need to know in order to write this story?
- Where would you find the necessary information?
- How does the author help you understand what the characters are feeling?
- What other options did the character have given this time and setting?
- Could this story have been told from another point of view?
- In what ways might this story have been different had it been set in our time and place?

*McTigue et al. (2012)*

Students can generate discussion questions for different historical genres.

With Bradbury's vivid images of Shiloh as introduction, Pamela asked students to carefully analyze a portrait projected on the white board. This was a picture of a man from a small town in Ohio, she explained. What clues could they find to the time when this person lived? Did they think this was a wealthy or poor person? As the students made their observations, Pamela recorded them on sheets of chart paper. Next, she showed them a primary source—a surgeon's report on an injury. This document, she told them, was a piece of evidence to help them figure out the identity of the person in the picture. As a class, they discussed the document, listing new information and new questions that were raised.

Over the course of the next several days, Pamela introduced a variety of other sources that she had collected and organized in folders:

- Public documents: Military records, surgeons' reports, and pension applications available from the National Archives.
- Family records: Obituaries, a county history that included Hugh McKay's family, and photographs. The pictures were from a family collection. The rest of the materials were from the county library and local historical society. Some collections also had photographs.
- Newspapers: Samples from Hugh's hometown paper included stories about secession as well as farming news, recipes for sorghum and butter, advice, poetry, and local politics. Old newspapers are digitized for online access through a number of different sources.
- Samples of personal writing: Other people witnessed the events Hugh lived through. Several diaries and collections of letters were available in the state historical society's online manuscript collection and periodicals such as *Civil War Times Magazine*.

- Other sources: Maps, drawings, photographs, and a time line of events from April 1861 through April 1865 provided a graphic framework for the other primary sources. Pamela used material from textbooks, online sources, and Civil War histories.

Each day's work was organized around a set of questions related to the sources with which students worked. For the obituary of Hugh's mother, for instance, students were asked how many siblings Hugh had and what had happened to them by 1898. Pamela also moved between groups, helping them decipher antique penmanship or asking probing questions: Was this document sufficient evidence for a particular interpretation? What seemed to be the general feeling of the new soldiers as they marched South? Although each group worked with the same set of documents, their interpretations were often quite different, and discussions at the end of work sessions were lively. Pamela found that she needed to make rules for polite debate and reasoned discussion and finally spent time establishing ground rules for "supportable interpretations":

*Students need clear rules for debate and discussion. Hess (2009), O'Reilly (1998)*

- Evidence must be from a reliable source. Check publication date, author, possible bias.
- Interpretations should be true to the values and social rules of the time. Think about how people thought *then* not now.
- You cannot move historic events around just to suit your interpretation. You have to account for the facts.

Pamela reminded students that historians have similar arguments and that agreement was not required, although supportable interpretations were. She also found that, although students enjoyed the "decoding" aspect of reading primary sources, some sources just produced frustration. In considering how to handle this, her students suggested developing a "primary source key," showing common forms of script for a specific time period. Pamela also decided that next time she would transcribe some of the most difficult sources.

*Teachers must make decisions about whether to use sources in their original form or transcribe them for classroom use. Nokes & de la Paz (2018)*

After each day's work, Pamela asked students to write a letter or diary entry based on what they had learned about Hugh. Writing encouraged students to think about what they knew and could support. It also required organizing information in some meaningful way. In the prior sample, the student author included details about the battle obtained from reading diary entries from other soldiers. He also incorporated an assessment of General Sherman based on a soldier's letter. Another student discovered that field hospitals were used at Shiloh and incorporated that information into her story, along with details from the surgeon's report on Hugh's injury:

Dear Diary,

Today I got shot in the hand. My hand is almost completely destroyed. My middle finger is completely gone. I went to the field tent. The doctors did not do anything because there were other more important patients. I am not writing this diary entry, my best friend is. I am telling him what to write.

*Writing helps students discover what they already know and still need to find out.*

This type of writing certainly gives the teacher clues as to how well students understand source materials, but it also challenges children's notions of the romance of war. There was little in Hugh's story, or in any of the other sources, about feathers, sabers, and gold tassels. Instead, soldiers' letters and diaries describe rain and mud, terror, injury, and death. In one vivid diary entry, a young soldier described struggling to find a place to sleep with no shelter from the pouring rain and discovering in the morning that he had spent the night sleeping against a pile of amputated limbs discarded behind the field hospital. In response, a student wrote about April 7, 1862:

Today is the worst day of my life. It seems as if all my friends are dead...We are being picked off like grapes off a grape vine.

Although Pamela felt that her main purpose was achieved by having the students write diary entries or letters home, other teachers who have used primary sources find that the students benefit from the experience of writing a final, more comprehensive narrative. This takes time and access to all the sources that students have used throughout their project. One sixth-grade teacher has students write historical fiction based on the sources they have investigated. The characters do not have to be real, but the historical context must be authentic. This allows students to fill in the gaps in the historical record while remaining true to the period or situation.

*Kiefer (2003)*

Although young children can make less use of some types of written primary sources, they are perfectly capable of using art, artifacts, and interviews to write and illustrate biographies based on living people. Children's picture books can often suggest different techniques to use in creating biographies. One first grader, for instance, created postcards to tell the story of her uncle, a soldier stationed in Germany. The idea for postcards came from an older book her teacher had read, *The Jolly Postman*. In another primary school classroom, children studied a series of illustrations arranged in chronological order to solve a mystery and build an explanatory narrative. They used elements of each illustration as evidence to help them decide what the story behind the illustrations might have been. Even very young students could decode the pictures to determine the status and attitudes of people far distant from them in time and place. They could infer cause and effect from one illustration to the next, and so on. They were familiar enough with basic story structure to find evidence of conflict and resolution, fear and joy, wealth and poverty. Fashions and other elements of material culture and technology provided enough evidence for them to categorize events as happening close to now, long ago, or very long ago, a process that made them decidedly curious about the "real dates" when they finished their analysis.

*Ahlberg & Ahlberg (1986), Arias-Ferrer et al. (2019)*

## ANALYZING STUDENTS' HISTORICAL NARRATIVES

As Pamela planned for the creation of historical narratives with her students, she considered different ways to assess their work. Although she intended to assess the *medium* or *surface* features of students' writing—control of grammatical structures, spelling, and the like—Pamela's main concern was with the *message* or *content* components of students' work. These included the use of sources to support interpretations, the completeness of the interpretations, the sequencing of events, and the degree to which interpretations were period appropriate as well as students' facility with letter and diary genres. Along with many of the teachers you have already met in this book, Pamela had experience assessing students' written work *as writing*. She worried, however, about finding ways to assess *historical* writing. Pamela decided that she could adapt some literacy strategies to history. She began with the "ground rules" she had already developed with her students. Figure 10.1 shows the analysis sheet Pamela developed, along with her comments on the work of one of her students, Andrea. A sample of Andrea's writing is shown in Figure 10.2.

For more on assessing message and medium components of written work, see *Pappas et al. (2005)*

Students need feedback on the historical as well as literary aspects of their writing. *Monte-Sano (2012)*

These analysis sheets proved most useful in conferences with students, parents, and guardians. Sometimes Pamela organized students in small groups; sometimes she worked individually with students, especially if they were having difficulty with a particular aspect of the task of reconstructing Hugh McKay's life. Over several years, she experimented with a variety of ways to assess this project. The assessment sheet proved useful for the diary entries, but Pamela decided she needed some way to help students step back and view Hugh's experience in a larger historical context. As you look at the "final exam" question Pamela developed (Figure 10.3), think about what this question would require of students and what scaffolding might be necessary to help them be successful. To begin with, the task asks students to *picture* history. Pamela encouraged students to use different media to create the three scenes—some used collage, others painted their scenes, while still others created three-dimensional dioramas. This sent them to the sources they had been using all along but required that they focus less on Hugh and more on the background—the geography, the placement of the people around Hugh, field hospitals, gunboats on the river, or life before or after Shiloh. Pamela also asked them to provide historical arguments for

Assessment tasks often require careful scaffolding.

| Student: Andrea | Date: |
|---|---|
| **Questions** | **Analysis/Observation** |
| How well does the student control the genre being attempted? | The first entry puts the action in the present tense, rather than as a reflection. The second entry sounds more "diary-like"—and very much like the Civil War diaries we read last week. She's picked up some of the language, too—"my dear Millie" and "determined woman." Still confusing desert/dessert. Is nonstandard spelling taken from other diaries or is it her own miscue? |
| Is the text historical? Could a reader identify the time, event, or issue depicted? | Andrea has made good use of the primary sources in each entry. She gives the reader some time markers (pending of the Northwest Territory, Confederates closing in) as well as during each entry. She is trying to capture the feelings of the time—seems to be making good use of the primary sources to help her think about what a person from that time might be feeling, thinking, concerned about. |
| Is information ordered to make sense? Is the order historically accurate? | I need to check on the desertion scenario in the first entry. Does Andrea have evidence for this? It seems too early in the war for desertion to be a big problem. I don't remember this is any of our sources. Perhaps she is using material from later in the war? |
| How well has the student used the available sources to build the interpretation? | Andrea seems good at reading sources for the emotional component, but doesn't always use them to provide telling historical detail. She doesn't name the "General" or talk much about why this battle is so difficult. Maybe this is a reflection of the kind of real diary entries she's been reading. |

**Suggestions:**

**For Teacher:**

1. Write one diary entry as a class, demonstrating how to incorporate more historical detail in their writing.
2. Have discussion about chronology—i.e.., was desertion an issue this early in the war? Make timeline of sources.
3. Remind students that diary entries are written after events more often than during events—you probably wouldn't sit down and write in your diary while under attack

**For student conference:**

1. Discuss which details are historically grounded, which are speculation.
2. Look at several of the real diaries, discuss how a historian might use them to understand what was happening to ordinary people during this time. What questions could the diaries help answer? What things don't they tell us? Why?

**FIGURE 10.1 Assessment guidelines for historical writing.**

why each scene was significant and credible. As a result, students thought more carefully, not just about whether a scene was historically plausible or accurate but about why it was historically important.

This kind of assessment is an integral part of learning to think historically. It benefits both students and teachers by promoting reflection on the content and process of doing

---

April 3, 1863

Dear Diary,

I am being fired at from all sides. It is still misty from last night's rain. I don't like war at all. I am now realizing that it is a very bad thing. But I have to fight for the North. There are too many who have already desserted. I am thinking about desserting myself.

It is getting worse now. My friend Johnny died and was carried away with the many wounded. I can hear the wounded crying for help. The General is calling my regiment. I will have to leave.

(at night) The Confederates are closing in, but I can no longer fight. I write this now because I may not survive the surgery. A bullet tore through my hand. I think most of one finger is gone. Maybe I am lucky.

November 29, 1888

Dear Diary,

Today I will marry my dear Millie. Millie is a determined woman. She raised four children after the death of her first husband. Maybe it is because of her pioneer family. Her family moved here when the Northwest Territory first opened up. She knows how to face bad times and make the best of very little. Since I was sent home from the army I have had to do that too. I am lucky that I saved some money while I worked on the freighter in Colorado. I think I can make a good life for Millie and her children.

**FIGURE 10.2   Sample of student's historical writing.**

---

**Putting Hugh McKay in Perspective**

A new play has been produced based on Hugh McKay's life. You are the set designer. Illustrate three scenes that you think would be important in helping theatre-goers understand the historical setting for Hugh's experiences. Provide an explanation for why you have chosen each one. Your explanation must show evidence that you understand the historical time period in which Hugh lived.

**FIGURE 10.3   Final assessment of Hugh McKay project.**

---

history. It also encourages increasing levels of self-assessment and self-confidence on the part of students. As the grounds for building historical narratives are made more clear, students become better able to establish criteria for judging the merits of their own and others' work—the self-regulated learning discussed in Chapter 8.

*Alleman & Brophy (1999), VanSledright (2013)*

Finally, this kind of assessment provides a rich source of data for explaining student progress to parents and guardians. Just as rubrics, scoring guides, and analysis sheets make clear the parameters of a study to students, they also let parents and guardians know something about the work that engages their children. When questions arise about expectations or about the basis for evaluation, teachers explain a student's progress with reference to a variety of samples of work and their accompanying criteria. They can clearly demonstrate the relationship between those criteria and the student's work and help parents or guardians understand where progress has already been made and where work remains to be done.

# CONCLUSIONS

I will tell you something about stories…

They aren't just entertainment.

Don't be fooled.

*Silko (2006)*

—Leslie Marmon Silko

History is expressed in a variety of genres, and students need experience in as many of them as possible.

*Henderson & Levstik (2016), Levstik (1995)*

The teacher's task is to help students make sense out of the literary and historical aspects of different genres. *Levstik (2003), Mayer (1998), Nokes & de la Paz (2018), VanSledright (2013)*

Bickford (2018), McTigue et al. (2012)

Different genres provide different historical insights and serve different social and cultural purposes.

*N. Rodríguez & Kim (2018), Vickery & Rodríguez (2020)*

It is important in the development of any mature historical understanding that learners see history as a human enterprise made up of interpretations, subject to revision, and expressed through a variety of genres. The structure of narrative encourages readers to recognize the human aspects of history and, with some help, to develop a better sense of its interpretive and tentative aspects. In addition, narrative may help students maintain a balance between the abstractions of history as an intellectual exercise and history as an ongoing, participatory drama. But narrative is only one piece of the puzzle, for history is more than narrative. It is also learning to sift evidence before it has been shaped and interpreted. It is putting one's own time and place into a broader perspective and seeing oneself as making choices that are, cumulatively, historic.

The task of the teacher is to help students judge the interpretations appearing in narrative, to make sense out of alternative points of view, and to make careful historical judgments. Questions of fact and interpretation raised in this context can be used to initiate historical inquiry, refer students to other sources—including the full array of non-narrative genres—and provide a forum for the presentation of student interpretations. This, we think, is a crucial and often overlooked component to thinking and learning in history. This type of mediation also helps guard against the uncritical acceptance of literary constructions of history. The power of narrative is not an unmitigated good. As noted previously, a good story can mask bad history and blind students to other interpretations. Children are likely to believe bad history if the narrative is compelling and ignore good history if the narrative is insipid. There is no evidence that a history curriculum based primarily on narrative and storytelling is either good teaching or good history. As one of Jeanette Groth's students notes, different genres provide different historical insights. The text, she explains, "told exact dates, places, names and etc. Other sources provide more explanations of why something happened or why someone was famous. They give more details of actual reasoning and even feelings. For instance, I was *inside* on who wanted the states split up, and why." As you read through this book, you will notice that, although teachers use narrative in both its fictional and non-fictional forms, they also provide many other ways for students to think and learn in history.

# 11

# OH, GOOD! WE GET TO HAVE...A REASONED DISCUSSION

## Putting Conflict in Context

Nick Antoncic's eighth grade U.S. history curriculum, stretching from the end of Reconstruction to the present, presents a dizzying array of historical controversies wrapped around issues of race, gender, class/caste, and the nature of protest. The early decades of this era saw passage of the 19th Amendment and the accompanying vicious attacks on women suffragists, often-violent confrontations associated with the Great Migration of Southern Blacks out of the Jim Crow South and into Northern cities, bloody racial violence during the 1919 "Red Summer," anti-immigration hysteria resulting in severely restrictive legislation, and a pandemic that gripped the world. Nick wanted to address these historical patterns honestly by emphasizing civic agency directed toward social justice rather than dealing with each issue as simply one of a string of "controversial issues" to be analyzed. In earlier years, he had hoped that beginning with inquiries into current events would establish a template for reasoned discussion across the curriculum and, just as importantly, prepare students for civic engagement. Nick's students used a variety of sources to determine different perspectives, possible conflict resolutions, and changes that might result from current disputes. Over the years, he refined his approach, putting more emphasis on the historical significance of each conflict by asking students to focus on two questions: *What caused this?* and *What might this mean for the future?* After investigating a controversy, students wrote down their best evidence-based hypothesis on what caused the conflict. Small groups of students developed short presentations explaining some aspect of the controversy from the perspectives of participants in the events as well as from the perspective of an imagined historian 50 years in the future.

Nick was reasonably satisfied with this approach, but the COVID-19 pandemic, a presidential campaign, and protests around racism, made his home state a political "hot spot," with animosities running high. As is often the case, discomforting challenges to the way we've always done something may ultimately encourage useful changes. Nick's changes began when he considered the links between the crisis-filled years immediately following Reconstruction and those his students were living through in their own time.

In fact, he decided that he wanted to focus on recurring historical struggles for social justice rather than begin with any of the highly volatile crises of the moment. This, he thought, would better align with his civic aims—to prepare students to face recurring challenges to creating a more just society. He was sure, too, that investigating these challenges offered a more realistic and powerful approach to understanding how differing human experiences in the past influenced present conceptions of historical significance and relevance.

See *L. King (2020)* for a discussion of differences in the perceived significance of historical events.

Nick introduced this approach as an opportunity for students to consider their own choices as civic agents in responding to recurring movements related to social justice. At first, this approach generated anxious questions from his students. They weren't quite sure what he expected of them. As Nick directed students to sources that traced the persistence of social justice movements and related resistance in the post-Reconstruction era, they became more invested in making sense of persistent dilemmas. Interest really spiked, however, in the aftermath of the invasion of the U.S. Capitol building on January 6, 2021.

DOI: 10.4324/9781003179658-11

On the evening of January 6, Nick's online class comment board lit up with posts from students. He spent time responding to students' strong feelings, reminding them that reasoned discussion relied on a willingness to hear each other out; to be respectful and compassionate, even across serious differences; and to provide evidence-based analyses to support or reject assertions. Over the next several days he noticed that students returned again and again to flaws they perceived in how democracy seemed to be working. At this point, Nick asked students to consider three related questions: First, how deeply rooted were the flaws they'd identified—where had they encountered them in their studies so far and in what forms? Second, which, if any, of these flaws could be "fatal" to democracy and under what conditions? And finally, how might studying past eruptions of these flaws offer help in responding to their current manifestations?

Initially, students identified lying, discrimination or prejudice, poverty, and violence as the flaws with the longest historical lineages and greatest potential to destroy democracy. As one student explained, it seemed that everyone *said* they wanted a democracy, but only a few acted like they really believed in democracy for everyone. Nick asked them to consider cause and effect. Could they identify triggering events where the "flaws" kicked in? What responses reduced their impact? Why did these flaws re-emerge over time? What actions had citizens taken in the past to address them? What actions had been ignored? This classroom context—evidence-based, reasoned discussion followed by deliberation about courses of action—offered students an opportunity to use the history they studied to help them respond to current crises. Nick also asked students to identify concrete examples of how different groups and individuals responded to such crises in the past. How did past decisions cast light or shadow on the present? How might the past inform actions students might take in response to current issues they had identified?

Bickmore (2017), Ni Cassaithe & Chapman (2021), Levstik (2000), Levy & Sheppard (2018), Matias et al. (2016)

Even in less fraught times, many teachers are afraid to engage students in difficult histories. They worry that their students will not be able to handle conflict and that parents and others will object if they try it. They also often perceive their task as helping people get along, not argue. Sometimes political leaders add to this tension by attempting to ban difficult histories from the classroom. Not surprisingly, teachers who strive for harmony in such disharmonious environments often long for consensus—some shared set of values at least—rather than conflict. In the 1940s and 1950s, U.S. historians of the consensus school also tried to focus on uncovering a broadly shared set of values that, they argued, overrode ethnic and class distinctions. They worried that diversity would cause fragmentation and that emphasizing conflict rather than consensus could lead to cynicism and the failure of citizens to participate in civic life. Echoes of the same charges and counter-charges continue to be heard in current debates over the place of history in the social studies curriculum and will likely continue long past the present moment.

A. Anderson, (2017), Matias et al. (2016)

We may long for consensus, but we live with dissension.

Goldberg & Savenije (2018), Levstik (1996a), Levstik & Thornton (2018), National Council for the Social Studies (2021)

Conflict is fundamental to democracy.

We, like Nick and other teachers in this book, argue a contrary position. Conflict is built into the fabric of our public and private lives. Democracy is rooted in a conflictual model. The American Declaration of Independence lays out a rationale for the right of people to overthrow governments that violate their rights, and the Bill of Rights begins with a guarantee of freedom of speech, including disagreeable speech. Democracies worldwide have similar foundations. Democratic governments are generally based on conflicting ideas, dissent, debate, negotiation, and even litigation. When we vote, the majority wins, even when some people think it should be otherwise. We also limit majority rule with laws intended to protect minority rights, and we use a court system to adjudicate disputes. In addition, our own lives daily force us to recognize the reality of conflict in the world—whether it be terrorism at home and abroad, ethnic wars in Europe or Africa, calls for disunion in francophone Canada or in Catalonia, calls for reunification in Cyprus, disputes over religion in schools in the U.S., or disagreements about environmental issues. We live in a contentious world. Yet research indicates that students are often unsure of how conflict might be managed or resolved or what happens when conflicts persist.

Carretero et al. (2017), Evans et al. (1999), Hess (2009), Pace (2021), Parker (1991a, 1996)

As you can see, assuming that conflict is something to avoid misunderstands and misrepresents the foundations of democracy and the nature of much of the world. We ignore it at our peril. At the same time, an unwillingness to negotiate and compromise when faced with conflict paralyzes democratic decision-making, leaving people exhausted, sad, cynical, and sometimes, as the students noted, violent. As Nick worked with his students, he was careful not to allow endless unevidenced debates. Instead, he directed students, first, to inquire into the historical roots of the perceived flaws they identified; second, to reasoned discussion about the nature of these flaws and their possible consequences; and third, to deliberation about how students might use what they were learning to respond to current events wisely and compassionately. Wisdom informed by compassion, Nick reminded his students, were the characteristics he hoped they would develop as they applied their study of the past to making sense of the present and acting as informed citizens.

*Barton & Ho (2022)*

We, too, suggest being more honest with students about conflict, dissent, consensus, and compromise. This requires shifting the focus of history instruction from an over-simplified emphasis on "progress"—every day in every way we are getting better and better—to more in-depth study of how groups and individuals now and in other times exercise agency publicly and privately, how society deals with competing claims between harmony and protest, and how political and social meanings are transmitted to individuals and groups. This certainly means that the history curriculum is more complex but not that it disintegrates. Instead, history moves from a single and dangerously incomplete mas-ter narrative to investigating the relationships among diverse historical actors, recogniz-ing differing conceptions of social reality, developing supportable interpretations based on that study, and considering how applying historical understandings could help build wiser, more compassionate, and more humane societies. In this aim, we share common ground with the National Council for the Social Studies' emphasis on developing "tools that inform [students'] decision-making processes" and support "more reasoned discus-sion rather than an immediate debate of one view versus an opposite view." The *reasoned discussion* necessary for thoughtful deliberation, however, requires considerable scaffold-ing across the curriculum before it becomes a comfortable part of students' intellectual repertoire.

*Hollinger (1997), McCully (2012), Pace (2021)*

*NCSS (2010), Levstik & Thornton (2018)*

*Gordon-Reed (2008), Hess (2009, 2002a, b), Matias et al. (2016), Sklar (1995), Takaki (2008)*

## LET'S TALK: PREPARING FOR REASONED DISCUSSION

It might seem that the last thing your students need is help with talking, but students need exactly that if they are to participate in the kinds of reasoned discussions we have in mind. Further, they need it from their earliest years in school. One of the most important things that children can learn in school is how to share public spaces, a primary requirement for democratic living. From establishing class rules and routines to resolving group and interpersonal problems, children begin to engage in reasoned discussion and deliberation about the common good. In contrast, that most frustrating of public spaces, a classroom where student agency is too limited and the common good too often ignored and submis-sion or rebellion are the only available choices, leaves children historically and civically impoverished.

Primary school teachers, especially, are generally quite experienced at helping students share public spaces and participate in all sorts of conversations. Some discussions focus on the past, perhaps what students did last summer, while others may address more immediate concerns, but all can build toward historically informed deliberation about civic engagement. For Lydia Ruiz, careful planning is key. She begins with a discussion of "how we can live in an interesting and peaceful community." Next, she and her first graders develop a list of rights and responsibilities to ensure the classroom is a safe public space for them all. In Lydia's view, safety is central as students encounter, inquire into, and celebrate human differences over time and across the world. In her first years as a teacher, she noted how often young children drew inaccurate and troubling conclusions about dif-ferences. She responded by joining an "international classroom" program sponsored by a nearby university. Guests from different parts of the world spent time with her students sharing insights and information about their home countries. Lydia encouraged her stu-dents to dictate stories based on these visits and then used the stories as the basis for class-room discussion. When she picked up on misconceptions she might ask, "Do we know this is true?" or introduce other possibilities through literature, storytelling, and class investigations. She hoped that over the course of the year, students would learn a language

*Levstik (2016)*

*See also UNICEF (2002)*

*P. Cooper (2011), McTighe et al. (2012)*

Field (2003)

Lindstrom (2020)

Kimmerer (2013), Sabzalian (2019)

Avery (2002), P. Cooper (2011), I-Care Language (2011)

Cazden (1988)

Teach for as well as with discussion. Hess (2009, 2002a, 2002b), Parker & Hess (2001)

of friendship and curiosity that inclined them to notice similarities as well as differences in perspectives across time and different cultures. Establishing this classroom climate made it much easier to engage her students in reasoned discussion about a long-standing concern in her high desert community, protecting and sharing sparce water resources. After reading Carole Lindstrom's award-winning picture book, *We Are Water Protectors,* she worked with the science specialist in her school to develop an integrated inquiry into "water-saving" that both teachers thought could connect past and present. The book introduces Indigenous people's long history as water protectors, resisting historical and current threats to safe water. Lydia and her colleague thought it might present an important opportunity to work with people in their community who shared this history.

The book emphasizes the power of storytelling in bringing people together for a common cause, which suggested a format for student investigations: Connecting stories past and present. Before long, the classroom boasted maps, illustrations, historical and current photographs, and stories based on interviews about water use and protection over time. Students took a water census and made a map showing the location of historical and current water features in their community. They also made a chart entitled "How Can We Become Water Protectors?" and, after considerable deliberation, dictated statements about what they thought they could do based on their study.

In introducing challenging topics, Lydia and teachers like her strive to help students sustain moral sensitivities and impulses while investigating the complexities and frustrations inherent in such conflicts. Some of their classrooms begin with relatively simple "I Care" standards that include listening to each other, caring about other's feelings and being responsible for one's own words and actions When enacted, these standards support the development of healthy patterns of friendship, sharing, and cooperation. These patterns, in turn, establish the grounds for negotiating a classroom-based common good and for discussing how such standards might apply in the world outside the classroom.

Unfortunately, this type of discussion occurs too rarely in school. Instead, an *Initiation-Response-Evaluation (IRE)* pattern prevails. In IRE, the teacher asks a question (initiation), a student answers (response), and the teacher either accepts or corrects the response (evaluation). Aside from game shows and, perhaps, courtrooms, there really isn't much "real world" call for this kind of talk. When people discuss the imposition of a dress code at a P.T.A. meeting, petition the zoning board for protection or development of resources, debate the relative merits of a noise ordinance, or serve on some other board, commission, or committee, they don't expect to be quizzed in this manner and would be rightfully annoyed if such a thing happened. On the other hand, civic life could certainly benefit if more of us learned to use evidence to support a position, listened respectfully when others differed with us, avoided ad hominem attacks, worked for consensus, and learned to live with disagreement. Most of the teachers in this book carefully plan for just this kind of experience by teaching *with* and *for* reasoned discussion and deliberation. In teaching *with* discussion, teachers use reasoned discussion and deliberation as instructional techniques in the service of some other purpose. They might, for instance, engage students in a discussion of Japanese American internment, not so much to promote good discussion as to help students understand the conflicting perspectives behind that decision and the ensuing human costs. The teachers in this book who include reasoned discussion in their instructional repertoire find that it motivates student interest in history and its impact on civic life.

As Josh Elliott began his first year of teaching, he too, wanted to use discussion as a fundamental part of his fourth-grade state history curriculum. He thought that discussions would be interesting and engaging for his students, of course, but he also expected to use discussion to turn his disparate students into a more cohesive community of inquiry. Unfortunately, Josh's first few attempts at engaging his fourth graders in discussion fell flat. It wasn't that his students didn't like to talk; they argued about just about everything—until he tried to organize a discussion about the state history they were supposed to be studying. He asked a question. A painful silence ensued. He probed. Students mumbled and shifted in their seats. A few provided desultory responses. Before serious management problems erupted, Josh moved on to review a homework assignment, wondering all the while what had gone wrong.

Josh's experience is not unusual. It took some time and experimentation for him to begin teaching *for* discussion so that he could better teach *with* it. While teachers in this chapter and throughout this book support high-quality academic discussion in a number of ways, Josh organized his instruction by:

- Carefully selecting discussion topics. Just as Dehea Smith, in doing the community history described in an earlier chapter, found that all questions weren't equally useful for inquiry, Josh quickly discovered that not all controversies were worth discussion. At one point, his students wanted to discuss a controversy over new state license plates, but Josh feared that pursuing a discussion of license plate illustration was unlikely to foster deep engagement with historical content. On the other hand, discussing the ways in which the region (part of Appalachia) was represented—on license plates, among other things—met several curricular goals. Josh knew that the state-wide assessment included questions about political cartoons, and these invariably include caricatures of people and places. He thought students would be better prepared to analyze such images by understanding the historical roots and repercussions of regional images on present-day situations. He thought his students would benefit from discussing regional stereotyping because such historically rooted practices affected them and would likely continue to do so. Rather than discuss what should be on a license plate, students investigated the historical and current manifestations of regional stereotypes and discussed their impact on their state and region.

  For scholarship on Appalachia that counters regional stereotypes, see *Billings & Kingsolver (2018)*, *Buck (2001)*, *Eller (2008)*, *Weise (2001)*.

- Preparing primary and secondary resources related to the topic. There's little point in discussion when participants lack sufficient resources to provide some common background information. As Josh soon discovered, there were plenty of primary and secondary resources to support discussion of regional stereotyping. He discovered cartoons and magazine illustrations, footage from movies and television, advertisements, and a wonderful set of photographs taken under the auspices of the Depression-era Works Progress Administration and Farm Service Administration. Fortunately, many of these sources could be printed from the Library of Congress's digital collection. The availability of resources related to a discussion topic is crucial to a high-quality discussion—whether in the classroom or in other public arenas. Many topics generate considerable heat, but without sufficient resources to support intelligent discussion, there's little light, learning, or understanding.

- Providing opportunities for small group background work. Initially, Josh hoped that he could save valuable time by giving students background material prior to class discussion. This just didn't work. Because students were unsure of exactly how to use materials, they tended not to look at them very carefully—if at all. As a result, Josh organized students into small groups to review selected resources. He began by presenting students with a proposition: Regional stereotypes make it difficult for people to respect groups and individuals from other regions. He asked students to work in small groups to find evidence for or against this proposition. First, students searched for regional representations. One group categorized a set of cartoons by types of stereotypes, another group looked for stereotypical images in a set of children's books, a third made a list of problems with stereotypes based on an article they read, and a fourth surveyed parents and other students about their ideas regarding different regions of the U.S. Before they engaged in discussion with their peers, students had a rich array of background information to draw on as well as at least a beginning understanding of different perspectives on the topic and proposition.

  Background study prepares students for discussion. *Hess (2009)*

Over the course of the school year, Josh found that carefully structured small-group discussions paved the way for richer full-class discussion. The small groups also had the advantage of involving more students more consistently than full-class discussions. As students built confidence in the small groups, he noticed that more students spoke during whole-class discussions.

Barton (2011), Colley (2019), Colley et al. (2021), den Heyer (2018), Levstik et al. (2014)

High-quality academic discussions not only prepare students for participation in democratic debate and negotiation, they also support important aspects of historical thinking, including better understanding of historical agency. *Agency* refers to the power to act. As we have already mentioned, we are all participants in the ongoing drama of history. We are both the subjects of history and its agents. We make history by the collective activities of our lives, including our participation in the ephemeral as well as enduring dilemmas of our times. Unfortunately, history instruction often loses exactly this sense of agency. To the extent that we make history seem both finished and inevitable, students have difficulty seeing themselves as having agency—the power to make history. Focusing historical inquiry on challenging and persistent issues helps students in discussing the arguments and evidence that surround such dilemmas, but it is also more likely to help students see themselves as having agency. Part of developing a sense of one's own agency is recognizing that there are alternative positions and alternative actions that could be taken. Imagine trying to represent the current political climate in the United States to your grandchildren. What perspectives would you have to explain? If most conflicts had only two perspectives, they might be easier to resolve, at least by voting, but there are obviously more than two ways of looking at such issues as military intervention in other countries, changes in voter access, or limits on campaign donations. A wide range of options and opinions are available to citizens in responding to each of these issues. Dealing with such complex issues challenges history teachers to consider how different historical contexts constrained and sustained groups' and individuals' historical agency.

*Hahn & Tocci (1990), Hess (2009), Hess & McAvoy (2014)*

*For more on special challenges facing beginning teachers of history, see Barton & Levstik (2010), Grant (2003), Seixas (1998, 1999), VanSledright (2002)*

## IT'S HAPPENING RIGHT NOW: STARTING WITH CURRENT EVENTS

Investigating current, unresolved issues has a sense of immediacy too often lacking in historical study. Because they are unresolved, current issues encourage students to speculate about how conflicts began and how they might turn out and provide a framework for analyzing other historical conflicts. Students learn to think about the options available to participants in a specific time and place, the likelihood that any particular option might be chosen, and the possible outcomes that might result. They learn to look for decision-makers—who has power, and how is it exercised? What can people distant from the immediate crisis or with limited influence or power do? How have such people reacted in the past? If, on the other hand, students perceive history as finished, it can be hard to get them involved in rethinking historic controversies much less in thinking about what those controversies might have to do with their own lives.

*Current conflicts encourage speculation about multiple causes and possible effects.*

One option for teaching history, then, is to begin with controversies that are still unresolved. This was certainly Dehea Smith's (Chapter 9) approach and one of the reasons she preferred to teach history in an integrated social studies framework. She used current events to help students see how conflicts changed their community and how groups and individuals influenced those changes. One current controversy—development of green space—was easily observed and lent itself to historic connections. Students could develop before and after illustrations to show shrinking green space, they could see how much construction altered their community, and they could debate whether development should be slowed, stopped, or left unfettered. In addition, the public librarian showed children how to access maps and photographs, newspaper articles, and blueprints showing how the city had coped with similar controversies in the past, and the local Trust for Historic Preservation provided boxes of primary and secondary materials, maps, photographs, children's literature, slides, and a video showing attempts to reclaim the site of the first White settlement in the area. By the time Dehea decided her students were ready to "argue" their first question, they had accumulated a good deal of information. Dehea had already introduced a new definition of "argument," changing it from her primary school students' idea of an angry disagreement to a tool that helped them build good, evidence-based reasons to persuade others to take action, agree with an idea, or change a point of view. Note how Dehea frames the term "arguing" as she gathers the class in a circle on the floor.

*Foster (2001), Foster & Yeager (1999), Levstik & Barton (2008), Levstik & Henderson (2016)*

*Teachers can work with librarians and history interest groups to help students access different types of sources.*

**140**

"Make the circle wide enough so that everyone can see and be seen," Dehea reminds her students.

"Oh, good, we get to argue!" announces one of the boys.

"Yes, I think we probably need an argument here, but remember that this is a special kind of argument," Dehea says, and then reviews the rules for turn taking, polite forms of disagreement, and the need for full participation, all of which are clearly listed on a bright pink poster taped to the wall.

For the next 25 minutes, the students discuss and debate issues surrounding the original settlement of Lexington. Twice, Dehea intervenes to remind students to sit back in the circle so that no one's view is blocked. She also asks several students to provide information based on their reading, has one student read a passage from an informational text, and replays relevant parts of a video. It is clear that the discussion could go on longer, but the bell signals lunch break.

Most of Dehea's third graders claimed to "love to argue," and Dehea worked hard to help them do so in constructive ways. They could disagree about ideas, she said, and various opinions were always sought because "it helps to think out different opinions before we start," but students could not attack people or make fun of their ideas. "If we did that, no one would speak up, and then we wouldn't have as many good ideas to work with," Dehea reminded one student who said an idea was "stupid." In general, though, students used a discussion model that scaffolded participation by giving them two discussion templates. The first template began with a child saying, "I agree/disagree with _____ because _____." Considerable emphasis was placed on being able to give a solid reason for agreement or disagreement. The second template allowed students to agree with part of someone's idea but disagree with or modify another part. Thus, a sentence might begin, "I agree with _____ about _____, but I disagree about _____ because _____." Using these templates allowed for quick reminders when students violated the rules for debate. Sitting in a circle also helped, as everyone could see and be seen, and Dehea could make sure that everyone participated.

Older students sometimes chaff at such formulaic debates and can be especially intractable if they have had little experience dealing formally with controversy. Some teachers prefer focusing discussion on the historical significance of controversies. Although students certainly engage in debate, their work is most often organized around comparing how a conflict might look in its own time relative to what historical significance it might assume in the future. "It helps to get a little distance on 'hot' topics," one teacher explains. "I ask them, 'How would a historian explain this controversy, or what would it look like to someone from another culture?' That makes them stop and think. Maybe not change their mind, but at least consider how it might look from another perspective."

*Reasoned discussion serves important functions in historical thinking.*

*Hahn & Tocci (1990), Kawashjima-Gionsberg & Junco (2018)*

*Templates for discussion and debate help scaffold students' participation in reasoned discussion.*

*Historical analysis helps students develop a broader view of current controversies.*

## WHAT IF IT COULD HAVE BEEN DIFFERENT?

Historical agency is an important concept because it is the aspect of historical thinking that helps students see themselves as historical actors. Just as the actions of people in the past produced history, so too do students' actions today and tomorrow make history. History is real and current. Unfortunately, textbooks too often make the outcomes of historical conflicts seem inevitable. Think about all the times you memorized the three causes of the Civil War or the major events leading up to World War I. Taught this way, history seems inexorable—a train moving along a track of someone else's devising. Yet one of the fascinating aspects of history is how easily events could have gone otherwise. What if Lincoln had not gone to the theater or Kennedy to Dallas? If Black parents had kept their children home, rather than let them face hatred and harassment in order to integrate schools? If Nelson Mandela had succumbed to his long imprisonment or Vladimir Putin had worked for peaceful coexistence?

As you might suspect by now, a train metaphor for history only works in retrospect. At any historic moment, all sorts of forces come into play. The economy takes a downturn and anti-immigration fervor mounts, a terrorist attack threatens peace negotiations, a pandemic and video conferencing technology change how workplaces are organized, and

*Barton (2011), Levstik et al. (2014), Gordon-Reed (2008), LePore (2018), Takaki (2008)*

*Ayers (2004)*

**141**

changes in attitudes toward legalizing marijuana and the easy availability of CBDs alter social and economic relations. And just as students need to see how current conflicts can alter by the moment, they also need to recognize that historic conflicts could also have played out differently. Conflict may be inevitable in human interaction, but the outcomes are dependent on human agency. The Freedman's Bureau could have redistributed land in the U.S. South instead of supporting a tenancy system in the wake of Civil War or the government of the People's Republic of China could have supported the freedoms outlined in Hong Kong's Basic Law instead of jailing reformers. People make choices, singly and collectively. Sometimes they take stands against overwhelming obstacles. Sometimes they succumb to the basest motivations. Often, they are unsure where reasonable solutions to dilemmas lie. In the end, however, each of these choices—and sometimes the lack of choice—makes history. Speculating about the outcomes of current conflicts certainly helps students see the potential impact of the decisions that are available to people.

"What if" activities are another way to help students think more carefully about the impact of conflicts, inventions, and events in the past. Look at the list in Figure 11.1 and think about the kind of background knowledge students might bring to each question and the kind of research they would need to do in order to make better grounded speculations. "What if" activities can also make vivid the longevity of historical dilemmas. Jim Farrell's eighth graders discovered this as they participated in a simulated Constitutional Convention with an interesting twist. The class had already studied the convention, along with the debates and compromises made to render the Constitution acceptable to its constituents. "Now," Mr. Farrell asked his students, "Consider what voices were left out of the original debates and what difference those voices might have made. What if women or Native peoples, Blacks, or non-landowners had been heard?" Groups of students were assigned different roles based on this discussion. Some represented the disenfranchised and others the original members of the convention. Rules were established (no filibustering allowed), and debate began.

Sometimes students found it hard to keep to the time period and use the arguments that might have been broached in 1787. For one thing, they discovered that some of these issues were very current. Gender turned out to be most volatile because it touched on problems students faced in the school every day. Did the Constitution need an Equal Rights Amendment? If there had been such a thing in 1787, how would life in the United States have altered? As the debate progressed, students were amazed at how difficult these issues remained in their own lives. In fact, several students found the simulation disturbing and sometimes threatening. "There's no sense talking about the past," one student announced, after a heated debate on gender. "I don't like to pick sides. People just get mad all over again. We're all equal now. Let's be done with it." Another retorted, "There's still problems in this school and in this class. Maybe it should come out, so we can deal with

*Holt (1990)*

*A variety of contingencies, including individual choices, influence historical outcomes.*

*Speculating about alternative outcomes helps students recognize that particular events are not inevitable.*

*Historical dilemmas are often longstanding.*

*Educators 4 Social Change (2021)*

---

What if ... ?
- George Washington had been crowned king, as many wanted?
- The United Nations had not been created?
- The Equal Rights Amendment to the U.S. Constitution had passed?
- Television had never been invented?
- Constantine had not become a Christian?
- There had been no anti-apartheid boycott of South Africa?
- There was no First Amendment to the U.S. Constitution?
- Labor unions had never formed in the United States?
- Conversos and Moriscos had not been expelled from Spain?
- Europeans had not colonized the Americas?

**FIGURE 11.1  Speculating about alternative outcomes in history.**

it." Similar controversy swirled around issues of race and class with frequent conversational shuttling between past and present. One student declared that, because everyone was essentially alike, it did not matter who had been left out and finally asked the teacher to "just tell us the information. Looking at all this controversial stuff is just confusing."

The student's responses and their sometimes poignant discomfort are not unusual; rather, they are an indicator of how powerful historical study can be. Hard intellectual work, especially when it touches areas of current sensitivity, is not comfortable, but it can be compelling and memorable. As one student wrote about racism and sexism, "I always thought people back then just didn't know. They did, though. So do we, but we don't do anything about it either." It would have been easy for Jim to back away from controversy and "just tell…the information." Had he done so, his students would have lost an opportunity to grapple with issues of historical agency not just in the past but also in their own lives. Certainly, the class discussions did not cure current social problems, but some issues that had been taboo were now public and students had a language to use in describing and responding to them. Pretending that such issues are not relevant or that there could be a simple right answer to persistent dilemmas would have misrepresented history and undermined an important instructional goal, preparing students to look at persistent issues in national and world history. Jim was impressed that his students made these issues their own and at least some of them found a degree of personal agency in the process.

Each of the teachers in this chapter found this kind of teaching rewarding, but in times of severe crisis, it can also feel overwhelming. You might wonder how this kind of history education could ever equip students to engage in reasoned discussion in the midst of a world mired in *unreason*, leading to public health dilemmas, environmental crises, and political catastrophes. Too often in the larger world, such challenges do not elicit the wisdom and compassion each of the teachers in this chapter sought from their students. As a result, a topic may seem too hot to handle with young students. Overall, though, students are often relieved to discuss complex issues as long as they do not feel pressured to agree with their teachers or each other. Their interest should not be surprising. History is intertwined with how people have organized to live together—the essence of civic and civil life—and studying it can offer hope and help in negotiating that process. That said, we don't want to underestimate the challenges teachers face in discussing contemporary or historical controversies. As we write, some legislators continue a long-standing pattern of attempts at banning discussion of difficult histories in schools. From our perspective, this violates the basic tenets of democracy, the aims of history education, and the obligations we have to prepare students for the reasoned discussion and deliberation vital to democratic living. We want to stress the importance of the work teachers do in preparing students to think constructively, with sufficient insight into the past, compassion, and a sense of personal and communal agency to make a positive difference in the world around them.

## IT ISN'T FINISHED YET: YOU CAN MAKE A DIFFERENCE

As we have said, one feature of historical agency is that things in the past could have been otherwise. An equally important aspect is that history is not final—some things can be undone. Certainly, responses to the COVID-19 pandemic show how complicated such changes can be. In other cases, laws once passed—"separate but equal" or apartheid, environmental protections, or immigration reform—can be rethought, revoked, or revised, sometimes for the better and sometimes not. And, perhaps more fundamentally, attitudes and beliefs—a "separate sphere" for women or the appropriateness of child labor—can alter. Choices rarely go unchallenged, a point Jeanette Groth makes in her eighth graders' study of the Bill of Rights.

As an assessment, Jeanette assigns them the task of proving that one of the first ten Amendments to the Constitution still has a direct impact on their lives. One group, assigned to the First Amendment, produced a video that began with a mock news report. As the anchorperson began delivering the news, there was an interruption. A message

*Contemporary issues challenge students to think differently about past and present.*

*Avery et al. (1992), Colley (2019), Levstik (2001)*

*When historical interpretations challenge our worldview, it can be discomforting—and compelling.*

*Culclasure (1999), Gerwin & Zevin (2011), Levstik & Groth (2002), Levstik et al. (2014), N. Rodríguez & Swalwell (2021)*

*Decisions made in the past can be changed in the present.*

**143**

flashed across the screen: "The President has declared a national emergency. All First Amendment Rights are suspended!" The anchorperson looked up from her desk: "Well, that means we're off the air!" The screen went dark. Moments later, the video showed a series of vignettes of life without the First Amendment: People being told they had to go to church (and which church they had to attend), a protester being led off to jail, and so forth. In each case, as the victims objected, they were reminded that the First Amendment no longer applied. At the close of the video, the students stood in front of an American flag and slowly read the First Amendment. Their video was certainly powerful and generated a good deal of discussion of possible limits on free expression that operated in their lives and were under debate in the country as a whole.

Jocelyn Erlich is also intentional in asking her fifth graders to consider historical contingencies, especially the agency available to people in exercising the freedoms described in the Bill of Rights. Drawing on materials from the *We the Civics Kids* program, her class discussed whether learning to read fell under the First Amendment. What, Jocelyn asked the class, did reading have to do with freedom? Following a lively discussion, small reading groups read short, well-illustrated biographies, either of Frederick Douglass, Booker T. Washington, or Sojourner Truth.

As they read, students took notes on how/if each person learned to read, challenges they faced in communicating their ideas to others, and how reading influenced their lives. Students drew on their own reading to build a comparison chart that led them to conclude not only that reading had a great deal to do with freedom—from allowing access to otherwise forbidden information to providing a platform for abolitionist argument—but also that not everyone benefitted equally from the rights listed in the Bill of Rights. Jocelyn suggested that they find out more about how, over time, people had worked to change this, again using a variety of children's literature. She explained that these were important ideas to think about throughout their study of U.S. history.

https://constitutioncenter.org/learn/educational-resources/we-the-civics-kids

*Myers (2017), Slade & Tadgell (2014), Turner & Ransome (2015)*

*Kawashima-Ginsberg & Junco (2018), Levy & Sheppard (2018), Pace (2021)*

## ASSESSING CONFLICT IN CONTEXT

Because students sometimes find discussions of conflict discomforting, it is especially important to provide them with opportunities to reflect on what they are learning. It is equally important to frame students' opportunities for reflection in ways that reinforce respect—not just for different perspectives but for thoughtful, supportable arguments and interpretations. As you have seen, the teachers in this book take seriously the challenge of finding ways to help students manage this kind of debate and disagreement. They are especially conscious of how easily assessment can stifle intellectual risk taking. As a result, they have developed a number of ways to encourage reflection and provide evaluations of student progress without leaving students feeling as if their ideas or opinions are under attack. Jeanette Groth has been particularly successful in this regard. In fact, one year, her middle-school students voted her tests "most interesting"—a pretty amazing vote of confidence from often test-weary adolescents. Take a look at two of the challenges Jeanette sets her students:

*Barton & Ho (2022), Bickmore (2015a, 2015b)*

- At the end of an eighth-grade unit on early culture contact in the Americas, students respond to this task: You have been invited to participate in a podcast entitled "Great Debates in History." In preparation, you have been asked to consider whether, in trying to help Native Americans, Bartolomé de las Casas did more harm than good. Write a paragraph to defend your position on this issue, then explain how this period in history may have affected your life today.
- In another class, students studying the history of racial violence in the United States are asked to imagine the following scenario. The local city council is considering how to address race relations after a series of recent conflicts, but a vocal group of residents opposes the effort and

argues that any measures will make the problem worse, not better. You've chosen to speak at the next meeting. What examples from your studies could you use to address this issue?

You will notice that each task provides latitude for students to express different points of view about the history they have studied. Each question also asks students to make a connection between past and present—how has a historical period influenced life today? How has a particular study broadened students' thinking? Jeanette is careful to explain that their responses will not be assessed on the basis of the position they take on an issue but on the quality of the support they marshal in support of a position.

Although there are many ways for students to express what they know and understand about historical conflicts and controversies, it often helps to introduce them to some of the social forms used to express and comment on different points of view. Sometimes Jeanette asks students to use these genres—cartoons, videos, art, and photographs—to explain either a particular position or alternate positions on historical conflicts. To ensure that she understands what her students are trying to communicate, she asks students to provide a key on the back of a cartoon or photograph. She finds that her students don't mind providing the key if it helps to make their point. They are generally appreciative of the opportunity to select a medium that allows them to best show what they know and want to make sure their teacher and peers fully understand the points they are trying to make. Jeanette also capitalizes on her students' interest in sharing their work with peers. "The pattern in my class," she explains, "is create, present, discuss." Repeated opportunities for students to explain their work—the "present and discuss" phases of this pattern—help students clarify their ideas. As they do so, Jeanette collects rich data on the progress of their thinking. During the "creation" phase, she informally observes student work, asks questions, and makes suggestions in regard to process and content. Observation and questioning also help her decide what kinds of "mini-lessons" need to be taught. If, for instance, students are struggling with a particular kind of source, Jeanette can plan for instruction directed at helping them better analyze or use the source. Similarly, she can identify other sources that might clarify a point, raise a new question, or present a different perspective. This kind of formative assessment is a crucial part of historical inquiry. No teacher can predict all the different turns an in-depth inquiry might take. Without careful monitoring of these turns, students can become frustrated and lose interest. Careful observation allows teachers to better anticipate students' needs and better scaffold their engagement with history.

The presentation and discussion phases are just as important as the creation phase in Jeanette's classroom. Once the students have a product—some form of historical interpretation or analysis—the opportunity to present that product to peers encourages more careful attention to the quality of the product. This only works, however, if presenters receive substantive feedback on their presentations and audience members have a reason to take the presentation seriously. Jeanette organizes presentations to maximize audience participation and provide useful feedback to presenters. "I always give them something to listen for," she explains. "Sometimes we put together an evaluation guide; sometimes we just list things on the board. But we always have something to focus on—to make sure they show their peers respect—for the work, of course, but for them as people, too." As students listen to their peers' presentations, they take notes. These notes, in turn, form the basis for follow-up discussion. During the discussion, the presenters are experts—they are expected to respond to questions, clarify points, and suggest places where further information might be located. In turn, they receive written feedback on their presentation from their peers (see Figure 11.2). This feedback includes commentary on content and presentation style. Students discuss appropriate ways to offer and receive feedback, and Jeanette monitors and models both. In this way, assessment in the classroom becomes part of an ongoing, substantive conversation in which teacher and students work together to build shared understandings of the past.

*Students need to learn the social forms for engaging in reasoned discussion.*

*Bickmore (2015b, 2017)*

*Formative assessment helps teachers plan for and with their students.*

*Larson & Kieper (2007)*

| Criteria for Presentation | Evaluation of Presentation |
|---|---|
| Connects to our unit of study | |
| Clearly communicates the content | |
| Provides interesting, accurate, and relevant details | |
| Identifies sources | |
| Keeps the audience's attention in positive ways | |

**FIGURE 11.2  Peer feedback form.**

## CONCLUSIONS

One of the functions of historical thinking is to help students make informed and reasoned decisions that promote personal as well as public good. When individuals begin to make such decisions, they are less likely to become the objects of manipulation and more likely to shape their own lives with dignity and respect for others. Individual decisions, however, are not made in a vacuum. In contemporary U.S. culture, students often see violence modeled as a primary means of solving conflicts and problem-solving rejected in favor of self-centered competition. It is not always easy or comfortable to alter these patterns, but we think it is worth the effort. If, as we argued in Chapter 1, history is fundamentally controversial, then we have an obligation to help our students recognize and respond intelligently to controversy. If, in addition, democracy is based on a conflictual model of decision-making, and if many of our public conflicts have historic roots, it becomes even more important to help students better understand how those conflicts played out historically and how students might participate in discussions about them. Finally, if exercising historical agency is embedded in how we respond not just to conflict but to peacemaking, then we have another powerful argument for encouraging our students not just to analyze conflicts but also to take reasoned and deliberate action to shape the future in respectful and, hopefully, peaceful collaboration with others.

This chapter focused on several related aspects of historical thinking—recognizing the impact of conflict, compromise, consensus, resistance, and justice-seeking in shaping historical agency. In Dehea's class, these aspects were dealt with in the context of a social studies thematic unit on *community* (see Chapter 9 for more detail on this unit). To help her students understand the impact of conflict and consensus in their community,

Historical agency influences how we respond to conflict, compromise, and consensus.

**146**

she explicitly related public conflict management to classroom protocols. Her emphasis on metacognition—establishing metaphors to describe tasks, modeling procedures, and then asking students to analyze them, thinking aloud with students as they outlined the parameters of a "good argument"—provided cognitive touchstones for students new to inquiry into contentious issues. In addition, because the class focused on those issues in the local community, where they could interview relevant people, write to local officials, and survey participants in decision-making, her students were initiated into the role of civic participant by participating in reasoned discussions. Not only did they learn that other people have historic agency, but they also practiced being responsible historical and civic agents themselves.

In each of the classrooms in this chapter, reflective inquiry helped students establish the significance of historic events and the impact of individual and collective agency—social participation—on the ways conflicts are managed. Although not every current or historic controversy requires such extensive treatment in the classroom, some issue, contention, or question lies at the heart of all historic inquiry. With no controversies, no questions to be resolved, and no perspectives to be understood, history is a lifeless thing—able to tell us little about how to live in harmony with others or seek justice in an interdependent, complex world full of difficult challenges that rarely result in broad consensus. In contrast, participation in communities of historical inquiry encourages students' willingness to engage in reasoned discussion with diverse others, proffers tools for sharing public spaces, and, at its best, offers hope even in difficult times.

# 12

## In My Opinion, It Could Happen Again

## How Attitudes and Beliefs Have Changed over Time

Throughout the year, Amy Leigh draws her fourth graders' attention to how ideas, attitudes, values, and beliefs have changed over time. Near the beginning of the year, for example, the class investigates changes in names. After talking about their own first names, students collect information on names in their own, their parents', and their grandparents' generations in order to analyze historical trends: Which names have become more or less common, how the length of names has changed, and how reasons for choosing names have varied. Students work in groups to record and analyze the data they collect, and they make presentations on their findings to the rest of the class. Afterward, they visit a nearby cemetery to collect information on names further back in time, and they read books about naming traditions in the United States and around the world.

Later in the year, Amy begins a unit on how social relations have changed over time. The class reads and discusses several works of children's literature that focus on attitudes, both in history and today, toward differences in race, gender, religion, or sexuality, such as Olugbemisola Rhuday-Perkovich's *Someday is Now: Clara Luper and the 1958 Oklahoma City Sit-in*; Rob Sanders' *Stonewall: A Building. An Uprising. A Revolution*; and Asma Mobin-Uddn's *My Name is Bilal*. Students respond through simulated journals, written dialogues, and other activities. Throughout this unit, Amy's focus is on the way people treat those who are different than themselves and the attitudes that underlie such treatment.

Later in the year, during a unit on life in Colonial America, students study the Salem witch trials. Amy begins by explaining how villagers' religious beliefs and their ideas about work and community influenced their attitudes toward each other. Over the next two weeks, students take on the roles of villagers and plan a simulated trial of a woman accused of witchcraft. Students have to plan their actions and statements based on the beliefs of people at the time. Jurors and witnesses decide what evidence would have been convincing to people at the time, not to people today.

Being able to recognize the perspective of people in the past is a requirement for meaningful historical understanding. To understand why people acted as they did, it's necessary to be familiar with the societal context that shaped their thoughts. Without examining the ideas, attitudes, values, and beliefs of people in history, their actions have no meaning. The institutionalization of racial slavery in British North America, for example, can only be understood with reference to Europeans' creation of ideas about differences between themselves and Africans, and the loss of Natives' land by reference to Europeans' use of ideas about what constituted civilization. This kind of perspective recognition requires understanding that the views of people in history may have been different than our own; we cannot explain the actions of a medieval serf or lord, an eighteenth-century Japanese merchant, or a Texas farm woman in 1890 by pretending that they're all just like us. Their worldviews, mentalities, and ideologies were different than those of people today, and

> Historical thinking involves understanding the perspectives of people in the past. *Barton & Levstik (2004)*

> *Dunbar-Ortiz (2014), Jennings (1975), Jordan (1968), Kendi (2016)*

DOI: 10.4324/9781003179658-12

those differences have to be taken into account—otherwise their actions may just seem irrational. Without understanding Salem villagers' attitudes toward God, the Devil, work, and community, for example, the practice of dunking people in water to determine whether they were witches looks like a flaw in logic. Most of us agree that there are no witches and that, even if there were, dunking them in water wouldn't prove much; if we apply our standards to Salem villagers, then, they all appear to be mentally defective.

And in fact, children often think precisely that until they have studied the perspectives of people in the past in more depth. We have emphasized that students come to school already knowing some things about how material life has changed over time. They quickly recognize historic clothes and technology, for example, and can put them in a relatively accurate chronological sequence. But students' understanding of changes in ideas is less sophisticated. They do know some things about the topic: They often recognize that people had different attitudes toward women and minorities in the past, and they may have learned that European settlers didn't consider Native peoples their equals. But rarely have they had the opportunity to see these attitudes as part of a larger system of beliefs—one different from their own. Instead, they tend to think of them as idiosyncratic and inexplicable mistakes, and they generally conclude that people in the past weren't as smart as we are. By consistently asking students to think about how people saw things differently in the past, though, Amy helps them develop a more complex understanding of how ideas have changed over time.

> Understanding people in the past means recognizing how they saw the world.

> Many children know that attitudes toward race and gender were different in the past. *Barton (2008)*

## CHANGES IN NAMES

Students' belief that people in the past were stupid often is striking. While reading *Immigrant Kids*, for example, students in Tina Reynolds's class (Chapter 5) began to discuss how people at the time washed their clothes; some thought they washed them in sinks because there were no washing machines, but one student was certain that there were indeed washing machines then—but that people were too stupid to use them! Clothing styles often inspired similar comments. For example, Tina found that students sometimes asserted that people long ago knew they were dressing "old fashioned" and realized that someday people would start doing things the right way. And in doing their family history projects, several students brought in their parents' high school yearbooks. "Why did they dress so nerdy?" they all wanted to know. The tendency of people in the past to wear such obviously unattractive clothes led several students to conclude that "they must not have known it was picture day." Never having systematically explored how ideas change over time, students had no way to explain older fashions other than outright ignorance.

> *Freedman (1980)*

> Children sometimes assume that people in the past were not as intelligent as people today. *Barton (2008), Levstik & Henderson (2016)*

Without understanding that people in the past did not consider themselves stupid or old fashioned, it's difficult to understand much about history. If students think that people would have used washing machines if someone had just shown them how, or would have dressed differently if they had known how bad they looked, then studying the past must appear as an exercise in futility; all it shows is that people needed to be shaken until they got some sense. Fortunately, Amy has found it easy to move students beyond their initial belief in historical stupidity and to help them recognize that people in the past considered themselves normal, not old fashioned—that they saw things from a different perspective than we do. The "Names Project" is the way she introduces students to this aspect of historical understanding.

Amy began the unit by reading *The Name Jar*, about a Korean newcomer who fears her classmates won't be able to pronounce her name and decides to change it—until she learns its significance and embraces it as part of her identity. Amy asked students about their own names: Have any of you ever wished you could change your name? Do any of you have nicknames? Do you know how you got your name? Their responses were passionate: They could barely stay in their seats, they were so excited about sharing what they knew about their names, whether they liked them, and what they wished they had been named. For homework, students had to find out three additional facts about their names—such

> *Choi (2003)*

> Literature and personal connections provide introductions to the study of historical topics.

as who they were named after or what other choices their parents considered—and share these in class the next day. They then used this information as the basis for essays that became part of their writing portfolios.

Having developed their interest in the topic, Amy later moved on to the more specifically historical aspects of the project. She asked whether they thought there were some names people used in the past that weren't common anymore, and most students could easily think of several—Gladys, Thelma, Lula, and so on. They also thought there were some names that were common now—Maykayla, Madison, Chloe—that weren't used in the past, although they were less sure of their examples. Noting that most of their suggestions were women's names, Amy asked whether they thought women's names had changed more over time than men's. Although again, they weren't sure, they thought they probably had. They began to investigate some of these questions more systematically by entering their own names and those of their family members into a Social Security website that displays changes in name popularity (https://www.ssa.gov/oact/babynames/rankchange .html), and Amy modeled how to read and interpret the bar graphs generated there. Before the end of the lesson, Amy asked whether they thought the reasons names were chosen were different in the past. Students were interested in the reasons for their own names, but most had no firm opinion on how those reasons may have changed over time; a few suggested that more people were named after family members a long time ago.

Amy then introduced students to an assignment that would allow them to investigate these questions in their own families. She gave each student a data collection sheet (Figure 12.1) on which they were to collect information on the names found in their generation, their parents', and their grandparents'. The next day, after giving students time to talk about what they had discovered, she divided them into groups and gave each group one of the following questions to answer:

- How have the reasons for men's names changed over time?
- How have the reasons for women's names changed over time?
- Are there some men's names that are found in only one generation or in all generations?
- Are there some women's names that are found in only one generation or in all generations?
- Have men's names gotten longer or shorter?
- Have women's names gotten longer or shorter?

Students can use mathematical procedures to draw historical conclusions.

Over the next week, students worked in groups to use their data sheets to answer these questions and design displays to communicate their findings.

The inquiry-oriented aspects of this project are obvious. But what does it have to do with recognizing the perspective of people in the past? This project did, in fact, go a long way toward helping students overcome their assumptions about the lack of intelligence long ago. As they were working on their projects, students frequently commented on some of the more unusual names they found, particularly in their grandparents' generation: "*Vivian*, I like that name," or "*LeRoy*, I *know* nobody's named that anymore!" Whenever such comments arose, Amy asked why they thought those names weren't used anymore. Students' initial responses sometimes reflected their previous idea that people didn't know any better: "You wouldn't want to have a really cute boy and name him *LeRoy*, or a really cute girl and name her *Mildred*." One student even suggested that people a long time ago weren't educated enough to be able to say all the letters of the alphabet, and thus couldn't pronounce all the names we can. But almost as soon as students made such suggestions, other students corrected them by pointing out that the names didn't sound funny back then, and that they sounded perfectly normal or even "high tone"—and other students quickly agreed.

Perhaps because the topic was a simple one such as names, or perhaps because the people being studied were their parents and grandparents, students began to understand that some things change because fashion changes and not because people in the past couldn't see how stupid they were. After this project, whenever anyone in the class mentioned how unusual or perplexing something in history seemed, other students could be counted on to interject, "But it wouldn't seem that way to *them*, it just seems that way to us because

**Names**

| Yours (you, siblings, cousins) | Your parents' (parents, aunts, uncles) | Your grandparents' (grandparents, great aunts/uncles) |
| --- | --- | --- |
| Name_____ | Name_____ | Name_____ |
| Reason chosen: | Reason chosen: | Reason chosen: |
| ___ liked the sound | ___ liked the sound | ___ liked the sound |
| ___ named after relative | ___ named after relative | ___ named after relative |
| ___ famous person | ___ famous person | ___ famous person |
| ___ unknown | ___ unknown | ___ unknown |
| ___ other _____ | ___ other _____ | ___ other _____ |
| Name_____ | Name_____ | Name_____ |
| Reason chosen: | Reason chosen: | Reason chosen: |
| ___ liked the sound | ___ liked the sound | ___ liked the sound |
| ___ named after relative | ___ named after relative | ___ named after relative |
| ___ famous person | ___ famous person | ___ famous person |
| ___ unknown | ___ unknown | ___ unknown |
| ___ other _____ | ___ other _____ | ___ other _____ |
| Name_____ | Name_____ | Name_____ |
| Reason chosen: | Reason chosen: | Reason chosen: |
| ___ liked the sound | ___ liked the sound | ___ liked the sound |
| ___ named after relative | ___ named after relative | ___ named after relative |
| ___ famous person | ___ famous person | ___ famous person |
| ___ unknown | ___ unknown | ___ unknown |
| ___ other _____ | ___ other _____ | ___ other _____ |
| Name_____ | Name_____ | Name_____ |
| Reason chosen: | Reason chosen: | Reason chosen: |
| ___ liked the sound | ___ liked the sound | ___ liked the sound |
| ___ named after relative | ___ named after relative | ___ named after relative |
| ___ famous person | ___ famous person | ___ famous person |
| ___ unknown | ___ unknown | ___ unknown |
| ___ other _____ | ___ other _____ | ___ other _____ |

**FIGURE 12.1  Data collection chart.**

we're not used to it." Moreover, students were very conscious, and even proud, of their change in understanding: They knew they hadn't quite gotten it before, and now they did. In addition to all the benefits of the process of historical inquiry, then, this project helped students begin to see how their perspective differed from people in the past—a fundamental characteristic of historical understanding.

*Students can understand that the perspectives of people in the past differed from their own.*

## CHANGES IN SOCIAL RELATIONS

There are, of course, more serious changes in perspective over time. Some of the most important involve the way people treat those who are different than themselves: Attitudes toward differences in race, religion, and gender have been responsible for many of history's most enduring and dramatic struggles. As noted in Chapter 8, however, none of Amy's students chose to investigate changes in social relations during their "History Museum" projects. Instead, they focused on aspects of everyday life they knew best—toys, clothes, cars, and so on. Amy knew that it would be her responsibility to expand students' understanding of changing perspectives on social relations, and for this, she relied primarily on children's literature.

Amy began this unit by asking students if any of them had ever wanted to do something and not been allowed. They all had examples, and Amy listed these on the board, along with the reasons they had been given for not being able to do what they wanted. She then asked which reasons they thought were fair and which ones weren't. Most students saw that some reasons were fair even if they disagreed with them—not being able to have a slumber party until the same age as a sister, for example, or not being allowed to ride a motorbike because of the danger. Others they considered clearly unfair: One boy said that his parents wouldn't let him stay overnight at his friend's house because he lived in a public housing project, and one girl pointed out that school rules prevented her from wearing box braids.

Amy had meant to spend this entire first lesson simply exploring the concepts of *fair* and *unfair* treatment and talking about how attitudes may influence people's treatment of each other. In the middle of the discussion, though, one student noted, "Hey, this sounds like prejudice and discrimination!" Several other students agreed with her, and Amy made the most of the opportunity—asking them if they knew of any times in history when people had been treated unfairly. One girl had recently read *Number the Stars* and *When Hitler Stole Pink Rabbit*, and she explained how Jews had been treated unfairly "during the war." Another mentioned slaves being treated unfairly because of "their color." Yet another student had read *Journey to Topaz* and explained that "the China people were treated bad just like the Jews." Students did not simply consider these issues a thing of the past: They knew many examples, both from personal experience and from the media, of racial and sexual discrimination in the present. The Black Lives Matter and #MeToo movements had been in the news, and although students did not have an in-depth understanding of these issues, they clearly recognized that they were related to discrimination.

This discussion indicates just how much historical knowledge children have. By fourth grade, many of them have encountered the topic of enslavement while learning about Harriet Tubman and have heard words such as *prejudice* and *discrimination* when studying Rosa Parks or Martin Luther King, Jr. Sources outside formal instruction provide an even wider range of information. Students often read historical fiction on their own, and the girl who had just read *Number the Stars* wasn't the only one who had heard about the Holocaust. Children sometimes also learn from their relatives, or other adults outside of school, about how women and minoritized communities were treated differently in the past. This information is often lacking in context and elaboration, and students will benefit from learning that it was Japanese Americans (not "the China people") who were sent to internment camps, and that both internment and the Holocaust happened in the 1940s during World War II. The fact that children already are familiar with both the concept of prejudice and specific historical examples, though, makes it easier for them to examine new information on the topic.

Over the next few weeks, Amy read aloud a variety of pictures books about people treated differently because of their race, gender, religion, or a combination of these—books such as *Ron's Big Mission* and *A Ride to Remember* (about racial segregation in the 1950s and 1960s); *The Blessing Cup* and *All the Lights in the Night* (about Jews fleeing persecution in czarist Russia); *The Bracelet* and *Baseball Saved Us* (about the internment of Japanese Americans during World War II); and *Marching with Aunt Susan* and *She was the First! The Trailblazing Life of Shirley Chisholm* (about women political leaders). Amy wanted students to achieve two main things during this unit: To understand the attitudes and beliefs that lead to unfair treatment and to explain some of the ways people respond to such treatment.

In discussing patterns of discrimination, students often were inclined to attribute attitudes solely to personal characteristics. Sometimes, for example, they assumed that men in the past were "bossy" or Whites were "mean," and that's why they discriminated against

Personal experience can provide an introduction to historical topics.

Lowry (1990), Kerr (1971), Uchida (1985)

Students often recognize that prejudice and discrimination are contemporary problems.

Students have learned about history from school, relatives, the media, and their own reading. Barton (2008)

Blue & Naden (2009), Langley (2020), Polacco (2013), A. Levine (1991), Uchida (1993), Mochizuki (1993), Murphy (2011), Russell-Brown (2020)

women or minorities. ("They didn't want to do anything around the house," as one student put it.) As a result, their initial response to most of the books was indignation: They were angry that anyone would mistreat others because of their race, religion, or gender. Amy encouraged them in their judgments about how wrong such actions were, but at first, she worried their moral responses were so strong, and so focused on individuals, that they were failing genuinely to take the perspective of people in the past. She realized that she needed to help students understand that people's actions derived from larger patterns of discrimination that justified the belief that women should be confined to the home, that Blacks were inferior, or that Japanese Americans couldn't be trusted. She also had to help them understand that there are always social circumstances that either enable or constrain action. Many of the activities she had planned for the class asked students to put themselves in the place of participants in these episodes and to make decisions about what they would have done—whether they would have tried to hide Jewish children in their homes during World War II, for example. At first students saw no reason to think they would have done otherwise (and frequently imagined themselves endowed with supernatural powers, able to hide every Jewish child in France or to lead all the slaves to freedom). They argued that people were stupid not to know that everyone is the same, and they were sure they wouldn't have been that stupid if they were around then.

Such responses were similar to students' reaction to names such as Mildred—why didn't they know any better? Rather than indicating a reversion to this earlier inability to understand the motivations of people in the past, Amy ultimately decided that they represented students' way of distancing themselves from the beliefs they were studying: They seemed to need this certainty to demonstrate their own moral and ethical sensibility. Once they got past their initial discussions, students demonstrated a more sophisticated inclination to understand the perspective of people in history. After reading *Butterfly* (about a French family hiding Jews during World War II), for example, students worked in pairs to complete decision charts (see Figure 12.2) that listed the reasons for and against hiding Jewish families. Although all students ultimately decided they would have done so, they gave much more complicated reasons than they had initially, and they were careful to explain why they thought the benefits outweighed the potential dangers. Rather than seeing it as an obvious decision that no rational person could avoid, they came to consider it a complicated one that would have been difficult to make. Similarly, all the girls in the class were, at first, convinced that they too would have been an advocate for women's rights in the nineteenth century; on further reflection, however, some realized that their own attitudes

*See also Bardige (1988) and Levstik (1986)*

*Polacco (2000)*

Decision charts allow students to record reasons for and against a course of action. *Alvermann (1991)*

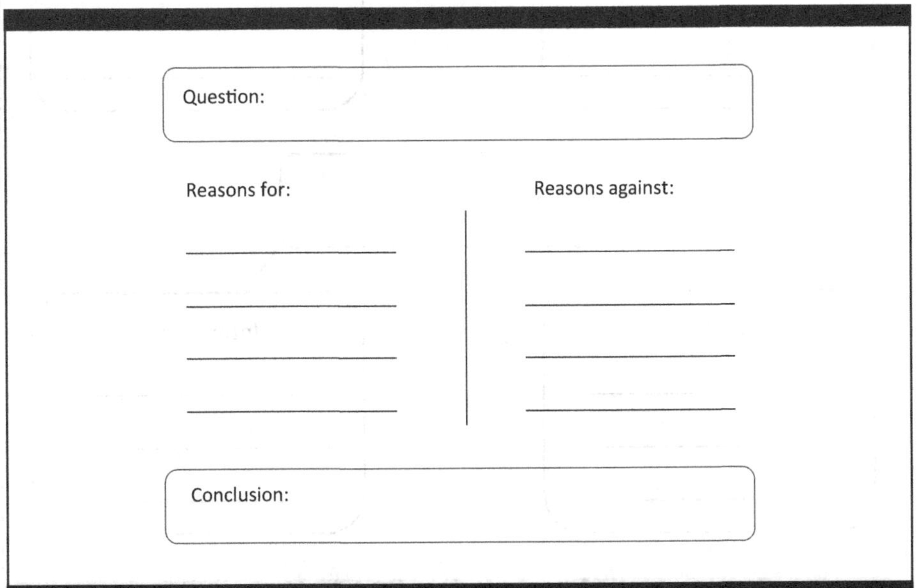

Question:

Reasons for:

Reasons against:

_____          _____

_____          _____

_____          _____

_____          _____

Conclusion:

**FIGURE 12.2 Decision chart.**

as women might have been different then. As one girl said, "If it were *me* going back in time, I would have fought for women's rights, but if I had been a woman *then*, I might have been too afraid of what people would think."

Amy also made sure that students were exposed to the variety of ways that people can respond to mistreatment. She wanted them to understand that there was no single response to difficult circumstances and no simple way of solving such problems. The books she read about the Holocaust, for example, included examples of people who went into hiding (*I Will Come Back for You*), who took part in the resistance (*The Cats in Krasinski Square*), and who relied on faith and tradition to sustain themselves and their communities (*The Secret Seder*). In addition, she called attention to how those who are not the direct victims of mistreatment can respond, whether by risking their own safety (*Butterfly* and *The Grand Mosque of Paris: A Story of How Muslims Rescued Jews during the Holocaust*), or in another context, publicly showing their support for others (*Teammates*, about Pee Wee Reese's support of Jackie Robinson in the face of racist abuse). She wanted students to recognize that even in difficult situations, people have agency: They can make choices about whether to go along with prevailing opinion, or to stand up to it in ways that their resources and abilities permit. This is a critical aspect of historical understanding, and it is also an essential characteristic of informed civic participation.

Amy's use of graphic organizers was an important part of helping students think about these issues in more sophisticated ways. After reading *Teammates*, for example, students were assigned to write a simulated journal entry from the perspective of either Robinson or Reese. Before having them do that, though, she had them complete character webs for each teammate (see Figure 12.3). Students had to take these characteristics into account in their writing. Rather than simply a knee-jerk response, they had to try to make their journals reflective of the traits they had identified. The webs, then, helped clarify how they could write from someone's perspective other than their own. Similarly, before writing a dialogue between Japanese American parents discussing how to respond when government agents were sent to detain them, students had to identify their goals, the information

*Russo (2011), Hesse (2004), Rappaport (2005)*

*Polacco (2013), Ruelle (2009), Golenbock (1990)*

*Agency* includes willingness and ability to act on the choices they make. Barton (2012), Levstik (2014a)

In simulated journals, students write diary-type entries from the perspective of people in history.

On character webs, students record information on traits such as goals, background, personality, and relationships.

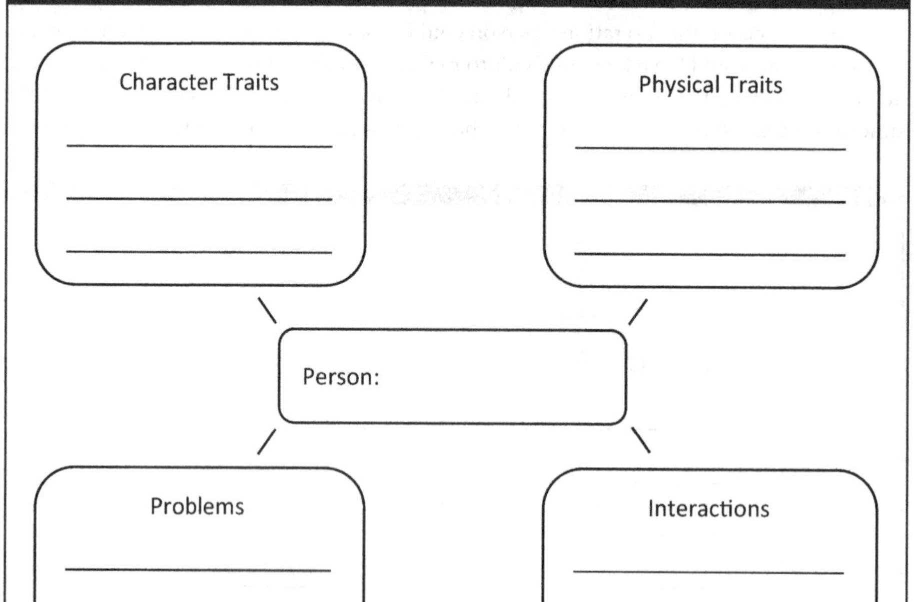

**FIGURE 12.3  Character web.**

they had, and how circumstances affected their options. Instead of thinking that any sensible person would have started a violent confrontation (as they were at first sure they would have done themselves), they understood why many Japanese Americans might have gone along peacefully in the hopes that matters would be resolved fairly. It was the graphic organizers that Amy used that required students to stop, think, and organize what they knew instead of leaping to unhistorical conclusions.

These response activities demonstrate how teachers can use children's literature effectively. Although many schools now buy trade books for use in classrooms, teachers often are at a loss as to what students can do with them, and they often turn to commercial publishers or online sources for worksheets to accompany many well-known trade books. These materials, though, often focus on low-level comprehension tasks and may lead students to dislike good literature as much as they dislike textbooks. In Amy's class, by contrast, students consider the content of what they read: They read literature to learn about themselves and the world. When the students have read the same book, she has them write dialogues, perform skits, or write simulated journals—all activities in which they take what they have learned and extend their understanding by putting it in a new form. During their independent reading, students keep a dialogue journal in which they respond to the work. Because students often aren't sure what to write when journal assignments are completely unstructured, many teachers assign focused but open-ended questions for students to use in formulating their responses. Rhoda Coleman, for example, assigns students to choose from among the following questions after reading each chapter:

- What is your reaction to the events and words in this chapter?
- What questions do you have for the author or characters?
- What would you want to say to the author or characters?
- What predictions can you make about what will happen next?
- How does this chapter relate to your own experience?

Unlike commercial worksheets, Amy's and Rhoda's activities help students understand what it means to engage with literature in authentic ways. When people read, they don't sit down and fill in blanks: They think about what they're reading—why an author wrote something the way she did, why a character acts in a particular way, and how the reading relates to their own experiences. Students learn that reading is a way to grapple with issues that are significant and meaningful not a prelude to easily graded school exercises.

This unit also encouraged students to see history itself as significant. We have sometimes heard people express hesitation at "exposing" young children to topics such as the Holocaust or enslavement out of concern that they are too innocent to learn about such violence. It's true that prolonged and detailed exposure to graphic elements of historical tragedies such as the Holocaust can be traumatic for some children, but few teachers take such an approach in elementary school. Instead, they hope to provide an initial awareness of events so that students can explore them in more detail in later years. In addition, compared with the violence students see every day in the media, children's literature is quite tame. What most students have not been exposed to, though, is what motivates people to mistreat others or what could be done to prevent such behavior. Without the kind of reflection Amy provides, students may come to think of violence as natural and inevitable. In this unit, though, they see that people make decisions about their actions: They choose to mistreat others, or they choose to condemn or resist such mistreatment. Informed by this understanding, students are much better equipped to make their own decisions in the future.

## CHOOSING PERSPECTIVE ACTIVITIES

Amy was careful about the kinds of perspectives she asked students to take, because not all such activities are acceptable in the classroom. On the one hand, to understand history,

*In written dialogues, students work in pairs to create an imaginary conversation between two historical characters.*

*Graphic organizers can lead to more thoughtful written responses.*

*Students read literature to learn about themselves and the world.*

*In dialogue journals, students respond to literature, and teachers respond to students' observations.*

*Open-ended questions can stimulate students' responses in dialogue journals.*

*Authentic responses to literature call for an engagement with content.*

*Schweber (2008)*

*History can help children analyze contemporary social issues.*

**155**

students must be able to recognize the perspectives of people in the past—their values, attitudes, ideas, and beliefs—and imagining how people thought and felt is a particularly effective way of doing that. Rather than seeing others from a distance, attempting to get inside their heads forces students to consider their perspectives more deeply and can help them move beyond the belief that they were "bossy," "mean," or had other personality defects. Often, these activities involve students imagining that they are inhabiting the lives of someone in the past, through simulated journals, dialogues, role plays, and other perspective-taking tasks. Sometimes, however, these activities go wrong—very, very wrong. News reports and social media continually call out teachers who have asked students to engage in perspective activities that are inappropriate, such as re-enacting auctions of enslaved families. Particularly for students who identify with members of oppressed groups, such activities are a form of curriculum violence, and students can be traumatized by being forced not only to imagine but participate in this kind of historical victimization.

How can teachers make use of perspective-taking activities while avoiding these abusive situations? One key distinction is whether the activity focuses directly on a situation of oppression. Any historical topic or period will involve conditions of inequality, but not every lesson will focus on those conditions. For example, in studying the Revolutionary Era, students might imagine the thoughts of a young apprentice deciding whether to join the military; in studying immigration in the nineteenth century, they might imagine how a woman finds community with others who are newly arrived in the country; or in learning about changes in daily life, students might re-enact games or school lessons from the past. These situations are unlikely to send any troubling messages, and no student is likely to be traumatized by participating.

Problems arise, however, when perspective-taking activities center the experience of oppression, and particularly when students are asked to take on the role of oppressors. Many educators seem enamored with simulations in which a class of students is divided by eye color or some other arbitrary characteristic, and one group is encouraged to mistreat the other for a day—purportedly so they will have firsthand experience with discrimination. Activities such as this are unethical. The most problematic re-enactments usually involve students taking part in this kind of oppression—asking them to imagine that they are racists, enslavers, Nazis, and so on, and are engaged in overt acts of cruelty or persecution. These exercises have no place in the classroom and certainly not in elementary or middle school. Encouraging children to behave cruelly, even in a historical simulation, is not part of a teacher's role and can do lasting damage. Let us state this as clearly as we can: Do not ever have students "pretend" to oppress each other. The world is an oppressive enough place already without giving students practice.

But what about activities that focus on the oppressed, rather than the oppressor? This is more complicated, because it depends on the nature of the activity. In some cases, it can be acceptable and appropriate for students to imagine the experiences of those experiencing discrimination, such as when Amy's students wrote a simulated journal from the perspective of Jackie Robinson. In Chapter 13, you will also read about teachers who have students write from the perspective of Africans being enslaved and Native peoples experiencing forced assimilation. These exercises can extend students' understanding and develop their compassion for those who have been victimized. However, teachers must keep three important qualifications in mind if they choose to use such activities:

- It is almost never acceptable to have students *physically* re-enact oppression, such as by simulating an auction of enslaved families, transportation to a concentration camp, or attacks on civil rights protestors. The very physicality of these simulations moves them beyond compassion and perspective into the realm of trauma.
- Asking students who identify as members of an oppressed group even to *imagine* experiencing that oppression should only be done under certain conditions. Teachers must have a thorough understanding of the historical context and must convey that context to students; they must have a clear purpose for the assignment and must explain that to students; and they must have good relationships with students and seek their consent before proceeding.

**156**

Students can be traumatized by perspective activities. *Jones (2020), L. King & Woodson (2016/2017)*

Activities that do not center on oppression are unlikely to create trauma.

Do not have students mistreat others, even as part of a simulation.

Do not have students physically re-enact an experience of oppression.

Asking members of oppressed groups to imagine oppression in history should be done only under certain conditions.

- Conditions of oppression should never be romanticized, such as by having students act out the so-called first Thanksgiving as though it were a pleasant meeting of friendly equals, or having them pretend to be enslaved men and women happily singing songs while picking cotton. These perpetuate historical myths and sweep oppression under the rug.

Do not romanticize oppression.

Clearly, teachers must be cautious about perspective-taking activities that involve oppression, and many such exercises should be avoided. There are two ways, however, that teachers can achieve the benefits of perspective tasks while avoiding their pitfalls. First, activities should highlight the agency of those experiencing oppression. For example, students can create a conversation among enslaved Africans deciding whether and how to join British forces during the American Revolution; a Jewish family discussing how to maintain their religious and cultural identity in czarist Russia or Nazi Germany; a group of civil rights activists planning strategies for a sit-in; children of an activist accompanying her on trips to organize farmworkers. These activities require an understanding of historical context—including values, attitudes, and beliefs—but they emphasize that people throughout history have been resourceful, knowledgeable, and creative individuals who can work against their oppression—a critical lesson for developing students' own civic agency.

Emphasize the agency of people who have been oppressed.

Second, teachers can have students imagine that they are by-standers in historical situations and are witnessing instances of oppression, rather than experiencing them themselves. In Amy's classroom, for example, some students wrote a simulated journal entry from the perspective of Jackie Robinson's teammate Pee Wee Reese, who chose to support Robinson despite the reaction he knew he would get from racist fans, friends, and teammates. Similarly, after reading *Passage to Freedom: The Sugihara Story* (about a Japanese diplomat in Lithuania who issues visas for Jews escaping Nazi persecution, in defiance of his government's orders), students can create a dialogue between Sugihara and his family about how to best help refugees and the risks they would encounter in doing so. Younger children reading *Busing Brewster*, about a Black student facing prejudice (and support) when bussed to a distant school during the 1970s, can imagine what students at the school might take into account as they consider how to make their new classmate feel welcome. These activities also stress agency, not of those experiencing oppression, but of those who may be in a position to do something about it, in large or small ways.

Have students imagine the responses of by-standers witnessing oppression.

*Bryant (2006), Mochizuki (1997)*

*Michelson (2010)*

## SALEM WITCH TRIALS

In studying the Salem witch trials, students encountered a set of beliefs that differed dramatically from their own. Amy began this topic in much the same way that she had the study of social relations. With students sitting on the carpet in the front of the room, she asked if any of them had ever been accused of something they hadn't done. Needless to say, students had a number of examples to volunteer, and the discussion of unfair accusations and how to counter them took up most of the first class. Much of this discussion focused on the reasons a person might be accused and the kinds of evidence that would be necessary to support or refute such accusations.

Personal experiences can provide an introduction to historical topics.

The next day, Amy (herself a descendant of Rebecca Nurse, who was hanged as a witch in Salem in 1692) used children's literature to help students understand witchcraft accusations in seventeenth-century Salem village—*Witches! The Absolutely True Tale of Disaster in Salem, The Salem Witch Trials: An Unsolved Mystery from History*, and selections from *Witch-Hunt: Mysteries of the Salem Witch Trials*. She focused primarily on the villagers' religious beliefs—not only that witches were real but also that idleness indicated a person was possessed by the devil. She also explained how a combination of physical disasters (such as an outbreak of smallpox and the death of livestock) and social tensions (revolving around the local church) made people particularly likely to look for someone on whom to blame their problems. Just as they had during previous lessons, students were eager to condemn these accusations—pointing out that witches don't really exist

*Schanzer (2011), Yolen (2004), Aronson & Anderson (2005)*

**157**

and that being lazy "doesn't mean that the devil is in you." Once again, though, this reaction seemed to be a way of distancing themselves from the people they were studying. After they had demonstrated, to their own satisfaction, how much wiser they were, they were ready to enter more fully into the mindset of Salem villagers—a perspective necessary for the central activity of this unit, the creation of a fictional witchcraft trial. Amy assigned students various roles to play—accused and accusers, prosecutors, defense attorneys, jury members, and witnesses for the prosecution and defense—and gave them general background information on their roles. (Because Amy's purpose was for students to learn about the perspective of people in the past—rather than the evolution of trial procedures—these roles more closely resembled contemporary courtrooms than the proceedings of seventeenth-century trials.)

There was no script for this trial; except for explaining procedures such as who got to call their witnesses first, Amy left the development of the trial to the students. For the next several days, they met in small groups to discuss their roles and what they entailed. Jury members decided what kinds of evidence they would listen for, witnesses wrote depositions on their knowledge of the accused, and attorneys planned their strategies. Of course, Amy was hardly idle during this time. She constantly met with students to help them perfect their plans. Through their discussions with her and their reading of the primary, secondary, and other sources she had provided, students largely were able to separate their contemporary perspectives from those of people at the time. For example, jury members decided that they would look for marks on the body of the accused, while defense attorneys prepared the accused to recite the Lord's Prayer as evidence of her innocence.

The trial itself was a big hit; several months later, most students said it was their favorite activity of the year. Many did their best to dress the part—judges wore black sweats to approximate robes—and several students used what they knew about the language of the time (with the occasional lapse, as when the defense attorney asked a witness why he thought the accused was "a slimeball"). Meanwhile, the accused repeatedly erupted into fits during the trial. Students' enthusiasm and flair notwithstanding, most of their learning had taken place before this point—during the discussion and planning that led up to it. It was while preparing what to say, what to ask, and what to listen for, that students were most actively engaged in learning about the period.

For this kind of activity to be a meaningful learning experience, students must be given responsibility for creating the drama based on their investigation of the issues of the day. If they are simply enacting a predetermined script, they may learn something about acting but will probably gain little insight into the historical period under study. With a script, the story is already in place, the characters and themes already set, and students have nothing to do but play their parts; when they are involved in creating a drama, though, they obviously have a much more active role. Using role play and other forms of drama to play out different interpretations or constructions of events can support recognition of historical perspectives. This demands historical inquiry, as students refine their questions, consult evidence, consider a range of responses, test possibilities, and examine the results. Without such inquiry, they could not have pulled off the performance. They would have had little idea what to say, could not have responded to unanticipated questions, and would not have known where they were going or how to get there.

## LONG-TERM ASSESSMENT OF HISTORICAL SKILLS

As we have emphasized throughout this book, teachers need to assess students' understanding by focusing on the specifically historical aspects of their work. Teachers in Chapters 4–6 emphasized students' understanding of historical concepts such as *causality*, *evidence*, and *significance*. In Chapters 7–9, students grappled with more complicated historical projects, and assessment focused on the soundness of their historical *interpretations*; those projects not only included attention to causality, evidence, and significance but also to students' descriptions of change over time and their use of historically accurate details.

**158**

*Students distance themselves from historical actions they consider unfair.*

*Students can take responsibility for planning dramatic activities. Fines & Verrier (1974)*

*Drama is one of students' favorite activities.*

*Preparing for role play requires learning about the period under study.*

*Effective drama involves students in inquiry. Fines & Verrier (1974)*

*Teachers need to assess the specifically historical aspects of students' work.*

In other chapters, including this one, we have highlighted the importance of another aspect of historical interpretation—*perspective recognition*.

Recognizing the perspective of people different than oneself, like most historical skills, can only be measured along a continuum; it is not a skill students lack one day and possess the next. When district or state curriculum guidelines are written as a series of discrete objectives, it is easy to regard them as a kind of checklist—Monday we'll teach understanding of time, Tuesday we'll do evidence, and Wednesday is perspective recognition. But like most important skills, perspective recognition cannot be taught, practiced, and mastered during a single lesson; it requires sustained attention in a variety of contexts over the course of many lessons, many units, and many years. As adults, for example, we still struggle to understand how people who were perceptive enough to write that "All men are created equal" could enslave others, or how devout Christians could persecute those whose beliefs or practices differed from their own. Assessing students' facility with perspective recognition, then, is not a matter of giving them 18 points out of 20 on a single assignment but of attempting to evaluate their gradual progress toward a complex and difficult component of sophisticated historical understanding.

Assessing such complex skills requires a more long-term approach than is typically found in the content areas, where short-term assignments and tests predominate. The scoring rubric in Figure 12.4 represents one way of thinking about the progress of

*Most historical skills can only be measured along a continuum.*

| Level | Indicators |
|---|---|
| Level 4 Distinguished | Student explains the actions of people in history by reference to the values, attitudes, beliefs, or experiences that were present at the time under study, including the ways they conflicted with each other or caused tensions; connects changes in behavior over time to a variety of interconnected factors, including changing values, beliefs, etc.; uses authentic language characteristics of the time, including slang, colloquialisms, and unusual or uncommon details; compares judgments based on values of the time and those based on contemporary values and suggests reasons for the differences |
| Level 3 Proficient | Student explains the actions of people in history by reference to the values, attitudes, beliefs, or experiences that were present at the time under study; connects changes in behavior over time to changing values, beliefs, etc.; uses language and details characteristic of the time; makes judgments about motivation based on values of the time |
| Level 2 Developing | Student recognizes historical differences in values, attitudes, beliefs, and experiences but does not completely connect those to changing behaviors; uses some language and details characteristic of the time, along with some anachronisms; makes judgments based on present day values but recognizes that people in the past may not have shared those values |
| Level 1 Novice | Student explains the actions of people in history by reference to their own values, attitudes, beliefs, or experiences; does not explain why people in the past acted differently than people in the present; uses language or other details characteristic of the present; makes judgments about motivation based on present-day values |

**FIGURE 12.4  Long-term rubric for perspective recognition.**

students' recognition of historical perspectives. Like the rubric in Chapter 9, it is not used to evaluate individual assignments (although it might be adapted for that purpose). On the contrary, a variety of individual assignments can be used to provide evidence for a student's location on the rubric. Amy's goal over the course of the year is for her students to move into at least the "Proficient" category. To assess whether they have done so, she gathers evidence from all the relevant assignments they have done—the "Names" project, literature response activities, the Salem witch trial re-enactment, and so on. This evidence includes anecdotal records, graded assignments, and portfolio entries. The result of all this is not the assessment of an assignment but the assessment of a student; it takes the form not of a numerical average but of a narrative report on that student's historical understanding.

The use of a long-term process like this illustrates another important characteristic of assessment—its ability to extend over more than one school year. Although schools have not traditionally put a premium on cross-grade organization and communication, many educators are aware of the need to coordinate students' experiences over a number of years. For example, some schools are experimenting with "looping," in which teachers change grades each year so they can stay with the same group of students as they progress through two or more levels. (We know one teacher who keeps the same set of students from Kindergarten through Grade 8.) Other schools have divided faculty into instructional teams that work together to guide students' learning across grades; although individual teachers may continue to have the same grade level each year, they take joint responsibility for a single group of students as they move through primary, intermediate, or secondary school. In both models, teachers report the advantages of getting to know students better and of having a more developed sense of their prior academic progress. A long-term rubric, such as that in Figure 12.4, can help add continuity to such efforts. If such rubrics are used by all teachers in a team—from Grade 4–Grade 6, for example, or Grade 6–Grade 8, depending on school and team structures—teachers can develop a more consistent set of expectations for students' achievement and track their progress over more than a single year. Teachers consistently report that the joint development of such scoring guidelines helps them more clearly think through what they expect out of students.

*Assessment should extend over more than a single school year.*

*Cross-grade school organization allows teachers to develop long-term relationships with students and better insights into their achievements.*

## EXTENSIONS

Throughout this chapter, we have emphasized the importance of helping students gain insight into the perspectives of people in the past. Dramatic activities, simulated journals, and other responses to historical literature are particularly useful in involving students in deeper interactions with history, and these can easily be extended to a wide range of historical topics, events, and people. Although it is not always necessary to use literature as a starting point for role playing, it does have some advantages. First, literature generally attempts to get inside the head of characters, and readers come to understand at least some of the ideas and emotions that motivated people in the past. In addition, historical literature often incorporates personal idiosyncrasies that enrich characterization.

*Literature highlights the ideas and motivations of people in history. O'Brien (1998)*

*Fleischman (2013)*

For instance, Paul Fleischman's *Bull Run* consists of a series of monologues representing different perspectives on the Battle of Bull Run. A Southern officer recalls the first shots at Fort Sumter, a young boy tells of signing on as a drummer because he is too young to be a soldier, a Minnesota woman laments her father's harshness that sent her brother to war, and another young man signs on with the Confederacy because the army promises him a horse. This book naturally lends itself to dramatic presentation. In Dee Hallau's fifth-grade class, for example, she asks students to role play characters from Fleischman's book. "These are people who never met each other," she tells her class. "Given what you have read about each of them, what might they say to each other? What questions might they ask each other? What questions would you want to ask them?" Three students are selected and assigned roles. They come to the front of the room and sit at a table where they can see each other and be seen by their classmates. Dee asks the rest of the class to write questions on index cards for the characters. She shuffles these, along with several questions she has written out, and then serves as moderator of the ensuing role play.

Note that students are not simply asked to "act like" a particular character. Instead, they are given a specific problem to resolve as they think their character would have responded. They are allowed to refer back to the book, but few of the questions can be answered only by reference to Fleischman's novel. Instead, they have to think about what motivated a particular person and, given the time and circumstances, how that person might have answered questions such as "If you had it to do over again, would you still join the Confederacy/Union?" or "How much do you think enslavement had to do with this war?" As the students respond from their characters' perspectives, Dee periodically stops and asks the class if they think a particular response is supportable, given their reading of the book, and students are encouraged to give each other suggestions. In addition, Dee occasionally switches role players so that most students have an opportunity both to ask questions and take on the perspective of one of the book's characters.

*Students use what they know about specific characters to respond to questions.*

Some teachers also use historical round tables, in which students take on the roles of specific individuals from history and other students serve as reporters who interview them. One round table discussion might focus on the Birmingham Children's Crusade of 1963 and include interviews with children, parents, political leaders, school officials, the police chief, and the mayor. Students could investigate the personal and political goals that motivated each of these individuals, the practical concerns that restrained their actions, and the courses of action they chose. Such round tables can also be organized around themes rather than specific events; one such round table might involve dialogue about independence movements among Gandhi (India), Jinah (Pakistan), Louverture (Haiti), Bolivar (South America), and Sam Adams (United States). Just as in the Salem witch trial drama, students would need a thorough understanding of diverse viewpoints to be able to carry out these projects.

*In historical round tables, students take on the roles of specific individuals from history.*

## CONCLUSIONS

Understanding the perspectives of people in the past is a fundamental aspect of historical understanding, yet students often have given the topic little thought—assuming, for example, that people were too stupid to know better than to mistreat others or give their children names such as Mildred. But by reading and discussing literature, making comparisons to their own experiences, and engaging in response activities, such as simulated journals, written dialogues, and drama, students can come to understand the ideas, attitudes, and beliefs that underlay the actions of people in the past and can begin to see them as part of a larger social context.

Such a program of study is not merely an academic exercise but an important means to help students see history as meaningful and relevant. People still face the kinds of problems described in this chapter—how to treat people from different backgrounds, how to help victims of discrimination, how to prevent exploitation. Focusing on the motivations and circumstances that influence such decisions helps students see history not as inevitable but as subject to human reason, and to see the *study* of history as a way to apply reason to contemporary problems. Many of Amy's students, in fact, drew precisely that conclusion: They thought people studied history so they would know what not to do in the future. They consistently pointed out that history was worth studying so that they would know not to mistreat Blacks, women, Jews, or newcomers to the country. Although some elementary students have a limited perception of contemporary racism, prejudice, and discrimination, others know from the media or their own experiences that these are indeed enduring issues in society. When asked whether she thought people's attitudes were different today than in the past, for example, one sixth-grade girl in a racially mixed urban area—whose class had been reading literature on the Holocaust—pointed to the skinheads, Klan, and "other kooks" in her neighborhood and concluded that not much had changed. "In my opinion," she said, "It could happen again."

*Focusing on attitudes and beliefs calls attention to the enduring human dilemmas at the core of historical study.*

**161**

Of course, not everyone we disagree with is a kook. Reasonable people can differ on many important issues—immigration or health care policy, limits to free speech, zoning regulations, and so on. Having different opinions does not always mean that one view is correct and others are ill-informed, selfish, or downright malicious. Often, conflicting perspectives arise when people see problems through different lenses, and this can lead them to assess costs and benefits of solutions differently. People who are genuinely concerned with meeting the needs of individuals experiencing housing insecurity, for example, may differ in their assumptions about the relative importance of job opportunities, affordable housing, personal circumstances, and individual choice and preferences. Such differences of opinion often arise from divergent social backgrounds or experiences. Learning about how perspectives differ may prevent students from rushing to judgment as soon as they encounter unfamiliar viewpoints.

On the other hand, some perspectives really are ill-informed, or informed by motives that are selfish or downright malicious. Some people have no interest in working toward just solutions to social problems; they may only want to make sure they gain the most rewards for themselves. Other people aim to perpetuate the privileges of their race, nation, religion, class, or gender. And many are unwilling to consider evidence or reasoned arguments. Once we hear the reasoning behind a viewpoint, we may choose to reject it as unworthy of public discussion. Participating in the public life of a democracy does not require that we accept all views as equally legitimate. There is no reason to engage sympathetically with claims that school shootings have not occurred, that violence toward racial or religious minorities is justified, or that those with differing gender expressions or sexual orientations are unworthy of dignity and respect. History can help us see where such views come from, and such knowledge can be useful when arguing against them. Learning about undemocratic views does not, however, mean accepting or encouraging them.

# 13

# Nosotros La Gente

## Honesty and Diversity in U.S. History

After reviewing the changes in the Virginia colony that led to new attempts to exploit labor, Rebecca Valbuena asks her fifth graders what they think of when they hear the word *slave*. Many of them have clear but fairly simple ideas, which Rebecca records on a chart—"they were whipped," "Black," "they had no freedom," "it was a long time ago," "they were always in chains." She explains that they are going to find out which of their ideas are correct and which they need to add to or change. After recording a list of their questions about enslavement on another chart, she selects several students to perform Readers' Theater scripts derived from firsthand accounts of the First, Middle, and Final Passages of enslavement. After reading each selection, students brainstorm words to describe what enslaved people might have heard, seen, and touched as well as what they might have said or felt. They then use these words and ideas to write poems describing the experiences of enslavement.

Over the course of this unit, students engage in several activities designed to extend and refine their understanding of enslavement. In their second lesson, for example, they work in groups to develop a list of basic *human rights*—they suggest such things as privacy, speech, feelings, religion, clean air, nature, life, freedom, being safe outside, and "being yourself." Rebecca then shows them examples of slave codes from colonial Virginia; students compare these restrictions to their own list of rights and analyze why enslavers considered such measures important and how these contributed to systematic oppression. The class concludes this lesson by discussing contemporary examples of violations of human rights. Some students' families come from Guatemala and El Salvador and can supply examples from those countries, while others make comparisons to what they have learned at school about the Civil Rights Movement, to media reports of the treatment of immigrants at the nation's borders, or to their knowledge of topics such as child abuse and sexual abuse.

\* \* \*

Rhoda Coleman's fifth graders begin their study of the nineteenth-century colonization of the U.S. West by reading two selections from their basal series—one a collection of tall tales popular among White settlers, the other a set of first-person accounts by Native peoples about the loss of their land. Earlier in the year, the class had studied the cultures of several Indigenous groups, as well as the earliest contacts between Europeans and Native peoples, so most students readily contribute to a Venn diagram comparing the experiences of Native peoples and settlers. Later, Rhoda leads the class in beginning a KWL chart on this period of history—recording what they know already and what they want to know.

At the beginning of this unit, Rhoda reads aloud several original source descriptions of this period. Yankton Sioux author and activist Zitkala-Ša, for example, wrote several accounts of her life growing up in South Dakota and attending a missionary boarding school, and portions of these

DOI: 10.4324/9781003179658-13

are collected into the children's book *Red Bird Sings*. Similarly, Waheenee-wea's memories of her life in a Hidatsa village are compiled in *Buffalo Bird Girl*, while *Dandelions* is the story of a White girl moving to the Nebraska Territory with her family. Working in groups of three, students develop a list of problems these individuals faced—either those they have just read about or others they know about or can imagine. Rhoda then asks several students to be on the "Hot Seat"—to come to the front of the room to portray different people during the period and to respond to questions from their classmates about their experiences. Later, students write letters home from the perspectives of Native children sent to boarding school or settler children who have moved with their families—in each case, detailing where they are, what their hopes are, and what they think and feel. Over the next weeks, students will continue to investigate a variety of books, internet sources, and original accounts to create simulated journals from the perspective of people during this period.

Many teachers cannot study whatever topics they or their students consider important: They don't have the option of exploring the Holocaust, Japanese American internment, the Salem witch trials, or family history. Particularly at fifth and eighth grades, when most states require U.S. history, teachers are expected to cover events that schools have traditionally identified as major events in the nation's past—European explorers, colonial life, creation of the U.S. Constitution, the Civil War, and so on. These expectations are not unreasonable, and we certainly hope that by the end of the middle grades, students will know about such topics. In the two classrooms profiled in this chapter, Rebecca Valbuena and Rhoda Coleman help students learn about two of the most important topics in U.S. history: The enslavement of Africans and the dispossession of Native lands by White settlers.

> "Covering" content does not lead to in-depth understanding.

> Textbooks are difficult to comprehend. *Beck & McKeown (1991), Berkeley et al. (2012)*

> Textbooks are particularly difficult for English Learners. *C. Brown (2007)*

Unfortunately, studying the content traditionally found in required curricula often means adopting a narrow range of perspectives and using unimaginative forms of instruction. These tendencies are amplified when instruction revolves around textbooks, which rarely present conflicting experiences or explore the contemporary relevance of historical events. Proceeding through a textbook also frequently leads to simple "coverage" of content and little in-depth understanding by students. Textbooks contain barriers to comprehension, and in classrooms like Rhoda's and Rebecca's—where few students speak English as a native language—textbooks in isolation would be practically unintelligible. Furthermore, because most of their students come from families who have immigrated to the United States only recently, the relevance of Jamestown or colonization of the West will need more explicit attention. Few textbooks make it clear to a 10-year-old Tongan girl in Los Angeles what the encounter between Native peoples and settlers has to do with her own life in the present.

> Literature and original sources develop students' understanding of the past.

Rhoda's and Rebecca's teaching shows how theory- and research-based methods of instruction can help students understand the content that too frequently is only "covered," and their approaches reflect important principles of history education. During the year, both Rebecca and Rhoda divide instruction into units that closely match their state's curriculum framework. However, neither relies primarily on textbooks, nor do they value the simple coverage of information or amassing of facts. Instead, both Rebecca and Rhoda rely on literature and original sources to develop students' understanding of the past. In addition, they devote systematic attention to aspects of U.S. history that are frequently ignored: The multiple and often conflicting experiences of diverse groups of people, and the agency of those involved in past events. For their students, most of whose families have immigrated only recently from Mexico, Central America, Southeast Asia, or the Pacific Islands, America's history really does become a story of *Nosotros La Gente* (We the People): They study the experiences, thoughts, and actions of real people, and they learn about the diversity that has been—and continues to be—part of the nation's history.

## DIVERSITY IN U.S. HISTORY

> America has always been diverse. *Dunbar-Ortiz (2014), Kendi & Blain (2021), Ortiz (2018), Takaki (2008)*

North America has always consisted of differing populations, and the United States has been culturally, racially, and religiously diverse since its inception as a nation. Before the first European explorers arrived, Indigenous inhabitants of the Americas were part of numerous autonomous and sovereign groups, spoke many different languages, and displayed an enormous range of cultural variation—as they still do. Once colonizers arrived, the variety of people increased: Scandinavian, Dutch, German, Spanish, English, French, and Scottish settlers populated the East Coast and interior waterways, while enslaved Africans further added to the population. By the mid- and late-1800s, immigrants from Ireland, China, Japan, and elsewhere had moved to many parts of the country, while millions of Mexicans became U.S. residents after the Mexican-American War. Immigration from Central America, the Caribbean, Asia, the Pacific Islands, and, indeed, every region of the world continues to add to one of the country's greatest strengths—its diversity.

*Diversity is one of the greatest strengths of the United States.*

Learning U.S. history requires understanding the role of each of these groups in the nation's past and present. Colonists and settlers did not simply take over unoccupied lands: They interacted with, and ultimately dispossessed, Native peoples who already lived there, and this involved a long process of trade, warfare, and political negotiation, all of which were central to the experience of Indigenous and non-Indigenous people throughout the periods covered in the curriculum. Economic development of the Colonies and the United States, meanwhile, depended on the exploitation of enslaved Africans, and later, on labor extracted from people of many racial and ethnic backgrounds. Maintaining this system of White supremacy required an elaborate set of legal institutions and social practices, and this, too, has been central to the experience of Americans throughout much of the nation's history. And, of course, women as well as men also have always been part of this experience: Farming, giving birth, doing housework, working in factories, operating businesses, becoming professionals, leading political movements, and all the other activities that have produced contemporary society. Without understanding the experiences of all these segments of the population, students cannot really understand the nation's past—or its present.

*Students must understand the experiences of all people in the nation's past.*

Children often fail to see this diversity in history and instead think of the past as a matter of simple and linear development, with everyone alive at a time living in similar ways. For example, they often think that all people in the Colonial Era lived in log cabins or that everyone in the 1800s dressed in formal clothes. Such perceptions are hardly surprising, given that students are rarely exposed to differences within a given period. Teachers like Rhoda and Rebecca, on the other hand, emphasize not just understanding people in the past but understanding *different* people. In studying colonial Williamsburg, for example, students learn about the lifestyles of the rich, poor, and "middling" segments of the population and about different roles for men and women. In learning about the American Revolution, they conduct debates between Patriots and Loyalists and write editorials from each viewpoint, as well as explore the effect of the war on women, Indigenous peoples, and those who were enslaved. When teachers consistently emphasize diverse experiences, it becomes a basic part of students' understanding. In examining pictures from colonial Boston, for example, students in Rebecca's classroom quickly noted the presence of Blacks, the different kinds of work done by men and women, and the variety of economic classes depicted. Similarly, students reading about settler experiences during colonization of the West in Rhoda's class often stopped to point out how Native peoples would have viewed events differently—noting, for example, that what the settlers called a "new home" was already someone else's home. These are the kinds of observations we typically hear only from students who have been taught to look for such differences.

*Students often fail to recognize diversity in history.*

*Students can learn to see diversity and conflicting perspectives as a basic characteristic of history.*

Most schools these days devote some attention to diversity in the nation's past, yet these attempts can suffer from several problems. As in Rhoda's classroom, students throughout the country learn about the life of Indigenous populations at the time of contact with Europeans. However, units on "Native American life" often reinforce stereotypes, convey misinformation, and send degrading messages about the humanity of Native peoples. Simplified stereotypes of generic "Indians"—usually headdress-wearing, horse-riding warriors who lived in tipis—are so pervasive in popular culture that teachers must work hard to help students develop more complete and differentiated understandings. Unfortunately, some widely circulated classroom materials depict all Native

*The study of "Native American Life" often reinforces stereotypes.*

*Smith (2009)*

**165**

peoples as sharing similar cultures; these include worksheets that purport to be about "Native American picture writing" or stories that claim to be "Native American legends." Teachers must avoid materials like these, which give the impression that Indigenous peoples of North America shared a single culture. Fortunately, most classroom resources these days (especially in the upper elementary grades) attend to at least a few examples of Native peoples, such as those who lived in the Southwest, Plains, Eastern Woodlands, Northwest Coast, and so on, and this can help students begin to understand the variety of Native life. Studying more specific Native peoples—Navajo, Cherokee, Choctaw, Sioux, and so on—provides an even better understanding of the rich diversity of Indigenous peoples.

Even when teaching about the variety of Native peoples in the past, however, schools may convey pernicious stereotypes. If students only learn about features of life such as clothing or homes, they may come away believing that all Native groups, despite their cultural diversity, led simple and uncomplicated lives: Woodland Indians were simple people who lived in wigwams, Plains Indians were simple people who lived in tipis, Northwest Indians were simple people who lived in longhouses. Many Indigenous communities were indeed small and relatively non-hierarchical, and they used natural resources carefully. Many others, though, were large settlements (sometimes with thousands or tens of thousands of inhabitants), often with complicated forms of agricultural production, extensive trade networks, and complex political structures. European colonists encountered not just a variety of simple people who happened to differ in culture but a daunting range of societies, often more sophisticated than the European ones with which they were familiar. Many settlers, in fact, lived near Native people who were more prosperous and more socially organized than they themselves were. Unless schools help students understand the complexity of historic Native peoples, they reinforce the false idea that they were more "primitive" than Europeans—and they implicitly justify colonialism as inevitable.

A related problem is the pattern of teaching about Native peoples and other groups only during certain periods: Indigenous people at the time of the first European settlement and the later colonization of the West, Blacks during enslavement and the Civil Rights Movement, Asian Americans during Japanese American internment, women during suffrage. This sends the message that these groups were important only when they played a prominent role in political events, rather than recognizing that their experiences always have been part of the nation's history. If women and non-Whites remain on the margins of the curriculum, then interactions and connections of diverse people in the nation's past will remain unclear. A meaningful understanding of U.S. history requires recognizing that, at any given time, the country has consisted of men and women; of people from many different racial and ethnic backgrounds; of those who were rich, poor, and everything in between.

Teachers like Rhoda and Rebecca make it a point to include a variety of experiences and perspectives, regardless of the time or topic they are teaching. Rebecca's students, for example, encounter Black life not just as part of enslavement but also when studying each period in history. This includes learning about well-known Revolutionary Era figures such as Crispus Attucks, Salem Poor, Phyllis Wheatley, and Benjamin Banneker, but also about those whose names and identities have been lost to history, such as Black soldiers who fought as part of Patriot forces and the larger number who fought for the British. In learning about the nineteenth century, they learn about free Black men and women in the North and West, including workers, activists, settlers, and those who came to be known as "Buffalo Soldiers." It is especially important for students to understand that not all Blacks before the Civil War were enslaved and that many made important artistic and intellectual contributions. Thoughtful teachers who cover later periods in history make sure to include Black life when they study the labor movement, sharecropping, urbanization, the Great Migration, the Harlem Renaissance, World War II, and so on.

Limiting the study of Native people to given periods of the past is especially damaging because it reinforces the idea—common among children and even adults—that

**Avoid materials that give the impression that Indigenous peoples shared a single culture.**

*Sabzalian (2019)*

**Many Native societies were large and complex.**

*Dunbar-Ortiz (2014), P. Smith (2009)*

**Portraying Native peoples as simple or "primitive" justifies colonialism.**

*An (2016), Busey & Walker (2017), Journell (2008); Shear et al. (2015)*

**All groups must be included throughout history, not only during certain periods.**

*L. King (2014)*

Indigenous peoples no longer exist in the United States. But of course, this is not true: Well over five million Indigenous Americans live in the country today, many as part of more than 500 federally recognized bands and nations, and around 150 Native languages are still spoken. In addition, Native groups have a status that is unlike that of other Americans, because most are not only U.S. citizens but also members of sovereign nations, with rights that derive from that membership. By law, federally recognized groups have a status equivalent to the U.S. national government and must be treated as nations, not as dependents. Treaties signed between the United States and many of these nations remain in force, even though these binding agreements often have been disregarded, and even though Native peoples must often pursue legal action to enforce them.

The survival of Indigenous peoples into the present means that they cannot appear only in the history portion of the curriculum; students must learn about Native peoples today. Yet this does not mean studying "exotic" cultural practices today in ways similar to learning about Native people who lived 500 years ago. Native peoples—like people anywhere in the world—combine beliefs, languages, practices, and fashions from a range of local, national, and global influences. In addition, although studying "other" cultures in the distant past is appropriate (because 500 years ago, all cultures were different than those today, even if they involve people of the same ethnicity), studying contemporary groups this way positions people as objects to be investigated the way students would examine specimens under a microscope. And crucially, depicting Native peoples as ethnic groups equivalent to any other, or as the "first immigrants," fails to recognize that they are the original inhabitants of North America, with continuing sovereignty and a unique legal status.

Including Native people in the study of life today requires incorporating their voices, perspectives, and experiences into the study of contemporary issues. This means, for example, learning about tribal governance (and treaty rights) as part of civics, alongside content about local, state, and federal institutions. It means learning about Native leaders, such as former Principal Chief of the Cherokee Nation Wilma Mankiller, congresswoman Sharice Davids, Secretary of the Interior Deb Haaland, activists Nathan Phillips and Madonna Thunder Hawk, and many others. Students also should learn about Native efforts to protect the environment, such as their opposition to oil pipelines and other forms of environmental destruction, and their use of ecological knowledge to mitigate the effects of climate change. Outside social studies, students should be reading works by Native authors such as Jo Harjo and Louise Erdrich. In each of these cases, students would be learning *from*, and not simply *about*, Native people, as they encounter ideas about governance, leadership, environmental protection, and the arts. Expanding students' understanding in this way, rather than simplifying and objectifying the lives of Native peoples, should be the goal of the curriculum.

Teachers must also recognize and avoid the many inappropriate, even offensive, ways that Native peoples and cultures often are incorporated in classroom lessons. Having students "dress up" as Native peoples, no matter how authentically (and it's almost never authentic), or create "Native American names" for themselves, does not in any way honor Indigenous groups; it reinforces White supremacy by portraying Native people as objects to be manipulated. Having students make kachinas, sand paintings, or pipes can be just as offensive. These are sacred or ceremonial objects meant to be used by special people in an honored way, and making such objects—sometimes even displaying them—has no place in the classroom. Teachers must also carefully attend to the language they use and that is used in classroom materials. Referring to creation stories as "myths" or "legends," for example, is demeaning, because in Native cultures these are often meant to be actual accounts of the original of natural phenomenon. Students also should not be exposed to offensive words such as *squ\*w* or stereotyped forms of ungrammatical "Tonto talk," which still appear in books and materials used in classrooms. When this language cannot be avoided (such as in historical sources), teachers must discuss the racist origins and societal consequences of using such terms, just as they would if students encountered other ethnic slurs.

Schools often reinforce the perception that Native peoples no longer exist. *Dunbar-Ortiz (2016), Sabzalian (2019), P. Smith (2009)*

Native Americans are members of sovereign nations in addition to being U.S. citizens. *Sabzalian (2019), Shear et al. (2018)*

*U.S. Department of Justice (2020)*

Students must learn about Native peoples in the present.

Studying culture can objectify people. *Sabzalian (2019), P. Smith (2009)*

Native peoples are not just one cultural group among many. *Sabzalian (2019), St. Denis, (2011)*

*National Council for the Social Studies (2018), Sabzalian (2019), Sabzalian et al. (2021) Shear et al. (2018)*

Students should learn from, and not just about, Native peoples. *Sabzalian (2019)*

Teachers must avoid offensive ways of teaching about Native peoples. *Sabzalian (2019)*

Sacred objects should not be art projects. *Hirschfelder & Beamer (2000)*

Do not expose students to offensive language. *Sabzalian (2019)*

## CONFLICT, OPPRESSION, AND AGENCY

Understanding U.S. history means recognizing not only that groups had fundamentally different experiences but also that these frequently came into serious—even violent—conflict, particularly when some groups tried to subjugate, exploit, or oppress others. Not only were Blacks enslaved for hundreds of years, but even after emancipation, they faced widespread political disfranchisement, economic subjugation, legal discrimination, and violence—and each of these continues into the present, with voter suppression, lack of economic opportunities, mass incarceration and its aftermath, and police brutality. Crucially, students must understand that oppression is not simply the result of personal prejudice or the moral failings of individuals. Too often, enslavement and other unjust social practices are portrayed as though they were historical aberrations—exceptions to the nation's story of social progress, or problems that were solved as individuals became more enlightened. Students must understand that racism and other forms of injustice do not lie primarily within individuals but are part of social systems—connected sets of laws, institutional structures, ideological beliefs, and systematic social practices that work together to perpetuate the privilege of those in power.

Blacks are hardly alone in facing such historical and ongoing problems. In addition to dispossession and disease, Native peoples have faced legal restrictions (not even becoming citizens until 1924) and a variety of economic and environmental setbacks, often resulting from intentional government policies. Immigrants and citizens from China and Japan faced pervasive social prejudice and legal restrictions for many years (with internment during World War II just being one consequence), and Asian immigrants and Asian Americans continue to suffer from both the limitations of the "model minority" myth and widespread prejudice and even violence. Those from Mexico and Central America, meanwhile, have faced a long history of lost land; housing, employment, and educational discrimination based on both ethnicity and language; mob violence; and deportation, even when U.S. citizens. The continuing incidence of hate crimes targeting specific groups—including persistent violence against Muslims as well as mass shootings at the Pulse nightclub in 2016, the Tree of Life Synagogue in 2018, and Asian spas in 2021—are recent examples of problems that have existed through the country's history.

Some people don't want students to learn about racism and other forms of oppression in the nation's history, much less in the present. Some politicians have even attempted to prohibit such teaching. No honest, ethical, or professional teacher, however, can omit such harsh realities, regardless of whether such content is required—or prohibited. Lying about the nation's history, even by omission, is just that: Lying. Withholding truths about the nation's complicated and conflicted history robs children of an understanding of how the country and its peoples have evolved, prevents their recognition of the ongoing effects of historical oppression and its modern-day parallels, and undermines their ability to engage in civic action to promote the common good. For students who identify with members of oppressed and marginalized groups, concealing this information amounts to denial of their very identity, as they are forced to spend a decade or more in institutions that refuse to acknowledge their background. Teachers cannot be complicit in this erasure: They must tell the truth about the past, even when it disturbs some people—and it is usually less disturbing to children than to adults who are invested in White supremacy and narrow forms of patriotism. Teaching history cannot be limited to a story in which it appears that everyone agreed with each other in a kind of happy consensus, free of exploitation, repression, or conflict.

Teachers also need to understand that excluding diverse experiences does not always take place in an overt way. One of the most significant problems with the way U.S. history is taught lies in the pervasive pattern of centering the perspectives and experiences of oppressors and thus ignoring, normalizing, or justifying that oppression. At one time, for example, it was common to treat enslavement as though it were an inevitable response to economic development in the colonies, and even to portray it as a benevolent institution that benefitted the enslaved. This approach is no longer as common (although it has

### Margin notes

*Alexander (2020), Kendi (2016), Rothstein (2018)*

*K. D. Brown & Brown (2010), Wills (2019)*

Racism is a societal system and not just personal prejudice.

*Dunbar-Ortiz (2014), McKinley & Brayboy (2006)*

*Lee (2016), Wu (2015)*

*Bonilla-Silva (2017), Ortiz (2018)*

Discrimination and violence have existed throughout U.S. history.

Some people are opposed to teaching the truth about oppression in U.S. history.

Omitting information on oppression is unethical.

Understanding oppression is essential for democratic civic participation.

Teaching the truth about history may be disturbing.

Focusing on oppressors justifies oppression. *Calderon (2014), McKinley & Brayboy (2006), Sabzalian (2019)*

not disappeared), but a similar perspective still underlies treatment of Native peoples in the curriculum. The unit that Rhoda teaches on colonization of the U.S. West, for example, is typically referred to as "Western Expansion" or "the Westward Movement." Not only do such units focus almost entirely on the experiences of White (and sometimes Black) settlers, but the very names of these units position students to identify with those who were "moving" and "expanding" and not with those who were being moved *out* and expanded *upon*. Similarly, studying White pioneers and settlers in state and local communities encourages a narrow form of identification that not only portrays a single racial group as the core of "Americanness" but obscures their impact on Native people and others. To the extent that Indigenous peoples are part of such lessons at all, they may be portrayed as either helpers to White settlers, or their opponents—but rarely as subjects of their own histories. Overcoming this pattern means centering the perspectives of diverse people rather than seeing them solely as contributors to White history or as its victims.

Being honest about differing experiences in the past, however, does not mean simply reversing the traditional story of U.S. history by portraying it as the story of victimization rather than noble conquest. Doing so reinforces the perception that there is a single story out there—one in which women, minorities, and the poor play a generally subordinate and inferior (albeit sympathetic) role. Teachers are sometimes shocked, for example, when Black students appear uninterested in hearing about enslavement: "It's their history, so why aren't they proud of it?" teachers ask. They're not proud of it because enslavement and segregation often are the only times Blacks show up in school history; it's hard to be proud of your past when you only encounter it in the context of someone beating up your forebears. Portraying people as victims—without choice, control, or initiative—is neither historically nor pedagogically sound. Students need to understand that throughout the nation's history, Blacks, Asian Americans, Indigenous people, people of Mexican and Central American ancestry, and others have actively fought against injustices aimed at themselves and others. Just as importantly, teachers must avoid simplifying and romanticizing groups of people. Portraying all Native peoples as spiritually advanced or environmentally conscious, for example, or all civil rights activists as educated and upstanding paragons of virtue, not only is historically inaccurate but also distances students from the more complicated realities they know from their own lives. If they fail to see people like themselves involved in history, it can also undermine their sense of civic agency.

History teaching, then, must respect the agency of people in the past. U.S. enslavement is one of history's worst violations of human rights, and those enslaved were ruthlessly and cruelly victimized in countless ways. But being honest about victimization in the slave system is different than thinking of individuals solely as victims. Portraying the enslaved as hapless and servile—even when doing so sympathetically—is a caricature that does nothing to illuminate life under enslavement. Despite their lack of political and economic freedoms, enslaved people made lives for themselves—they married, had children, hunted, fished, raised gardens, learned skilled trades, and fought back against the system. Indeed, one of the most fascinating aspects of this period in history is the way people developed vibrant and meaningful traditions under trying circumstances—yet this is not always a part of the way the topic is presented in school.

In Rebecca's class, students learned not only about how enslavement violated human rights but also about how enslaved people adapted and persisted. An important part of the unit, for example, focused on storytelling. Rebecca began by talking about how those who were enslaved had to survive in a challenging environment and how they passed on what they learned to each other and to their children. Students knew that some of the most important ways they themselves learn—schools and reading—weren't available to the enslaved, and Rebecca explained that storytelling fulfilled many of those same purposes. Students read several stories from *The People Could Fly* and other sources and discussed the lessons that each might have been meant to express. They concluded, for example, that one story demonstrated the importance of not telling everything you know—a lesson they thought was as useful today as during enslavement. After learning about the elements of stories and storytelling, students wrote and performed their own stories designed to teach a lesson.

*Calderon (2014), O'Brien (2010), Sabzalian (2019)*

Focus on the perspectives of diverse groups in history.

Oppressed people have not only been victims.

*Busey & Walker (2017)*

*L. King (2020), P. Smith (2009), Woodson (2016)*

Enslaved Africans and their descendants developed vibrant cultural traditions. *Joyner (1984), Mintz & Price (1992), Morgan (2010), L. Levine (2007)*

*Hamilton (1985)*

**169**

These lessons portrayed enslaved people not as stereotypical victims but as creative and insightful human beings—people who gained wisdom from their experiences and developed sophisticated art forms to convey those lessons. Through their own experience writing and performing stories, students saw just how difficult that was: They had to structure a story to teach a meaningful lesson, follow appropriate conventions, and learn techniques of performance. Finding out how much work and creativity was involved in such artistic products helped students see the richness and complexity of life during enslavement rather than perpetuating their initial stereotypes of people who were "always in chains." One student even pointed to this as his favorite activity during the year: "It was something they did," he pointed out, "and we were doing the same thing."

Learning about the culture of Indigenous groups may seem to address this concern with agency by focusing on how various groups have lived (assuming that these portrayals are not oversimplified or relegated only to the past). However, focusing exclusively on the idea of culture can obscure the agency and even intelligence of Native peoples. Sometimes cultures are presented as though they are simply differing preferences; it may even seem as though culture exists outside of the people who are part of them, as though they are at the mercy of unreflective beliefs over which they have no control. But elements of culture, such as clothing, home construction, agriculture, and hunting (including resource management), do not simply reflect differing preferences or random variation. The idea that "everyone has a culture" (or worse, other people have culture, while "we" do things the normal way) obscures the fact that many elements of culture represent ingenious adaptations to social and natural environments. As we have noted, students tend to think of lives that are different than their own—whether historical or contemporary—as deficient. Even when studying Indigenous peoples of the Americas in the distant past, students need to understand that hunting with bows and arrows, traveling in kayaks, using plants to treat illnesses, and building pueblos from stone, adobe, and wood, were impressive technological achievements.

## MAKING HUMAN SENSE OF HISTORY

Although textbooks and curriculum guidelines are typically organized around events—wars and battles, political changes, migrations—learning history requires understanding *people* in their historical contexts. What decisions did people make in the past, and how were those affected by their goals, beliefs, and circumstances? These are the questions that historians study, and for anyone who is not part of the academic discipline, the importance of people in history is even more pronounced. Stories of courage, heroism, or simple endurance are more likely to strike a responsive chord than the analysis of political or legal affairs in history. Without the emphasis on people, history would be an abstract—and not particularly interesting—subject.

In the past three chapters, we have drawn attention to the importance of helping students make *human sense* of history, particularly through various forms of narrative, and Rebecca's and Rhoda's classrooms show how this approach can be applied to a variety of topics. Just as in Amy's classroom (Chapter 12), many of their activities require students to use what they have learned to imagine the lives and thoughts of historical actors. After reading accounts of enslavement, for example, Rebecca's students wrote "I Am" poems, in which they used a basic outline (Figure 13.1) to explain what people might have heard, seen, felt, and so on. The examples in Figure 13.2 show how students were able to draw conclusions not only about the physical environment in which enslaved people found themselves but also about how those circumstances affected their thoughts and feelings.

Rhoda's "Hot Seat" activity is an advanced form of role-playing. After students discussed accounts of Natives and Whites in the nineteenth century U.S. West, several of them took on the roles of people at the time and answered questions about their feelings, motivations, and hardships. In doing so, they not only had to demonstrate their

Students should see enslaved people not just as victims but as creative and insightful human beings.

Native ways of life reflected creativity and intelligence. *Sabzalian (2019)*

For a description of this kind of study, see *Levstik et al. (2014)*.

People make history interesting.

*Rosenzweig & Thelen (1998)*

In "I Am" poems, students explain what people in history may have heard, seen, felt, and thought.

In a "Hot Seat," students answer questions from the perspective of people in history.

I am _____

I wonder _____

I hear _____

I see _____

I want _____

I am _____


I pretend _____

I feel _____

I touch _____

I worry _____

I cry _____

I am _____


I understand _____

I say _____

I dream _____

**FIGURE 13.1  "I Am..." poem outline.**

I am African
I wonder what is going to happen
I hear whipping
I see White people
I want to go home
I am very sad

I pretend to be with my family
I feel very worried and confused
I touch my irons
I worry about my family
I cry because I'm very sad
I am miserable

I understand nothing
I say, Is this happening?
I dream about my home in Africa
        by Anglea

I am an African
I wonder if I'll ever go back home
I hear the cries of relatives
I see those evil people
I want my freedom
I am a slave

I pretend it's not so bad though it is
I feel really miserable without my people
I touch nothing but chains
I worry for my family
I cry for the wooziness I feel
I am a prisoner

I understand not a word they say
I say, You are the most hideous thing on Earth
I dream that one day I'll have freedom
        by Genoveve

**FIGURE 13.2  "I Am..." poems.**

understanding of the circumstances of these events but also had to consider how these would have affected people's lives. One of the main assignments for this unit, meanwhile, was for students to develop a simulated journal written from the perspective of someone moving West to settle, or a Native child sent to a boarding school; these journals had to contain information on people, places, and hardships as well as the writer's reaction to these. Again, this assignment required that students understand not only the factual content of the unit but also how people reacted to their circumstances.

In a simulated journal, students write about events from the perspective of an individual in history.

**171**

These perspective recognition assignments are a basic feature of instruction for most historical topics in Rhoda's and Rebecca's classrooms. In studying life during the Colonial Era, for example, students wrote broadsides announcing the availability of apprenticeships; in doing so, they had to decide how to persuade a young, seventeenth-century city-dweller to take on the position. (Phrases included, "Dost thou need room and board?" and "Come hither to learn silversmithing.") In another assignment, they took the perspective of supporters of Anne Hutchison and wrote letters explaining why she should not be prosecuted for her religious beliefs. And in studying the American Revolution, students wrote journals from the point of view of British soldiers stationed in Boston; created a colonial newspaper with news items, editorials, and interviews; and conducted debates between Patriots and Loyalists.

The "I Am" poems in Figure 13.2 show the seriousness and passion with which students approached such assignments. In both classrooms, students consistently pointed to these kinds of perspective recognition activities as one of the primary reasons they enjoyed studying history. Several noted that they hadn't liked history in previous years, when they were just reading about it from a book or writing about it on paper; what they liked, as one girl pointed out, was acting things out—pretending to be people in the past. A classmate agreed: "It gives you a chance to be in their places—how did it feel, like the real thing."

As we have noted, historical fiction is a particularly effective way to help students recognize the perspective of people in the past. Fiction is inherently subjective in nature; it invites readers to understand the mindset of the characters they read about. It is important to understand, however, that perspective recognition activities are not simply exercises in creative writing, nor is their purpose to instill some vague sense of sympathy for people in the past; their purpose is to develop historical understanding, and therefore, they must be based on evidence. Without emphasizing the role of evidence, such activities might amount to little more than asking students to imagine that they're elephants; because an elephant doesn't have human thoughts and feelings, anything students create is equally valid—there are no clear criteria for judging whether a student really recognizes the perspective of an elephant. People, however, can explain what they're thinking, and they leave behind both direct and indirect evidence of their ideas; these expressions of their perspectives form the basis for historical interpretations.

Both Rhoda and Rebecca connect their perspective recognition activities to original historical sources. Rebecca, for example, had students write their "I Am" poems after having read and discussed firsthand accounts of Africans describing enslavement; in another lesson, students used advertisements for the return of those who had escaped enslavement to make inferences about their lives—concluding, for example, that because advertisements sometimes noted that an individual could read, most probably could not. Similarly, Rhoda's students based their "Hot Seat" role play on literature derived from sources written by people who were alive at the time and directly experienced the events that they were studying, such as *Dandelions*; *Buffalo Bird Girl: A Hidatsa Story*; *Red Bird Sings: The Story of Zitkala-Ša, Native American Author, Musician, and Activist*; *Black Elk's Vision: A Lakota Story*; *Red Cloud: A Lakota Story of War and Surrender*; and *Wounded Knee: An Indian History of the American West*.

Students' own experiences often provide a valid basis for attempting to imagine the thoughts and feelings of people in the past. Despite all the differences in worldview and experience between a Mexican American 10-year-old today and a West African adult in the 1600s, their feelings about being separated from their families probably have some important similarities. At the same time, though, teachers must stress that part of the reason for such perspective activities is to understand how attitudes are both similar and different across time and place—and that these conclusions must be based on evidence. When Rhoda asked students how Native peoples felt about forced assimilation or dispossession of land, they initially reacted with their own intuitive judgments—"sad," "mad"—but she consistently directed their attention back to the primary sources they had been reading—"What did they *say* they felt?" she asked. When missionaries cut Zitkala-Ša's

Students usually enjoy activities in which they explore the perspective of people in the past.

Historical perspective recognition depends on evidence.

Original sources can provide insight into the perspectives of people in the past.

D. Brown (1993), Bunting (2001), Capaldi & Pearce (2011), Nelson (2010, 2012, 2017)

Students' own experiences can help them recognize the perspective of people in the past.

Historical perspective recognition helps students make connections to people from different times and places.

**172**

hair—a practice that her people normally used only for mourners and defeated warriors—her feelings went beyond being "sad." Upon losing her hair, she wrote,

> I lost my spirit. Since the day I was taken from my mother I had suffered extreme indignities. People had stared at me. I had been tossed about in the air like a wooden puppet. And now my long hair was shingled like a coward's! In my anguish I moaned for my mother, but no one came to comfort me. Not a soul reasoned quietly with me, as my own mother used to do; for now I was only one of many little animals driven by a herder.

*Zitkala-Ša (1900, p. 187)*

An original passage such as this not only expands students' understanding of the nuance and complexity of human emotions but helps them place those emotions in their social and cultural context. Having their own hair cut may seem unimportant, but Zitkala-Ša's memoir illustrates why a Yankton Sioux girl, who had experienced a string of indignities, would be so anguished that she describes the event as having caused her to lose her spirit. Students will not always be able to separate their own contemporary perspectives from those of people in the past, but using historical sources can expand students' views in order to recognize different perspectives.

## DEVELOPING KNOWLEDGE

Like many teachers, both Rhoda and Rebecca had several students who were English learners as well as several who came from other countries. It's important not to conflate these two groups. Some immigrants are proficient in English. Those from India, Nigeria, Jamaica, and other countries may have learned it as their first language, even if their wording and pronunciation differ from those of their U.S. teachers. At the same time, some students who are born in the United States grow up in households where English is not the primary language, especially if their parents moved here shortly before they were born. Teachers must be sensitive to both cultural and linguistic characteristics of their students, without mistaking these for being the same thing. Some students need to develop their English skills, some need to become familiar with U.S. cultural and historical contexts, and some need to do both.

*Not all students from other countries are English language learners.*

*Not all English learners are from other countries.*

This combination of cultural and linguistic elements means that teachers always must pay attention to three tasks: Teaching content, teaching language, and teaching how to complete tasks. In previous chapters, we've stressed strategies for developing language—giving students rich opportunities to read, write, speak, and listen; providing feedback on English usage; and modeling academic language. In a later section, we return to the topic of assessing students' knowledge of historical content. In this section, we focus on building and developing knowledge. This is important for all students, but it takes on heightened significance for those from differing cultural and linguistic backgrounds.

*Teachers must help students with content, language, and assignments. Cruz & Thornton (2013), Short (1998)*

Because of students' diverse backgrounds, neither Rhoda nor Rebecca could be sure of what prior knowledge they had that would help them make sense of distant events in U.S. history, so they saw their first task as helping students develop networks of understanding that would allow them to put topics such as enslavement and the colonization of the West into context. An important step was activating what students already knew. Rebecca, for example, recorded students' ideas about enslaved people on a web in the front of the classroom; Rhoda listed what students knew about the colonization of the West on a KWL chart. They did not limit such exercises to the beginning of new units, however; they also frequently structured individual lessons around students' prior knowledge—as, for example, when Rebecca had students develop a list of what they considered basic human rights before introducing slave codes and then had them compare this to what they knew about contemporary human rights violations. Beginning lessons and units this way activated students' prior knowledge—it reminded them of what they already knew. Students from other countries almost always have understandings that will help them make sense of what they learn in school, but the connections may not be obvious unless teachers attempt to uncover students' ideas.

*A web (also known as a semantic map) shows relations among concepts and ideas.*

*Teachers can support students in drawing from their diverse funds of knowledge. Salinas et al. (2006)*

*Discussion, KWL charts, and webs activate students' prior knowledge. Duke & Bennett-Armistead (2003), Duke & Pearson (2009)*

**173**

Activities that activate prior knowledge provide insight into students' understanding.

Activities such as webbing and KWL charts also have a purpose beyond activating prior knowledge: They give teachers insight into what they need to address in upcoming lessons and how much attention to devote to various aspects of the topic. Sometimes it becomes clear that students have already learned a great deal about a topic from relatives, the media, or their own reading. In Chapter 12, for example, we saw how Amy discovered that her students were already so familiar with the concept of *prejudice* that some of the introductory content she had planned was unnecessary. Other times, students' knowledge is inaccurate or—more frequently—incomplete, and webs and KWL charts alert teachers to the information they need to address in upcoming lessons. A teacher might not know ahead of time that students think enslaved people were always kept chained to each other, yet if she didn't address that misconception, students would have trouble understanding the topic. Because she had students web out their ideas, Rebecca knew that she would have to include more information (especially visual images) on daily life in upcoming lessons.

Teachers accept students' ideas as approximations. *Pappas et al. (2005)*

During activities such as webbing, teachers must accept students' ideas as approximations of more sophisticated understandings. Most of us are tempted to correct students when they say something inaccurate, but no one modifies their conceptual understanding just because someone tells them they're wrong. At best, they may place what they hear in school in a separate category of "school knowledge" unrelated to what they really know. If school knowledge conflicts with the understanding students have gained elsewhere, they will believe it only if they can confirm it through new experiences. In Rebecca's classroom, reading firsthand accounts and looking at pictures of the daily life of enslaved families provided new evidence about whether they were always kept in chains, and this gave students the chance to modify their understanding.

Students modify their understanding based on new experiences.

Webs and KWL charts can help students see how their understanding has changed.

Accepting students' ideas and recording them on webs and KWL charts also provides students a chance to reflect on their knowledge, and this kind of metacognition is an important element of preparing them for a life of civic participation. Too often, people make decisions based on limited or inaccurate knowledge, and they may not ever pause to ask themselves if they know enough or if their ideas are well-grounded. In the classroom, such reflection requires that exercises in which students reflect on their knowledge—such as webs and KWL charts—be used throughout a unit. When Rebecca's class returned to their web, for example, they were quick to point out that they had been mistaken about enslaved people always being kept in chains. They were not only willing but even eager to point out their previous mistakes: They were proud that they knew more than they did before. If, on the other hand, Rebecca had simply told students, "No, enslaved people weren't always kept in chains, so I'm not going to write that on the web," she would have transformed an activity aimed at building knowledge into nothing more than a pre-test of factual details. Not only would students have learned little, but they also might have stopped contributing to the discussion.

Students can reflect on the reasons for what they know and don't know. *Sabzalian (2019)*

Having students reflect on what they know—and don't know—also can help them better understand the larger societal context of knowledge. This is a crucial aspect of learning history and of being prepared for civic participation. Rhoda's students, for example, realized that their initial ideas about White settlers were both more detailed and more accurate than those about Native peoples. This led to a discussion of why that was, as they reflected on likely sources of their information (and misinformation), including cartoons, movies, and other elements of popular culture. And critically, they discussed *why* these sources might distort or omit some kinds of information and what the consequences of those choices were. As one student said, "I can't believe I didn't know about boarding schools for Indians before. That's a pretty important thing to know about."

Students may know abstract words without understanding the concepts they refer to.

Another important aspect of helping students develop knowledge is *concept development*. Some students may be familiar with words for abstract concepts—*independence, religion, society*, and so on—but they may not fully understand the ideas those words refer to. English learners may have even less idea what abstract terms mean, because these are not usually part of everyday conversation. Looking up definitions, however, would do nothing to help them understand these ideas. In preparing to study the American Revolution, for example, Rebecca knew that students would have to understand the concept of *rebellion*; as a result, she devoted an entire lesson to exploring the topic. She read examples of people who had been dissatisfied with something and had taken action, as well as examples of people who had not taken action; the class discussed the similarities and differences among the examples, constructed a Venn diagram comparing them, and worked in groups to develop their own definitions of *rebellion*. Finally, they took events from their own lives and from the news and considered whether they could be classified as examples of rebellion. When they moved into the events leading up to the American Revolution, they frequently had occasion to refer to these discussions. For historical topics to have meaning and relevance, students must have enough conceptual understanding to see how specific topics relate to broader themes and issues. Focusing on the concept of *human rights*, for example, helped students put their study of enslavement into a broader context—one with relevance to many times and places, including their own backgrounds and experiences.

> Students develop concepts by identifying critical attributes through discussion of examples and non-examples. *Larson & Keiper (2007), Parker (1991b)*

> Focusing on *concepts* as well as *topics* makes history more relevant.

## SUPPORTING STUDENTS' LEARNING

Teachers must provide students with the structure they need to be successful. Creative and stimulating lessons sometimes fall apart when students begin independent or group assignments—hands fly up, and the room is filled with cries of, "I don't know what to do!" The most imaginative, stimulating, creative assignments will yield few results if students aren't given the scaffolding to complete them. To build on the enthusiasm that well-designed readings, discussions, and presentations can produce, teachers must help students make the transition to their own work. Having students design colonial newspapers, write "I Am" poems, or perform stories that teach lessons, will not go smoothly unless the teacher shows them how to use what they are learning to complete their assignments. This is especially important for newcomers and English learners, who may have little idea what they're being asked to do. They may come from educational settings in which activity-oriented lessons aren't common, or they may not be able to pick up on the nuances of instructions and assignments.

> Students need structure to be successful with open-ended assignments.

One important means of supporting students is class discussion. Although students may listen or read carefully, they invariably learn more when their interaction with texts is accompanied by discussion with the teacher and other students. Rhoda, for example, stopped frequently while reading to ask questions. Sometimes she simply checked for comprehension, but more often, she aimed to stimulate thoughtful analysis and discussion among students—for example, by asking, "If you were traveling West, or being sent to a boarding school, and you could only take one thing, what would it be?" Some books benefit from uninterrupted reading, but more interactive reading is usually necessary when students are unfamiliar with the content. Especially with historical works, students depend on discussion to help them fully understand the context, to see the connection between events, and to gain insight into the perspectives of the people involved. When English learners in these classrooms were asked what advice they had for teaching history, several said that teachers shouldn't just read something out loud or tell students to read it—they should stop to talk about it so students will understand.

> Discussion promotes interest and develops comprehension. *Altieri (2017), Duke et al. (2012), Pierce & Gilles (1993)*

The collaborative nature of such activities is a critical part of this process. Asking individual students what they know about enslavement or colonization of the West may prompt the response, "Nothing." But when they work together, each student's contribution reminds others of information they can add; often, students don't realize they have relevant knowledge until they hear their classmates' comments. For English language learners, collaboration is often more effective in small groups—two to four students—than as a whole class (at least initially). Many students are hesitant to take risks before the entire class, and teachers sometimes find themselves calling on the same three or four students repeatedly. But working in small groups before coming together as a whole class helps more students contribute; those who are less confident—either of their language abilities or their knowledge—are more likely to take part in class discussion when they have had a chance to try out their ideas in small groups first.

> Collaboration helps students activate prior knowledge.

> Small groups encourage students to take more risks than whole-class discussion.

**175**

| Those who were enslaved might have ... | | | | | |
|---|---|---|---|---|---|
| | Felt | Heard | Seen | Said | Touched |
| First Passage | | | | | |
| Second Passage | | | | | |
| Third Passage | | | | | |

**FIGURE 13.3  Passages of enslavement graphic organizer.**

Teachers can also support students' learning by allowing them to decide on questions they want to answer during a unit. We have already pointed out that education is a joint responsibility of teachers and students. Letting students develop questions builds on their underlying interest in history and treats them as self-directed learners who can use a variety of resources to learn more. By starting with students' questions, teachers are also more likely to engage the ideas and interests of students who come from differing backgrounds. Investigating questions of their own choosing, though, means that students will need to use a variety of resources and that they will have to learn how to use them critically and effectively. These resources include non-fiction literature written for children and adolescents, as well as internet sources, and students will need help in finding, using, and evaluating each of these, as we have described in Chapter 8. Teachers cannot always anticipate what topics will be of interest and, therefore, cannot plan lessons explicitly designed to address them. What they can do, though, is make sure that they provide access to the resources students may need. As Rhoda points out, "My room is more chaotic that way, but the learning is better."

Graphic organizers are also a key means by which Rhoda and Rebecca help students develop knowledge. Reading about enslavement may have produced a great many ideas, but most students would not have been able immediately to write a poem about an enslaved person's thoughts and feelings, and many English learners would have balked at the prospect of producing such complicated and extended text. The basic outline of the poem (Figure 13.1) was one step in helping students get their ideas on paper, but even more important was the graphic organizer the class filled out together: As they read and discussed each passage, they kept track of what an enslaved person would have felt, seen, heard, and thought (Figure 13.3). Similarly, even students who had studied colonization of the U.S. West in depth might have had trouble knowing what to write in a simulated journal. By leading students in webbing out their ideas beforehand, Rhoda ensured that they would have many more words and ideas from which to draw.

## ASSESSING STUDENTS' KNOWLEDGE OF HISTORICAL CONTENT

Throughout this book, we have emphasized the assessment of students' historical skills: Their ability to explain historical changes, use historical evidence, create historical interpretations, and so on. Most teachers, though, are also expected to assess how well students retain specific knowledge—the factual content of history. Assessing knowledge of content, however, does not mean that teachers must turn their back on the principles of constructive assessment, and it certainly does not mean that they should bombard students with

Education is a joint responsibility of teachers and students.

Students need help finding, using, and evaluating resources.

Graphic organizers promote learning by helping students visually organize information. *Fisher & Frey (2018), Hattie (2009)*

multiple-choice tests, lists of items to be matched, or sentences in which they fill in blanks. Such tasks neither assess what students know nor improve the instructional process; they simply allow the teacher to shake loose a set of largely meaningless grades. The assessment of knowledge, like the assessment of skills, must play a constructive role in the classroom—one that provides students and teachers with authentic information on how the schema-building process is coming along. Chapter 14 deals with the role the arts can play in assessing students' knowledge; in this chapter, we deal primarily with the use of writing.

Written language is one of the most common forms of evaluation, and in our experience, students often learn by writing in history. To provide constructive information on learning, written assignments must be open ended: They must allow for a variety of correct responses. Good instruction and good resources usually present more information than any single student can be expected to remember, and an open-ended assignment allows each student to draw from that body of information to reach conclusions or make evaluations. After studying colonization of the U.S. West, for example, teachers should expect that students could give examples of hardships faced by settlers or Native peoples; they should not expect, though, that all students would give the same examples. Different students will be interested in different details, and thus, the knowledge they retain will vary. This is not the same as saying that any answer is equally correct, because each response must make use of the facts, concepts, and relations that have been covered in the unit.

One problem with using writing as a means of assessment, however, is that students who struggle with it—including English learners—may appear to have little understanding of content, when what they really have is limited familiarity with writing. This means that teachers have to give writing assignments that allow students to use language in ways they are familiar with, and they must provide the scaffolding necessary to help them do so. One effective way to assess students' understanding through writing is the use of "Magic Words" (see Figure 13.4). "Magic Words" are prepositions and subordinating conjunctions; they're called "magic" not only because that sounds more exciting, but because their use magically improves the quality of writing. These words call attention to the relations that lie at the heart of history—how one thing causes another, what events came before or after others, and so on—and using them requires that students demonstrate their understanding of these relations. Most students, including English learners, know and use many of these words in speech, but they rarely do so in writing. They can with help, though, and their writing then provides insight into their understanding of content. At the end of a

> Assessment must play a constructive role in the classroom.

> Open-ended writing assignments provide insight into learning. *Knipper & Duggan (2006)*

> Responses can show knowledge of facts, concepts, and relations in different ways.

> "Magic Words" call attention to the relations that underlie historical interpretations. *Barton (1996)*

| | | | |
|---|---|---|---|
| about | because | for | though |
| above | before | from | through |
| across | behind | if | to |
| after | below | in | unless |
| against | beneath | in order to | until |
| along | beside | like | when |
| although | between | near | whenever |
| among | behind | of | where |
| around | by | on | wherever |
| as | down | past | while |
| as if | during | since | whoever |
| at | except | sothat | with |

Adapted from Barton (1996)

**FIGURE 13.4 "Magic Words."**

lesson or unit, for example, Rebecca's students write several sentences about what they've learned. They can write anything at all about the topic, but each sentence has to contain a "Magic Word," and therefore they can search through all the information they have gained to show what they know about time, causation, and so on. The following examples of "Magic Word" sentences come from her class and others:

> Because the ground [at Jamestown] is watery, they can't plant corn.
>
> Because Francis Drake stole money and land, he was a hero to England.
>
> In a new settlement, slaves were in high demand because the colonists needed a lot of work done.
>
> Although the Indians were not lazy and stupid, the Spanish thought they were.
>
> Whenever a slave was bought, almost every time a family was split up.
>
> Although the Indians lived here first, the Spanish said they owned the land.
>
> After a woman was bought as a slave, she begged her master to buy her children too.

By expanding or narrowing the topic for assessment, teachers can vary the level of detail they obtain on student's understanding. For example, at the end of a unit on enslavement, Rebecca might ask students to write five sentences using any of the "Magic Words"; after a week of studying the economic structure of the institution, she might be more specific and ask students to write two sentences on economic relations and to use the word *because* in each. In either case, this strategy is a clear example of giving students the chance to show what they know rather than what they don't know: They must demonstrate their understanding and retention of content, but not all are expected to have learned exactly the same set of facts.

A more structured task is the use of open-ended questions. Such questions also allow for a range of possible answers, but they require a more focused response than "Magic Words." Productive open-ended questions generally ask students to pull together different aspects of what they have learned in order to identify patterns, draw conclusions, or make evaluations. Amy, for example, followed her "History Museum" projects by having students respond to the question, "How has the United States changed over the last 100 years?" Although each student used different examples, all had to draw on information to support a generalization about patterns of change. When used as assessment, such questions are sometimes called *performance tasks*. They evaluate whether the final product or performance sustains a supportable interpretation given the available information (and the level of experience of the writer); to do so, such writing must be grounded in substantial historical knowledge. This is not just a matter of getting the facts right, but of showing how those facts are related to each other and to the writer's larger interpretation. This is true even with the youngest writers. When LeeAnn's primary school students in Chapter 6 wrote about Columbus, they included such telling details as Columbus "trading fake jewels for real gold" and kidnapping the Taino as support for their interpretation of his claim to fame. Although an older student might make a more complex argument, these young children are novices, and the fact that they marshal evidence to support a position is an important beginning point.

Often, good written tasks ask students to organize what they have learned into forms other than expository sentences and paragraphs. After studying the "Columbian Exchange," for example, Rebecca had students write dialogues between a reporter and a student protesting either a Columbus Day celebration or a school's cancellation of such a celebration. In writing the dialogue, students had to draw on their knowledge of why Columbus is regarded as either a villain or a hero—they had to use historical information to support a position on a contemporary social issue. Similarly, Amy had students write a dialogue between a Japanese American parent during World War II and the government agent sent to detain him or her; again, students had to use what they had learned to support a position in a real-life setting. Using information in this way leads to more meaningful writing—and better assessment—than simply trying to get students to reproduce a set of facts, definitions, or concepts. It also allows English learners to use their knowledge of conversational English to participate in complex academic tasks.

*Constructive assessment emphasizes what students know and not what they don't know.*

*Open-ended questions ask students to identify patterns, draw conclusions, or make evaluations.*

*Performance tasks are opportunities for students to present supportable interpretations.*

*Historical writing must be grounded in knowledge. Newmann et al. (1995)*

**178**

# EXTENSIONS

Throughout this chapter, we have emphasized the importance of focusing on the agency of people in the past and the diversity of perspectives and experiences that have characterized any moment in history. For any topic that teachers wish (or are required) to teach, they should ask, "Who else was involved in this, and what did they think about it?" In teaching about World War II, for example, it is important not to limit the focus to the battles and political leaders that may quickly leap to mind. Instead, students might study the effect of the war on daily life in the United States and other countries by learning about the internment of Japanese Americans, changes in employment opportunities for women, U.S. anti-Semitism, opposition to the war, and the war's economic consequences. Even when learning about the military, students could study experiences such as those of the Tuskegee Airmen, Navajo code talkers, Japanese American and Chinese American soldiers, and women of the Women's Army Corps and other units. These topics allow students to explore the variety of perspectives and experiences during the time and to understand the choices that varied people made.

All historical topics should include the study of diverse experiences and perspectives.

Similarly, the American Revolution is one of the most frequently covered topics in both fifth and eighth grades, yet when asked about it later, students often remember only a string of unrelated people, events, and documents, and their understanding of its significance is limited to observations such as, "It's important so we wouldn't be bossed around by the queen anymore." Rarely do they learn that many colonists opposed the war or that Patriots tarred and feathered Loyalists, nor do they learn about the effect of the war on women, Blacks, or daily life in general. Rather than seeing the American Revolution as a pivotal and controversial event in their country's history, students are presented with a single, finished story—a story that has no clear immediacy and whose details they remember in only the most superficial way. Students would gain a more complete understanding of the Revolution if they examined novels on the period describing a variety of experiences—works such as *Soldier's Secret: The Story of Deborah Sampson* (about a girl who dresses as a man in order to fight in the Colonial Army), *Chains* (about two girls promised freedom from enslavement but who are, instead, sold to a family in New York), and *The Arrow Over the Door* (about an encounter between a Quaker boy who struggles with his family's pacifism, and an Abenaki boy whose family was murdered by settlers). By working in literature response groups, students can analyze and compare these novels and the experiences they represent.

*Levstik & Barton (2008), McKeown & Beck (1990), VanSledright (1995)*

*Klass (2009), L. Anderson (2008a), Bruchac (2002)*

As we described however, narrative is such a powerful medium that students tend to regard what they read without a critical eye. They can investigate the accuracy of the books they are reading by comparing them with informational texts such as *Answering the Cry for Freedom: Stories of African Americans during the American Revolution*; *Liberty or Death: The Surprising Story of Runaway Slaves Who Sided with the British during the American Revolution*; *1776: A New Look at Colonial Williamsburg*; *Growing Up in Revolution and the New Nation, 1775–1800*; and *Independent Dames: What You Never Knew about the Women and Girls of the American Revolution*. Unfortunately, as far as we are aware, there are no full-length informational texts on Native peoples during the Revolutionary War, so teachers may need to curate extracts from works of history or internet sources to provide more information on their experiences.

*Woelfle (2016), Blair (2010), Kostyal (2009), B. Miller (2002), L. Anderson (2008)*

*Sawyer (2020), Schmidt (2014)*

# CONCLUSIONS

Some of the teachers in this book have substantial control over their history curriculum, but many teachers, particularly in fourth grade and above, are required by state standards or informal (but very real) expectations to teach specific topics in state, U.S., or world history. As Rhoda and Rebecca demonstrate, though, teaching the required content of the curriculum does not mean following a textbook in lockstep fashion or using unimaginative forms of instruction. Principles of effective teaching and the elements of historical thinking can be applied to any topic a teacher wants or needs to teach. At first glance, most of Rhoda's and Rebecca's students have little reason to be interested in the major events of U.S. history. Most are immigrants from poor or working-class families, and their ancestors rarely show up in stories of the British colonies, the American Revolution, or the Civil War. But by focusing on human agency and multiple perspectives, Rhoda and Rebecca not only keep their students interested in history but also make it clear why the topic is relevant to them. Focusing on people—real human beings who live, work, play, create art, and make decisions—allows students to make connections across time and place.

These students also learn that the United States has always been diverse and that attention to any topic must include the experience of different ethnic groups, of men and women, of rich and poor. Every historical period is characterized by varied experiences and perspectives, often as the result of attempts by some groups to subjugate others—such as racist doctrines grounded in efforts to exploit the labor of the enslaved and maintain the social status of Whites. This is often overlooked in school history, and students are presented with an image of widespread consensus in which everyone held the same opinions on events of the day. Yet if students are going to take part in meaningful public discussion, they need to understand that differing perspectives are a normal part of social interaction, and that these are often based on differing experiences. If students think that everyone in a given country or community agreed on public issues in the past, they will have few resources for understanding why people disagree today, and they will have little reason to take others' ideas seriously. The attention to diversity shown throughout this chapter may not guarantee that students will see the importance of understanding perspectives that differ from their own, but it should at least help them see that such differences are an unavoidable element of social life.

*Kendi (2016)*

# 14

# THE ARTS MAKE US ALL PART OF HUMANKIND

## Cognitive Pluralism in History Teaching and Learning

What makes a culture unique, where are the commonalities that we share if it isn't the arts? The arts make us all a part of humankind. When you think of learning as a whole instead of little pieces, the arts give you the whole picture. So, in seventh grade when I teach ancient civilizations, how could I teach about Greece and not teach about drama? How could I teach about Greece and not teach about architecture? And in eighth grade, it's really been interesting to watch the student who studied Mozart and found out that he was a contemporary of George Washington…The arts also give us a window. Sometimes, we don't give students an opportunity to share with us what they do know because we restrict their vehicle of expression. If I only accept what they know about the Bill of Rights in written form, then I've eliminated children that want to share that information with me in a picture or a drama or those kinds of things. The arts give them a vehicle to share with me what they really do know.…And sometimes you help a child develop areas they wouldn't have otherwise. They would have said that's not my strong suit, that's not something I do, but because it is a way that we express ourselves in the classroom—sometimes it's on some kind of assessment—that child makes an attempt to do it and becomes stronger as a result.

—Jeanette Groth, middle school teacher Grades 6, 7, & 8

Jeanette Groth's classroom is always full of art, music, and movement. When studying the Constitution, eighth-grade students carve feather pens, make ink (after finding a period recipe), and try their hands at drafting resolutions. A recording of Mozart's music using period instruments plays in the background as they work. A few weeks later, seventh graders transform the classroom into a medieval castle. Jeanette removes the classroom door and installs a "drawbridge" for the duration of their study. In her sixth-grade class, students make kente cloth and study the West African tradition of preserving history in the archives of a griot's memory. At other times, the arts of ancient Japan, Mali, and Mesopotamia compete for wall space with more recent images of U.S. history. As one observer notes, the juxtaposition of images creates "harmonious chaos." Jeanette nods, "I like it because my room is mostly student created, and so I think they feel comfortable with their own work, and I think it calls to mind things that they have learned." Three brief vignettes provide some of the flavor of Jeanette Groth's arts-infused curriculum.

\* \* \*

DOI: 10.4324/9781003179658-14

**181**

Garrett is, he says, doing a "non-research paper" on Ulysses S. Grant for his eighth-grade U.S. history class. His task is to study the life of Grant and then put together a "Jackdaw"—a packet of information and artifacts that will illuminate his subject. Jeanette's instructions direct him to "*visually represent* your topic, supply notes or digitized images of information with relevant details highlighted, provide pictures and replicas of relevant artifacts." "Then," Garrett says, "We get to present our Jackdaw to the class." Jeanette explains that this assignment involves gathering all the sources for a research paper, "except you don't write the paper." Garrett compares it to an archaeological dig in reverse: Rather than presenting a written interpretation based on artifacts, he has to present interpretive artifacts based on written sources. So far, he has decided to include a cigar and an empty whiskey bottle, along with a set of "letters from the field"—perhaps to Abraham Lincoln—and maps of Civil War campaigns.

*"Jackdaw" is also the trade name for a series of historical primary source and activity packets. (https://www.jackdaw.com/)*

\* \* \*

The school choir is planning a program of Middle Eastern music that coincides with the sixth graders' study of the Middle East. Jeanette challenges her students: Use what you have learned about the Middle East to help the choir director develop the concert. As a follow-up assessment, Jeanette asks the students to develop program notes explaining what they considered to be the distinctive elements of Middle Eastern music. Students compare the smaller intervals, different rhythms, and instrumentations common to Middle Eastern music with those used in European music and discuss vocal sound production—comparing the "loose" throat vocalizations of Western music with the "tighter" throat more common to Middle Eastern music.

\* \* \*

Jeanette's seventh graders are deeply involved in studying Islamic influences on Spain. The Alhambra, a fortress and castle in Granada, Spain, seems to be a perfect example of how war and conquest can disperse other aspects of culture, including art and architecture. Building a replica of the Alhambra might work, the students decide, but they really want visitors to be able to see, in detail, the kind of art introduced to the region by Muslims, and they definitely want to try their hand at reproducing these artistic styles. Perhaps they could try some of the art and hang it around the room? Or they could do what they had seen students do last year with the medieval castle! Before long, the students turn their classroom into a replica of the Alhambra, complete with examples of Islamic art. Student guides conduct visitors on a tour of historic Western Islamic art and architecture, explaining its political and religious significance as they point out the distinctive style of portrait painting and mosaics. Although students are enthusiastic in their admiration for Islamic art and respectful of the culture that produced it, they are also impressed with their own production. Hannah smiles when complimented on her work, and says "It really is beautiful, isn't it?" She then points out some details of the time period they have included "because this style lets you know exactly when it was built."

Because she teaches all the sixth-, seventh-, and eighth-grade social studies in this small arts magnet school, Jeanette sees her students develop over time. She worries, too, about what will happen to them when they leave this school. "Some teachers are afraid to integrate the arts," Jeanette says. "They feel that they'll have more behavior problems. I think that the reverse is true, but I have trouble convincing people of that. They think they can't let children create a piece of music or a piece of art—that they'll miss some content because the arts are taking up their time. In reality, they are probably not going to be so frustrated in their learning. They see the whole picture. In other words, they may learn separate parts, but I want them to see how it fits in the whole. We may relate a concept from early in the year—early African and Indian slavery—and then that fits in with the picture of what happened in the Civil War, and then we might talk about what happens with a racial situation here."

*The arts help students see the "whole picture." Martin (2021), Sterman (2018)*

In our view, the arts are an integral part of history—part of what makes civilizations unique. Think about how the musicals *Hamilton* or *In the Heights* speak to the life and experience of the early decades of the twenty-first century, how songs such as *Hair* or *Blowin' in the Wind* represented the counter-culture or anti-war movements of the 1960s and 1970s in the United States, or how Picasso's 1937 *Guernica* powerfully captured the

*Bell (2019), Flanagan (2016)*

**182**

**FIGURE 14.1 Historical art.**

horrors of the Spanish Civil War. Think, too, about the variety of official uses of art: Memorial statues and monuments, political posters, and the like. As you look at the historical art in Figure 14.1, consider how each artist attempts to manipulate your emotions. In the original artwork, lurid red and orange firelight illuminates the faces of Hitler and Hirohito, emphasizing the whites of Hitler's hypnotic eyes and the bit of liquid dripping from Hirohito's oversized teeth, conjuring up images of hell. Out of the black and red night, Hitler stares directly at the viewer; Hirohito shifts his view to the side, implying that he can see into the shadows. In the second example, the artist directs your eye to a mother and child. The lines are softer, and the picture is meant to recall the sentimentality and safety of a Madonna and child. In this instance, too, textual graphics call attention to safety—she's good enough to be your baby's mother—and then to the point of the illustration—therefore, she's good enough to vote with you.

The impact of each poster is greater, too, if you consider the historical context as well as the artistry of the rendering. Who was the audience for each piece of art? To what fears did each speak? The first, of course, is a World War II propaganda poster; the second is a 1918 song sheet. Although this song—from an early twentieth-century commercial sheet-music company—was a parody of the woman suffrage movement, it no doubt captured the attention of women and encouraged them to attain a direct political voice. As Jeanette explains, the "arts are situated in a historical context, in a culture, in a society. I think the arts can help the students speculate about what the purpose of a specific art form in a particular historical context or a particular historical time might be."

## THE ARTS ADDRESS SIGNIFICANT HISTORICAL QUESTIONS

The historical arts help students address different questions than do more traditional primary sources. A variety of print sources, for instance, might help students respond to a question such as: Could the conflicts between Indigenous peoples and White settlers in the post-Civil War era have been avoided? Students might read U.S. and Canadian government documents and census records, analyze statements by military leaders such as General Philip Sheridan ("The only good Indian is a dead Indian"), study U.S. government policies intended to destroy tribal cohesiveness ("Kill the Indian, save the man"),

The arts are political as well as aesthetic.

The arts exist in an historical context. *Eisner (1988), Sizemore (2011)*

*Bell (2019), Marable-Bunch (2020), P. Smith (2009)*

On the Native Knowledge 360° Education Initiative, see *Marable-Bunch (2020).*

**183**

and consider Sitting Bull's call for his people not to surrender the sacred Black Hills ("We want no white men here. The Black Hills belong to me. If the whites try to take them, I will fight"). Using these sources, students could build and defend positions regarding the inevitability of hostility or develop an explanation of, and suggest alternatives to, the United States' genocidal policies toward Indigenous nations. These are important, but limited, questions to consider in making sense of this historical era.

By working with the historical arts, students focus on a different—though related—sort of historical question: What was it like to be a Sioux or one of their allies during the period surrounding the Battle of Little Big Horn? This question deals more explicitly with a people's "way of being in the world." Consider what sources students might use to answer this question. They might study examples of the decorative arts—clothing, basketry, body art—that evoke aspects of Sioux culture. They could use photographs taken of Sioux and Cheyenne children as they first entered boarding schools (separated from their families, home communities, and language) and again, after workers at the schools cut their long hair and replaced their familiar clothing with European styles. Photographs of an Arapaho camp, a Lakota woman packing a travois, or a young Comanche on horseback could be juxtaposed with images of boarding school life. Further, photographs of the massacre at Marias River, cartoons expressing outrage at Custer's defeat, posters for Buffalo Bill Cody's Wild West show, and Sioux artwork showing the death of Sitting Bull and Crazy Horse all provide insight into the human experience behind the myth of "Custer's last stand" and the attempted subjugation of the Sioux (and other Indigenous peoples) as well as their long-term *survivance*—not just their survival over time, but their resistance to historical and cultural erasure. These historical arts provide different vantage points from which to view history and make explicit the powerful emotions that often defy the power of words to fully express. This does not discount more traditional historical sources; rather, together they develop the "whole picture" that Jeanette seeks for her students.

Developing the whole picture is clearly important to Jeanette. Although her small classroom is often crowded with work from three different grades, she feels strongly that this apparent chaos really is harmonious. Students regularly see each other's work, borrow ideas from each other, and are reminded that the "separate parts" they study each year fit in a larger framework. In building this framework, Jeanette focuses on several aspects of the arts related to thinking and learning in history. First, she uses the arts as source material for historical study. This involves understanding and making judgments about art as well as coming to appreciate art from different times and places. Second, she encourages (and regularly requires) students to use the arts as vehicles for the expression of their historical understanding. Different artistic symbol systems allow them to think with and express their thinking through the arts. Although these processes are interrelated in the context of Jeanette's classroom, it is useful to consider the separate contributions of the arts as historical data and as ways to express historical understanding.

## THE ARTS AND MATERIAL OBJECTS AS SOURCE MATERIAL FOR HISTORICAL STUDY

The arts serve as primary source documents that help us understand the time and place in which they were produced. As Jeannette says, it is hard to imagine teaching about ancient Greece without reference to its art, literature, and architecture. Indeed, it should be equally difficult to imagine ignoring the rich artistry of such African empires as Benin or Mali or of the Aztecs and Mayans. While much of Western knowledge of these civilizations was based on the reports of European explorers, each empire also left at least a partial record of its *own* worldview in its arts and material culture (the arts of everyday life). An ivory mask from Benin, for instance, depicts a row of Portuguese sailors in a position intended to represent the power of the people of Benin over these strangers. Similarly, the art and architecture of the ancient Maya indicate a sophisticated understanding of

*Bensen (2001), Welch (2007)*

Historical arts complement, extend, and sometimes counter more traditional historical sources.

*Bensen (2001), Greene (1995), P. Smith (2009), Sabzalian (2019)*

The arts provide different historical vantage points.

The arts are data sources for history as well as vehicles for expressing historical understanding.

*Bell (2019), Brandt (1988), Arias-Ferrer et al. (2019), Eisner (1988), Renyi (1994)*

math and astronomy as well as a rich cosmology and elaborate social and political life. In North America, the art of Sioux and Cheyenne—pictures drawn in ledger books and on skins and fabric to explain events from an Indigenous perspective—provide eyewitness accounts of the Plains wars in the late 1800s (see Figure 14.2). These material objects are sources of information on the *content* of these cultures, from clothing and recreation to religious beliefs and technology, from gender roles and child rearing practices to political and natural cataclysms. But the *form* of the arts is also historically important. Just as culture gives direction to art—providing religious ideas, for instance—so art shapes our perceptions of the world by embodying ideas in sensory images—a Russian Orthodox icon, perhaps. More fully understanding history, then, means studying how the form and content of the arts express that history.

It is easy to recognize World War II posters and ledger art as artifacts of the times in which they were created. We sometimes forget, however, that when the arts depict the past, whether in a painting of George Washington crossing the Delaware, in a movie such as *Judas and the Black Messiah*, or as part of a mosaic or stone carving, they do so through the perspectives of the time in which they were created. Perhaps you have seen the 1990 movie *Dances with Wolves*. Unlike older "Westerns" in which Indigenous peoples were generally villainous and the cavalry rode to the rescue of White settlers, *Dances with Wolves* presented the Lakota as a heroic people stalked by the evil U.S. Cavalry. At first glance, this may seem a more realistic and culturally sensitive interpretation—it was certainly hailed as such when it was released—but it was just as much an artifact of its time as were earlier and more obviously inaccurate and stereotypical Westerns. Movies such as this tell

*Eisner (1988), Hodder (2012), Levstik et al. (2014), Levstik & Henderson (2016), P. Smith, (2009)*

*Deloria (2004), Sabzalian (2019), P. Smith, (2009), Welch (2007)*

*Marcus et al. (2010), Mihesual (2009)*

**FIGURE 14.2** An unknown Hunkpapa Lakota artist's rendition of the arrest and killing of Sitting Bull (North Dakota Historical Society).

us more about White U.S. society in the 1990s than they do about the complex lives of either Indigenous peoples or the U.S. Cavalry in the years following the Civil War. And our students' ideas of life in the West—or during the Eisenhower administration, or the civil rights era—are at least as likely to be shaped by such movies as by the history they encounter in school. As a result, we help our students most when we teach them to consider the interpretive eye behind the visual arts just as we do for other historical sources.

Levstik & Barton (2008), Stoddard (2012), Stoddard & Marcus (2017), Stoddard et al. (2017)

Just as in Jeannette Groth's middle school classroom, Jocelyn Erlich draws on music, dance, drama, literature, and the visual arts in her fifth-grade classroom. Students in both classes expect the arts to be integral to their historical study. Their contrasting approaches to a unit on the Constitution illustrate the flexibility of the arts as source material as well as the avenues through which students share their own evidence-based interpretation of the past. In this instance, Jeanette uses children's literature and documentary sources describing hot and miserable conditions surrounding the Constitutional Convention, then focuses on a 1940 painting by Howard Chandler Christy of the signing of the Constitution. After students discuss their responses to the first sources, noting how "hot and muggy" the room was, with "flies buzzing around, windows closed" to keep things "secretive," they work as "art critics." Jeanette reminds them to use some of the work they have done with costume, clothing, art, and artifacts of the time period, asking them to evaluate the painting based on three questions:

> What kind of job do you think the artist did? Did the artist make an accurate portrait of what happened at that time? Inaccurate? What makes you think so?
> Where is attention focused in the painting? What do you think the artist is trying to do here?
> What are the aesthetic elements of this painting? What are the political uses this painting might be put to?

Seeing often supports believing. Arias-Ferrer et al. (2019), Levstik & Henderson (2016)

Working in small groups, the students begin noting details that conflict with other sources they have used. The men in the painting seem cooler and less uncomfortable than other sources indicated; curtains and windows are open, also contrary to most sources. They notice that George Washington is centered in the painting, the light focusing on him so that "he becomes the main figure," while the men who did most of the writing are minor figures in the painting. Carter explains that seeing the painting helped him visualize what the delegates looked like: "It really assisted me…knowing which figure was which."

Fritz (1987)

Jocelyn Erlich begins a bit differently, starting with "The Room Where It Happened" from *Hamilton,* then moving to Jean Fritz's book, *Shh! We're Writing the Constitution.* She divides the class into small groups and invites each group to examine portraits and brief biographies of prominent convention members. They identify things these people might have in common and what might separate them and discuss the ways in which people are portrayed in each medium. Jocelyn asks them about people who were not "in the room where it happened." While students work, "History Has Its Eyes on You," also from *Hamilton,* plays in the background. As Jocelyn notes, "We are going to imagine that room and the decisions made there. We'll look through the eyes of the people who wrote the Constitution, artists like the ones who painted the portraits you just examined, and like Lin-Manuel Miranda, who wrote the music you just heard, as well as historians, to see if we can figure out what ideas and arguments led to the U.S. Constitution that came out of that room in 1787. We'll also think about what ideas never even made it into the room. How might those ideas have changed history? Or maybe they did!"

In both classrooms, students comment on how the artwork helped them see how interpretations varied. Interestingly, Carter, one of the students in Jeanette's class, mentions that, despite "knowing" how many delegates had been in attendance, "I didn't realize how many delegates participated…until I saw that picture. There were quite a few, you know." Carter's experience may be familiar to you. Think back to the first time you saw a favorite ballet, heard a soul-stirring concert, or stood before a powerful piece of art or architecture—not on film or reproduced in a textbook, but live, perhaps in a theater, concert hall, gallery, museum, or wandering down some city street. Perhaps the experience jolted

Bell (2019), Epstein (1994), Greene (1995), Sizemore (2011)

you out of familiar ways of seeing. You understood, to some degree, not just an event or idea, but a world of feelings. As you gained experience—perhaps heard a recording of the concert or saw the play performed a second time, you noticed dimensions of the work you missed the first time or caught echoes of architectural styles in other buildings. These experiences enriched your feelings for the work; perhaps you also shared it with someone else and re-experienced it through their eyes. In a sense, this kind of aesthetic experience is a bit like unravelling a mystery—one in which there is no final scene in which all is made clear. It engages both your intellect and your emotions, and often moves beyond the power of words to explain. As Isadora Duncan said, "If I could *tell* you what I mean, there would be no point in dancing."

*Platt (n.d.), Martin (2021)*

In history, too, there is an element of mystery, of searching for some key to explain not just what happened, but why it happened—what web of emotions, values, and ideas connects a set of events. Perhaps because of this air of mystery, students are likely to recognize voice and intention in the arts more readily than in textbooks. As students think about the mind behind the historical image, however, it is important to consider not only the viewpoint represented but also how the artist used a medium to express that viewpoint. Some children's books explore just this connection between artist and art, intention and action. Powerful illustrations bring perspectives young readers might not have found in the text alone. Consider Kadir Nelson's illustrations in *The Undefeated*, a book that celebrates Black America across time and different walks of life, or Michaela Goade's illustrations for *We are the Water Protectors* about Indigenous-led environmental protection movements. They don't repeat the texts, they extend them, and they use different artistic genres to do so.

History and the arts share an element of mystery. *Gerwin & Zevin (2011)*

*J. Brown et al. (1989), Platt (n.d.), Sterman (2018)*

*K. Alexander (2019), Lindstrom (2020)*

Unfortunately, the very thing that students find appealing—the emotion and intention of the arts—sometimes leads them to discount the arts as "biased." Students may assume that the worldview of a textbook is "objective" precisely because it has, from their perspective, no recognizable voice or intention. This is not an argument against using the arts; rather, we think that an arts-infused curriculum in which children analyze the intentional nature of all modes of expression will help children think more carefully about the nature of historical perspective, wherever encountered.

*Epstein (1994), Gabella (1994), Zhensun & Low (1991)*

*Levstik & Barton (2008), Suh (2013)*

Students should learn to recognize the voice and intention of all modes of expression.

Analyzing visual sources has several advantages for students. Unlike the events they represent, for instance, visual images are fixed in time. When you analyze a still image (or stop a moving one), you are undisturbed by the changing moment, by movement, or the emotional fluctuations that were part of the actual event. You can go back to an image repeatedly, searching its multiple dimensions, asking new questions, bringing new information and experience to bear. Of course, this presents its own set of problems. Something that was, in fact, ephemeral can gain undue significance simply because it was preserved. Think how easily a single photograph from your family album, taken out of context, could misrepresent your family history. Archaeologists face an even more daunting task as they attempt to interpret a past for which the only records may be the art and artifacts that survive the wear and tear of time.

*Levstik & Henderson (2016), Mazur (1993), Salomon (2012)*

Visual images allow students to examine and re-examine historical moments.

Taking a historical moment out of context can lead to incomplete interpretations.

Children enter school having been exposed to an enormous variety of visual images. Although they may be more adept at making sense of cartoons or animated computer graphics than historical art, they already have a store of visual clues at their disposal. From their earliest years, sighted and hearing children infer relationships between visual and aural data and their own social situations and background experiences. In fact, many children communicate through the arts long before they achieve fluency with reading and writing, and they may prefer drawing to writing despite increasing fluency in writing. In addition, children often have a rich visual symbology that helps them interpret their own and others' art. In Figure 14.3, for instance, a 7-year-old's response to the *Little House* books uses only one word but incorporates many details from the story—high-button shoes, water pails, a barn with square nails, Laura's clothing—along with more iconographic symbols that were already part of the child's artistic shorthand—the imaginary house and yard and the bird. (And as with all art, it's important to note what is *not* represented, such as the Native people whose land the girl's family was settling on.)

*Hodder (2012)*

*Freedman (2003), N. Smith (2007)*

**FIGURE 14.3 Visualizing the past.**

As children gain more background knowledge in history (often from non-print media), they use that information in their own artistic productions and in interpreting the historical arts. In general, they are more fluent in describing and interpreting material culture—technology, clothing, architecture, food—where they can make connections between the historical image and their own lives—or the lives they see displayed on television, in movies, and in books. Children looking at a photograph of a Victorian schoolroom, for instance, associated it with Samantha, a character (and doll) from the *American Girls* books and recognized various elements in the photograph based on their experience with these materials.

It is clear that children in a variety of settings find the arts a rich part of their historical study. Old Town Elementary, a school not too far from the arts magnet school where Jeanette teaches, is in a neighborhood where many families are experiencing poverty. Old Town has no special arts programming, and few of its teachers began their teaching

Historical information can be garnered from many sources, including the media.

**188**

careers with more than the rudimentary background in the arts provided by introductory undergraduate courses, yet the school overflows with art. Murals of Black history stretch down one hall, a display of masks produced by different cultures around the world hangs from the ceiling in the entryway, a display of Chinese musical instruments left over from a study of China lingers in a corner, and photographs of an Indonesian visitor demonstrating a lion dance to a group of primary children are displayed on a classroom door. In the first grade, students invite a guest to try their hand at brass rubbing. Several classmates are carefully rubbing crayons across paper-covered brass reliefs. The reliefs (raised images on a flat background) represent British historical figures; as the children rub their crayons across the surfaces of the reliefs, they comment on the images emerging on their paper, reminding each other of medieval symbology:

*In some cultures, masks are ceremonial objects and should not be displayed in public settings.*

*The arts can speak across race, class, and cultural differences. Bell (2019)*

| | |
|---|---|
| *Erin:* | This one is a king. |
| *David:* | He's a knight, cause he's got a sword, see? |
| *Erin:* | Yeah, but there's a…see down by his feet. |
| *Aggie:* | A lion. |
| *Erin:* | Uh-huh. That lion means he's a king. Kings get lions [this had been a small note on a picture seen earlier in the year]. |
| *Catrina:* | The lady's got something. |
| *Jake:* | A dog. |
| *Catrina:* | Yeah, a dog. She's not a queen, I don't think. |

As the children continue their work, they rearrange these visual elements for their own purposes. Two of the boys label their rubbings in Norse (one of the artifacts they have been working with includes a Norse alphabet). Another girl turns her rubbings into stick puppets, and several others follow suit, intent on turning their work into a puppet show. David cuts out each of his figures and pastes them on different backgrounds, creating a picture that looks much like a medieval tapestry. In surrounding themselves and their students with the visual arts, these teachers are learning to read the historical arts as well as teach with them. Their students analyze the arts from historical and aesthetic perspectives and learn to associate specific questions with each of these analytical stances. From a historical perspective, for instance, students look for the details of daily life, asking:

*Students use visual arts for their own purposes.*

*Students learn to read the arts historically and aesthetically.*

*Platt (n.d.)*

- What parts of life are shown? Young children studying changes in child rearing practices might study art for information on child labor, recreation, family activities, religious events, or schooling.
- What are the artist's feelings about these activities? A Norman Rockwell picture, for instance, might celebrate certain aspects of family or small-town life, while simultaneously poking fun at some traditions or conventions.

Students also consider the arts as social and political commentary. They ask questions such as:

- How do artists shape historical and political thinking? Older students might consider what works of art, such as *The Rake's Progress*, *Guernica*, or *América Tropical*, tell them about the social and political world of the artists.
- How do interpretations change over time? For example, how do Pops Peterson's reinterpretations of Rockwell's paintings reflect the social and political concerns of a different era?
- How controversial might this commentary have been in its own time? Now? This question might send students to other sources to provide a context for their interpretations.

From an aesthetic perspective, students study how the elements of the arts relate to each other and to the historical content, asking:

- How does each artist approach the subject (style and technique)? Students might compare different artists' interpretations of the same idea, event, or emotion, as Jeanette's and Jocelyn's students did with the Constitutional Convention.
- What do these styles and techniques say about the worldview of the people who create them? For example, how does Roger Shimamura's use of Japanese compositional techniques enhance his reinterpretation of *Washington Crossing the Delaware*? Younger children might study a group of line drawings of Martin Luther King, Jr., and discuss which make him appear as a person of dignity and respect and which portray him as cartoonish—and why different sources may have made the choices they did.

As students apply these questions to the historical arts, they become better able to interpret the arts from historical and aesthetic perspectives.

## IMAGINING IN YOUR MIND: LEARNING TO READ THE HISTORIC ARTS

You'd have to take this picture, imagine it in your mind, and go through time. Based on what you know, you come to a conclusion.

—Rodney, Grade 5

[Looking at a picture of a mass gathering in front of a large building] You have like protests about race…the soldier's uniforms, well it could be about like Black rights… but I don't see any Black people, but I guess they could be carrying the signs.

—Evan, Grade 5

[After looking at pictures of the antebellum United States] It looks real interesting because there's a lot of stuff in it that makes you think it's older, like it has lots of boats and old buildings in it, and a hot air balloon, and it makes you think that it's older because the hot air balloon was invented a long time ago…and a lot of the people, it looks like they're homeless, they lost their homes…I think it would just be neat to see what they did and talk to them and see what they'd look like and see what the land would look like without anybody on it.

—Haveli, Grade 6

Each of these students is eager to look carefully and "imagine in their minds" what might be going on in a piece of art. Students can become equally immersed in the details of a medieval tapestry, an intricately carved jade sculpture from China, rock art in Botswana, or Seurat's pointillism. Yet we have all followed along on museum tours in which docents find it hard to keep children focused on even the most exquisite works of art. Feet get sore, attention wanders, the gift shop beckons, and art is ignored. Interest and attention to art, as with so many other things that adults think are good for children, has much to do with context—with attending to children's purposes.

As the teachers described in this chapter began making more use of the arts, they discovered that context really was crucial. Their students were more likely to immerse themselves in art if there was a reason for close attention. Each of the children quoted earlier, for example, had been asked to think about the time sequence of a set of visual images. They pored over the details of each picture, analyzing them for clues to the mystery of time. Other primary, intermediate, and middle school students enthusiastically responded to the same task, discussing the historical images, comparing pictures, and making reference to other sources of historical information. In still other classes, students focus critical attention and discussion on selecting the images for a comparative time line.

Making sense of the arts, like making sense of a written text, does not come automatically. Although we are probably born able to perceive patterns in different sensory modalities, experience and culture clearly influence how we interpret the arts. To a large extent, what we expect to see (or hear) influences what we do see (or hear). When something violates our expectations, we try to impose order on it, seeking to make sense out of our

*Authentic tasks encourage close attention to the arts.*

*Barton (2001), Levstik & Barton (2008), Henderson & Levstik (2016)*

*Kisida et al. (2020), Kisida et al. (2020), Martin (2021), Mitchell (1995)*

**190**

experiences. Although students certainly recognize some cultural ways of representing an object, idea, or emotion (downward curving lines indicate sadness, the forward lean of a figure indicates motion), there are others that are quite confusing. Young children who assume that a Japanese print depicts a wedding because the people wear white would certainly make a more supportable interpretation if they knew that, in Japan, white is generally the color of death and mourning. In the same way, children who learn some of the complex language of hand gestures typical of traditional Indonesian dance are better able to appreciate the performance of an Indonesian dancer.

The kind of teacher mediation necessary to help students accomplish these tasks varies, of course, with the degree of familiarity the students have with the arts and their background knowledge of the history depicted. When Liza Flornoy was assigned to teach fourth grade, she knew her students would be studying their state's history. Because she had only recently arrived in the state, she was nervous about her competence in handling this curriculum. She had been quite successful in using the arts in her old school but had few resources for this new assignment. In addition, she was worried because she had been told that her school was "in transition"—redistricting was shifting the school population to include a more even balance of low- and middle-income students. Many of her students would be unfamiliar with the school and the surrounding neighborhood, and some, she had been told, might be actively hostile. When Liza expressed her concerns to her team teacher, Mrs. Kadahota suggested she look at state history materials developed by a local heritage group. Liza liked the emphasis on public art and architecture and thought that, with a few adjustments, the materials might work well. She decided to start with the built environment surrounding her school. This had several advantages. Because the school was located in the state capital, there were a number of buildings and monuments with obvious political and aesthetic significance. The school bordered an area of newly gentrified older homes, a small business and shopping district, and a public housing development, so there would be a variety of public art, from signs and gardens to architecture and graffiti. Liza did some background reading and began adapting the materials from the heritage council and from an archaeology-based program, *Project Archaeology: Investigating Shelter*.

As she had expected, her students had little experience either with buildings and monuments as sources of historical information or with the neighborhood around the school, so Liza planned two introductory experiences on data retrieval. She began with a set of five images of different types of public and private buildings and monuments in the area and introduced several themes that might be related to each building: privacy, values, culture, change over time, social behavior, creativity, and history. Students identified evidence of each theme: An ornate plaster ceiling medallion for creativity, an electrified gas lamp as change over time, a recreation room for social behavior, family photographs as history, art and sculpture as both values and culture, and so forth. Liza then distributed data retrieval charts for the children to use in collecting information from a place of their own choosing— their own home, a favorite vacation spot, a store or recreation area. The data retrieval chart consisted of one sheet of paper. On the front, students filled in columns headed with each theme. On the back, they answered three questions about the building they selected: What is the purpose or function of the place you selected? How does the look, feel, and smell of this place make you think and feel? How important are the social things that happen there— how you are treated, whom you are with, what you do together (or apart)?

Not surprisingly, the children found that the categories listed on the data retrieval chart often overlapped. Two children listed the Bible as evidence of values, for instance, whereas another listed it as social behavior. Several children indicated that separate bedrooms for children was evidence of privacy. "Isn't that a value, too?" asked another child. "And what's the difference between history and change over time? Aren't they pretty much the same things?" Another child declared that "all of it is culture." As a result, the students altered the chart, limiting their categories to privacy, values, change over time, social behavior, and creativity. They also categorized buildings by use—commercial, educational, governmental, industrial, recreational, religious, residential, and transportation related—and compared how each theme was represented in each category. They noted that

Helping students make sense of the arts requires attention to background knowledge. *Sizemore (2011)*

Public art is generally free and accessible.

*Letts & Moe (2009)*

Teachers need to help students collect and organize data.

Specific questions help students organize data collection.

Initial data collection often generates more researchable questions.

several buildings had changed categories over time. A former gas station, for instance, was now an ice cream parlor, and several residences had become commercial buildings. They began compiling a list of questions they wanted to investigate: What caused buildings to change use? Why were older buildings more elaborately decorated? Why were people paying so much more to move into older buildings, rather than buy newer houses in the suburbs? What did the graffiti on some of the buildings mean?

Next, Liza organized a study of two buildings within walking distance of the school. Each student received a research guide—directions for observations and data collection, as well as follow-up activities—a clipboard, and materials for sketching and texture rubbings, as well as a camera. Working in small groups, students collected data on each building. As you look at the task outlined in Figure 14.4, notice that, although it includes

---

Step One: Observe

Carefully examine the building from as many angles and sides as possible. Look for the details and study the overall shape and size. Identify any sounds, smells, and tastes that may be associated with the building. Try to recognize the variety of building materials and textures related to the building. Look for any changes that may have accrued since its construction.

Step Two: Document

Answer as many of the following questions as possible from your observations
1. Name of the building.
2. Describe the location and setting of the building.
3. What is the foundation material?
4. What are the building materials?
5. Sketch or film the different types of windows and doors, as well as decorative materials and designs used on he building.
6. Make texture rubbings of different parts of the building (check with me first!)
7. Are there any chimneys? How many? Draw a picture of the chimney(s).
8. Describe any signs or words on the building
9. What was the building built for?
10. How many stories (floors) does the building have?
11. Describe, draw, or film any evidence of each of our themes.
12. What is the current use of the building?
13. Sketch a floor plan of the first floor of the building.

Step Three: Research

Be a historical detective! Find out as much as you can about the history of our buildings. You will have a chance to talk to a local historian, so think carefully about what questions you might want to ask her. You may also use materials in the folder marked "Built Environment."

Step Four: Interpret

We will be writing and producing a documentary on these buildings. As you plan your work, think about including the following:
1. A drawing or model of what you think the original setting of the building was.
2. Reenactments of some of the historical events the building "lived through."
3. An interview with the builder and/or original owners, discussing what the building meant to each of them.
4. Pictures and discussion of what this building means to the community today.
5. A poem or reader's theater showing what is unique or special about the building.

**FIGURE 14.4  Read-a-Building (adapted from materials developed by the Built Environment Education Consortium, [1990]).**

elements of the arts, it also uses other forms of historical documentation, such as interviews and printed information. Liza also asks her students to use this combination of data sources in their final product, requiring that students express their historical interpretations through visual images as well as different written genres.

When the arts are an integral part of historical study, students are surrounded by a rich array of images that let them see what things looked like, what people did, how they did them, and how people saw themselves or were seen by others. Art is studied as a product of human intention through which an artist or artists create alternate worlds and respond to the worlds created around them. From this perspective, making sense in art—just as in history—requires careful observation and a willingness to consider multiple interpretations. It is not enough, however, for children to be consumers of the historical arts; as they experience the multiple worlds expressed in the arts, they also need to express their own historical perspectives through the arts.

> The arts should be an integral part of historical study.

> Sizemore (2011), Sterman, (2018), Stoddard & Marcus (2017) Stoddard et al. (2017)

## THE ARTS AS VEHICLES FOR EXPRESSING HISTORICAL UNDERSTANDING

Nathan stands before the class about to present his report on the French Revolution: "I kind of thought of it as looking like *The Highwayman* sounds…sort of dark and dangerous." He holds up a charcoal drawing of a street scene in Paris. The paper is black, with white buildings whose faces (literally) stare down into the street or lean back with their windows (eyes) shut. In the street, white figures out of Munch's *The Scream* gather around a red guillotine.

\* \* \*

Jeanette asks her students "What picture comes to your mind when you hear the words *living Constitution?* I'd like you to find different ways to express your ideas…show why the Constitution has lasted so long. For us to be living, we need water, air, food, light.… What kind of things does it take for the Constitution to be living?" One student responds by drawing the Constitution as an eagle in flight, with legs, wings, and beak. Another student writes:

Concepts of freedom
Open minds
Nation as one
States as a union
Timeless set of laws and rights
Ideas accepted
Thoughts spread
Understanding of citizen's desires
Time of brainstorming
Indifferent laws
Outstanding results
No one's rights denied

Each of these students is learning to think *with* and *in* the arts. As they blend feeling and ideas to create art, they make their inner conceptions public. Jeanette recognizes in the list, for instance, that she needs to address the issue of rights denied in the Constitution and the long history of rights movements and calls for redress for rights denied. Further, the process of selecting representations for their inner conceptions shapes students' historical understanding. Where students otherwise might have relied largely on written language to convey ideas, they now have a wider repertoire of forms and symbols available to them. And, as Jeanette notes, when class work includes the arts, "you can't remain an observer very easily. You have to become a participant and when you become a participant, you have a way of learning by doing."

> The arts provide a wider expressive repertoire.

Opportunities to produce
art are as important as
opportunities to view art.

Producing your own historical art is quite different than using the arts as historical data. It is like the difference between reading a novel and writing one. Making historical art, in particular, can seem like a very risky business to a youngster. Faced with the problem of combining the symbology of art and the requirements of history, students will need plenty of supportive instruction. It helps, then, to think of producing historical arts as both problem solving and intellectual risk taking, components of the inquiry-based approach to history used throughout this book.

Art is a form of problem solving
and intellectual risk taking.

## THE ARTS AS PROBLEM SOLVING

Jeanette has asked her eighth graders to represent a portion of the Constitution in some way that will make clear its most significant elements. She tells students to think first about what information they want to convey and then how best to represent it to their peers. Students work in four groups, first discussing the task and then drawing sketches to illustrate to each other how their ideas might best be presented. One group discusses the use of circles "because these things keep repeating." Another debates the appropriateness of cartoon characters that represent the different sides of an issue; a third sketches ideas, playing with spatial relationships, symbols, and colors. Individual groups divide up the work, sending a couple of students off to draw pictures, others to compose the text, and still others to mock up the full presentation on a piece of poster board. Jeanette moves between the groups, asking them questions and making suggestions. She asks one group if Congress has ever chosen a president who did not receive "a majority of the actual votes." She mentions to another group that all people did not receive equal rights in the original Constitution. "Look through the amendments. Whose rights are guaranteed later?" She also comments that one group "has a very good idea, here. Their chart gives you two alternatives; it tells you what happens when there is a majority and what happens when there isn't. How has this changed from the way the Constitution was originally written?" She asks another group if they copied an idea from another source or made it up themselves. "What does this mean?" she asks them. "Tell us about that."

The final products are an interesting mix of art and text. One group presents an illustrated flow chart of the 12$^{th}$ amendment to the U.S. Constitution (election of president and vice president). They have arranged a series of branching choices that must be made in electing the President and Vice President. At each decision point, they have an illustration showing some actual historical event that coincides with the decision that must be made. A hand dropping a vote into a ballot box illustrates the first step when electors meet. Further down the chart, an illustration of what happens when there is a majority vote shows Richard Nixon with his arms above his head, his fingers making the "V" for victory sign. A bubble over his head says, "I am not a crook." Another illustration shows angry Congressmen negotiating the election of Thomas Jefferson. After 2020, students might include the violence surrounding the 2020 electoral college vote.

Clearly, Jeanette's students do not do art as an afterthought to inquiry or as icing on an otherwise less palatable cake. Rather, art is fundamental to the way in which students solve problems in history. The problems that Jeanette sets for her students sometimes require a particular medium—perhaps a dramatization or the selection of music to fit a historical event or period—but more often require that students select their own form of representation. Notice that Jeanette has developed a vocabulary for this type of assignment. Her use of "represent," for instance, operates on several levels: It signals an arts-inclusive activity, refers back to the language used in students' art classes, and, finally, reminds the students that, in this instance, the arts are intended to represent historical content. As she moves between groups, she challenges students to better develop both the art and history in their representations. This can be a real challenge for a teacher, especially when one piece of the work is clearly stronger and better grounded than another. In one group, for instance, the students want to get on with the art without having to carefully construct the history. They confuse the statement of equality in the Declaration of Independence with the Constitution and are preparing an illustration that credits the Constitution with guaranteeing equal rights "to everyone." Jeanette sends them back to their historical sources and leaves them with the more complicated problem of deciding how to visually represent the ideal of universal political equality with the reality of inequity.

**194**

Note, too, how the students use the potential for double entendres in their art. The text on the chart for the 12th Amendment, for instance, is quite straightforward, explaining that when a majority of members of the electoral college vote for a candidate that person becomes president or vice president. The accompanying illustration, however, shows Richard Nixon declaring both his victory and his innocence of wrongdoing. The juxtaposition of text and image speaks volumes about the students' perceptions of the challenges of the democratic process. As historical problem solvers, then, Jeanette's students often transform linguistic information into visual representation. In doing so, they select and retrieve relevant information, generate ideas, and form new concepts. They ponder the organization of shapes and ideas, play with how colors influence each other, how to create spatial as well as historical depth, and how to indicate structural as well as historical relations. It takes courage for children to risk all this, especially in the face of possible misinterpretation by the adults who assess them.

## THE ARTS AS INTELLECTUAL RISK TAKING

Representing ideas through the arts can seem quite risky, particularly to students used to more linguistic modes of expression. They may be unsure of the parameters within which they are working, of the language of interpretation, or the symbol systems open to them. Overall, students are more willing to discuss and use the arts when their teacher accepts and encourages a range of interpretations. They also gain confidence as they listen to and learn from their peers. Not surprisingly, students with little experience with the arts can become quite concerned with "getting it right." In fact, some children become so uncomfortable with their inability to render an image with photographic accuracy that they are stymied in their ability to express themselves.

*Epstein (1994)*

It is not particularly useful at this point to tell students that there is more to art than realism. What seems to work more effectively is to give students choices in terms of medium, practice in using different media, and specific help so that they can create art that is satisfying to them. Dehea Smith found that her students loved to project images, trace them, and then manipulate them for their own purposes. They would draw the background to a picture, for example, and then trace a car or people, and so forth. This worked well early in the year, but their teacher also wanted them to be a bit more adventurous. For one project, then, she helped the students to develop a shadow puppet theater and play. She demonstrated how shadow puppets worked, showed them examples of shadow puppets from different cultures, and then set them to work making their own. It soon became clear that their tiny figures with details drawn on were not going to show up effectively as shadows. Freed from the need to draw realistically, the students began paying attention to shape and space. They experimented with different materials, sizes of puppets, and distance from the screen. With well-timed suggestions from their teacher, the children developed an interesting set of props and puppets using a much wider array of materials than they had tried before. As the children became more confident with these images, their teacher encouraged them to add music and movement to their plays. She also asked the art teacher to teach the students specific techniques to satisfy their desire for realism. He worked with two-point perspective and figure drawing. Later in the year, parents with some experience in stage design took the students to their studio and demonstrated simple techniques to make images feel peaceful, spooky, dangerous, and so forth. By the time the students painted their own stage sets for a series of historical skits, they were able to use some of the techniques they had learned and were more confident in expressing themselves artistically.

*Collaboration with teachers in the arts enriches historical study.*

The art in children's literature can also serve as a beginning point in helping children experiment with different techniques. You might share a book with a distinctive technique—collage, charcoal, crayon resist—and then let students try their hand at the same technique. One class, fascinated with pop-up books, created pop-up illustrations for stories about early settlement in their community. Another class, after reading George Littlechild's *This Land Is My Land* (1993), in which the artist combines photographs,

*Children's literature can be a rich source of visual art.*

*Kiefer (2003), Littlechild (1993)*

**195**

painting, resists, and realia, tried combining these elements. Littlechild's book is auto-biographical, describing his life as a Cree and an artist. The children did much the same thing. They brought in family photographs, cut pictures from magazines, and found other images online that represented the story they wanted to tell. Their teacher photographed children in class, too. She digitized the photographs so that her students could select and print out the parts they wanted to use. The students drew illustrations in crayon resist and paint and glued the pieces of photographs to their pictures. They added shells and bits of lace, as had Littlechild. One girl glued sand below a picture of a bare foot (cut from a magazine). She scratched birds into the crayoned sky, glued on cotton puff clouds, and titled her picture "My first walk on the beach." The result delighted her and inspired her classmates to try some of her techniques.

In a fifth-grade class where students had studied the art of the Sioux and Cheyenne, they decided to see whether they could show what they knew about a historic event using only pictures. One group decided that they would tell the story of the first Norse explorations of North America. Another gave a child's eye view of the Plimouth Colony, and a third presented a Chinese immigrant's view of building the transcontinental railroad. In creating these images, they went back through their history text as well as other sources they had used in studying U.S. history. Their teacher suggested they also review some of the literature they had read on each of these topics, such as *Strange Footprints on the Land: Vikings in America, Meet the Real Pilgrims: Everyday Life on a Plymouth Plantation in 1627, The Seekers*, and *Dragon's Gate*. Although none of these books were recent publications, and not all richly illustrated, they reminded the students of the feelings as well as facts that might be represented in their drawings. A couple of the finished pictures were stick figure renditions of battles, but most provided interesting perspectives on how the students understood—and misunderstood—the events and people they had studied thus far. From a child's eye view, for instance, adults in Plimouth are huge, the forest threatening, plates and bowls empty. All accurate. At the same time, the Wampanoags who populated that part of North America go missing. In other renderings, Vikings sail between icebergs beneath a vast sky of stars with arrows pointing in the direction of a tiny—and unpopulated—North America; Chinese men in baskets dangle next to ice covered mountains while their White bosses sit warm and safe inside a nearby cabin. In the follow-up discussion, omissions were noted, but their teacher also began planning for an end-of-the year wrap up that would involve specific attention to connections between events, perspectives lost, and long-term impacts highlighted.

An important feature of art infused classrooms is that children's artwork is on display. By carefully mounting and arranging students' work, teachers honor the intensity of effort and trust that went into its production. They find that art, like writing, thrives when it has a respectful audience and especially when that audience goes beyond the teacher. One Boston school displays children's art and writing so that adults will see it as they walk their youngsters to class each morning. As a father stops to admire a mural of Native peoples living on the Great Plains, his daughter explains her work to him, pointing out the decorations on tipis, the place where a smudged bear became a large bush, and so forth. Her classmates join her, eagerly sharing other features of the mural, and explaining how each element matched something they had learned about how different Native nations adapted to life on the Great Plains: "See, this is a buffalo. The tipis are made out of buffalo hide, and they use the horn and everything. That's why there's a buffalo painted on this tipi. It has a zigzag lightning thing going from its mouth. We saw that in a book we read. Want to see the book?" Meanwhile another parent compliments a child on how realistic the buffalo looks. "Oh," the child smiles. "We looked at lots of pictures. It was hard to find one that had a whole buffalo, though. At first it looked just like a horse with a *very* big head. Buffaloes have very strange shapes." One friend explains that chickens are easier to draw, but she didn't find evidence that the Plains people kept chickens. "Maybe different birds," another child chimes in.

By displaying student work, teachers provide multiple audiences as well as multiple opportunities for students to discuss the aesthetic and historical choices they have made.

Historical images can be found on the websites of the Smithsonian Institution (*https://www.si.edu*), the National Archives (*https://www.archives.gov*), and the Library of Congress (*https://www.loc.gov*)

*Plimouth* was the original spelling, used beginning in the seventeenth century. The Plimouth Plantation historical site uses that spelling to distinguish it from the nearby community of *Plymouth*. You will find children's literature with either spelling.

Irwin (1980), Loeb (1979), Dillon (1986), Yep (1994)

Literary imagery can inspire visual imagery.

Displaying student art honors the students' problem solving and risk taking in an authentic way.

Through these discussions, they are encouraged to be more experimental—turn bears into bushes, if need be, but care about historical accuracy, and not worry about an experiment that did not come out entirely as planned. In our experience, when student's artwork is displayed and discussed, students become more confident and produce much more interesting, historically sound artwork. As Jeanette explains:

> The arts give children who learn in a different way a lot of different opportunities to learn. I think that it gives them a chance to integrate material or to review what they learn in another way, too. Sometimes a child will seem to be over their head, and when you use a different form, it becomes something they can learn. It certainly provides more interest to teaching. It's more fun for me as a teacher, and I think that makes it more interesting for the students. With the arts…you take what you learn into your being.

## ASSESSMENT AND THE ARTS

As we noted earlier, most of the teachers with whom we work are reasonably comfortable assessing writing processes and products in history and often have established routines for selecting portfolio pieces and sharing student progress with parents and guardians. Although many of these teachers have also used the arts in teaching history, they are less sure of how to assess this aspect of their curriculum. In fact, many of the assessment issues teachers fear in the arts are similar to ones they are already successfully handling in writing. Just as with writing, one issue is how to draw the line between credible and incredible interpretations or renditions. Sometimes, despite everyone's best efforts, students create artwork that reproduces stereotypes, ignores supportable historical interpretations, or is just silly. The work may be attractive or interesting artwork, but it is poor history. When you have worked hard to encourage students to take the risk and use the arts, this can be a real dilemma. How do you respond to the art without encouraging bad history and to the history without discouraging good art? This is particularly problematic when the teacher is insecure about assessing non-representational art. At this point, it may seem easier to rely on linguistic modes of expression—just let students tell you what they know. But that, of course, is exactly what they are doing. They are letting you know that something is missing in their historical thinking. In responding to historical art, it is important to remember that just as with any written historical interpretation, students' work must be historically plausible or possible. In other words, the work must be both *historically sound* and *historically bound*. *Historically sound interpretations* are those that are credible in terms of the history represented in the art. A picture depicting a bus driver happily inviting Rosa Parks to sit in the front of the bus (and not intended as satire) would not be true to events surrounding the Montgomery bus boycott. Such an interpretation, no matter how aesthetically pleasing, cannot be historically sound.

*Historically bound interpretations* are those that make sense within the broader historical context within which an event takes place. In other words, the interpretation is plausible given the time period and culture being studied. Although Jeanette's students did not know for sure that delegates to the Constitutional Convention listened to music by Mozart, it is plausible that they might have done so. In the same way, a fifth grader's representation of cowboys in the 1800s enjoying a televised football game is not historically bound—it would have been impossible for this activity to have taken place.

Jeanette and Jocelyn deal with these issues in two ways. First, students participate in a number of activities that are presented to peers for discussion and suggestion. Although few students make blatant errors with historical soundness, they do sometimes have difficulty with historical boundedness. They have the specific events right, but there are anachronisms—usually items of material culture that would not have appeared in the particular time and place represented. By asking students to explain their work and respond to suggestions, both teachers provide opportunities for students to self-correct or put non-representational art into historical context. Students in both classes also receive written peer evaluations of their work. Jeanette and her students jointly develop a scoring

*Hiebert & Hutchinson (1991), Marcello (1999)*

Assessment in writing and the arts is often quite similar.

*Epstein (1994)*

As with other historical genres, historical art can be assessed on its use of historical evidence.

Historical art can be assessed on its relationship to a broader historical context.

Anachronisms are ideas, events, or situations that are out of their proper historical time.

In explaining their own work, students have an opportunity to put that work in historical perspective or correct anachronisms.

rubric addressing the artistic and historical aspects of each performance. One expectation, for instance, is that the art must expand on any written information, not simply illustrate it. Thus, a poster explaining the electoral college has a straightforward text, but its illustrations comment on and expand the text through political cartoons. In Jocelyn's class she provides a general scoring rubric and students add items that apply to a specific product. All products are judged on historical accuracy, for instance, but students might include specific historical elements of Constitutional history that they think should be addressed in a presentation on that topic.

After peer evaluation, Jeanette also provides feedback on the content as well as the form of presentation. She will compliment students for creative imagery, on the one hand, and tell them to recheck their historical interpretation, on the other. Her students seem to understand the distinction and expect her critique to include both parts of their work. These are, after all, the same distinctions they are asked to make when they analyze other forms of historical art. In this sense, Jeanette insists that students give their own artwork the same respect and close reading accorded other artists.

Sometimes it is not essential that aesthetic merit be assessed, even when the arts are the medium of expression. Younger children, especially, may be able to say what they know through the arts in ways they are not yet able to do linguistically. Thus, providing students with the opportunity to use the arts frees them to say more than they could otherwise manage. Especially with younger students, some teachers find "sketch-to-stretch" activities useful in helping students think about the historical soundness of their ideas. A sketch-to-stretch activity involves creating at least two different images of the same concept, event, or era. At the beginning of their study, children are asked to draw things they associate with some aspect of history. In one classroom, primary school students drew things they associated with Africa *long ago* and things they associated with Africa *now*. Initial pictures combined elements of Disney's *The Lion King*, with jungle scenes, grass huts, and masks. One or two pictures included images of war and starvation. For the most part, however, there was little distinction between *long ago* and *now*. As they studied the history and culture of three different countries within Africa, students compared what they were learning with these first pictures. Sometimes they found elements that were accurate for a particular time and place. More often they found that many of the countries they were studying were quite different from their old ideas—and always had been.

As the unit progressed, the children drew new pictures of *long ago* and *now* for each of the countries. These new pictures combined images drawn from children's literature (*Shaka: King of the Zulus*; *Where Are You Going, Manyoni?*; *Sundiata*; and *14 Cows for America*), and photographs of each country. As children drew their new pictures, it was clear that their view of African countries was changing. Their *now* pictures concentrated on the contrast between urban and rural communities, whereas several of the *long ago* pictures depicted historical figures such as Shaka and Sundiata. Follow-up discussions allowed children to explain why they had included particular things in their pictures or left others out. There were still misunderstandings. One child drew a *now* picture of a young man from Chad who had visited the class. In the drawing, the young man and his sister ride an elephant to the student's school. As he shared his picture, the child explained: "I hope he comes visit our school again, but next time I want him to bring his sister and ride an elephant."

As you may have noticed by now, constructive evaluation shifts the focus from a remediation model for teaching and learning to the construction of a community of inquiry in which students rehearse, refine and revise, and communicate in a distinctive "voice" or style while solving substantive intellectual problems. Such an approach is closer to the way in which adults operate when they are working and is certainly more congruent with the ways in which teachers and students work throughout this book.

We have emphasized that the best assessment exercises have an authentic audience, and much of the work students have done in these classrooms clearly is directed at audiences beyond the teacher. We should also point out that some of the most meaningful assessment occurs when students are writing and creating art for themselves. The benefit of many of the techniques discussed throughout this book is that they give students a chance

Assessment addresses both historical and aesthetic aspects of performance.

Student work is worthy of the same respect and close reading accorded to other artists.

Freedman (2003), Kisida & Bowen (2019)

D. Stanley & Vennema (1988), Stock (1993), Wesniewski (1992), Deedy (2008)

Sketch-to-stretch pictures allow teachers to see where students' misconceptions persist.

M. King et al. (2015)

to demonstrate to themselves what they have learned. During a lesson or a unit, students may have picked up a great deal of information, but it often remains in a somewhat vague or disorganized form. Constructive evaluation provides a chance for students to reflect on their learning in order to identify organizing themes, patterns, and structures—it becomes a way for them to say, "Hey, I know what's going on here, and here's how I know it."

## CONCLUSIONS

You may have noticed the broad array of historical sources used by the students in these chapters during their inquiries. In addition to written documents and manuscripts, their teachers employ art and artifacts, buildings, landscapes, and oral interviews. Teachers carefully scaffold their use, finding that a variety of sources sparks interest and offers opportunities for different ways of learning at different levels of difficulty (see Chapter 4). They encourage students to use an equally wide range of expressive genres to share what they know.

This is not because these sources are somehow simpler to read than documents. Rather, opportunities to use a variety of sources offers students deeper and richer ways of inquiring into the past. Students glimpse other people's ways of being in the world through their arts and artifacts as well as through other types of sources. They consider how sources elicit powerful emotions, and how artists express what the world looks like to them through symbols that speak to different times and places.

If you compare paintings by artists Pops Peterson and Norman Rockwell, for instance, you will notice the ways in which each artist's paintings speak to changing conceptions of similar historical and human experiences. In one pair of paintings, each artist captures a citizen exercising "freedom of speech." Rockwell centers attention on a man speaking in a male-dominated gathering. Peterson centers his painting on a young woman in a more mixed gathering. In another pair of paintings, both artists depict a girl daydreaming before a mirror. Rockwell's subject gazes between her own image and that of a movie star. Peterson's subject sees herself in the mirror, but as a Boy Scout. The contrast invites close observation of each piece of art, conversation about the historical contexts for each painting, speculation about viewers' responses in different time periods, and consideration of how each painting speaks to the present moment.

*Pops Peterson (https://www .popspeterson.com), Norman Rockwell Museum (https://www .nrm.org)*

As the students and teachers in this chapter demonstrate, the arts do not simply illustrate the past described in written form, although they certainly can do that. More importantly, the arts offer students a glimpse of how diverse the world has been and continues to be while providing a wider expressive repertoire for students' own interpretations of the worlds they are investigating. Such experiences hold the promise of fulfilling what historian Gerda Lerner saw as the purpose of history. She wrote

*Lerner (1998 p. 211)*

Being human means thinking and feeling; it means reflecting on the past and visioning into the future. We experience; we give voice to that experience; others reflect on it and give it new form. That new form, in its turn, influences and shapes the way next generations experience their lives. That is why history matters.

# REFERENCES

Afflerbach, P. (2017). *Understanding and using reading assessment, K-12* (3rd ed.). Association for Supervision and Curriculum Development.

Ahlberg, J., & Ahlberg, A. (1986). *The jolly postman and other people's letters.* MSD Holdings.

Aitken, G., & Sinnema, C. (2008). *Effective pedagogy in social sciences/tikanga ā iwi: Best evidence synthesis iteration.* New Zealand Ministry of Education.

Albert, M. (1995). *Impact of an arts-integrated social studies curriculum on eighth graders' thinking capacities.* [Doctoral dissertation, University of Kentucky]. ProQuest Dissertations & Theses Global.

Alexander, K. (2019). *The undefeated.* Versify/Houghton-Mifflin.

Alexander, M. (2020). *The new Jim Crow: Mass incarceration in the age of colorblindness* (10th anniversary ed.). New Press.

Aliki, M. (1983). *Medieval wedding.* HarperCollins.

Alleman, J., & Brophy, J. (1998). Assessment in a social constructivist classroom. *Social Education, 62*(1), 32–34.

Alleman, J., & Brophy, J. (1999). Current trends and practices in social studies assessment for the early grades. *Social Studies and the Young Learner, 11*(4), 15–17.

Altieri, J. L. (2017). From sketchnotes to think-alouds: Addressing the challenges of social studies text. *Social Studies and the Young Learner, 30*(1), 8–12.

Alvarez, J. (2009). *Return to sender.* Alfred A. Knopf Books for Young Readers.

Alvermann, D. E. (1991). The discussion web: A graphic aid for learning across the curriculum. *The Reading Teacher, 45*(2), 92–99. https://www.jstor.org/stable/20200818

Amnesty International (2016). *We are all born free: The Universal Declaration of Rights in pictures.* Lincoln Children's Books.

An, S. (2016). Asian Americans in American history: An AsianCrit perspective on Asian American inclusion in state U.S. history curriculum standards. *Theory & Research in Social Education, 44*(2), 244–276. https://doi.org/10.1080/00933104.2016.1170646

Anand, B., Fine, M., Perkins, T., & Surrey, D. D. (2002). *Keeping the struggle alive: Studying desegregation in our town: A guide to oral history.* Teachers College Press.

Anderson, A. (2017). The stories nations tell: Sites of pedagogy, historical consciousness, and national narratives. *Canadian Journal of Education/Revue Canadienne De l'éducation, 40*(1), 1–38. https://journals.sfu.ca/cje/index.php/cje-rce/article/view/2143

Anderson, L. H. (2008a). *Chains.* Simon & Schuster Books for Young Readers.

Anderson, L. H. (2008b). *Independent dames: What you never knew about the women and girls of the American Revolution.* Simon & Schuster Books for Young Readers.

Andrade, H. G. (2000). Using rubrics to promote thinking and learning. *Educational Leadership, 57*(5), 13–18.

Andrade, H. L., Du, Y., & Wang, X. (2008), Putting rubrics to the test: The effect of a model, criteria generation, and rubric-referenced self-assessment on elementary school students' writing. *Educational Measurement: Issues and Practice, 27*(2), 3–13. https://doi.org/10.1111/j.1745-3992.2008.00118.x

Appleby, J., Hunt, L., & Jacob, M. (1994). *Telling the truth about history.* Norton.

# References

Arias-Ferrer, L., & Egea-Vivancos, A. (2019). Who changes the course of history? Historical agency in the narratives of Spanish pre-service primary teachers. *History Education Research Journal, 16*(2), 322–39. https://doi.org/10.18546/HERJ.16.2.11

Arias-Ferrer, L., Egea-Vivancos, A., & Levstik, L. S. (2019). Historical thinking in the early years: The power of image and narrative. In K. Kerry-Moran & J. Aerila (Eds.), *Story in children's lives: Contributions of the narrative mode to early childhood development. Literacy, and learning* (pp. 175–198). Springer. https://doi.org/10.1007/978-3-030-19266-2_10

Arnheim, R. (1981). *Visual thinking.* University of California Press.

Aronson, M., & Anderson, S. (2005). *Witch-hunt: Mysteries of the Salem witch trials.* Atheneum Books for Young Readers.

Ashby, R., & Lee, P. J. (1998, April). Information, opinion, and beyond. Paper presented at the Annual Meeting of the American Educational Research Association, San Diego.

Atwell, N. (1987). *In the middle: Writing, reading, and learning with adolescents.* Boynton/Cook.

Avery, P. (2002). Political socialization, tolerance and sexual identity. *Theory and Research in Social Education, 30*(2), 190–197. https://doi.org/10.1080/00933104.2002.10473190

Avery, P., Bird, K., Johnstone, S., Sullivan, J. L., & Thalhammer, K. (1992). Exploring political tolerance with adolescents. *Theory & Research in Social Education, 20*(4), 386–420. https://doi.org/10.1080/00933104.1992.10505680

Ayers, E. (2004). *In the presence of mine enemies: The Civil War in the heart of America, 1859–1864.* Norton.

Bakhtin, M. M. (1986). *Speech genres and other late essays* (V. W. McGee, Trans.). University of Texas Press.

Baldwin, J. (1963/1998). *James Baldwin: Collected essays.* The Library of America.

Baldwin, J. (1988). A talk to teachers. In R. Simonson & S. Walker (Eds.), *Multi-cultural literacy* (pp. 3–12). Graywolf.

Barber, B. J. (1992). *An aristocracy of everyone: The politics of education and the future of America.* Ballantine.

Bardige, B. (1988). Things so finely human: Moral sensibilities at risk in adolescence. In C. Gilligan, J. V. Ward, & J. M. Taylor (Eds.), *Mapping the moral domain: A contribution of women's thinking to psychological theory and education* (pp. 87–110). Harvard University Press.

Barton, K. C. (1996). Using magic words to teach social studies. *Social Studies and the Young Learner, 9(2),* 5–8.

Barton, K. C. (2001). A picture's worth. *Social Education, 65*(5), 278–278.

Barton, K. C. (2002). "Oh, that's a tricky piece!": Children, mediated action, and the tools of historical time. *Elementary School Journal, 103*(2), 161–185. https://doi.org/10.1086/499721

Barton, K. C. (2008). Students' ideas about history. In L. S. Levstik & C. A. Tyson (Eds.), *Handbook of research in social studies education* (pp. 239–258). Routledge.

Barton, K. C. (2009). The denial of desire: How to make history education meaningless. In L. Symcox & A. Wilschut (Eds.), *National history standards: The problem of the canon and the future of teaching history* (pp. 265–282). Information Age Publishing.

Barton, K. C. (2011). History: From learning narratives to thinking historically. In W. B. Russell (Ed.), *Contemporary social studies: An essential reader* (pp. 119–138). Information Age Publishing.

Barton, K. C. (2012). Agency, choice and historical action: How history teaching can help students think about democratic decision making. *Citizenship Teaching and Learning, 7*(2), 131–142. https://doi.org/10.1386/ctl.7.2.131_1

Barton, K. C. (2015). Reconsidering religion in the curriculum. In J. H. James (Ed.), *Religion in the classroom: Dilemmas for democratic education* (pp. 67–78). Routledge.

Barton, K. C. (2022). Schematic templates and diverse populations in the United States: Narrative limitations in young people's understanding. In I. B. de Luna & F. van Alphen (Eds.), *Reproducing, rethinking, resisting national narratives. A sociocultural approach to schematic narrative templates in times of nationalism* (pp. 79–95). Information Age.

Barton, K. C., & Avery, P. G. (2016). Research on social studies education: Diverse students, settings, and methods. In Bell, C. A., & Gitomer, D. (Eds.), *Handbook of research on teaching* (5th ed.) (pp. 985–1038). American Educational Research Association.

Barton, K. C., & Ho, L. C. (2022). *Curriculum for justice and harmony: Deliberation, knowledge, and action in social and civic education.* Routledge.

Barton, K. C., & James, J. H. (2010). Religion in history and social studies. *Perspectives: Newsmagazine of the American Historical Association, 48*(5). https://www.historians.org/publications-and-directories/perspectives-on-history/may-2010/religion-in-history-and-social-studies

Barton, K. C., & Levstik, L. S. (2004). *Teaching history for the common good.* Routledge.

Barton, K. C., & Levstik, L. S. (2008). History. In J. Arthur, C. Hahn, & I. Davies (Eds.), *Handbook of education for citizenship and democracy* (pp. 355–366). Sage.

Barton, K. C., & Levstik, L. S. (2010). Why don't more teachers engage students in interpretation? In W. C. Parker (Ed.), *Social studies today: Research and practice* (pp. 35–42). Routledge.

Barton, K. C., & McCully, A. (2005). History, identity and the school curriculum in Northern Ireland: An empirical study of secondary students' ideas and perspectives. *Journal of Curriculum Studies, 37*(1), 85–116. https://doi.org/10.1080/0022027032000266070

Barton, K. C., & Smith, L. A. (1997). Practical issues in literature study groups: Getting the most out of historical fiction in the middle grades. *Social Science Record, 34*(1), 27–31.

Bates, C. C., Schenck, S. M., & Hoover, H. J. (2019). Anecdotal records. *YC Young Children, 74*(3), 14–19.

Beck, I. L., & McKeown, M. G. (1991). Social studies texts are hard to understand: Mediating some of the difficulties. *Language Arts, 68*(6), 482–490. https://www.jstor.org/stable/41961894

Bell, L. A. (2019). *Connecting narrative and the arts in antiracist teaching.* Routledge.

Bender, L. (2013). *Invention.* DK Children.

Bennett, P. S. (1967). *What happened on Lexington Green: An inquiry into the nature and methods of history. Teacher and student manuals.* Office of Education, Bureau of Research. (Eric Document Reproduction Service No. ED 032 333).

Bensen, R. (Ed.) (2001). *Children of the dragonfly: Native American voices on child custody and education.* University of Arizona Press.

Berkeley, S., King-Sears, M. E., Hott, B. L., & Bradley-Black, K. (2012). Are history textbooks more "considerate" after 20 years? *The Journal of Special Education, 47*(4), 217–230. https://doi.org/10.1177/0022466912436813

Bernstein, W. (2013). *Masters of the word: How media shaped history from the alphabet to the internet.* Grove Press.

Bial, R. (2007). *Ellis Island: Coming to the Land of Liberty.* HMH Books for Young Readers.

Bickford, J. (2018). American authors, September 11th, and Civil War representations in historical fiction. *Journal of Social Studies Education Research, 9*(2), 1–27 https://dergipark.org.tr/en/pub/jsser/issue/37944/438279

Bickmore, K. (1999). Elementary curriculum about conflict resolution: Can children handle global politics? *Theory & Research in Social Education, 27*(1), 45–69. https://doi.org/10.1080/00933104.1999.10505869

Bickmore, K. (2015a). Incorporating peace-building citizenship dialogue in classroom curricula: Contrasting cases of Canadian teacher development. In R. Malet, & S. Majhanovich (Eds.), *Building democracy through education on diversity.* Sense Publishers. https://doi.org/10.1007/978-94-6300-259-2_2

Bickmore, K. (2015b). "Keeping, making, and building peace in school." In W. Parker (Ed.), *Social studies today: Research and practice* (2nd ed., pp. 238–245). Routledge.

Bickmore, K. (2017). Conflict, peacebuilding, and education: Rethinking pedagogies in divided societies. In K. Bickmore, R. Hayboe, C. Manion, K. Mundy, & R. Read (Eds.), *Comparative and international education: Issues for teachers* (pp. 268–302). Canadian Scholars.

Billings, D., & Kingsolver, A. E. (Eds.) (2018). *Appalachia in regional context.* University of Kentucky Press.

Blain, K. N., & Kende, I. X. (2021). *Four hundred souls: A community history of African America,* 1619–2019. One World.

Blair, M. W. (2010). *Liberty or death: The surprising story of runaway slaves who sided with the British during the American Revolution.* National Geographic Children's Books.

Blos, J. (1993). Perspectives on historical fiction. In M. O. Tunnell & R. Ammon (Eds.), *The story of ourselves: Teaching history through children's literature* (pp. 11–18). Heinemann.

Blue, R., & Naden, C. J. (2009). *Ron's big mission.* Dutton Children's Books.

Bolgatz, J. (2005). Revolutionary talk: Elementary teacher and students discuss race in a social studies class. *The Social Studies, 96*(6), 259–264. https://doi.org/10.3200/TSSS.96.6.259-264

Boner, P. (1995). New nation, new history: The history workshop in South Africa, 1977–1994. *Journal of American History, 81*(3), 977–985. https://doi.org/10.2307/2081437

Bonilla-Silva, E. (2017). *Racism without racists: Color-blind racism and the persistence of racial inequality in America* (5th ed.). Rowman & Littlefield.

Bradbury, R. (2013). *Bradbury Stories: 100 of his most celebrated tales.* Harper Collins.

Brandt, R. (1988). On assessment in the arts: A conversation with Howard Gardner. *Educational Leadership, 45*(4), 30–34.

# References

Brophy, J., & VanSledright, B. (1997). *Teaching and learning history in elementary schools.* Teachers College Press.

Brown, C. L. (2007). Strategies for making social studies texts more comprehensible for English-language learners. *The Social Studies, 98*(5), 185–188. https://doi.org/10.3200/TSSS.98.5.185-188

Brown, D. (1993). *Wounded Knee: An Indian history of the American West.* (Adapted for young readers by Amy Ehrlich from Dee Brown's *Bury my heart at Wounded Knee.*) Henry Holt.

Brown, J. S., Collins, A., & Duguid, P. (1989). Situated cognition and the culture of learning. *Educational Researcher, 18*(1), 32–42. https://doi.org/10.3102/0013189X018001032

Brown, K. D., & Brown, A. L. (2010). Silenced memories: An examination of the sociocultural knowledge on race and racial violence in office school curriculum. *Equity & Excellence in Education, 43*(2), 139–154. https://doi.org/10.1080/10665681003719590

Brown, M. (2020). *Side by side: The story of Dolores Huerta and Cesar Chavez/Lado a lado: La Historia de Dolores Huerta y Cesar Chavez.* HarperCollins.

Bruchac, J. (2002). *The Arrow over the door.* Puffin.

Bruner, J. (1986). *Actual minds, possible worlds.* Harvard University Press.

Bryant, J. A., Jr. (2006). What is good citizenship? The story of Chiune Sugihara. *Social Studies and the Young Learner, 19*(2), 13–15.

Buck, P. (2001). *Worked to the bone: Race, class, power and privilege in Kentucky.* Monthly Review Press.

Built Environment Educational Consortium. (1990). *Assessment tasks submitted to the Kentucky Council on School Performance Standards.* Unpublished report.

Bunting, E. (2001). *Dandelions.* HMH Books for Young Readers.

Bunting, E. (2014). *Washday.* Holiday House.

Busey, C. L. (2017). *Más que Esclavos*: A BlackCrit examination of the treatment of Afro-Latin@s in U.S. high school world history textbooks. *Journal of Latinos and Education, 18*(3), 197–214. https://doi.org/10.1080/15348431.2017.1386102

Busey, C. L., & Walker, I. (2017). A dream and a bus: Black critical patriotism in elementary social studies standards. *Theory & Research in Social Education, 45*(4), 456–488. https://doi.org/10.1080/00933104.2017.1320251

Calderón, D. (2014). Uncovering settler grammars in curriculum. *Educational Studies: Journal of The American Educational Studies Association, 50*(4), 313–338. https://doi.org/10.1080/00131946.2014.926904

Campbell, N. (2005). *Shi-she-etko.* Groundwood Books, House of Anansi Press.

Capaldi, G., & Pearce, Q. L. (2011). *Red Bird sings: The story of Zitkala-Ša, native American author, musician, and activist.* Carolrhoda Books.

Carretero, M., Psaltis, C., & Cehajic-Clancy, E. (2017). *History education and conflict transformation: Social psychological theories, history education and reconciliation.* Palgrave Macmillan. https://doi.org/10.1007/978-3-319-54681-0_1

Casanova, U. (1995). An exchange of views on "The great speckled bird." *Educational Researcher, 24*(6), 22.

Cazden, C. B. (1988). *Classroom discourse: The language of teaching and learning.* Heinemann.

Certo, J., Moxley, K., Reffitt, K., & Miller, J. A. (2010). I learned how to talk about a book: Children's perceptions of literature circles across grade and ability levels. *Literacy Research and Instruction, 49*(3), 243–263, https://doi.org/10.1080/19388070902947352

Choi, Y. (2003). *The Name Jar.* Dragonfly Books.

Chrisp, P. (2009). *Atlas of ancient worlds.* DK Publishing.

Coerr, E. (1994). *Sadako.* Putnam.

Cohen, E. G. (1986). *Designing groupwork: Struggle for the heterogenous classroom.* Teachers College Press.

Cole, H. (2012). *Unspoken: A story from the Underground Railroad.* Scholastic.

Colley, L. (2019). (Un) Restricting feminism: High school students' definitions of gender and feminism in the context of the historic struggle for women's rights. *Theory & Research in Social Education, 47*(3), 426–455. https://doi.org/10.1080/00933104.2019.1593268

Colley, L., Mueller, R., & Thacker, E. (2021). "We just followed the lead of the sources": An investigation of how teacher candidates developed critical curriculum through subject matter knowledge. *The Journal of Social Studies Research.* https://doi.org/10.1016/j.jssr.2020.12.001

Collier, J. L., & Collier, C. (2012). *My brother Sam is dead.* Blackstone Publishing.

Colman, P. (2015). *Thanksgiving: The true story.* Henry Holt and Company.

Cooper, H. (2014). *Writing history 7–11: Historical writing in different genres.* Routledge.

Cooper, P. M. (2011). *The classrooms all young children need: Lessons in teaching from Vivian Paley.* University of Chicago Press.

Cope, B., & Kalantzes, M. (1990). Literacy in the social sciences. In F. Christie (Ed.), *Literacy for a changing world* (pp. 118–142). Australian Council for Educational Research.

Cornbleth, C., & Waugh, D. (1995). *The great speckled bird: Multicultural politics and educational policy making*. St. Martin's Press.

Cribb, J. (2005). *Money*. DK Children.

Crocco, M. (1998). Putting the actors back on stage: Oral history in the secondary school classroom. *The Social Studies, 89*(1), 19–24. https://doi.org/10.1080/00377999809599817

Crocco, M. S. (2018). Gender and sexuality in history education. In S. A. Metzger & L. M Harris (Eds.), *The Wiley international handbook of history teaching and learning* (pp. 335–364). Wiley. https://doi.org/10.1002/9781119100812.ch13

Cruz, B. C., & Thornton, S. J. (2013). *Teaching social studies to English language learners* (2nd ed.) Routledge.

Culclasure, S. (1999). *The past as liberation from history*. Lang.

Cushman, K. (1994). *Catherine, called Birdy*. Clarion.

Darling-Hammond, L. (2008). *Powerful learning: What we know about teaching for understanding*. Jossey-Bass.

Darling-Hammond, L. (2010). *The flat world and education: How America's commitment to equity will determine our future*. Teachers College Press.

Deedy, C. A. (2018). *14 cows for America*. Holiday House.

Deloria, P. J. (2004). *Indians in unexpected places*. University of Kansas Press.

den Heyer, K. (2018). Historical agency: Stories of choice, action, and social change. In S. Metzger & L. M. Harris (Eds.), *The Wiley international handbook of history teaching and learning* (pp. 227–252). Wiley. https://doi.org/10.1002/9781119100812.ch9

Dennis, M. (2002). *Red, white, and blue letter days: An American calendar*. Cornell University Press.

Dewey, J. (1929). *The quest for certainty: A study of the relation of knowledge and action*. Putnam.

Dewey, J. (1933). *How we think: A restatement of the relation of reflective thinking to the educative process*. Heath.

Dewey, J. (1990). *The school and society and the child and the curriculum*. University of Chicago. (Original work published 1900 and 1902).

Dickinson, J. (1993). Children's perspectives on talk: Building a learning community. In K. M. Pierce & C. J. Gilles (Eds.), *Cycles of meaning: Exploring the potential of talk in learning communities* (pp. 99–116). Heinemann.

Dillon, E. (1986). *The seekers*. Scribner's.

Donaldson, M. (1978). *Children's minds*. Norton.

Douglass, F. (1852). Oration, delivered in Corinthian Hall, Rochester by Frederick Douglass, July 5, 1852. Lee, Mann & Co. https://archive.org/details/orationdelivered00fred/page/n1/mode/2up

Duke, N. K., & Bennett-Armistead, S. (2003). *Reading and writing informational texts in primary grades: Research-based practices*. Scholastic Teaching Resources.

Duke N. K., & Pearson P. D. (2009). Effective practices for developing reading comprehension. *Journal of Education, 189*(1–2):107–122. https://doi.org/10.1177/0022057409189001-208

Duke, N. K., Halvorsen, A.-L., & Knight, J. A. (2012). Building knowledge through informational text. In A. M., Pinkham, T. Kaefer, & S. B. Neuman (eds.), *Knowledge development in early childhood: Sources of learning and classroom implications*(pp. 205–219). Guilford Press.

Dunbar-Ortiz, R. (2014). *An indigenous people's history of the United States*. Beacon Press.

Dunbar-Ortiz, R. (2016). *"All the real Indians died off" and 20 other myths about Native Americans*. Beacon Press.

Dunn, R. E. (2012). *The adventures of Ibn Battuta*. University of California Press.

Echevarria, J., Vogt, M. E., & Short, D. (2017). *Making content comprehensible for English learners: The SIOP® model* (5th ed.). Pearson.

Educators for Social Change. (2021). Teaching about gender identity. https://educators4sc.org/topic-guides/teaching-about-gender-identity/

Ehlers, M. G. (1999). "No pictures in my head": The uses of literature in the development of historical understanding. *Magazine of History, 13*(2), 5–9. https://doi.org/ 10.1093/maghis/13.2.5

Ehrenhalt, J. (2019). Authors of their own stories. *Learning for Justice, 63*. https://www.learningforjustice.org/magazine/fall-2019/authors-of-their-own-stories

Eisner, E. (1988). *The role of discipline-based art education in America's schools*. Getty Center for Education in the Arts.

Eller, R. (2008). *Uneven ground: Appalachia since 1945*. University Press of Kentucky.

# References

Elshtain, J. B. (1981). *Public man, private woman: Women in social and political thought.* Princeton University Press.

Epstein, T. L. (1994). The arts of history: An analysis of secondary school students' interpretations of the arts in historical contexts. *Journal of Curriculum and Supervision, 9,* 174–194.

Epstein, T. L. (2009). *Interpreting national history: Race, identity, and pedagogy in classrooms.* Routledge.

Erekson, J. (2014). *Engaging minds in social studies classrooms.* Association for Supervision and Curriculum Development

Evans, R. W. (1988). Lessons from history: Teacher and student conceptions of the meaning of history. *Theory & Research in Social Education, 16*(3), 203–225. https://doi.org/10.1080/00933104 .1988.10505565

Evans, R. W. (2004). *The social studies wars: What should we teach the children?* Teaches College Press.

Evans, R. W., Avery, P. G., & Pederson, P. V. (1999). Taboo topics: Cultural restraint on teaching social issues. *The Social Studies, 90*(5), 218–244. https://doi.org/10.1080/00377999909602419

Faruqi, R. (2015). *Lailah's lunchbox: A Ramadan story.* Tilbury House.

Field, S. L. (2003). Using children's literature and the universals of culture to teach about Mexico. *The Social Studies, 94*(3), 123–127. https://doi.org/10.1080/00377990309600194

Fines, J., & Verrier, R. (1974). *The drama of history: An experiment in co-operative teaching.* New University Education.

Fisher, D., & Frey, N. (2018). The uses and misuses of graphic organizers in content area learning. *The Reading Teacher, 71*(6), 763–766. https://doi.org/10.1002/trtr.1693

Flanagan, L. (2016, March 14). How teachers are using "Hamilton" the musical in the classroom. *Mindshift.* https://www.kqed.org/mindshift/44137/how-teachers-are-using-hamilton-the-musical-in-the-classroom.

Fleischman, P. (1992). *The whipping boy.* HarperCollins.

Fleischman, P. (2013). *Bull run.* HarperCollins.

Floca, B. (2013). *Locomotive.* Atheneum.

Flournoy, V. (1985). *The Patchwork Quilt.* Dial Books for Young Readers.

Foner, E. (2002). *Who owns history? Rethinking the past in a changing world.* Hill and Wang.

Forbes, E. (1967). *Johnny Tremain.* Houghton Mifflin.

Foster, S. J., & Yeager, E. A. (1999). "You've got to put together the pieces": English 12-year-olds encounter and learn from historical evidence. *Journal of Curriculum and Supervision, 14*(4), 286–317.

Fox, R. A., Jr. (1993). *Archaeology, history, and Custer's last battle.* University of Oklahoma Press.

Fránquiz, M. E., & Salinas, C. S. (2011). Newcomers developing English literacy through historical thinking and digitized primary sources. *Journal of Second Language Writing, 20*(3), 196–210. https:// doi.org/10.1016/j.jslw.2011.05.004.

Freedman, K. (2003). *Teaching visual culture: Curriculum, aesthetics, and the social life of art.* Teachers College Press.

Freedman, R. (1980). *Immigrant kids.* Dutton.

Freedman, R. (2002). *Confucius: The golden rule.* Arthur A. Levine.

Freedman, R. (2006). *Freedom walkers: The story of the Montgomery bus boycott.* Holiday House.

Fritz, J. (1967). *Early thunder.* Coward-McCann.

Fritz, J. (1983). *The double life of Pocahontas.* Putnam.

Fritz, J. (1987). *Shh! We're writing the constitution.* Putnam.

Gabella, M. S. (1994). Beyond the looking glass: Bringing students into the conversation of historical inquiry. *Theory & Research in Social Education, 22*(3), 340–363. https://doi.org/10.1080/00933104 .1994.10505728

Gaddis, J. L. (2002). *The landscape of history: How historians map the past.* Oxford University Press.

Gallavan, N. P., & Kottler, E. (2007). Eight types of graphic organizers for empowering social studies students and teachers. *The Social Studies, 98*(3), 117–123. https://doi.org/10.3200/TSSS .98.3.117-128

Garrison, D. R., & Akyol, Z. (2013). Toward the development of a metacognition construct for communities of inquiry. *The Internet and Higher Education, 17*(April), 84–89. https://doi.org/10 .1016/j.iheduc.2012.11.005

Garza, C. L. (1996). *In my family/En mi familia.* Children's Book Press.

Gerdner, L. (2008). *Grandfather's story cloth.* Shen's.

Gerwin, D., & Zevin, J. (2011). *Teaching U.S. history as mystery* (2nd ed.). Routledge.

Giff, P. R. (2005). *Willow Run.* Random House Children's Books.

Glazewski, K. D., & Hmelo-Silver, C. E. (2019). Scaffolding and supporting use of information for ambitious learning practices. *Information and Learning Sciences, 120*(1/2), 39–58. https://doi.org/10 .1108/ILS-08-2018-0087

Goldberg, F., & Savenije, G. M. (2018). Teaching controversial historical issues. In S. Metzger & L. M. Harris (Eds.), *The Wiley international handbook of history teaching and learning* (pp. 503–526). Wiley. https://doi.org/10.1002/9781119100812.ch19

Goldenberg, C., & Coleman, R. (2010). *Promoting academic achievement among English learners: A guide to the research*. Corwin.

Golenbock, P. (1990). *Teammates*. Harcourt Brace.

Göncü, A., & Gauvain, M. (2012). Sociocultural approaches to educational psychology: Theory, research, and application. In K. R. Harris, S. Graham, T. Urdan, C. B. McCormick, G. M. Sinatra, & J. Sweller (Eds.), *APA educational psychology handbook, Vol. 1. Theories, constructs, and critical issues* (pp. 125–154). American Psychological Association. https://doi.org/10.1037/13273-006

Gonzalez, N., Moll, L. C., & Amanti, C. (2005). *Funds of knowledge: Theorizing practice in households, communities, and classrooms*. Routledge.

Goodrich, H. (1996/1997). Understanding rubrics. *Educational Leadership, 54*(4), 14–17.

Goodwin, B. (2011). *Doing what matters most to change the odds for student success*. Association for Supervision and Curriculum Development.

Gordon-Reed, A. (2008). *The Hemingses of Monticello: An American family*. Norton.

Gordon, L. (1990). U.S. women's history. In E. Foner (Ed.), *The new American history* (pp. 185–210). Temple.

Grant, S. G. (2003). *History lessons: Teaching, learning, and testing in U.S. high school classrooms*. Routledge.

Gravel, E. (2019). *What is a refugee?* Schwartz & Wade.

Greenblatt, S. (2011). *The swerve: How the world became modern*. WW Norton & Company.

Greene, M. (1995). Art and imagination: Reclaiming the sense of possibility. *Phi Delta Kappan, 76*(5), 378–382. https://www.jstor.org/stable/20405345

Griffin, A. F. (1992). *A philosophical approach to the subject-matter preparation of teachers of history*. National Council for the Social Studies.

Hahn, C., Bernard-Powers, J., Crocco, M., & Woyshner, C. (2007). *Gender equity in social studies* (2nd ed.). In S. Klein, B. Richardson, D. A. Grayson, L. H. Fox, C. Kramarae, D. S. Pollard, & C. A. Dwyer (Eds.), *Handbook for achieving gender equity through education* (pp. 365–388). Routledge.

Hahn, C. L., & Tocci, C. M. (1990). Classroom climate and controversial issues discussion: A five nation study. *Theory & Research in Social Education, 18*(4), 344–362. https://doi.org/10.1080/00933104.1990.10505621

Hamilton, V. (1985). *The people could fly*. Knopf.

Hannah-Jones, M. (2019, April 14). Our democracy's founding ideals were false when they were written. Black Americans have fought to make them true. *New York Times Magazine*. https://www.nytimes.com/interactive/2019/08/14/magazine/black-history-american-democracy.html

Harris, T. A. (Director). (2006). *The twelve disciples of Nelson Mandela* [Film]. California Newsreel.

Harrison, C., et al. (2005). *Guns, germs, and steel* [Film]. National Geographic.

Hart, D. (1994). *Authentic assessment: A handbook for educators*. Addison-Wesley.

Hart, D. (1999). Opening assessment to our students. *Social Education, 65*(6), 343–345.

Hattie, J. (2009). *Visible learning: A synthesis of over 800 meta-analyses relating to achievement*. Routledge.

Hattie, J., & Timperley, H. (2007). The power of feedback. *Review of Educational Research, 77*(1), 81–112. https://doi.org/10.3102/003465430298487

Haynes, C. C., & Thomas, O. (2007). *Finding common ground: A first amendment guide to religion and public schools*. First Amendment Center.

Hemphill, S. (2011). *Wicked girls: A novel of the Salem witch trials*. Recorded Books.

Henderson, A. G., & Levstik, L. S. (2016). Reading objects: Children reading material culture. *Advances in Archaeological Practice, 4*(4) 503–516. http://doi.org/10.7183/2326-3768.4.4

Hess, D. (2002a). Teaching controversial public issues discussions: Learning from skilled teachers. *Theory & Research in Social Education, 30*(1), 10–41. https://doi.org/10.1080/00933104.2002.10473177

Hess, D. (2002b). Teaching to public controversy in a democracy. In J. J. Patrick & R. S. Leming (Eds.), *Education in democracy for Social Studies teachers: Principles and practices for the improvement of teacher education*. ERIC/ChESS.

Hess, D. (2009). *Controversy in the classroom: The democratic power of discussion*. Routledge.

Hess, D., & McAvoy, P. (2014. *The political classroom: Evidence and ethics in democratic education*. Routledge.

Hesse, K. (2004). *The cats in Krasinski Square*. Scholastic Press.

Hickey, M. G. (2006). Family stories and memorabilia: Oral history projects in elementary schools. In B. A. Lanman & L. M. Wendling (Eds.), *Preparing the next generation of oral historians: An anthology of oral history education* (pp. 181–194). Altamira Press.

# References

Hicks, D., van Hover, S., Doolittle, P. E., & VanFossen, P. (2012). Learning social studies: An evidence-based approach. In K. R. Harris, S. Graham, T. Urdan, A. G. Bus, S. Major & H. L. Swanson (Eds.), *APA educational psychology handbook: Vol. 3. Application to learning and teaching* (pp. 283–307). American Psychological Association. https://doi.org/10.1037/13275-012

Hiebert, E. H., & Hutchinson, T. A. (1991). Research directions: The current state of alternative assessments for policy and instructional uses. *Language Arts, 68*(8), 662–668. https://www.jstor.org/stable/41961920

Hinojosa, M. (2020). *Once I was you.* Atria Books.

Hirschfelder, A., & Beamer, Y. W. (2000). *Native Americans today: Resources and activities for educators, grades 4–8.* Teacher Idea Press.

Hodder, I. (2012). *Entangled: An archaeology of the relationship between people and things.* Wiley-Blackwell.

Hodder, I. (Ed.) (2009). *Archeology as long-term history.* Cambridge University Press.

Hoffman, M. (2002). *The color of home.* Phyllis Fogelman Books.

Hollinger, D. A. (1997). National solidarity at the end of the twentieth century: Reflections on the United States and liberal nationalism. *Journal of American History, 84,* 559–569.

Holt, T. C. (1990). *Thinking historically: Narrative, imagination, and understanding.* College Entrance Examination Boards.

Holton, W. (1999). *Forced founders: Indians, debtors, slaves, and the making of the American revolution in Virginia.* University of North Carolina Press.

Hoose, P. M. (2009). *Claudette Colvin: Twice toward justice.* Melanie Kroupa Books/Farrar Straus Giroux.

Hopkinson, D. (2006). *Up before daybreak: Cotton and people in America.* Scholastic.

Hughes, J., Jewson, N., & Unwin, L. (Eds) (2007). *Communities of practice: Critical perspectives.* Routledge.

Hundorf, S. (2001). *Going native: Indians in the American cultural imagination.* Cornell University Press.

Hunter, B. T. (2005). *The girls they left behind.* Fitzhenry & Whiteside.

I-Care Language. (2011, October 7). *DBS school counselor.* http://dbsschoolcounselor.blogspot.com/2011/10/i-care-language_07.html

Irwin, C. (1980). *Strange footprints on the land: Vikings in America.* Harper.

Iseke-Barns (2009). Unsettling fictions: Disrupting popular discourses and trickster tales in books for children. *Journal of the Canadian Association for Curriculum Studies, 7*(1), 24–57. https://jcacs.journals.yorku.ca/index.php/jcacs/article/view/17988

James, J. H. (2008). Teachers as protectors: Making sense of preservice teachers' resistance to interpretation in elementary history teaching. *Theory & Research in Social Education, 36*(3), 172–205. https://doi.org/10.1080/00933104.2008.10473372

James, J. H. (2009). Addressing subjectivity in historical thinking: Who was Christopher Columbus? In E. Heilman (Ed.), *Social studies and diversity education: What we do and why we do it* (pp. 141–144). Routledge.

James, J. H., & McVay, M. (2009). Critical literacy for young citizens: First graders investigate the first Thanksgiving. *Early Childhood Education Journal, 36,* 347–354. https://doi.org/10.1007/s10643-008-0296-6

Jennings, F. (1975). *The invasion of America: Indians, colonialism, and the cant of conquest.* University of North Carolina Press.

Jobe, R., & Dayton-Sakari, M. (2003). *Info-kids: How to use nonfiction to turn reluctant readers into enthusiastic learners.* Pembroke Publishers, Ltd.

Johnson, D. W., Johnson, R. T., & Holubec, E. J. (1993). *Circles of learning: Cooperation in the classroom* (4th ed.). Interaction Book Company.

Johnston, P. (1992). *Constructive evaluation of literate activity.* Longman.

Jones, S. P. (2020). Ending curriculum violence. *Teaching Tolerance, 64.* https://www.learningforjustice.org/magazine/spring-2020/ending-curriculum-violence

Jordan, W. D. (1968). *White over black: American attitudes toward the Negro, 1550–1812.* University of North Carolina Press.

Journell, W. (2008). When oppression and liberation are the only choices: The representation of African Americans within states social studies standards. *Research in Social Studies Education, 32*(1), 40–50.

Joyner, C. (1984). *Down by the riverside: A South Carolina slave community.* University of Illinois Press.

Kadohata, C. (2009). *Weedflower.* Atheneum.

Kammen, M. (1991). *Mystic chords of memory: The transformation of tradition in American culture.* Knopf.

Kansteiner, W. (1993). Hayden White's critique of the writing of history. *History and Theory, 32*(3), 273–293. https://doi.org/10.2307/2505526

Kaplan, S. N., & Gould, B. (2005). *The flip book, too.* Educator to Educator.

Kawashima-Ginsberg, K., & Junco, R. (2018). Teaching controversial issues in a time of polarization. *Social Education, 82*(6), 323–329.

Kendi, I. X. (2016). *Stamped from the beginning: The definitive history of racist ideas in America.* Nation Books.

Kendi, I. X., & Blain, K. N. (Eds.) (2021). *Four hundred souls: A community history of African America, 1619–2019.* One World.

Kermode, F. (1980). Secrets and narrative sequence. *Critical Inquiry, 7*(1), 83–101. https://www.jstor.org/stable/1343177

Kerr, J. (1971). *When Hitler stole pink rabbit.* Coward, McCann, & Geoghegan.

Kiefer, B. (2003). Nonfiction literature to study the arts. In J. Kristo & R. Salesi (Eds.), *Nonfiction children's literature in the K-8 classroom* (2nd ed.). Christopher-Gordon Publishers.

Kiefer, B. Z., Tyson, C., Barger, B. P., Patrick, L., & Reilly-Sanders, E. (2022). *Charlotte Huck's children's literature: A brief guide* (4th ed.). McGraw-Hill.

Kilgore, D. (1999). Understanding learning in social movements: A theory of collective learning. *International Journal of Lifelong Education, 18*(3), 191–202. https://doi.org/10.1080/026013799293784

Kimmerer, R. W. (2013). *Braiding sweetgrass: Indigenous wisdom, scientific knowledge, and the teachings of plants.* Milkweed.

King, L., & Kasun, G. S. (2013). Food for thought. A framework for social justice in social justice education. *Focus on Middle School, 25*(3), 1–4.

King, L. J. (2014). More than slaves: Black founders, Benjamin Banneker, and critical intellectual agency. *Social Studies Research and Practice, 9*(3), 88–105.

King, L. J. (2016). Teaching black history as a racial literacy project. *Race, Ethnicity and Education, 19*(6), 1303–1318. https://doi.org/10.1080/13613324.2016.1150822

King, L. J. (2019). Critical family history as a strategy for multicultural history education. In Hinnant-Crawford, B. N., Platt, C. S., Newman, C. R., & Hilton, A. (Eds.), *Comprehensive multicultural education in the 21st century: Increasing access in the age of retrenchment* (pp. 59–79). Information Age Publishing.

King, L. J. (2020). Black history is not American history: Toward a framework of black historical consciousness. *Social Education, 84*(6), 335–341.

King, L. J., & Woodson, L. (2016/2017). Baskets of cotton and birthday cakes: Teaching slavery in social studies classrooms. *Social Studies Education Review, 6*(1), 1–18.

King, M. B., Newmann, F. M., & Carmichael, D. L. (2015). Authentic intellectual work: Common standards for teaching social studies. In W. C. Parker (Ed.), *Social studies today: Research and practice* (2nd ed., pp. 53–64). Routledge.

King, R. (2012, 9 November). 10 tips to promote global citizenship in the classroom. *The Guardian.* https://www.theguardian.com/teacher-network/2012/nov/09/global-citizenship-10-teaching-tips

Kisida, B., & Bowen, D. (2019). New evidence of the benefits of art education. *Brown Center Chalkboard.* https://www.brookings.edu/blog/brown-center-chalkboard/2019/02/12/new-evidence-of-the-benefits-of-arts-education/

Kisida, B., Goodwin, L., & Bowen, D. H. (2020). Teaching history through theater: The effects of arts integration on students' knowledge and attitudes. *AERA Open, 6*(1). https://doi.org/10.1177/2332858420902712

Kitson, A., & Husbands, C. (2011). *Teaching and learning history 11–18: Understanding the past.* Open University Press.

Klages, E. (2006). *The green glass sea.* Viking Children's Books/Penguin Young Readers Group.

Klass, S. S. (2009). *Soldier's secret: The story of Deborah Sampson.* Henry Holt Books for Young Readers.

Knipper, K. J. and Duggan, T. J. (2006), Writing to learn across the curriculum: Tools for comprehension in content area classes. *The Reading Teacher, 59*(5), 462–470. https://doi.org/10.1598/RT.59.5.5

Kostyal, K. M. (2009). *1776: A new look at Colonial Williamsburg.* National Geographic Children's Books.

Krakow, K. (2002). *The Harvey milk story.* Two Lives Publishing.

Krashen, S. (2003). *Explorations in language acquisition and use.* Heinemann.

Kristo, J. V., & Bamford, R. A. (2004). *Non-fiction in focus: A comprehensive framework for helping students become independent readers and writers of nonfiction, K–6.* Scholastic Professional Books.

Kroll, S. (2009). *Barbarians!* Dutton Children's Books.

Lainez, R. C. (2010). *From North to South/Del Norte al Sur.* Children's Book Press.

# References

LaMotta, V. M., & Schiffer, M. B. (2001). Behavioral archaeology: Toward a new synthesis. In I. Hodder (Ed.), *Archaeological theory today* (pp. 14–64). Polity Press.

Langley, S. (2020). *A ride to remember: A civil rights story*. Abram's Books for Young Readers.

Larson, B. E., & Keiper, T. A. (2007). *Instructional strategies for middle and high school*. Routledge.

Lave, J., & Wenger, E. (1991). *Situated learning: Legitimate peripheral participation*. Cambridge University Press.

Lee, E. (2016). *The making of Asian America: A history*. Simon & Schuster.

Leinhardt, G. (1994). A time to be mindful. In G. Leinhardt, I. O. Beck, & C. Stainton (Eds.), *Teaching and learning in history* (pp. 209–255). Routledge.

Lemke, J. (1991). *Talking science: Language, learning, and values*. Ablex.

LePore, J. (2018). *These truths: A history of the United States*. Norton

Lerner, G. (1998). *Why history matters: Life and thought*. Oxford University Press.

Letts, C. A., & Moe, J. (2009). *Project Archaeology: Investigating shelter*. Montana State University.

Lévesque, S. (2008). *Thinking historically: Educating students for the twenty-first century*. University of Toronto Press.

Levine, A. (1991). *All the lights in the night*. Tambourine Books.

Levine, L. W. (2007). *Black culture and Black consciousness: Afro-American folk thought from slavery to freedom*. Oxford University Press.

Levine, P. (2012, October 11). What we need to do about civic education. *HuffPost*. http://www.huffingtonpost.com/peter-levine/what-we-need-to-do-about-_b_1957948.html

Levine, P. (2013). *We are the ones we have been waiting for: The promise of civic renewal in America*. Oxford University Press.

Levstik, L. S. (1986). History from the bottom up. *Social Education, 50*(2), 1–7 (insert).

Levstik, L. S. (1989). Historical narrative and the young reader. *Theory into Practice, 28*(2), 114–119. https://doi.org/10.1080/00405848909543389

Levstik, L. S. (1993). Interpreting the past: History and narrative in the elementary curriculum. In Cullinan, B. (Ed). *Literature across the curriculum: Making it happen*. International Reading Association.

Levstik, L. S. (1995). Narrative constructions: Cultural frames for history. *The Social Studies, 86*(3), 113–116. https://doi.org/10.1080/00377996.1995.9958381

Levstik, L. S. (1996a). NCSS and the teaching of history. In O. L. Davis (Ed.), *NCSS in retrospect* (Bulletin 92, pp. 21–34). National Council for the Social Studies.

Levstik, L. S. (1996b). Negotiating the history landscape. *Theory & Research in Social Education, 24*(4), 393–397.

Levstik, L. S. (1997). "Any history is someone's history": Listening to multiple voices from the past. *Social Education, 61*(1), 48–51.

Levstik, L. S. (1999). "The boys we know; The girls in our school": Early adolescents understanding of women's historical significance. *International Journal of Social Studies, 12*(2), 19–34.

Levstik, L. S. (2000). Articulating the silences: Teachers' and adolescents' conceptions of historical significance. In P. Stearns, P. Seixas, & S. Wineburg (Eds.), *Knowing, teaching, & learning history* (pp. 284–305). New York University Press.

Levstik, L. S. (2001). Daily acts of ordinary courage: Gender equitable practice in the social studies classroom. In P. O'Reilly, E. M. Penn, & K. de Marrais (Eds.), *Educating young adolescent girls* (pp. 191–214). Routledge.

Levstik, L. S. (2003). "To fling my arms wide": Students learning about the world through nonfiction. In R. A. Bamford & J. V. Kristo (Eds.), *Making facts come alive: Choosing quality nonfiction literature K–8* (pp. 221–234). Christopher-Gordon.

Levstik, L. S. (2007). In pursuit of a usable past. In R. Wade (Ed.), *Community action rooted in history: The CiviConnections model of service-learning* (pp. 6–11). (Bulletin 106). National Council for the Social Studies.

Levstik, L. S. (2013). Learning to work it out: Social education for young students. In R. Reutzel (Ed.), *Handbook of research-based practice in early education* (pp. 395–412). Guilford Press.

Levstik, L. S. (2014a). *Historical agency in book sets*. National History Education Clearinghouse. http://teachinghistory.org/teaching-materials/teaching-guides/22365

Levstik, L. S. (2014b). What can history and the social sciences contribute to civic education? In J. Pagés & A. Santisteban (Eds.), *Una mirada al pasado y un proyecto de futuro*. Asociación de Professorado de Didáctica de las Ciencias Sociales.

Levstik, L. S. (2016). Outside over there: *My Book House* divides the world, 1919–1954. *Theory & Research in Social Education, 44*(4), 455–478. https://doi.org/10.1080/00933104.2016.1209450

Levstik, L. S., & Barton, K. C. (2008). *Researching history education: Theory, method, and context*. Routledge.

Levstik, L. S., & Groth, J. (2002). "Scary thing, being an eighth grader": Exploring gender and sexuality in a middle school U.S. history unit. *Theory & Research in Social Education*, *30*(2), 233–254. https://doi.org/10.1080/00933104.2002.10473193

Levstik, L. S., & Groth, J. (2005). "Ruled by our own people": Ghanaian adolescents' conceptions of citizenship. *Teachers College Record*, *107*(4), 563–586.

Levstik, L. S., & Henderson, A. G. (2016). A human dependence on things: Fifth-Graders' conceptions of human intelligence, innovation and agency. In M.-A. Éthier & É. Mottet (Eds.), *De nouvelles voies pour la recherche et la pratique en Histoire, Géographie et Éducation à la citoyenneté* (pp. 15–240). De Boeck Supérieur.

Levstik, L. S., & Pappas, C. C. (1987). Exploring the development of historical understanding. *Journal of Research and Development in Education*, *21*(1), 1–15.

Levstik, L. S., & Smith, D. B. (1996). "I've never done this before": Building a community of historical inquiry in a third-grade classroom. In J. Brophy (Ed.), *Advances in research on teaching, vol. 6: Teaching and learning history* (pp. 85–114). JAI Press.

Levstik, L. S., & Smith, D. B. (1997). "I have learned a whole lot this year and it would take a lifetime to write it all": Beginning historical inquiry in a third grade classroom. *Social Science Record*, *34*, 8–14.

Levstik, L. S., & Thornton, S. J. (2018). Reconceptualizing history for early childhood through early adolescence. In S. Metzger & L. M. Harris (Eds.), *The Wiley international handbook of history teaching and learning* (pp. 473–501). Wiley. https://doi.org/10.1002/9781119100812.ch18

Levstik, L. S., Henderson, A. G., & Lee, Y. (2014). The beauty of other lives: Material culture as evidence of human ingenuity and agency. *The Social Studies*, *105*(4), 1–9. https://doi.org/10.1080/00377996.2014.886987

Levstik, L. S., Henderson, A. G., & Schlarb, J. S. (2005). Digging for clues: An archaeological exploration of historical cognition. In R. Ashby, P. Gordon, & P. Lee (Eds.), *Understanding history: International review of history education 4* (pp. 34–49). Routledge.

Levy, S. (2014). Heritage, history, and identity. *Teachers College Record*, *116*(6), 1–34.

Levy, S., & Sheppard, M. (2018). "Difficult knowledge" and the Holocaust in history education. In S. Metzger & L. M. Harris (Eds.), *The Wiley international handbook of history teaching and learning* (pp. 365–387). Wiley. https://doi.org/10.1002/9781119100812.ch14

Lindstrom, C. (2020). *We are water protectors*. Roaring Brook Press.

Linenthal, E. T. (1994). Committing history in public. *Journal of American History*, *81*(3), 986–991. https://doi.org/10.2307/2081438

Lipscomb, G. (2002). Eighth graders' impressions of the Civil War: Using technology in the history classroom. *Education, Communication and Information*, *2*(1), 51–67. https://doi.org/10.1080/1463631022000005025

Littlechild, L. (1993). *This land is my land*. Children's Book Press.

Loeb, R. H. (1979). *Meet the real Pilgrims: Everyday life on a Plymouth plantation in 1627*. Clarion.

Lowry, L. (1990). *Number the stars*. Dell.

Lyster, R. (2007). *Learning and teaching languages through content: A counterbalanced approach*. John Benjamins.

Macaulay, D. (1977). *Castle*. Houghton Mifflin.

Macaulay, D. (1979). *Motel of the mysteries*. Graphia.

Manfra, M., & Hammond, T. C. (2006). Teachers' instructional choices with student-created digital documentaries: Case studies. *Journal of Research on Technology in Education*, *41*(2), 223–245. https://doi.org/10.1080/15391523.2008.10782530

Manning, P. (2003). *Navigating world history: Historians create a global past*. Palgrave Macmillan.

Marable-Bunch, M. (2020, December 28). Transforming teaching and learning about Native Americans. *Smithsonian Education*. https://www.smithsonianmag.com/blogs/smithsonian-education/2020/12/28/transforming-teaching-and-learning-about-native-americans/

Marcello, J. S. (1999). A teacher's reflections on teaching and assessing in a standards-based classroom. *Social Education*, *65*(6), 338–342.

Marcus, A., Metzger, S. A., Paxton, R., & Stoddard, J. (2010). *Teaching history with film*. Routledge.

Martin, D. (2021). Using visual fine arts to enrich understanding. *Ask a Master Teacher*. https://teachinghistory.org/teaching-materials/ask-a-master-teacher/24271

Mathis, G. (2015, August 24). Inquiry-based learning: The power of asking the right questions. *Edutopia*. https://www.edutopia.org/blog/inquiry-based-learning-asking-right-questions-georgia-mathis

Matias, C. E., Montoya, R., & Nishi, N. W. M. (2016). Blocking CRT: How the emotionality of whiteness blocks CRT in urban teacher education. *Educational Studies*, *52*(1) 1–19. https://doi.org/10.1080/00131946.2015.1120205

Mayer, R. H. (1998). Connective narrative and historical thinking: A research-based approach to teaching history. *Social Education, 62*(2), 97–100.

Mayer, R. H. (1999). Use the story of Anne Hutchinson to teach historical thinking. *The Social Studies, 90*(3), 105–109. https://doi.org/10.1080/00377999909602399

Mazur, J. (1993). *Interpretation and use of visuals in an interactive multimedia fiction program.* [Doctoral dissertation, Cornell University]. ProQuest Dissertations & Theses Global.

McClafferty, C. (2018). *Buried lives: The enslaved people of George Washington's Mount Vernon.* Holiday House.

McCully, A. (2012). History teaching, conflict and the legacy of the past. *Education, Citizenship and Social Justice, 7*(2), 145–159. https://doi.org/10.1177/1746197912440854

McDonald, F. (1997). *How would you survive in the Middle Ages?* Topeka Bindery.

McGinnis, K. (1991). *Educating for a just society: Grades 7–12.* The Institute for Peace and Justice.

McGovern, A. (1999). *…If you lived 100 years ago.* Scholastic.

McIntyre, E. (2007). Story discussion in the primary grades: Balancing authenticity and explicit teaching. *The Reading Teacher, 60*(7), 610–620. https://doi.org/10.1598/RT.60.7.1

McKeown, M. G., & Beck, I. L. (1990). The assessment and characterization of young learners' knowledge of a topic in history. *American Educational Research Journal, 27*(4), 688–726. https://doi.org/10.3102/00028312027004688

McKinley, B., & Brayboy, J. (2006). Toward a tribal critical race theory in education. *Urban Review, 37*(5), 423–446. https://doi.org/10.1007/s11256-005-0018-y

McNeill, R., & McNeill, W. (2003). *The human web: A birds-eye view of world history.* Norton.

McTighe, J., & Wiggins, G. (2012). *Understanding by design framework.* Association for Supervision and Curriculum Development.

McTighe, J., & Wiggins, G. (2013). *Essential questions: Opening doors to student understanding.* Association for Supervision and Curriculum Development.

McTigue, E., Thornton, E., & Wiese, P (2012). Authentication projects for historical fiction: Do you believe it? *The Reading Teacher, 66*(6), 495–505. https://doi.org/10.1002/TRTR.1132

Megill, A. (1989). Recounting the past: "Description," explanation, and narrative in historiography. *American Historical Review, 94*(3), 627–653. https://doi.org/10.2307/1873749

Meltzer, M. (1994a). *Cheap raw labor: How our youngest workers are exploited and abused.* Viking.

Meltzer, M. (1994b). *Nonfiction for the classroom: Milton Meltzer on writing, history, and social responsibility.* Teachers College Press.

Menkart, D. (2014). Mything Mandela. *Rethinking Schools, 28*(3), 57–58.

Metro, R. (2020). *Teaching world history thematically: Essential questions and document-based lessons to connect past and present.* Teachers College Press.

Meyers, W. D. (2017). *Frederick Douglass: The lion who wrote history.* Harper.

Michelson, R. (2010). *Busing Brewster.* Knopf Books for Young Readers.

Mihesuah, D. (2009). *American Indians: Stereotypes and realities.* Clarity Press.

Miller, A. (2007). *"Getting it right" and "keeping it real": Using narrative soundtracks as a transmediatory activity in secondary school.* [Doctoral dissertation, University of Cincinnati]. ProQuest Dissertations & Theses Global.

Miller, B. M. (2002). *Growing up in revolution and the new nation, 1775 to 1800.* Lerner Publishing Group.

Milson, A. J. (2002) The Internet and inquiry learning: Integrating medium and method in a sixth grade social studies slassroom. *Theory & Research in Social Education, 30*(3), 330–353, https://doi.org/10.1080/00933104.2002.10473200

Milson, A. J., & Brantley, S. M. (1999). Theme-based portfolio assessment in social studies teacher education. *Social Education, 63*(6), 374–377.

Mintz, S. W., & Price, R. (1992). *The birth of African-American culture: An anthropological perspective.* Beacon.

Misco, T., & Patterson, N. C. (2009). An old fad of great promise: Reverse chronology history teaching in social studies classes. *Journal of Social Studies Research, 33*(1), 71–90.

Mitchell, W. J. T. (1995). *Picture theory: Essays on visual and verbal representation.* University of Chicago Press.

Mochizuki, K. (1993). *Baseball saved us.* Lee & Low.

Mochizuki, K. (1997). *Passage to freedom: The Sugihara story.* Lee & Low.

Monte-Sano, C. (2008). Qualities of historical writing instruction: A comparative case study of two teachers' practices. *American Educational Research Journal, 45*(4), 1045–1079. https://doi.org/10.3102/0002831208319733

Monte-Sano, C. (2012). What makes a good history essay? Assessing historical aspects of argumentative writing. *Social Education, 76*(6), 294–298.

Morgan, J. L. (2010). Gender and family life. In G. Heuman & T. Burnard (Eds.), *The Routledge History of Slavery* (pp. 138–152). Taylor and Francis. https://doi.org/10.4324/9780203840573-15

Moser, S. (2001). Archaeological representation: The visual conventions for constructing knowledge about the past. In I. Hodder (Ed.), *Archaeological theory today* (pp. 262–283). Polity Press.

Mouradian, K. (2021). *The resistance network: The Armenian genocide and humanitarianism in Ottoman Syria, 1915–1918.* Michigan State University Press.

Murphy, C. R. (2011). *Marching with Aunt Susan: Susan B. Anthony and the fight for women's suffrage.* Peachtree.

Myers, W. D. (2007). *Harlem summer.* Scholastic Press.

Nahum, A. (2011). *Flight.* DK.

Nash, G., Crabtree, C., & Dunn, R. (1997). *History on trial: Culture wars and the teaching of the past.* Knopf.

National Archives. (2020). Teaching six big ideas about the Constitution. https://www.archives.gov/legislative/resources/education/constitution

National Constitution Center. (n.d.). We the civics kids lesson 3: The Bill of Rights. https://constitutioncenter.org/learn/educational-resources/lesson-plans/we-the-civics-kids-lesson-3-the-bill-of-rights

National Council for the Social Studies. (2010). *National curriculum standards for social studies: A framework for teaching, learning, and assessment.* National Council for the Social Studies.

National Council for the Social Studies. (2013). *College, career and civic life (C3) Framework for state standards frameworks.* National Council for the Social Studies.

National Council for the Social Studies (2014). *The Study of religion in the social studies curriculum: A position statement of the National Council for the Social Studies.* https://www.socialstudies.org/position-statements/study-of-religion-in-social-studies

National Council for the Social Studies. (2016). A vision of powerful teaching and learning in the Social Studies. *Social Education, 80*(3), 180–182.

National Council for the Social Studies. (2018). Toward responsibility: Social studies education that respects and affirms Indigenous peoples and nations. *Social Education, 82*(3), 167–173.

National Council for the Social Studies (2021). Saving American history? *Try teaching American history.* https://www.socialstudies.org/current-events-response/saving-american-history-start-teaching-american-history

Nelson, K. (2013). *Heart and soul: The story of America and African Americans.* Balzer & Bray.

Nelson, S. D. (2010). *Black Elk's vision: A Lakota story.* Abrams Books for Young Readers.

Nelson, S. D. (2012). *Buffalo Bird girl: A Hidatsa story.* Abrams Books for Young Readers.

Nelson, S. D. (2017). *Red Cloud: A Lakota story of war and surrender.* Abrams Books for Young Readers.

Newkirk, T. (1989). *More than stories: The range of children's writings.* Heinemann.

Newmann, F. M., & Associates. (1996). *Authentic achievement: Restructuring schools for intellectual quality.* Jossey-Bass.

Newmann, F. M., Secada, W. G., & Wehlage, G. (1995). *A guide to authentic instruction and assessment: Vision, standards and scoring.* Wisconsin Center for Education Research.

Newmann, F. M., Carmichael, D. L., & King, M. B. (2015). *Authentic intellectual work: Improving teaching for rigorous learning.* Corwin Press.

Ni Cassaithe, C., & Chapman, A. (2021). History education in a climate of crisis. *Public History Weekly, 9*(1). https://doi.org/10.1515/phw-2021-17415

Noah, T. (2020). *Born a crime.* Yearling.

Nokes, J. (2012). *Building students' historical literacies: Learning to read and reason with historical texts and evidence.* Routledge.

Nokes, J., & de la Paz, S. (2018). Writing and argumentation in history education. In S. Metzger & L. M. Harris (Eds.), *The Wiley international handbook of history teaching and learning* (pp. 551–578). Wiley. https://doi.org/10.1002/9781119100812.ch21

O'Brien, J. (1998). Using literary themes to develop historical perspective. *The Social Studies, 89*(6), 276–280. https://doi.org/10.1080/00377999809599870

O'Brien, J. (2010). *First and lasting: Writing Indians out of existence in New England.* University of Minnesota Press.

O'Dell, S. (1980). *Sarah Bishop.* Houghton Mifflin.

O'Donnell, A. M. (2012). Constructivism. In K. R. Harris, S. Graham, T. Urdan, C. B. McCormick, G. M. Sinatra, & J. Sweller (Eds.), *APA educational psychology handbook, Vol. 1. Theories, constructs, and critical issues* (pp. 61–84). American Psychological Association. https://doi.org/10.1037/13273-003

O'Reilly, R. (1998). What would you do? Constructing decision-making guidelines through historical problems. *Social Education, 61*(1), 46–49.

Ogle, D. M. (1986). K-W-L: A teaching model that develops active reading of expository text. *Reading Teacher, 39*(6), 564–570. https://doi.org/10.1598/RT.39.6.11

Oppenheimer, J. (2006). *Dear Miss Breed.* Scholastic.

Ortiz, P. (2018). *An African American and Latinx history of the United States.* Beacon Press.

Osborne, M. P. (2002). *Favorite Medieval tales.* Scholastic Inc.

Owen, D., & Vista, A. (2017, November 15). Strategies for teaching metacognition in classrooms. *Education Plus Development.* https://www.brookings.edu/blog/education-plus-development/2017/11/15/strategies-for-teaching-metacognition-in-classrooms/

Oyler, C. (1996). *Making room for students: Sharing teacher authority in Room 104.* Teachers College Press.

Pace, J. (2021). *Hard questions: Learning to teach controversial issues.* Rowman & Littlefield.

Pappas, C., Kiefer, B., & Levstik, L. (2005). *An integrated language perspective in the elementary school: An action approach* (4th ed.). Allyn & Bacon/Longman.

Pappas, C. C. (1991). Fostering full access to literacy by including information books. *Language Arts, 68*(October), 449–462. https://www.jstor.org/stable/41961890

Park, L. S. (2013). *When my name was Keoko.* University of Queensland Press.

Parker, W. C. (1991a). Searching for the middle: A critique of the critiques of the Report of the National Commission on Social Studies in the Schools. *Social Education, 55*(1), 27–28, 65.

Parker, W. C. (1991b). Teaching an IDEA. *Social Studies and the Young Learner, 3*(3), 11–13.

Parker, W. C. (1996). "Advanced" ideas about democracy: Toward a pluralist conception of citizen education. *Teachers College Record, 98*(1), 104–125.

Parker, W. C. (2003). *Teaching democracy: Unity and diversity in public life.* Teachers College Press.

Parker, W. C., & Hess, D. (2001). Teaching with and for discussion. *Teaching and Teacher Education, 17*(3), 273–289. https://doi.org/10.1016/S0742-051X(00)00057-3

Passe, J., & Whitley, I. (1998). The best museum for kids? The one they build themselves! *The Social Studies, 89*(4), 183–185. https://doi.org/10.1080/00377999809599849

Peace Corps World Wise Schools. (1998). *Looking at ourselves and others.* Peace Corps.

Peacock, L. (2007). *At Ellis Island: A history in many voices.* Atheneum Books for Young Readers.

Peck, R. (2007). *On the wings of heroes.* Dial Books for Young Readers.

Pelta, K. (1991). *Discovering Christopher Columbus: How history is invented.* Lerner.

Penyak, L. M., & Duray, P. B. (1999). Oral history and problematic questions promote issues-centered education. *The Social Studies, 90*(2), 68–71. https://doi.org/10.1080/00377999909602393

Perdue, T., & Green, M. (2005). *Cherokee removal: A brief history documents.* Bedford/St. Martins.

Pierce, K. M., & Gilles, C. J. (Eds.) (1993). *Cycles of meaning: Exploring the potential of talk in learning communities.* Heinemann.

Pilgrim Explorations. (2008, November 2). *Plymouth vs. Plimouth.* https://uspilgrims.wordpress.com/2008/11/02/plymouth-vs-plimouth/

Platt, E. (n.d.). Photographic memory: Using historical images to improve student learning. *TeachArchives.org.* Brooklyn Historical Society. https://teacharchives.org/articles/using-images/

Polacco, P. (2000). *The butterfly.* Philomel Books.

Polacco, P. (2013). *The blessing cup.* Simon & Schuster Books for Young Readers.

Polacco, P. (2014). *Fiona's Lace.* Simon & Schuster.

Popham, J. W. (1997). What's wrong—and what's right—with rubrics. *Educational Leadership, 55*(2), 72–75.

Prawat, R. S. (1989a). Promoting access to knowledge, strategy, and disposition in students: A research synthesis. *Review of Educational Research, 59,* 1–41.

Prawat, R. S. (1989b). Teaching for understanding: Three key attributes. *Teaching and Teacher Education, 5,* 315–328.

Purves, A. C. (1990). *The scribal society: An essay on literacy and schooling in the information age.* Longman.

Putnam, R. D. (2000). *Bowling alone: The collapse and revival of American community.* Simon and Schuster.

Rabinowitz, P. J. (1987). *Before reading: Narrative conventions and the politics of interpretation.* Cornell University Press.

Rappaport, D. (2005). *The secret Seder.* Hyperion Books for Children.

Rappaport, D., & Collier, B. (2007). *Martin's big words.* Hyperion.

Renyi, J. (1994). The arts and humanities in American Education. *Phi Delta Kappan, 75*(6), 438–440, 442–445. https://www.jstor.org/stable/20405137

Resnick, L. B. (1987). The 1987 presidential address: Learning in school and out. *Educational Research*, *16*(9), 13–20. https://doi.org/10.2307/1175725c.v

Rivière, A., Núñez, M., Barquero, B., & Fontela, F. (1998). Influence of intentional and personal factors in recalling historical texts: A developmental perspective. In J. F. Voss & M. Carretero (Eds.), *International review of history education: Vol. 2. Learning and reasoning in history* (pp. 241–226). Woburn.

Roberts, D. (2019). *Suffragette: The battle for equality*. Walker Books.

Rochman, H. (1990). *Somehow tenderness survives*. HarperTeen.

Rodríguez, H. M., Salinas, C., & Guberman, S. (2005). Creating opportunities for historical thinking with bilingual students. *Social Studies and the Young Learner*, *18*(2), 9–13.

Rodríguez, N. N. (2020). Focus on friendship of fights for civil rights? Teaching the difficult history of Japanese American incarceration through *The Bracelet*. *Bank Street Occasional Papers*, *44*(Article 6), 48–59. https://educate.bankstreet.edu/occasional-paper-series/vol2020/iss44/6

Rodríguez, N. N., & Ip, R. (2018). Hidden in history: (Re)constructing Asian American history in elementary social studies classrooms. In S. B. Shear, C. M. Tschida, E. Bellows, L. B. Buchanan, & E. E. Saylor (Eds.), *(Re)imagining elementary social studies: A controversial issues reader* (pp. 319–339). Information Age Publishing.

Rodríguez, N. N., & Kim, E. J. (2018). In search of mirrors: An Asian critical race theory content analysis of Asian American picturebooks from 2007–2017. *Journal of Children's Literature*, *44*(2), 16–33.

Rodríguez, N. N., & Swalwell, K. (2021). *Social studies for a better world: An anti-oppressive approach for elementary educators*. Norton.

Rogoff, B. (1990). *Apprenticeship in thinking: Cognitive development in social context*. Oxford University Press.

Rosenzweig, R., & Thelen, D. (1998). *The presence of the past: Popular uses of history in American life*. Columbia University Press.

Rothstein, R. (2018). *The color of law: A forgotten history of how our government segregated America*. Liveright.

Rowe, D. W. (2003). The nature of young children's authoring. In N. Hall, J. Larson, & J. Marsh (Eds.), *Handbook of early childhood literacy* (pp. 258–270). Sage.

Ruelle, K. G. (2009). *The Grand Mosque of Paris: A story of how Muslims saved Jews during the Holocaust*. Holiday House.

Russell-Brown, K. (2020). *She was the first! The trailblazing life of Shirley Chisholm*. Lee & Low Books.

Russo, M. (2011). *I will come back for you: A family in hiding during WWII*. Schwartz and Wade.

Sabzalian, L. (2019). *Indigenous children's survivance in public schools*. Routledge.

Sabzalian, L., Shear, S. B., & Snyder, J. (2021). Standardizing indigenous erasure: A TribalCrit and QuantCrit analysis of K–12 U.S. civics and government standards. *Theory & Research in Social Education*. https://doi.org.10.1080/00933104.2021.1922322

Salinas, C., Fránquiz, M. E., & Guberman, S. (2006). Introducing historical thinking to second language learners: Exploring what students know and what they want to know. *The Social Studies*, *97*(5), 203–207. https://doi.org/10.3200/TSSS.97.5.203-207

Salomon, G. (2012). *Interaction of media, cognition, and learning: An exploration of how symbolic forms cultivate mental skills and affect knowledge acquisition*. Routledge.

Sancha, S. (1983). *The Luttrell village: Country life in the middle ages*. Ty Crowell Company.

Sánchez, J. G., & Sáenz, R. Y. (2017). Stories, counterstories, and tales of resistance: Family history projects in World History classrooms. In P. T. Chandler & T. S. Hawley (Eds.), *Race lessons: Using inquiry to teach about race in social studies* (pp. 213–230). Information Age Publishing.

Santiago, M. (2019). A framework for an interdisciplinary understanding of Mexican American school segregation. *Multicultural Education Review*, *11*(2), 69–78. https://doi.org/10.1080/2005615X.2019.1615246

Saul, E. E. (Ed.) (1994). *Nonfiction for the classroom: Milton Meltzer on writing, history, and social responsibility*. Teachers College Press.

Sawyer, W. (2020). *The six nations confederacy during the American Revolution*. National Park Service. https://www.nps.gov/fost/learn/historyculture/the-six-nations-confederacy-during-the-american-revolution.htm

Saye, J. W., & Brush, T. (2007). Using technology-enhanced learning environments to support problem-based historical inquiry in secondary school classrooms. *Theory & Research in Social Education*, *35*(2), 196–230. https://doi.org/10.1080/00933104.2007.10473333

Saye, J. W., & Brush, T. (2004), Scaffolding problem-based teaching in a traditional social studies classroom. *Theory and Research in Social Education*, *32*(3), 349–378. https://doi.org/10.1080/00933104.2004.10473259

# References

Schanzer, R. (2011). *Witches: The absolutely true tale of disaster in Salem*. National Geographic Books for Children.

Schlitz, L., & Byrd, R. (2008). *Good masters! Sweet ladies! Voices from a medieval village*. Candlewick.

Schmeichel, M. (2011). Feminism, neoliberalism, and social studies. *Theory & Research in Social Education, 39*(11), 6–31. https://doi.org/10.1080/00933104.2011.10473445

Schmidt, E. A. (2014). *Native Americans in the American Revolution: How the war divided, devastated, and transformed the Early American Indian world*. Praeger.

Schul, J. E. (2010). The mergence of CHAT with TPCK: A new framework for researching the integration of desktop documentary making in history teaching and learning. *THEN:Technology, Humanities, Education, & Narrative, 7*(Spring). http://thenjournal.org/index.php/then/article/view/44

Schunk, D. H. (2012). Social cognitive theory. In K. R. Harris, S. Graham, T. Urdan, C. B. McCormick, G. M. Sinatra & J. Sweller (Eds.), *APA educational psychology handbook: Vol. 1. Theories, constructs, and critical issues* (pp. 101–123). American Psychological Association. https://doi.org/10.1037/13273-005

Schweber, S. (2008). "What happened to their pets?" Third graders encounter the Holocaust. *Teachers College Record, 110*(10), 2073–2115.

Scott, D. D., Fox, R. A., Jr., Connor, M. A., & Harmon, D. (2000). *Archaeological perspectives on the battle of the Little Bighorn*. University of Oklahoma Press.

Segall, A. (1999). Critical history: Implication for history/social studies education. *Theory & Research in Social Education, 27*(3), 358–374. https://doi.org/10.1080/00933104.1999.10505885

Seixas, P. (1993). Historical understanding among adolescents in a multicultural setting. *Curriculum Inquiry, 23*(3), 301–327. https://doi.org/10.1080/03626784.1993.11076127

Seixas, P. (1998). Student teachers thinking historically. *Theory & Research in Social Education, 26*(3), 310–341. https://doi.org/10.1080/00933104.1998.10505854

Seixas, P. (1999). Beyond "content" & "pedagogy": In search of a way to talk about history education. *Journal of Curriculum Studies, 31*(3), 317–337. https://doi.org/10.1080/002202799183151

Shabazz, I. (2014). *Malcolm Little: The boy who grew up to become Malcolm X*. Atheneum Books for Young Readers.

Shama, S. (1992). *Dead certainties: Unwarranted speculations*. Vintage.

Shear, S. B., Knowles, R. T., Soden, G. J., & Castro, A. J. (2015). Manifesting destiny: Re/presentations of Indigenous peoples in K–12 U.S. history standards. *Theory & Research in Social Education, 43*(1), 68–101. https://doi.org.10.1080/00933104.2014.999849

Shear, S. B., Sabzalian, L., & Buchanan, L. B. (2018). Affirming indigenous sovereignty: A civic inquiry. *Social Studies and the Young Learner, 31*(1), 12–18.

Sheinkin, S. (2013). *Bomb: The race to build—and steal—the world's most dangerous weapon*. Macmillan.

Shemilt, D. (2018). Assessment of learning in history education: Past, present, and possible futures. In S. A. Metzger & L. A. Harris (Eds.), *The Wiley international handbook of history teaching and learning* (pp. 449–471). Wiley. https://doi.org/10.1002/9781119100812.ch17

Shepard, L. A. (1991). Negative policies for dealing with diversity: When does assessment and diagnosis turn into sorting and segregation? In E. H. Hiebert (Ed.), *Literacy for a diverse society: Perspectives, practices, and policies* (pp. 279–298). Teachers College Press.

Shepard, L. A. (2000). *The role of classroom assessment in teaching and learning*. Technical Report, Center for Research on Evaluation, Standards, and Student Testing, Los Angeles, CA. Eric Document Reproduction Service No. ED443880.

Sheppard, M., & Mayo Jr., J. B. (2013). The social construction of gender and sexuality: Learning from two spirit traditions, *The Social Studies, 104*(6), 259–270. https://doi.org/10.1080/00377996.2013.788472

Short, D. J. (1998). Social studies instruction and assessment: Meeting the needs of students learning English. In H. Fradd & O. Lee (Eds.), *Creating Florida's multilingual global workforce: Educational policies and practices for students learning English as a new language* (pp. 1–12). Florida Department of Education.

Short, D. J., Vogt, M. E., & Echevarria, J. (2011). *The SIOP model for teaching history-social studies to English learners*. Pearson.

Silko, L. M. (2006). *Ceremony*. Penguin.

Sizemore, J. (2011). Integrating social studies and the arts: Why, when & how. *Kentucky Teacher*. https://www.kentuckyteacher.org/wp-content/uploads/2011/06/Integrating-Social-Studies-Arts.pdf

Sklar, K. K. (1995). *Florence Kelley & the nation's work: The rise of women's political culture, 1830–1900*. Yale University Press.

Slade, S., & Tadgell, N. (2014). *With books and bricks: How Booker T. Washington built a school.* Whitman & Company.

Smagorinsky, P. (2001). If meaning is constructed, what's it made from? Toward a cultural theory of reading. *Review of Educational Research, 71*(1), 133–169. https://doi.org/10.3102/00346543071001133

Smith, L. A., & Barton, K. C. (1997). Practical issues in literature study groups: Getting the most out of historical fiction in the middle grades. *Social Science Record, 34,* 27–31.

Smith, N. (2007). The flowering of identity: Tracing the history of Cuba through the visual arts. *Social Education, 71*(4), 182–186.

Smith, P. C. (2009). *Everything you know about Indians is wrong.* University of Minnesota Press.

Sokoni, M. A. (1991). *Mchesi goes to market.* Jacaranda Designs.

Speare, G. E. (1958). *The witch of Blackbird Pond.* Houghton Mifflin.

St. Denis, V. (2011). Silencing Aboriginal curricular content and perspectives through multiculturalism: "There are other children here." *Review of Education, Pedagogy, and Cultural Studies, 33*(4), 306–317. http://dx.doi.org/10.1080/10714413.2011.597638

Stanley, D., & Vennema, P. (1988). *Shaka: King of the Zulus.* Morrow.

Stanley, J. (1994). *I am an American: A true story of Japanese internment.* Crown.

Stearns, P. N. (Ed.) (2008). *World history in documents: A comparative reader.* (2nd ed.). New York University Press.

Sterman, C. (2018). Arts infuses joy and student voice into daily instruction. *Principal, 97*(3). https://www.naesp.org/resource/arts-integration-improves-school-culture-and-student-success/

Stiggins, R. J. (2001). *Student-involved classroom assessment* (3rd ed.). Merrill/Prentice-Hall.

Stock, M. A. (1993). *Where are you going, Manyoni?* Morrow.

Stoddard, J. (2012). Film as a "thoughtful" medium for teaching history. *Learning, Media, and Technology, 37*(3), 271–288. https://doi.org/10.1080/17439884.2011.572976

Stoddard, J., & Marcus, A. (2017). Media and social studies education. In M. M. Manfra & C. M. Bolick (Eds.), *The Wiley handbook of social studies research* (pp. 477–498). Wiley-Blackwell.

Stoddard, J., Marcus, A., and Hicks, D. (2014). The burden of historical representation: The case of/for Indigenous film. *The History Teacher, 28*(1), 9–36. https://www.jstor.org/stable/43264376

Stoddard, J., Marcus, A., Hicks, D. (2017). *Teaching difficult history through film.* Routledge.

Stoddard, J. D. (2012). Film as a "thoughtful" medium for teaching history. *Learning, Media and Technology, 37*(3), 271–288. https://www.doi.org/10.1080/17439884.2011.572976

Sturner, F. (1973). *What did you do when you were a kid? Pastimes from the past.* St. Martin's.

Suh, Y. (2013). Past looking: Using arts as historical evidence in teaching history. *Social Studies Research and Practice, 8*(1), 135–159. https://www.socstrpr.org/wp-content/uploads/2013/09/MS_06372_Spring2013.pdf

Swan, K., & Hofer, M. (2013). *And action … Directing documentaries in the social studies classroom.* R&L Publishing.

Takaki, R. (2008). *A different mirror: A history of multicultural America* (Revised ed.). Back Bay Books.

Tennant, D. & Boyne, J. (2016). *We are all born free (The Universal Declaration of Human Rights in pictures).* Amnesty International.

Thornton, S. J. (1991). Teacher as curricular-instructional gatekeeper in social studies. In J. P. Shaver (Ed.), *Handbook of research on social studies teaching and learning* (pp. 237–248). Macmillan.

Thornton, S. J. (2005). *Teaching social studies that matters: Curriculum for active learning.* Teachers College Press.

Timberlake, A. (2013). *One came home.* Yearling.

Ting, R. (2009). *Chinese history stories: Volume 1, Stories from the Zjou Dynasty.* Shen's Books.

Touhill, L. (2012). Inquiry-based learning. *National Quality Standard Professional Learning Program Newsletter, 45.* https://wudinnakgn.sa.edu.au/wp-content/uploads/2019/08/Inquiry-based-learning.pdf

Trease, G. (1983). Fifty years on: A writer looks back. *Children's Literature in Education, 14*(3), 149–159. https://doi.org/10.1007/bf01142202

Trigger, B. (2006). *A history of archaeological thought.* Cambridge University Press.

Tschida, C. M., & Buchanan, L. B. (2015). Teaching controversial topics: Developing thematic text sets for elementary social studies. *Social Studies Research and Practice, 10*(3), 40–56.

Tschida, C. M., & Buchanan, L B. (2017). What makes a family? Sharing multiple perspectives through an inclusive text set. *Social Studies and the Young Learner, 30*(2), 3–7.

Turner, A. (1992). *Katie's trunk.* Aladdin.

Turner, A., & Ransome, J. (2015). *My name is Truth: The life of Sojourner Truth.* HarperCollins.

# References

Turner-Vorbeck, T., & Marsh, M. M. (Eds.) (2007). *Other kinds of families: Embracing diversity in schools.* Teachers College Press.

Uchida, Y. (1985). *Journey to Topaz.* Creative Arts.

Uchida, Y. (1993). *The bracelet.* Philomel.

Uhlberg, M. (2010). *Dad, Jackie, and me.* Peachtree.

UNICEF. (2002). *For every child: The rights of the child in words and pictures.* Red Fox Books.

United States Department of Justice. (2020). *Native American policies.* https://www.justice.gov/otj/native-american-policies

Van Oers, B., & Wardukker, W. (1999). On becoming an authentic learner: Semiotic activity in the early grades. *Journal of Curriculum Studies, 31*(2), 229–249. https://doi.org/10.1080/002202799183241

Vanderpool, C. (2010). *Moon over manifest.* Yearling Books.

VanSledright, B. A. (1995). "I don't remember--The ideas are all jumbled in my head": Eighth graders' reconstructions of colonial American history. *Journal of Curriculum and Supervision, 10*(4), 317–345.

VanSledright, B. A. (2002). *In search of America's past: Learning to read history in elementary school.* Teachers College Press.

VanSledright, B. A. (2010). *The challenge of rethinking history education: On practices, theories, and policy.* Routledge.

VanSledright, B. A. (2013). *Assessing historical thinking and understanding.* Routledge.

VanSledright, B. A., & Brophy, J. (1992). Storytelling, imagination, and fanciful elaboration in children's historical reconstructions. *American Educational Research Journal, 29*(4), 837–859. https://doi.org/10.3102/00028312029004837

Vickery, A. E., & Rodríguez, N. N. (2021). "A woman question and a race problem": Attending to intersectionality in children's literature about women in the long civil rights movement. *The Social Studies, 112*(2), 57–62. https://doi.org/10.1080/00377996.2020.1809979

Vygotsky, L. (1978). *Mind in society: The development of higher psychological processes.* Harvard University Press.

Wade, R. C. (2007). Service-learning for social justice in the elementary classroom: Can we get there from here? *Equity & Excellence in Education, 40*(2), 156–165. https://doi.org/10.1080/10665680701221313

Warga, J. (2019). *Other words for home.* Balzer + Bray.

Weatherford, C. B. (2018). *Voice of freedom: Fannie Lou Hamer.* Carolrhoda Books.

Weatherford, C. B. (2021). *Unspeakable: The Tulsa race massacre.* Carolrhoda Books.

Weaver, R., & Dale, R. (1993). *Machines in the home.* Oxford University Press.

Weise, R. S. (2001). *Grasping at independence: Debt, male authority, and mineral rights in Appalachian Kentucky, 1850–1915.* University of Tennessee Press.

Weitzman, D. L. (2009). *Pharaoh's boat.* Houghton Mifflin Books for Children.

Welch, J. (2007). *Killing Custer: The battle of the Little Bighorn and the fate of the Plains Indians.* WW Norton & Company.

Wellman, H. M., & Gelman, S. A. (1992). Cognitive development: Foundational theories of core domains. *Annual Review of Psychology, 43,* 337–375. https://doi.org/10.1146/annurev.ps.43.020192.002005

Wells, C. G. (1999). *Dialogic inquiry: Towards a sociocultural practice and theory of education.* Cambridge.

Wells, C. G., & Chang-Wells, G. L. (1992). *Constructing knowledge together: Classrooms as centers of inquiry and literacy.* Heinemann.

Wertsch, J. V. (1998). *Mind as action.* Oxford University Press.

Wesniewski, D. (1992). *Sundiata.* Clarion.

White, M. (1965). *Foundations of historical knowledge.* Harper & Row.

White, H. (1980). The value of narrativity in the representation of reality. *Critical Inquiry, 7*(Autumn), 5–27. https://www.jstor.org/stable/1343174

White, H. (1992). Historical emplotment and the question of truth. In S. Friedlander (Ed.), *Probing the limits of representation: Nazism and the "final solution"* (pp. 37–53). Harvard University Press.

Wiggins, G. (1992). *The case for authentic assessment.* United States Department of Education, Office of Educational Research and Improvement, Educational Resources Information Center.

Wiggins, G. (2012). Seven keys to effective feedback. *Educational Leadership, 70*(1), 10–16.

Wilde, O. (1982). *The artist as critic: Critical writings of Oscar Wilde.* University of Chicago Press.

Wilkerson, I. (2020). *Caste: The origins of our discontents.* Random House.

Wilkinson, P. (2006). *Christianity.* DK Children.

Wilkinson, P., & Margan, P. (2006). *Buddhism.* DK Children.

Williams, K., & Mohammed, K. (2009). *My name is Sangoel.* Eerdmans Books for Young Readers.

Willingham, D. T. (2009). *Why don't students like school? A cognitive scientist answers questions about how the mind works and what it means for the classroom.* Jossey-Bass.

Wills, J. S. (2019). "Daniel was racist": Individualizing racism when teaching about the Civil Rights Movement. *Theory & Research in Social Education, 47*(3), 396–425.

Wilson, M. (2006). *Rethinking rubrics in writing assessment.* Heineman.

Woelfle, G. (2016). *Answering the cry for freedom: Stores of African Americans and the American Revolution.* Calkins Creek.

Wohlman, L. (n.d.) *Roman art and architecture, 500 BCE-400 CE.* World History for Us All. https://whfua.history.ucla.edu/downloads/download.php?file=E4CU5.1

Wolf, P. (2006). Settler-colonialism and the elimination of the native. *Journal of Genocide Research, 8*(4), 387–409. https://doi.org/10.1080/14623520601056240

Wood, D., Bruner, J. S., & Ross, G. (1976). The role of tutoring in problem solving. *Journal of Child Psychology and Psychiatry, and Allied Disciplines, 17*(2), 89–100. https://doi.org/10.1111/j.1469-7610.1976.tb00381.x

Woodson, A. N. (2016). We're just ordinary people: Messianic master narratives and Black youths' civic agency. *Theory & Research in Social Education, 44*(2), 184–211. https://doi.org/10.1080/00933104.2016.1170645

Wu, E. D. (2015). *The color of success: Asian Americans and the origins of the model minority.* Princeton University Press.

Yell, M. (1999). Multiple choice to multiple rubrics: One teacher's journey in assessment. *Social Education, 63*(6), 326–329.

Yep, L. (1994). *Dragon's gate.* HarperCollins.

Yin. (2001). *Coolies.* Philomel.

Yolen, J. (2004). *The Salem witch trials: An unsolved mystery from history.* Simon & Schuster Books for Young Readers.

Young, C. (1994). Change and innovation in history curriculum: A perspective on the New South Wales experience. In K. J. Kennedy, O. F. Watts, & G. McDonald (Eds.), *Citizenship education for a new age* (pp. 29–46). The University of Southern Queensland Press.

Zhensun, J., & Low, A. (1991). *A young painter: The life and paintings of Wang Yani: China's extraordinary young artist.* Scholastic.

Zitkala-Ša. (1900, February). School days of an Indian girl. *Atlantic Monthly, 85*(508), 185–194.

Zusak, M. (2007). *The book thief.* Picador Australia.

# Index

Page numbers in *italics* represent figures, while page numbers in **bold** represent tables.

# Index

# Index

Little Bighorn Battlefield National Monument 68
*Little House* book series 187, *188*
Littlechild, George 195
local history, and migrations 58

McKay, Hugh B. 128–29
Maggard, Grace 31–33
"magic words" *177*, 178
"Makers and Shakers in World History" project 87–88
Mankiller, Wilma 167
*Marching with Aunt Susan* (Murphy) 152
marginalization: teaching about 3, 168, *see also* minorities
Martin, Steve 77, 83
material culture 86, 104, 131; changes in 93
material resources, school provision of 45, 71
meaning construction 12, 14, 21, 79, 84, 128
meaningful learning 15
medieval studies 127–28
*Medieval Wedding* (Aliki) 128
*Meet the Real Pilgrims: Everyday Life on a Plymouth Plantation in 1627* (Loeb) 195–96
Meltzer, Milton 120–21, 125–26
memorization, and learning 12
metacognition 19, 109, 146, 174
#MeToo movement 16, 152
Middle-Eastern music 182
migration: extensions of 58–60; importance of 49; wall chart *53*
minorities: different treatments of 152; English language learners as 41; historical exclusion of 6–7
Miranda, Lin-Manuel 186
misinformation, and interpretations 30
mobiles 86
Monticello nail factory 120, 125–26
moral response stances 2
Morgan, Donte 61, 65
Mott, Abby 34, 127–28, 153–54
movies 185–86
murals 196; at Old Town Elementary School 188–89
*My Brother Sam is Dead* (Collier & Collier) 121
*My Name is Bilal* (Mobin-Uddn) 148
*My Name is Sangoel* (Williams and Mohammed) 48
*Mything Mandela* article 69–70

*The Name Jar* (Choi) 149
names, discussions of 65, 148
"Names Project" 149–50, *151*
narratives 5–6, 118–19, 122, 133; believing 121; and critical reading 121, 134; defining 119; "History of Me" project 39–40; and morals 121; students creating 88, 128–29, 131; vs. textbooks 118–19, 121–22, *see also* books; historical accounts; *specific projects*; storytelling
National Archives 87
National Council for the Social Studies 116–17, 126, 137
"Newspapers of the Reformation" project 78, 81, 85
*Nickajack* (Conley) 123

Noah, Trevor 64
non-fiction 124–26, 179; errors in 125; student use and discussion 124
Northern Ireland, history education 15
*Notable Books for a Global Society* 126
*Notable Social Studies Trade Books for Young Readers* 126
note-taking 111–12; "quick writing" 107; teaching 51–52
*Number the Stars* (Lowry) 152

Old Town Elementary School 188–89
*On The Wings of Heroes* (Peck) 123
*One Came Home* (Timberlake) 124
opposition, teaching about 3
oppression: centering 168–69; and perspective-taking 156–57
*Other Words for Home* (Warga) 119, 121

papal indulgences 128
Parks, Rosa 14
participatory democracies: characteristics of 9; preparation for 105
*Passage to Freedom: The Sugihara Story* (Mochizuki) 157
past, complexity of 1–2
*The Patchwork Quilt* 48
peer-based feedback 145, *146*; of art 197
peer-review, by students 88
people, emphasis on 170, 180
*The People Could Fly* (Hamilton) 169
perspective-taking activities 161, 170–72, 180; assessment of 158, *159*; cautions about 155–58; extensions 160–61; and reasonable people 161–62
Peterson, Pops 189
Phillips, Nathan 167
photographs: as primary sources 25, 93, 105, 129; resources for 139; student analysis of 25, 129; using 93; using in the "History of Me" project 40
physical artifacts 93–96; Grant assignment 182
pluralist democracies: history education for 9–10, 47, 60, 105, 137; and perspective-taking 161–62
pluralist perspectives 3
Plymouth plantations 195–96
*Pocahontas* (Bruchac) 125
portable archives 32, 70
portfolios: assessment portfolios 34; Friday portfolios 34; and inquiry-based instruction 33; learning portfolios 33–34; and scoring guides 56; writing portfolios 150
position papers 73, *74–75*
postcards 131
prejudice 1, 57, 152, 174
present day controversies, history leading to 135–36
presentations: and assessment 21, 72; Christopher Columbus 72–73; and the "create, present, discuss" methodology 145; on Greek society 63; Lexington project 113, *114*, 115; medieval studies 128
primary sources 85–87; art as 83, 183–85, *185*, 186; artifacts 5, 93, 95–96; keys for 130; photographs as 25, 93, 105, 131; and

# Index